'The book can be considered a guiding companion for those who are concerned about fintech.'
Dr Mohd Daud Bakar, *Founder of Amanie Group & International Islamic Finance Advisor*

'The book provides students, academics, scholars, and practitioners with a detailed description of theoretical and philosophical speculations on digital transformation in Islamic finance.'
Abu Umar Faruq Ahmad, *Chair, Shariah Governance Curriculum Review Committee, AAOIFI*

'The book offers an important insight as to how technology is going to shape the future of finance.'
Professor Dr Mohammad Hashim Kamali, *Founding CEO, International Institute of Advanced Islamic Studies (IAIS), Malaysia*

DIGITAL TRANSFORMATION IN ISLAMIC FINANCE

The ongoing digital transformation is shaping the Islamic mode of financial intermediation and the impact on the faith-based financial mode has been multifaceted. This has raised a host of interesting questions: what is the degree of penetration of Islamic finance in the fintech industry? Are Islamic financial institutions (IFIs) or banks ready to embrace fintech? Is fintech an enabler or barrier to achieve the intended purpose of Islamic finance? Will technology narrow the division between Islamic and conventional finance in the future? These are existential questions for Islamic finance and the book endeavors to examine the impact of financial technology on the industry.

The book assesses various fintech business models and how they could be a threat or an opportunity. It also examines whether fintech provides IFIs an edge to serve clients following the Shariah norms and how the adoption of fintech in the Islamic mode is required for meeting the maqasid Al Shariah. The book discusses applicability of fintech like blockchain, digital currency, big data, and AI to different branches of Islamic finance.

This book will interest students, analysts, policymakers, and regulators who are working on Islamic finance, financial economics, Islamic economics, and development finance.

Yasushi Suzuki is a Professor at Ritsumeikan Asia Pacific University, Japan.

Mohammad Dulal Miah is an Associate Professor at the University of Nizwa, Oman.

Islamic Business and Finance Series
Series Editor: Ishaq Bhatti

There is an increasing need for western politicians, financiers, bankers, and indeed the western business community in general to have access to high quality and authoritative texts on Islamic financial and business practices. Drawing on expertise from across the Islamic world, this new series will provide carefully chosen and focused monographs and collections, each authored/edited by an expert in their respective field all over the world.

The series will be pitched at a level to appeal to middle and senior management in both the western and the Islamic business communities. For the manager with a western background the series will provide detailed and up-to-date briefings on important topics; for the academics, postgraduates, business communities, manager with western and an Islamic background the series will provide a guide to best practice in business in Islamic communities around the world, including Muslim minorities in the west and majorities in the rest of the world.

Institutional Islamic Economics and Finance
Edited by Ahsan Shafiq

Islamic Finance in the Financial Markets of Europe, Asia and America
Faiza Ismail

The Informal Economy and Islamic Finance
The Case of Organization of Islamic Cooperation Countries
Shabeer Khan

Digital Transformation in Islamic Finance
A Critical and Analytical View
Edited by Yasushi Suzuki and Mohammad Dulal Miah

For more information about this series, please visit: www.routledge.com/Islamic-Business-and-Finance-Series/book-series/ISLAMICFINANCE

DIGITAL TRANSFORMATION IN ISLAMIC FINANCE

A Critical and Analytical View

Edited by
Yasushi Suzuki and
Mohammad Dulal Miah

LONDON AND NEW YORK

First published 2023
by Routledge
4 Park Square, Milton Park, Abingdon, Oxon OX14 4RN

and by Routledge
605 Third Avenue, New York, NY 10158

Routledge is an imprint of the Taylor & Francis Group, an informa business

© 2023 selection and editorial matter, Yasushi Suzuki and Mohammad Dulal Miah; individual chapters, the contributors

The right of Yasushi Suzuki and Mohammad Dulal Miah to be identified as the authors of the editorial material, and of the authors for their individual chapters, has been asserted in accordance with sections 77 and 78 of the Copyright, Designs and Patents Act 1988.

All rights reserved. No part of this book may be reprinted or reproduced or utilised in any form or by any electronic, mechanical, or other means, now known or hereafter invented, including photocopying and recording, or in any information storage or retrieval system, without permission in writing from the publishers.

Trademark notice: Product or corporate names may be trademarks or registered trademarks, and are used only for identification and explanation without intent to infringe.

British Library Cataloguing-in-Publication Data
A catalogue record for this book is available from the British Library

Library of Congress Cataloging-in-Publication Data
Names: Suzuki, Yasushi, editor. | Miah, Mohammad Dulal, editor.
Title: Digital transformation in Islamic finance : a critical and analytical view / edited by Yasushi Suzuki and Mohammad Dulal Miah.
Description: First Edition. | New York, NY : Routledge, 2023. | Series: Islamic business and finance series | Includes bibliographical references and index. |
Identifiers: LCCN 2022036670 | ISBN 9781032200910 (hardback) | ISBN 9781032200934 (paperback) | ISBN 9781003262169 (ebook)
Subjects: LCSH: Finance—Islamic countries. | Banks and banking—Technological innovations—Islamic countries. | Financial institutions—Technological innovations—Islamic countries.
Classification: LCC HG187.4 .D54 2023 | DDC 332.091767—dc23/eng/20221006
LC record available at https://lccn.loc.gov/2022036670

ISBN: 9781032200910 (hbk)
ISBN: 9781032200934 (pbk)
ISBN: 9781003262169 (ebk)

DOI: 10.4324/9781003262169

Typeset in Bembo
by codeMantra

CONTENTS

List of figures xi
List of tables xiii
List of contributors xv
Foreword xix
Preface xxiii
Acknowledgements xxv

    Introduction 1
    Yasushi Suzuki and Mohammad Dulal Miah

Part I
Theoretical and philosophical speculations on digital transformation in Islamic finance 13

  1 Digital transformation in Islamic finance: a critique of perfectionist's views on Islamic fintech 15
    Yasushi Suzuki and Mohammad Dulal Miah

  2 A typology of financial business models on digital transformation ('DX'): expected impacts on commercial banks 44
    Yasushi Suzuki and Mohammad Dulal Miah

  3 Fintech, technomania, and persistent socio-civilizational challenges 64
    Mohammad Omar Farooq and Muhammad Dulal Miah

Part II
Empirical studies 81

4 Business risk mitigation through "Value-Chain Integrated" financing in Islamic Peer-to-Peer Lending in Indonesia: PT Qazwa Mitra Hasanah's experience 83
Sigit Pramono, Dikry Paren, M. Iqbal Ramadhan and Muhammad Razikun

5 Prospects and opportunities of Islamic crowdfunding in Bangladesh 101
S. M. Sohrab Uddin, Rima Akter and Md Imran Hossain Anik

6 Empirical assessment on digital transformation in Islamic banking 118
Abideen Adeyemi Adewale and Rifki Ismal

7 Fintech in Islamic banking in Bangladesh: opportunities and threats 142
Md. Joynal Abedin, Syed Mahbubur Rahman and Riyashad Ahmed

8 Exploring digital banking patronage in the Netherlands 154
Muhammad Ashfaq, Abdul Rauf, Mai Tran and Rashedul Hasan

9 Can Islamic FinTech best serve the migrants' interest in remittance services? The South and Southeast Asian perspective 172
S. M. Sohrab Uddin and Tasfika Khanam

10 The impact of central bank digital currency (CBDC) on the operations of Islamic Banks 190
A.K.M. Kamrul Hasan

11 Takafultech reflects the Maqasid al-Shariah ethos in takaful 203
Amirul Afif Muhamat and Norfaridah Ali Azizan

12 Digital transformation and IFRS 17 accounting issues in takaful industry: the case of Indonesia 218
Ersa Tri Wahyuni

13 Dilemma and challenges for fintech application in *Waqf* administration/regulation in contemporary Muslim majority countries: a case of Bangladesh 235
A. K. M. Kamrul Hasan

14 Breaking the barriers of Zakat management system through Islamic Fintech: the case of Bangladesh 251
S. M. Sohrab Uddin and Afroza Sultana

15 An inquiry into the application of artificial intelligence on *Fatwa* 273
Ali Polat, Shoaib Khan and Usman Bashir

Conclusion 288
Yasushi Suzuki and Mohammad Dulal Miah

Index 297

FIGURES

Chapter 1
1   Functions and components of a financial system   20
2   Category of Gray-Zones in Islamic Finance   27
Chapter 4
1   Indonesia's Fintech compositions by business model   86
2   AFTECH members from 2016 to Q2 2020   86
3   P2P lending business scheme   90
4   Qazwa's "value-chain integrated" financing approach   94
5   Supply chain–financing model workflow   96
Chapter 5
1   Reward-based crowdfunding model   111
2   ECF model   112
Chapter 6
1   Reasons why IBs engage in digital transformation   121
2   Proportion of IBs that 'Strongly Agree' with Reasons for Digitalisation   122
3   Status of IBs Implementation of Digital Transformation   124
4   Proportion of IBs digital operation and most recent IT budget spent   124
5   Technological advances adopted by Islamic Banks   126
6   Technological advancement being currently expended on as part of IBs' digital transformation process   129
7   Digital transformation risks facing IBs   130
8   Challenges to IBs' digital transformation   133
9   Regulatory approaches to digital transformation   135
Chapter 8
1   Trends in the Dutch banking sector   157
2   Digital banking account holders across gender   160

3	Digital payments by gender	161
4	Digital payments by age	162
5	Digital banking patronage among consumers with technological expertise	163

Chapter 9

1	Drawbacks of SWIFT system	183
2	Blockchain based remittance transfer reducing the drawbacks of traditional SWIFT system	184
3	Contribution of Islamic FinTech in Transferring Remittance under Blockchain	186

Chapter 10

1	Liquidity management dilemma for IFIs	196

Chapter 11

1	Death rate from suicides 2017	206
2	Major *maqasid* al-Shariah and their link to the takafultech	216

Chapter 12

1	Optimism level on overall insurance industry	219
2	Takaful models used globally	220
3	Top countries in Islamic Finance Assets 2019	222
4	Timeline of accounting standards for insurance contracts in Indonesia	229

Chapter 13

1	Parties involved in *waqf* estates management	241
2	Administrative structure of the Office of the *Waqf* Administrator	242
3	Decision-making process at the Office of *Waqf*	242
4	Adaptation of fintech in cash *waqf*	246
5	Adaptation of fintech in non-cash *waqf*	247

TABLES

Chapter 1
1   Domestic credit (by banks) to private sector (% of GDP) in 2020   19
Chapter 2
1   The working Fintech taxonomy and classification by CCAF   45
2   Expected impacts of digital lending on commercial banks   49
3   Expected impacts of digital capital raising on commercial banks   50
4   Expected impacts of digital banking on commercial banks   51
5   Expected impacts of digital savings on commercial banks   52
6   Expected impacts of digital payments on commercial banks   53
7   Expected impacts of digital assets exchange on commercial banks   54
8   Expected impacts of digital custody on commercial banks   55
9   Expected impacts of Insurtech on commercial banks   55
10   Expected impacts of Wealthtech on commercial banks   57
Chapter 4
1   List of Indonesia's Fintech regulations   87
2   Fintech lending company overview   90
Chapter 5
1   CFPs in Bangladesh   106
2   Volume of alternative finance in South Asian countries   109
3   NPL and ROA of different banks   110
4   Crowdfunding regulatory policies of different countries   113
Chapter 7
1   Profile of the respondents   147
Chapter 9
1   Year-wise remittance collection through formal sector from year 2015 to year 2020   178

2	Country-wise inward remittance and remittance percentage of GDP at the end of 2020	178

Chapter 10
1	Core features of CBDC	192
2	Implication of Shariah-based CBDC	198

Chapter 11
1	Benefits of drone in *takaful* operation	211

Chapter 12
1	Total Islamic insurance industry players in five years	223
2	The adoption of IFRS 17 on takaful contract across some jurisdictions	227

Chapter 13
1	Salient features of *Waqf* Ordinance 1962	240

Chapter 14
1	*Zakat* collections and disbursements (rounded in a million) of key representatives of the member countries of the World Zakat Forum	255
2	Contributions of Islamic banks of Bangladesh to the *zakat* funds for the last ten years (figures are rounded to a million)	265

Chapter 15
1	Shari'ah conformity matrix	279

CONTRIBUTORS

Md. Joynal Abedin is an Assistant Professor at the Department of Finance, American International University-Bangladesh.

Abideen Adeyemi Adewale is the Head of Research – Islamic Financial Services Board (IFSB).

Riyashad Ahmed is an Assistant Professor at BRAC Business School, BRAC University, Dhaka, Bangladesh.

Rima Akter is an undergraduate student at University of Chittagong, Bangladesh.

Md Imran Hossain Anik is an undergraduate student at University of Chittagong, Bangladesh.

Muhammad Ashfaq is a Lecturer in Business Administration at Wittenborg University of Applied Sciences University, the Netherlands.

Norfaridah Ali Azizan is a Postgraduate Student, Universiti Teknologi, MARA, Malaysia.

Usman Bashir is an Assistant Professor, University of Bahrain, Sakhir, Kingdom of Bahrain.

Mohammad Omar Farooq is an Assistant Professor at Gulf University, Kingdom of Bahrain.

Contributors

A. K. M. Kamrul Hasan is a Senior Lecturer of Finance at School of Business and Economics, Westminster International University Tashkent, Uzbekistan.

Rashedul Hasan is a Lecturer at Coventry University, United Kingdom.

Rifki Ismal is a Deputy Director – Bank Indonesia and Assistant Secretary-General – Islamic Financial Services Board (IFSB).

Shoaib Khan is an Assistant Professor, University of Ha'il, Kingdom of Saudi Arabia.

Tasfika Khanam is a Lecturer at the Department of Business Administration in Finance & Banking, Bangladesh University of Professionals, Bangladesh.

Mohammad Dulal Miah is an Associate Professor at the University of Nizwa, Oman.

Amirul Afif Muhamat is an Associate Professor at Universiti Teknologi, MARA, Malaysia.

Dikry Paren is a CEO and Founder of Qazwa Mitra Hasanah, Indonesia.

Ali Polat is an Associate Professor, Ankara Yildirim Beyazit University, Ankara, Turkey.

Sigit Pramono is a Chairman at SEBI School of Islamic Economics, Indonesia.

Syed Mahbubur Rahman is Associate Professor at BRAC Business School, BRAC University, Bangladesh.

M. Iqbal Ramadhan is a CFO of Qazwa Mitra Hasanah, Indonesia.

Abdul Rauf is a Lecturer in HRM at Wittenborg University of Applied Sciences University, the Netherlands.

Muhammad Razikun is a Founder of MUC Consulting Group and Lecturer at SEBI School of Islamic Economics, Indonesia.

Afroza Sultana is a Lecturer at the Department of Business Administration, Premier University, Chattogram, Bangladesh.

Yasushi Suzuki is a Professor at Ritsumeikan Asia Pacific University, Japan.

Mai Tran is graduate student, Wittenborg University of Applied Sciences University, the Netherlands.

S. M. Sohrab Uddin is a Professor, Department of Finance, University of Chittagong, Bangladesh.

Ersa Tri Wahyuni is an Associate Professor in Accounting at the Faculty of Economics and Business, Universitas Padjadjaran, Indonesia.

FOREWORD

The global financial crisis (GFC) of 2007–2009 caused an unprecedented suffering for the financial world. While financial institutions were concentrating on restoring themselves overcoming the adversaries resulted from the GFC, it was the COVID-19 pandemic that hit the global economy and financial system again. Restrictions on people's movement, frequent lock-down of national economies, and prolonged closure of production and distribution wrecked a serious havoc on real and financial activities globally. Despite the devastating effects unfolded by these two consecutive events within a decade, the financial world has proved its resilience and learned how to survive, thanks to its continuous innovative capacity to utilize technology in designing and delivering financial products and services. The use of technology to enable and support financial products and services is simply known as fintech.

Fintech is the buzzword of the time. Blockchain, crowdfunding, robo-advising, artificial intelligence (AI), cloud-computing are just few examples of how technology is constantly shaping finance world. Although it is difficult to accurately estimate the size of fintech market owing to its wider scope, KPMG estimates that global fintech market reached US$210 billion in 2021. Digital payment is the leading and major element of fintech in terms of transaction amount. Another report published by US-based Grand View Research shows that AI in the global fintech market is estimated to reach US$41.16 billion between 2022 and 2030, a cumulative annual growth rate of about 16.5%. Venture capital and private equity firms are the major investors in Fintech, the report shows.

The penetration of technology in the financial market is believed to disrupt the traditional financial system. Although the impacts of fintech on conventional banking and finance have explored extensively, the same is not observed for Islamic finance industry. The applicability of technology in Islamic finance and its repercussion for the industry have remained largely unexplored. In particular, the adoption of fintech by Islamic financial institutions (IFIs) may raise numerous concerns. Among them, the primary is the Shariah compliance. Hence, it raises a host of interesting questions as such: how IFIs cope with the disruptive trend of fintech? Is technology going to be an enabler or barrier to IFIs? How IFIs can utilize the promising features of technology to harness their competitive edge and successfully compete with tech-based and quasi-financial institutions? This edited volume is a novel attempt to answer these questions and follows a holistic approach to achieve this objective. It helps readers understand the broader picture of fintech applied in IFIs. Moreover, the arguments raised in this book are substantiated by necessary data and statistics.

As a Professor of Islamic finance and editor of several academic journals, I have found Professor Suzuki Yasushi and Mohammad Dulal Miah passionate contributors, avid readers, and keenly interested in Islamic finance. They always strive to update them about the changes taking place in their relevant fields. Professor Suzuki has accumulated significant practical experience working in the industry for a long time and gained knowledge by contributing intellectually to the literature of Islamic banking and finance though regularly publishing books and articles. This has enabled him to effectively integrate contemporary theories with practice, which has been reflected in this edited volume.

The chapters are well organized, written in a plain language, and equally suitable for specialized and non-specialized readers. Moreover, a fine balance between theory and practice has been maintained. Cases are carefully selected from Muslim majority countries to illustrate practical applications of fintech and explore other potentials fintech has to offer for Islamic finance industry. From this vantage point, I can say that the book would be a timely collection for graduate and undergraduate students of Islamic banking and finance as a reference book. Moreover, policymakers may find the book an interesting guide for appropriate policy intervention.

M. Kabir Hassan
Professor of Finance
University of New Orleans
2016 IsDB Prize winner in Islamic
banking and finance

When I am writing this foreword, the market for cryptocurrency, one of the most obvious examples of fintech, experienced yet another tumultuous phase. Bitcoin, the leader of crypto market, saw a plunge in its price to the lowest since November 2020. In a span of less than three months until June 2022, Bitcoin (most other cryptos as well) lost more 60% value. As many central banks worldwide are contemplating to introduce digital currency, it raises a concern as to how financial institutions, particularly Islamic banks which are prohibited to deal with *Riba* (interest) and *Gharar* (uncertainty), can deal with digital currency and other such sophisticated technologies. This book is an insightful attempt to raise such practical issues which are pertinent to Islamic finance and require careful observation from the policymakers and regulatory authorities for materializing the benefits offered by the trend of current digital disruption.

Fintech is making an inroad into our daily lives. Mobile payment is now an everyday phenomenon; money transfer using blockchain is a new reality. Texting a Chatbot embedded with a customer care software of a financial service provider is not surprising at all. Paying bills by cryptocurrency has been gaining momentum despite numerous hurdles. Figuring out customers' buying patterns from a large pool of data using complex algorithm and offering products and services matching their preferences are now easier and more realistic than ever before. Delivery of actuarial service relying on data stored in a cloud platform is more efficient and effective than the traditional one. These examples, which are nothing but the tips of a large iceberg of fintech, imply that technology is destined to usher in a new era for finance.

The intellectual curiosity of Professor Suzuki Yasushi and his associate, Dr. Mohammad Dulal Miah, has motivated them to capture a snapshot of how fintech is shaping Islamic finance. The current project, seemingly a well-timed and trending in finance, is not their first endeavor to edit a volume; rather, the duo has successfully accomplished numerous projects including several edited volumes as well as research monographs. In addition, they have widely published about Islamic finance and banking. The distinctive feature of their works relies on the ability to examine contemporary issues of finance through the prism of practicality. As students of new institutional economics, Professor Suzuki and Dr. Miah have always attempted to introduce new facts and evidence in an unconventional and holistic manner. They have followed the same tradition in this book as well. Apart from contributing several chapters on their own, the editors were meticulous in selecting chapters. Care has been taken to ensure that selected cases expose readers to new facts and ideas that would hopefully enrich their understanding about fintech in Islamic finance.

As usual, certain limitations apply to this project. Readers may perceive that some concepts, including regulatory issues about Shariah compliance of fintech, ethical concerns, and political economy of digital transformation of Islamic finance, could have been given more space. However, the editors have set the scope of the book at the outset. They focus on bringing practices of fintech among IFIs including banks, micro-finance institutions, insurance companies, etc. In addition, the book explores the future potentials of technology that would positively affect IFIs. The book emphasizes that IFIs should seriously consider tapping those potentials for modernizing their services and successfully competing with the conventional banking system. If the book is assessed through the lens of the above-articulated goals, it has certainly met the stated objectives. Therefore, the book could be a useful read for those who wish to know more about the applicability and future prospects of fintech in IFIs.

Professor Yasushi Kosugi
Director, Asia-Japan Research Institute
Ritsumeikan Asia-Japan Research Organization
Ritsumeikan University

PREFACE

The trend of Digital Transformation (DX) is likely to give a critical impact on the *geography* of Islamic finance because the information & communication technology (ICT) is considered to de-territorialize human experience in general. ICTs have made regional borders porous or, in some cases, entirely irrelevant. Perhaps, the Islamic mode of financial intermediation is open to anyone, irrespective of their religious belief, who are engaged in commercial transactions – *mu'amalat*. In practice, however, the *shari'ah*-compliant mode of financial intermediation has been developed and thoroughly used in the *Muslim* community. On the one hand, the Islamic mode of financial intermediation is expanding beyond a sovereign territorial unit, while the DX in Islamic finance is expected to intensify the penetration of the *shari'ah*-compliant mode in the Muslim community. On the other hand, the trend of DX in financial contracts – financial technology (Fintech) – is exposing severer competitions to IFIs in competing with conventional financial institutions both in domestic and international financial markets, beyond the geography of Muslim community. The adoption of technologies is considered an essential endeavour for any financial service provider to remain competitive in the post-pandemic period. In other words, fintech is going to be a decisive factor in determining the success and failure of financial service providers in the future.

Scholars and practitioners of Islamic finance are concerned about how the on-going DX would shape the Islamic mode of financial intermediation and services, specially, during the time of 'globalization' as well as 'internationalization' of financial services. The argument on 'what is feasible' (reality) should be outweighed rather than that on 'what is desirable' (idealistic expectations). This book aims to analyze how DX is giving a critical impact on the faith-based financial mode in multifaceted ways. Part I of this book is addressed to provide theoretical and philosophical speculations on DX in Islamic finance, while Part II collects 12 empirical studies related to digital lending, digital capital raising, digital banking, digital payments, *takaful*-tech (insurtech), *waqf*-tech, *zakat*-tech, *shari'ah*-tech (legaltech). We would be happy if this book facilitates further discussions on the 'reality' faced by the Islamic mode of financial intermediation, as well as discussions on how it is essential to adopt the DX in financial contracts – 'Fintech' – for a harmonious co-existence with the internationally prevailing mode, that is, the conventional mode of financial intermediation and services.

Yasushi Suzuki and Mohammad Dulal Miah
June 2022

ACKNOWLEDGEMENTS

The editors would like to thank Routledge/Taylor & Francis Asia Pacific for their guidance and continuous support towards the publication of this book. *Yasushi* would like to acknowledge that his work was supported by JSPS Grant-in-Aid for Scientific Research (C), Grant Number, 19K01749. He would like to thank Akiko Suzuki for her constant support and motivation. Special thanks go to Professor Yasushi Kosugi whose deep and insightful thoughts of Islamic Studies always inspire the editors. *Dulal* would like to thank Prof. M. Kabir Hassan, Dr. Samsul Alam, Dr. Md. Nurul Kabir, and Dr. Md. Safiullah for sharing their views and ideas about Islamic finance. He would also like to thank Mir Ferdousi for her continuous support and motivation.

INTRODUCTION

Yasushi Suzuki and Mohammad Dulal Miah

Digital revolution, digitalization, and digital transformation (DX) have become the most frequently used phrases in this last decade. The term 'digital transformation' has no universal definition because it encompasses a diverse set of concepts like digital supply chain, digitalization of services and products, and so on (Hazik and Hassnian, 2019). Solis and Szymanski (2014) define DX as 'the realignment of, or new investment in, advanced technology and business models to more effectively engage digital customers at every touchpoint in the customer experience lifecycle'.

Financial institutions are, perhaps, the pioneers in embracing the ongoing DX with an aim to harness their efficiency and performance. Moreover, the adoption of technologies is considered an essential endeavor for financial service provider to remain competitive and survive in the market. As a result, technology-enabled financial transactions such as wealth management, robo-advising, peer-to-peer (P2P) lending, crowdfunding, and digital payments have spawned recently. According to Forbes, digital banking amounted to US$7.7 billion in 2019, whereas digital insurance (insurtech) recorded transactions amounting to US$6.8 billion, and the digital payment summed up to US$15.1 billion at the same time.

Although the DX has received enormous attention worldwide especially during and after the COVID-19 pandemic, financial institutions attempted to modernize services throughout the ages. History shows that the building of Transatlantic Cable in 1858 between the UK and the USA and the introduction of Fedwire in 1918 marked the beginning of the modernization of financial services. They were the early steps that facilitated the electronic transfer of funds using information technology. Subsequently, the introduction of the first ATM in 1967 by Barclays Bank changed the course of financial transactions people

DOI: 10.4324/9781003262169-1

used to know them before. Furthermore, the establishment of NASDAQ in 1971 added a new dimension to stock trading because it paved the way for online trading of financial assets. This was followed by the introduction of SWIFT in 1973 which brought a revolutionary change in interstate transfer of funds. Since then, the finance world experienced an increased penetration of technologies which can be attributed to the invention of mainframe computers in the 1980s. As a result, remarkable changes have been observed in payment systems, fund transfers, cashless transactions, etc.

The global financial crisis of 2007–2009, triggered by the US subprime mortgage crisis, changed the landscape of modern finance. In particular, the role of fiat money has been challenged on the ground that the centralized control of fiat currency distorts its intrinsic value by changing the supply of money single-handedly by the central bank, sometimes at a consideration that does not mean to enhance social welfare. In addition, the regulatory control over fiat money limits the freedom of money transfer because all transfers through formal financial system must seek approval from the relevant authority. In addition, the conventional process of financial transactions is time-consuming and expensive. With the promise to mitigate such problems, Satoshi Nakamoto (pseudonym) invented Bitcoin in 2009, followed by thousands of other cryptocurrencies subsequently. At its peak, the market capitalization of Bitcoin alone surpassed trillion-dollar mark. This particular invention is considered the biggest disruptive technology related to finance and vows to redefine the payment system (Thakor, 2020).

Undoubtedly, the COVID-19 pandemic has accelerated the adoption of fintech at an unprecedented pace. During the peak of the pandemic, countries across the world were forced to introduce home-office, nationwide lockdown, and social distancing. This 'new normal' economic circumstance required business organizations to extensively rely on technology-based solutions. For example, business and individuals relied on cashless transactions to avoid physical contact as an attempt to restrict the spread of Novel Coronavirus. Fu and Mishra (2022) estimate that the rate of daily download of finance-related mobile applications during the pandemic increased between 21% and 26%. They further show that more than half of the downloads belonged to the traditional incumbents and about half of the top downloads pertain to general banking apps. Among other popular finance apps, lending, payment, investment, and insurance were highly demanding apps during the pandemic. Najaf et al. (2021) report that the volume of P2P lending increased by 23% on average between January 2019 and June 2020 compared to the pre-pandemic period.

How does the ongoing technological disruption affect the course of financial landscape we used to know it? The development of fintech and its increased application during the COVID-19 has created a general perception among people that banks can provide better services through greater use of technology. With the onset of the post-pandemic new normal, such perception is deemed to persist and customers will no longer be interested in leaving the use of technology and returning to the traditional transacting system using physical facilities.

This has a significant repercussion for the overall finance industry, in general, and banking system, in particular. Banks, which have set up more branches by adopting branch expansion strategies to capitalize on the competitive advantage offered by the economies of scale, are believed to have more fixed assets than they require in the new normal. As a result, banks with huge sunk cost invested in property and plant are perceived to suffer from excess and unused capacity which, in turn, hampers their cost-cutting strategy. While large banks may be plagued by excess physical capacity, small and medium-sized banks, which are much weaker in terms of financial strength, tend to face mounting challenges in integrating information technology with financial services. At the same time, commercial banks are likely to face intense competition from technology-enabled non-banking financial institutions as well as fintech-based startups. These types of financial services providers are gradually turning into direct competitors to mainstream commercial banks by capitalizing on the advantage of fintech.

Increased competition brought about by fintech is believed to provide customers with better services in terms of reducing time and cost of transactions. On the service providers end, fintech is likely to enhance efficiency and squeeze traditional-style physical facilities, paving the way for the emergence of boutique banks in the future. Moreover, technology-driven P2P lending, use of apps to pay fees and bills, robo-advising, crowdfunding, direct transfer of funds using block chain technologies as well as cryptocurrencies imply less demand for traditional banking services, which may result in financial disintermediation. Hence, the survival of the banking sector hinges critically on the adoption of technologies or establishing a link with the tech-based firms.

While the impacts of fintech on conventional banking system are well documented in the contemporary finance literature, much less is known as to how the ongoing DX affects Islamic banking system. Islamic financial institutions (IFIs) co-exist with their conventional counterparts and hold a commendable market share worldwide. According to Islamic Financial Services Board's (IFSB, 2019) stability report, Islamic financial service industry's total worth grew remarkably over the last few years to reach an accumulated amount US$2.44 trillion as of the second quarter of 2019. The ongoing DX is, undoubtedly, going to impact the faith-based financial mode in multifaceted ways. Hence, scholars and practitioners of Islamic finance are concerned about how the DX would reshape the Islamic mode of financial intermediation and services, especially, during the time of 'globalization' as well as 'internationalization' of financial services. Globalization, in this context, refers to the trend in which the Islamic mode of financial intermediation and services is being expanded on a global scale. On the other hand, 'internationalization' means the trend that the Islamic mode of financial intermediation and services needs a harmonious co-existence with the internationally prevailing mode, i.e. the conventional mode of financial intermediation and services.

The trend of DX is likely to give a critical impact on the *geography* of Islamic finance because the information & communication technology (ICT) is considered to de-territorialize human experience in general. As Floridi (2014) points out, ICTs have made regional borders *porous* or, in some cases, entirely irrelevant. Perhaps, the Islamic mode of financial intermediation is open to anyone, irrespective of their religious belief, who are engaged in commercial transactions – *mu'amalat*. In practice, however, the *shari'ah*-compliant mode of financial intermediation has been developed and thoroughly used in the *Muslim* community. On the one hand, the Islamic mode of financial intermediation is expanding beyond a sovereign territorial unit, while the DX in Islamic finance is expected to intensify the penetration of the *shari'ah*-compliant mode in the Muslim community. In parallel, the trend of DX in financial contracts – financial technology (fintech) – is exposing severer competitions to IFIs in competing with conventional financial institutions both in domestic and international financial markets, beyond the geography of Muslim community. The adoption of technologies is considered an essential endeavor for any financial service provider to remain competitive in the post-pandemic period. In other words, fintech is going to be a decisive factor in determining the success and failure of financial service providers in the future. Intuitively, we would say that the trends of globalization as well as internationalization of Islamic mode of financial intermediation and services should be promoted. However, what is the justification for promoting the globalization as well as internationalization of Islamic mode? To what extent the globalization as well as internationalization of Islamic mode should be promoted? Is fintech going to be an enabler or barrier to achieve the intended purpose of Islamic finance, *Maqasid Al shari'ah*? Is fintech going to narrow the division between Islamic and conventional finance in the future?

These questions are existential for Islamic financial service industry because a delay in the adoption of technology is feared to throw IFIs out of the competition. On the other hand, IFIs must filter the compatibility of technology-enabled financial techniques through the lens of *shari'ah* norms. The extant literature on finance focuses extensively on the benefits fintech may offer to the society. While it is always welcoming to decipher the benefits of new technology, we should, at the same time, attempt to assess the broader picture of the impacts. As mentioned earlier, fintech would provide customers with cost-reducing, timely, and intervention-free transaction experience. However, DX may lead to financial disintermediation. How beneficial would such disintermediation be for Islamic finance industry which is still at its developing stage?

Islamic perfectionists emphasize the fact that transactions such as P2P lending can avoid financial intermediaries; crowdfunding can help increase equity-based finance instead of intermediary-based lending; cryptocurrency can facilitate the transfer of funds beyond the formal banking channel. These processes increase compliance with shari'ah compared to traditional banks-based system. On the other hand, digitalization can accelerate the rate of wealth transfer but may erode the possibility of wealth creation through the help of financial intermediaries. Hence, there is debate as to whether Islamic financial system has already created enough wealth to facilitate its transfer or IFIs should concentrate on creating wealth through the formal banking system instead of accelerating financial disintermediation. Bakar (2021) calls for bridging a divide between the 'temporary solution approach' for the needs of the contemporary Muslim society and the society's – seemingly mainstream – 'perfectionists' expectation for a complete profit and loss sharing (PLS)-based Islamic financial system. Bakar insists that *maqasid shari'ah* could potentially be the most powerful device in *shari'ah* orientation, not only to spur a new policy and value proposition but also to change certain established policies and standards in Islam. The knowledge of *maqasid shari'ah* is overwhelmingly backed by 'collective, cumulative and compounding' insights of a bundle of Divine texts (Bakar, 2021, p. 13). To ensure the 'collective, cumulative and compounding' perspective, in other words, in order to avoid any 'personally-and-emotionally biased perspective', Bakar proposes, 'the knowledge of *maqasid shari'ah* should be fairly structured, quantified, and most importantly scientific (Bakar, 2021, p. 14).

The above discussion entails that financial technology is essential for IFIs not only for achieving operational efficiency and competitiveness but also for transition from a 'temporary solution' for the needs of the contemporary Muslim society to an ideal PLS-based Islamic finance. In other words, the question is not if IFIs should adopt fintech or not, the right question is how Islamic financial intermediaries can continue their primary task of wealth creation utilizing the trend of DX without compromising shari'ah guidelines. This book attempts to contribute to this stream of literature. It aims to examine if DX provides IFIs with an edge to serve clients following *shari'ah* norms. Simultaneously, this book aims to critically assess how each DX in the Islamic mode is required for meeting the *maqasid* objectives for society.

To achieve the above-stated objectives, this book collects evidence through case studies from a diverse set of countries. It focuses on the applicability of financial technology including blockchain and digital currency, big data, and artificial intelligence (AI) to versatile areas of Islamic finance including Zakat funds, Waqf management, Islamic SMEs, crowdfunding, P2P lending, remittance flow, etc. In addition, Islamic finance is basically a faith-based system founded on Islamic principles which strongly embody ethical and moral values. On the other hand, technology generates a host of ethical concerns as far as financial transactions are concerned. Hence, ethics has been considered an important element in assessing the feasibility of adopting financial technology for Islamic financial service providers.

The field of Islamic finance and economics is expanding at a rapid pace due to its relevance to the development and social justice issues not only in Muslim majority countries but also in other parts of the world. This edited volume is a noble attempt to help fostering Islamic finance further by identifying strengths and weaknesses in integrating financial technology to harness their operation. Inferences and arguments made in this book are substantiated by theory and evidence. The first part of the book lays the theoretical foundation by discussing several theories relevant to Islamic finance and critically evaluates the feasibility of clubbing finance with technologies. The second part of the book provides evidence analyzing cases drawing from a diverse area of Islamic finance. Moreover, the cases are collected mostly from the Muslim majority countries where Islamic finance claims a significant share of financial assets so that the selected cases unveil what is happening on the ground. These distinctive features of the book make it a useful read for students, analysts, policymakers, and regulators interested in Islamic finance, financial economics, Islamic economics, and development finance.

Structure of the book

Part I of the book comprises three chapters. Chapter 1 critically evaluates the impact of fintech on the financial industry. The computing power of digital systems is becoming stronger, faster, and cheaper at an exponential rate. How feasible it is to achieve the socio-economic objectives through Islamic financing powered by technology? It is certain that the scope of operation of financial intermediaries is going to shrink in the future when high-tech firms would take a significant share of fee and commission-based operations of banks. In addition, intense competition from shadow banking as well as tech-based firms would erode bank's earning capacity. In such a circumstance, Islamic banks would struggle to capture 'rent' required to ensure shariah compliance of their product. While Islamic perfectionists strongly advocate a shift of financial activities from traditional financial intermediaries to technology-enabled firms, the motto of wealth creation in the society is overshadowed by wealth distribution. Critics of contemporary Islamic finance, however, have paid much less attention to this fundamental issue than it really deserves. In Chapter 1, the authors attempt to find an explanation in which this divide can be bridged.

Fintech embodies a wider scope. Hence, it is difficult to precisely conceptualize the term. Chapter 2 aims to review the working taxonomy and proposes a typology of 'Fintech' business models, to provide a platform for further academic and professional debate toward predicting how fintech and DX in financial contracts would reshape the current mode of financial intermediation and financial contracting. This working taxonomy is believed to help understanding the scope of fintech activities. The authors particularly, focus on identifying the major stakeholders (who have a keen interest) in promoting each fintech business model. In addition, the authors assess the impacts of fintech on commercial banks through the lens of these major stakeholders.

One of the critical aspects of integrating technology with finance is that sometimes the hype of technology may overshadow the intrinsic values and principles on which society's foundation is built. Everyone is now enamored with the prospect of fintech, and no one wants to be left behind. In light of the past contributions and impacts of technology in general, there might be good reasons to be excited about fintech too. However, just like technology can reshape our lives and the services and conveniences we enjoy, there can also be technomania, obsessive enthusiasm about technology. To benefit from fintech properly and adequately, it is important that fintech does not succumb to technomania. Chapter 3 explores what potentials fintech may offer to mankind beyond ease, convenience, sophistication, efficiency, and diversity of the ways to do things. The humanity and the Muslim world face some ongoing challenges, including few existential ones. The authors have pointed out few key challenges, examined how fintech may or may not contribute toward addressing those challenges, and suggested some parameters that might enable fintech to properly interact with the ongoing and persistent human challenges.

The empirical part of the book starts with a case, P2P lending experience of an SME, in Chapter 4. The authors provide an overview of the recent progress of online 'P2P' financing platforms for supporting SMEs in Indonesia. As mentioned earlier, the P2P lending mechanism has emerged as a potential alternative to mainstream financing which eliminates the need for intermediation. Some attractive features of P2P lending include quick processing, low-cost transactions, and ease of management. Through the prisms of these features, the experience of PT Qazwa Mitra Hasanah Indonesia, which aims at linking Islamic finance with the technology, has been assessed. In addition, the authors have explored how Qazwa's 'value-chain integrated' financing scheme plays a critical role in mitigating associated business risks. The authors further prescribe some policy recommendations which may ameliorate the persistent problems hindering the expansion of P2P lending especially in SMEs.

Like P2P lending, crowdfunding has been growing profusely, though small in scale. Chapter 5 discusses the scenarios of Islamic crowdfunding in Bangladesh. The history of crowdfunding of the country, as the chapter highlights, is rather a new phenomenon. Due to lack of enthusiasm among people, and perhaps lack of trust about the success of funding initiatives, the first attempt of crowdfunding in Bangladesh apparently failed. However, there are evidence that some projects have been able to manage funds successfully. Analyzing the success and failures of crowdfunding in Bangladesh, this chapter recommends for establishing proper infrastructure, enacting investors-friendly rules and regulations, and creating appropriate investment opportunities for the potential entrepreneurs for a thriving crowdfunding environment in Bangladesh. The chapter further points out that the Islamic financial industry will be revolutionized by the implementation of crowdfunding if a legit and convenient platform of investment for the general people can be ensured.

Chapter 6 conducts an empirical analysis to identify antecedents that motivate Islamic banks to adopt technology. The authors conduct a survey that covers 80 Islamic banks across 21 jurisdictions to assess the rationales for digitalization, current status, and the technologies being adopted by Islamic banks. The chapter further investigates the regulatory approaches, challenges, prudential risks, and financial stability implications of digitalization of Islamic banking. Analysis shows that the Islamic banking digitalization process is still in progress but has gained momentum since the outbreak of the COVID-19 pandemic. Survey responses show that strengthening competitiveness, enhancing operational efficiency, and improving customer satisfaction are the main driving force of Islamic banks' digitalization drive. However, some obstacles such as legal infrastructure, lack of requisite human resources, and open banking infrastructure impede Islamic banking digitalization drive.

While questionnaire survey provides valuable insights about the drivers facilitating the adoption of technologies by Islamic banks, Chapter 7 embarks on an interview method to explore opportunities and threats for launching and innovating Fintech in Islamic banks in Bangladesh. To achieve this objective, the chapter collects data through in-depth interviews with relevant bank officials. Analysis shows that awareness about fintech among the bankers is confined to mobile banking services only. Lack of technological expertise has been pointed out as a hinderance toward promoting Fintech in Islamic banks. While the central bank of the country does not force banks to adopt technologies, customers are found to be demanding for tech-based banking services. The interview further reveals that bankers perceive digitalization as a potential driver that helps minimize banks' operating costs. Moreover, a lack of skilled human resources is identified as a barrier toward digitalizing banking services. Based on these critical findings, the chapter offers some policy options for regulatory authorities.

So far, we have presented cases from Muslim majority countries. How is the experience of fintech in non-Muslim majority countries where the penetration of Islamic finance is relatively low but expanding at a good pace? Chapter 8 presents the case of the Netherlands. Adopting a qualitative research methodology and a case study approach, the chapter critically reviews the development of Islamic digital service delivery in the Netherlands. A distinct contribution of this chapter relies on its systematic analysis of security threats stemming from the adoption of technology by financial institutions. Analysis shows that customers' suspicion about data protection keeps them away from using fintech. This distrust is a function of customers' technical knowledge. Customers' adequate technical knowledge is a positive factor impacting their perception about data protection quality, which in turn, results in increased use of digital banking services.

While the above-mentioned security concern is real, technology has advanced well to mitigate such problems. Blockchain as a disruptive technology has appeared to tighten the security concern embedded with the technology. Under the blockchain mechanism, a transaction is recorded in a ledger once it occurs. Each page of this ledger is like a block. The number of pages created will continue to be added to the ledger as a chain-like block. Everyone who uses blockchain technology has their own copy of the ledger to create an integrated transaction record. The software records each new transaction exactly as it happens and updates each copy of the new blockchain at the same time, keeping all records uniform and accurate. Because every transaction has a digital record and signature that guarantees identification, validity, preservation, and sharing, blocks are protected from the risk of deletion, tampering, or any other changes. Although the blockchain was initially meant for cryptocurrency, its use has been extended to other areas of businesses as an attractive technology to solve real-world problems. Chapter 9 assesses how this promising technology (blockchain) can facilitate cross-border payment, remittance, in a timely, transparent, and cost-effective manner. Considering South Asia as a case, the chapter argues that blockchain-enabled transfer payments can reduce the fraudulent activities in the system as the operations of Islamic banks and other financial institutions are profoundly supervised and monitored by *shari'ah* Supervisory Board.

The blockchain-based cryptocurrency shows the promise to make P2P transactions quick, economic, and hassle-free without compromising the confidentiality of the transaction and interference from the central authority. If cryptocurrency becomes successful and earns trust from users, it would be an existential threat for the traditional fiat money. Central banks would lose control over money supply, which sometimes may prove augur ill for the overall economy. To avoid such awkward future circumstances, some central banks have already initiated or declared to issue digital currency known as Central Bank Digital Currency (CBDC). China is the pioneer in piloting a CBDC, and the Fed is seriously considering introducing central bank-backed stable-coin. Chapter 10 examines how the CBDC would affect the operations of Islamic banks. The chapter asks: is the use of CBDC going to augment Gharar (uncertainty), for Islamic banks? If so, how can Islamic banks address increased uncertainty? The chapter derives its logic from *shari'ah* scholars' divided opinion (in favor and against) regarding Shariah compliance of cryptocurrency. CBDC would share some common features with cryptocurrency. The chapter points out that price fluctuation in CBDC may be a *shari'ah* concern for IFIs due to *Gharar*. The author, thus, recommends Islamic banks to use asset-backed CBDC as a potential safeguard against CBDC-embedded uncertainty.

The impact of technology on banks usually receives a wide coverage in the literature due to the scope and scale of banking sector in the industry compared to other subunits of a financial system. For instance, the insurance industry is an integral part of any financial system. Like their banking counterparts, insurance companies are also believed to be affected significantly by the ongoing digital disruption. Chapter 11 takes this issue into account and attempts to discuss the potentials of takafultech (Takaful+technology) to bring closer takaful (Islamic terminology of insurance) operator to fulfil the *shari'ah* objective (maqasid al- *shari'ah*). The analysis in this chapter focuses on takaful participants or the policyholders who, although not part of the management, are one of the principals in the takaful operations. Moreover, policyholders are concerned about the rise of their liabilities such as payment of higher premium. Based on this analytical underpinning, the chapter identifies challenges which need to be addressed for a thriving technology-enabled takaful industry.

Undoubtedly, accounting issue would be a critical challenge for takaful industry in the Muslim world. Chapter 12 examines how DX poses a threat to accounting issue of takaful industry in Indonesia. The chapter finds analyzing survey data that DX in the takaful industry is much slower than the conventional insurance. One of the critical reasons highlighted in the chapter is the lack of insurtech ecosystem in most Muslim countries including Indonesia. The small size of the industry may have contributed to the lack of appetite to invest in the IT system to embrace the insurtech opportunity. The chapter further shows that takaful industry in Indonesia faces a greater uncertainty stemming from the adoption of International Financial Reporting Standard (IFRS) 17, which must be implemented by 2025. Since takaful operators in Indonesia are mostly the wing of conventional insurance companies, a different system for the takaful wing will complicate the implementation of IFRS 17. The chapter also points out some strategies as remedies for this problem.

Chapter 13 focuses on the *Waqf* administration. The existing regulations and administration of the Waqf estates in most of the Muslim majority countries (especially which are in the developing economies category) are obsolete, so to say. This chapter first explores the historical background of the *Waqf* system, the regulations, monitoring arrangement, and how it works in Bangladesh. Second, the chapter explores avenues for modernizing *Waqf* administration by adopting technologies. Specially, the chapter brings forth the issue of monitoring and governance costs of *Waqf* management. Hence, the chapter illustrates how adoption of fintech in *waqf* administration can minimize monitoring costs and ensure transparent governance.

Like *waqf* management, *Zakat* (obligatory payment) management is also a critical issue in Muslim society. *Zakat* is the most influential Islamic social fund and a powerful Islamic economic instrument to achieve equitable distribution of wealth and poverty alleviation. Chapter 14 shows that fintech has the potential to help *Zakat* Management by campaigning, calculating, collecting, distributing, and ensuring *shari'ah* compliance of Zakat. Furthermore, this chapter is of the opinion that fintech can help ensure flexible, efficient, timely, and less costly services in the financial services industries. Moreover, fintech might solve the challenges of low performance, mismanagement, weak governance, and inefficiency of the Zakat system.

In Shariah-based transactions, certain issues require scholarly interpretation regarding their compliance with Shariah because Quran and Hadith do not explicitly articulate a clear guideline about them. Only qualified Islamic scholars (Fiqh scholar) can assess compliance or non-compliance of a particular financial transaction with Shariah. The entire Islamic financial industry suffers from shortage of Fiqh scholars who can issue fatwa. As a result, it is quite common that one Fiqh scholar sits in multiple boards of Islamic banks worldwide. This practice has been widely criticized in the contemporary Islamic finance literature. Fintech has ushered a possibility that AI can reduce the work requirements of Fiqh scholars. The final chapter (Chapter 15) of the book assesses the feasibility of introducing AI in fatwa issue. In addition, this chapter analyzes how Islamic scholars can use fintech in delivering fatwa and whether issued fatwas can be analyzed using AI to assess their applicability in multiple area of Islamic finance.

Hence, analysis of this chapter is critically important because of its pragmatic policy relevance.

References

Bakar, M. D. (2021). *Maqasid Shariah*: The face and voice of Shariah embedded with big data analytics & artificial intelligence. Kuala Lumpur: Amanie Media Sdn Bhd., in press.

Floridi, L. (2014). *The fourth revolution: How the infosphere is reshaping human reality.* Oxford University Press, Oxford.

Fu, J., & Mishra, M. (2022). Fintech in the time of COVID-19: Technological adoption during crises. *Journal of Financial Intermediation, 50,* 100945. https://doi.org/10.1016/j.jfi.2021.100945

Hazik, M., & Hassnian, A. (2019). *Blockchain, Fintech, and Islamic Finance: Building the Future in the New Islamic Digital Economy.* Berlin: Walter de Gruyter.

Islamic Financial Services Board. (2019). Islamic Financial Services Stability Report, 2019.

Najaf, K., Subramaniam, R. K., & Atayah, O. F. (2021). Understanding the implications of FinTech Peer-to-Peer (P2P) lending during the COVID-19 pandemic. *Journal of Sustainable Finance & Investment, 12*(1), 87–102.

Solis, B., Li, C., & Szymanski, J. (2014). *The 2014 State of Digital Transformation.* Altimeter Group.

Thakor, A. V. (2020). Fintech and banking: What do we know? *Journal of Financial Intermediation, 41,* 100833. https://doi.org/10.1016/j.jfi.2019.100833

PART I
Theoretical and philosophical speculations on digital transformation in Islamic finance

1
DIGITAL TRANSFORMATION IN ISLAMIC FINANCE

A critique of perfectionist's views on Islamic fintech

Yasushi Suzuki and Mohammad Dulal Miah

1 Introduction

Financial institutions are the pioneers in embracing the on-going 'digital transformation' (DX) with an aim to harness their efficiency and performance. Though the term 'DX' does not have a universal definition due to its diversity in meaning, the term encompasses various dimensions like digital supply chain, digitalization of services and products, and so on (Hazik and Hassnian, 2019). The adoption of technologies by financial institutions – shortly termed 'FinTech' – is considered an essential endeavor for any financial service provider – including Islamic financial institutions – to remain competitive and survive in the market. Defined broadly, FinTech encompasses advances in technology and changes in business models that have the potential to transform the provision of financial services through the development of innovative instruments, channels, and systems (CCAF, 2020, p. 24).

FinTech-enabled business models invented so far are overwhelming and diverse. A recent study – *The Global Covid-19 FinTech Market Rapid Assessment Study* – by Cambridge Centre for Alternative Finance developed a working taxonomy that brings together a coherent conceptualization of FinTech activities while appreciating the sector's diversity and differentiated business models (see Table 1 in Chapter 2). This working taxonomy includes 13 discrete primary FinTech verticals and 103 sub-verticals. These have been further categorized into two overarching groups – *Retail Facing* (providing financial products and services with a focus on consumers, households, and micro, small- and medium-sized enterprises [MSMEs], and more likely to be B2C) and *Market Provisioning* (those which enable or support the infrastructure or key functionalities of FinTech and/ or Digital Financial Services markets, thus more likely to be B2B).

DOI: 10.4324/9781003262169-3

DX has become the most frequently used word in the last decade.[1] Islamic financial providers are also exposed to the trend of DX under the name of 'Islamic FinTech'. Hence, it is logical to ask: is there any uniqueness in Islamic FinTech compared to conventional FinTech? In other words, can we differentiate technologies based on the type of financial institutions, Islamic or conventional, adopted them? Oseni and Nazim Ali (2019) insist that fintech is merely a means to an end and not the end itself; therefore, it should not necessarily carry the full 'Islamic' label. We concur to this view. Oseni and Nazim Ali (2019, p. 5) further state 'the *Shari'ah* principles will only apply to each of the components or applications after a careful study of the specific details rather than the generic term "Fintech"'. From this viewpoint, the terms 'Islamic FinTech' is used as the terms of '*Shari'ah*-compliant Fintech' or 'DX solutions in Islamic finance', rather than to demonstrate the uniqueness of fintech solutions in Islamic finance.

On the other hand, we observe that many Islamic scholars tend to expect that fintech is a natural form of Islamic finance. Oseni and Nazim Ali (2019, p. 6) contend 'the ability to mobilize funds for a common or communal cause through crowdfunding, which in some cases is more of donation or interest-free loans, presents a new mode of financing that mirrors the traditional Islamic principles of social finance'. Some experts say fintech financing is inherently Islamic, as it connects owners (*rabb al-mal*) and users of capital directly (Gassner and Lawrence, 2019). Moreover, Islamic finance is concerned with the wellbeing of the community and the transparency of the transaction (De Anca, 2019). Among Islamic scholars, it is believed that fintech has the potential of promoting financial inclusion. Accordingly,

> Islamic finance has more areas of convergence with the socially responsible investment (SRI) movements than any other financing model and automating such processes through fintech will help to emphasize and promote the social element in Islamic finance as it relates to the higher objectives of Islamic law, *maqasid al-Shari'ah*.
>
> *(Oseni and Nazim Ali, 2019, p. 7)*

It is widely believed among Islamic economists that Islamic banks must not only follow the *Shari'ah* principles as the legal system of pragmatism and convenience but also uphold the guiding spirit of *maqasid al-Shari'ah*. From the Islamic economic perspective, *maqasid* can be observed in two dimensions: the *Shari'ah* (law) and the objective of *mukallaf* (religiously responsible or accountable). Obviously, most Islamic banks comply with the *Shari'ah*. However, they must reflect the spirit of *Shari'ah* on their performance by striving to achieve justice, equity, and fairness. Dusuki and Abozaid (2007, p. 144) states, 'the values which prevail within the ambit of the *Shari'ah*, are expressed not only in the details of its transactions but also in the breadth of its role in realizing the *maqasid al-Shari'ah*'. Unlike conventional banks, the maxim of profit-maximization alone is unsuited to *maqasid al-Shari'ah;* but rather, profit should be accompanied by justice and fairness at all levels of human interaction (Chapra, 2000). In this sense, Islamic banks must not exploit their customers *ex-ante* and *ex-post*. As Qur'an mentions, 'Allah has imposed no hardship (*haraj*) upon you in religion' (22:78). And again, 'Allah does not burden a soul beyond its capacity' (2:286). Qur'an reiterates, 'Allah desires not to inflict any hardship upon you' (5:6).

This belief leads us to ask; to what extent – rather automatically or structurally – could we expect the *Shari'ah*-compliant FinTech to help achieving the *maqasid al-Shari'ah*? This chapter aims to critically assess the mainstream and 'perfectionist' or 'idealist' view on Islamic fintech. In so doing, the chapter brings an array of concepts that are at the core of achieving *maqasid al-Shari'ah* and how FinTech can facilitate or obstruct achieving this goal by Islamic financial institutions.

The rest of the chapter is structured as follows: Section 2 assesses the impact of Fintech on Shari'ah-compliance financial disintermediation and how does it affect the society. Section 3 examines the impact of fintech and DX on the performance of Islamic finance. Section 4 analyzes if Shari'ah compliance is both a necessary and sufficient condition for *maqasid al-Shari'ah*. Section 5 identifies potential areas where Islamic banks can focus to materialize the benefits offered by the on-going digitalization. Section 6 points out some issues, such as altruism and reciprocity, that may affect or be affected by the adoption of Fintech. This is followed by a brief conclusion that summarizes the chapter.

2 Is *Shari'ah*-compliant financial disintermediation good for societies?

Most of the Islamic finance industry is concentrated in banking assets and the Islamic finance industry is primarily defined by products developed and sold by banks. According to an investigation by the Islamic Finance Development Report, Islamic banking is continuously the largest sector in the Islamic finance industry amounting to US$1.99 trillion, which accounts for 69% of the industry's assets in 2019. Many Islamic 'perfectionist' views cast doubt on its debt-focused nature and its deviation from the pure mode of profit-loss sharing (PLS) that is suggested by the contractual structures, *musharakah* (investment partnership) and *mudarabah* (investment partnership where one party is named the manager of capital) (Irfan and Ahmed, 2019). More perfectionists propose that financial technology (fintech) which leads to 'disintermediation' may be better suited than the banking industry to achieve the objectives of *Shari'ah*. 'Fintech has the advantage of democratizing the provision of finance, disrupting the standard business models of banks and allowing for risk-sharing asset classes to emerge, all three of which are lacking in the present-day model of Islamic banking' (Irfan and Ahmed, 2019, p. 24).

From the viewpoint of 'temporary solution approach', for instance, Bakar (2021) laments the newest trend and phenomenon of *maqasid shari'ah* in Islamic finance which have been skewed toward putting a lot of expectation on PLS and the equitable distribution of wealth. He criticizes the trend in which many

Muslim thinkers have relied extensively on *maqasid shari'ah* – as they call it – to argue that Islamic finance must attain this *maqasid shari'ah*.

> According to them [Muslim thinkers], all Islamic financial institutions must incorporate this *maqasidic* feature of profit and loss sharing in their product offerings. Otherwise, there could potentially be a structural problem within Islamic banking practice. As far as *maqasid shari'ah* and Islamic finance are concerned, would this be a fair and legitimate expectation?
>
> *(Bakar, 2021, p. 317)*

The temporary solution approach or the 'pragmatist' view gives a warning that Islamic economics advocate 'wealth distribution' while forgetting a much more important element, 'wealth creation'. Bakar (2016) casts doubt on the naive conclusion by Islamic economists that equity-based financing be prioritized to debt-based financing upon the naive assumption that *mudarabah* and *musharakah* financing can be provided on a big scale without affecting the capital adequacy requirement. For instance, the participatory financing of Islamic banks is risker than the debt-like financing which implies that an increase in this mode of finance is likely to increase risk-weighted assets at a higher percentage. This literally implies that Islamic banks which have substantial share in the participatory mode of investment would be required to maintain a higher amount as statutory reserve. Since banks are not earning any return on statutory deposit but pay profit to depositors, the overall cost of banks tends to rise. Thus, under a regulatory environment in which Islamic and conventional banks must maintain a fixed capital adequacy ratio, it is rational for Islamic banks not to dedicate too high of an amount to the participatory mode of finance.

Apparently, the perfectionist expectation on the *Shari'ah*-compliant financial disintermediation underestimates the correlation between financial deepening (in particular, bank credit penetration) and economic development. It is widely argued that the economic development is associated with financial deepening through the function of credit (money) creation by commercial banks.

Table 1 demonstrates that the stage of economic development has a correlation with the level of domestic credit to private sector. We can see that the financial deepening level in developed countries is, in general, higher, while the financial deepening in developing countries stays at a lower level. The average ratio of domestic credit to private sector in OECD members reached 161.9% of their GDP, while that ratio in Arab World stays at 57% of their GDP in 2020. Except Malaysia, financial deepening in Asian Muslim-majority countries including Bangladesh, Indonesia, and Pakistan stays at a low level.

Banks play the role as financial intermediaries of mediating *idle* or, in the Marxian term, *stagnant* money in the household sector to financing mainly the investment by corporate sector. In addition to this role of financial intermediation, commercial banks are expected to be engaged in the role of 'credit (money) creation' because the majority of bank deposits is originally created by banks

TABLE 1 Domestic credit (by banks) to private sector (% of GDP) in 2020

Countries	Financial deepening level
Bangladesh	**45.2 (45.1)**
China	182.4 (182.4)
Egypt	27.3 (27.3)
Indonesia	**38.7 (33.2)**
Iran	66.1 (66.1) [in 2016]
Japan	194.6 (120.4)
Malaysia	**134.1 (134.1)**
Oman	75.1 (75.1) [in 2019]
Pakistan	**17.1 (17.0)**
Singapore	132.7 (132.7)
United Kingdom	146.4 (145.9)
United States	216.3 (54.4)
[Average]	
World	149.6 (99.1)
OECD members	**161.9 (84.7)**
LDC	30.2 (29.5)
Arab World	**57.0 (54.9)**

Source: World Bank (2021).

issuing new loans. This function of credit creation is backed by the central bank which is the primary source of money supply in an economy through the circulation of currency.[2] The circulation as well as the process of credit creation are based on the public confidence on the banking system such that each commercial bank's liquidity risk is well-monitored and mitigated through the so-called 'last-resort facilities' by the central bank or the government to avoid potential chain bankruptcies of banks or bank runs.

Digital lending is the process of offering loans that are applied for, disbursed, and managed through digital channels, in which lenders use digitized data to inform credit decisions and build intelligent customer engagement (Stewart et al., 2018). The online platform enables individuals and companies to lend and borrow money by connecting lenders with borrowers 'directly' through an online peer-to-peer (P2P) lending platform. The fundamental nature of P2P lending is 'direct finance' (see Figure 1). Here, we should note the mode of direct finance (financial disintermediation) cannot be automatically replaceable from the mode of indirect finance (financial intermediation through banks backed by the last-resort facilities by the central bank). The developing countries, in general, with the lack of capital accumulation, need the function of credit creation by banks. In other words, a certain accumulation of capital in societies is a prerequisite for transforming toward the mode of direct finance. At least, P2P lending is to be backed by large and diversified investors who are willing to absorb various types of credit risks and uncertainties as well as to absorb the associated

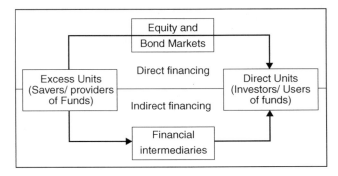

FIGURE 1 Functions and components of a financial system.
Source: Wanniarachchige et al. (2017).

transaction cost of screening and monitoring. Otherwise, a shallow banking and financial market, which often interlocks the economic backwardness in developing countries, would be just succeeded by a shallow P2P lending market. Around $2.88 trillion of assets were attributed to the global Islamic finance industry in 2019. Even on the global scale, within that asset base, the *Shari'ah*-compliant asset-management industry – an expected substitutable financial base for P2P lending – represents only 4% of the total assets (World Bank, 2021).

It would be naïve to just expect the P2P lending under the slogan of 'financial inclusion' to function as a substitute for the mode of indirect finance. In passing, we should note that the market size of P2P lending seems still limited. According to International Banker, Lending Club as the P2P lending industry leader arranged about 56,600 loans totaling only US$0.79 billion in the first quarter of 2014, while the US commercial bank of JP Morgan Chase delivered consumers loans with no less than US$47 billion over the same time frame. The size may depend on further capital accumulation in the risk-averse investors and/or further provision of proper credit information to shift their risk preference closer to risk-neutral. Rather, in our view, it should be outweighed to argue on how to incubate the Islamic banking industry to facilitate its financial penetration in the Muslim-majority countries for accumulating and mobilizing more financial resources in their societies. At least, the argument of Islamic banking penetration should be argued simultaneously with the movement of financial disintermediation upon FinTech.

It is reported through various media that the market share of Islamic banking assets to the total banking system in Malaysia reached 34.2% in 2020. In Bangladesh, the market share of *Shari'ah*-based banks in the country's banking sector increased to 27.5% in the January–March quarter of the year 2021 as two more conventional banks have started Islamic banking since January 2021. In Pakistan, the market share of Islamic banking assets and deposits in the overall banking industry stood at 17.0% and 18.7%, respectively in June 2021. Reportedly, Islamic financial institutions contribute up to 9.03% to the financial system in Indonesia as of April 2020. Taking into account the overall financial (banks) deepening ratio in Table 2, the estimated impact (% of GDP) of Islamic banking penetration can be calculated; 45.8% (134.1% × 34.2%) in Malaysia, 12% (45.1% × 27.5%) in Bangladesh, 2.9% (17.0% × 17.0%) in Pakistan, and 2.9% (33.2% × 9.03%) in Indonesia. As is suggested by Irfan and Ahmed (2019), whether there is a maturing process that Islamic finance must undergo in order to become truer to the spirit of *Shari'ah* remains to be seen. Except Malaysia, so far, we have to say that the impact of Islamic banking and finance has been very limited or marginal at its national level even in Asian Muslim-majority nations. Even in Malaysia, the so-called '*murabahah* and *tawarruq* syndrome' – the conservative credit portfolio strategy by Malaysian Islamic banks – has been long criticized by Islamic perfectionist scholars. It is observed that more than 90% investment of Islamic banks take the form of *murabahah* (mark-up or cost-plus investment) which includes *bai murabaha*, *bai muajjal*, and *ijara*. PLS modes of finance such as *musharakah* and *mudarabah* constitute only a small percentage of the total investment. To be specific, the share of these financing remains only at 1.7% by the end of 2019 (Miah, Suzuki and Uddin, 2021).

We should be instrumentally rational for attempting to bridge a divide between the 'temporary solution approach' for the needs of the contemporary Muslim society and the society's 'perfectionists' view. It is impractical to expect the acceleration of the participatory financing without preserving a much higher margin for security to cover further PLS risk. *Shari'ah* scholars, the regulatory authority, and other professionals need to design an appropriate financial architecture which can create different (and socially acceptable) levels of margin opportunities for Islamic banks to avail the benefit from the variety of Islamic financing as declared by *Shari'ah*.

How feasible is it to achieve the socio-economic and *Shari'ah* objectives through Islamic financing under the contemporary Islamic epistemological foundation as well as financial set-up? The concurrent interpretation of Islamic epistemology does not convincingly clear an apparent paradox generated by Islamic financing principles. For instance, Islam encourages PLS financing. At the same time, it prohibits associated uncertainty (*gharar*). An attempt to increase PLS financing implies embracing fundamental uncertainty of entrepreneurs. Critics, however, have paid much less attention to this fundamental issue than it really deserves.

So far as a sufficient level of wealth and capital has been accumulated in the society and the sufficient number of investors are ready and willing to absorb various types of credit risk and uncertainty, the P2P mode of financial intermediation and services would be feasible and, perhaps, desirable for including more ultimate investors and users of financial products and services. As was discussed earlier, one of the questions here is that if such a sufficient level of wealth and capital has not yet been accumulated, particularly observed in developing countries, can we simply conclude that the trend of digitalization would be desirable? In developing countries, we may still need the role of commercial banks as financial intermediaries by mediating idle/stagnant funds held by households to the industrial sector in a considerably large scale. In theory, so far as a sufficient level of wealth and capital has been accumulated enough to meet the financial demand on a global scale including that in developing countries, the trend of digitalization would be feasible. However, there is no guarantee of always ensuring the stable and sufficient circulation and flows of fund from an investor to a user of fund.

3 How would fintech affect the performance of Islamic banks?

FinTech and Digitalization would give other financial servicers a chance to penetrate the traditional financial products and services monopolized by the commercial banking unit in the past; in particular, *deposit taking* (Digital Savings), *payment settlement* (Digital Payments), and *mediating financial resources from depositors to corporations* (Digital Lending). Also, the services related to *money dealing* (cash and exchange) would be penetrated by newcomers in Digital Banking, Digital Asset Exchange, and Digital Custody. The 'P2P' financial services would erode the monopolistic/oligopolistic market in lending, payments, and money dealing operated so far mainly by commercial banks.

On the other hand, FinTech and Digitalization would give commercial banks an opportunity to expand the scope of business as well as to diversify risks and uncertainty with ultimate investors. In our view, (1) the lending business upon securitization (Collateralized Debt Obligation) and crowdfunding (Digital Lending and Digital Capital Raising) for diversifying credit risks, (2) the sale and utilization of the accumulated credit/client information to other financial service providers and platforms (Digital Banking and Digital Asset Exchange), (3) the business related to 'Private Banking' (wealth management) upon FinTech (Wealth Tech) for reducing the fund management cost would give commercial banks an opportunity to seek for a new profit base. We should note that the shift to the lending business upon securitization and crowdfunding would mean that the business of commercial banks would be shifted from 'indirect' to 'direct' finance. At the same time, the sales and utilization of credit information would bring commercial banks a 'fee' based business opportunity. Also, we should note that the wealth management (private banking), in its nature, is an 'investment banking'.

Roughly speaking, the P2P mode of financial intermediation and services would make traditional commercial banks extremely difficult to earn a sufficient profit (bank rent) to maintain their franchise value. Some innovative commercial banks may reshape their mode of business for their survival with the direction to P2P and 'direct-finance' mode of financial intermediation and services upon the technology of digitalization. However, such innovative commercial banks would not be called 'commercial banks' anymore.

The analysis of *bank rents* has provided an effective tool as an institutional approach to investigating the important role of banks. According to the definition by Khan (2000), *rents* refer to 'excess incomes' which, in simplistic models, should not exist in efficient markets. More precisely, 'a person gets a rent if he or she earns an income higher than the minimum that person would have accepted, the minimum being usually defined as the income in his or her next-best opportunity' (Khan, 2000, p. 21). The widely known 'financial restraint' regulation of creating bank rent opportunities (Hellmann, Murdock and Stiglitz, 1997) was an important institutional setting, for instance, in the Japanese traditional financial system. This institutional setting contributed to creating and maintaining an effective monitoring system in which the Japanese main banks played important roles as prudent financial intermediaries and monitors in the heyday of the system. Meanwhile, the stability in the Japanese main bank system was partly achieved by interest rate controls, with a wide margin between deposit and lending rates, so that the major banks could earn profits (Aoki, 1994; Suzuki, 2011). In the same fashion, Islamic banks must earn profits to maintain their 'franchise value' as prudent monitors. This leads us to ask; under the Islamic mode of financial intermediation, how do Islamic banks earn profits to preserve their 'reputation' as prudent *Shari'ah*-compliant (Islamic law-compliant) lenders?

Suzuki and Uddin (2014) proposed a fairly new conceptualization of the 'Islamic bank rent' that is defined as the extra profits enough to compensate for the unexpected loss and the displaced commercial risk to which Islamic banks are facing. In other words, the excess profit is required for maintaining banks' franchise value and reputation as prudent *Shari'ah*-compliant lenders. The unexpected loss is associated with the difficulty in sharing PLS and hence, can also be regarded as 'PLS sharing risk'. As an illustration, the displaced commercial risk and the PLS sharing risk are associated with the 'α' in the following equation:

Spread earned by Islamic banks = (risk-adjusted) risk premium + α,
where spread = rate of profit received − rate of profit paid.

We call 'α' as 'Islamic bank rent' (in a narrower sense) in terms of the extra profits to cover the PLS sharing risk and the transaction cost for the *Shari'ah* compliance in order to maintain the franchise value as prudent Islamic financial providers. Risk premium in the equation should be reflected in the credit risk of each borrower. If the bank acquires perfect skills of screening and pricing, in theory, no bank rent opportunity may exist. However, since perfect screening is impossible under conditions of uncertainty, all the commercial banks are expected to earn the extra profits by adding the subjective risk premium to cover the unmeasurable risk or uncertainty that the banks are exposed to. Islamic banks are also exposed to the general uncertainty. Therefore, they also must charge the risk-adjusted risk premium covering the measurable risk plus associated uncertainty as the conventional banks charge. Beyond the premium, Islamic banks are assumed to earn the extra profits to maintain the franchise value as prudent *Shari'ah*-compliant lenders (we may call this additional risk premium to cover the uncertainty plus 'α' in the equation also as Islamic bank rent in a broader sense). It is, thus, hypothesized that the spread in total earned by Islamic banks should be larger than that by conventional banks.

Linking this *Shari'ah*/PLS sharing risk with the current lending practice of Islamic banks, it is highly likely that they choose low-risk assets for their portfolio so far as the risk-adjusted return is still satisfactory. Of course, PLS sharing modes of investments are highly recommended under Islamic *Shari'ah*, even though Zaher and Hassan point out, 'Islamic banks are not expected to reduce credit risk by systematically requiring collateral or other guarantees as a pre-requisite for granting profit-and-loss-sharing facilities' (Zaher and Hassan, 2001, p. 176). But, from the practical point of view, asset-based modes including *murabaha* are more contributing for protecting their rents compared to fully *Shari'ah*-driven *mudarabah* and *musharakah*, although the asset-based lending, in particular, the credit exposure uncovered by the collateral, does not always offset the PLS sharing risk of Islamic banks. Moreover, in this competitive and liberalized market framework, Islamic banks have to compete with their conventional counterparts in spite of the fact that the risk management tools commonly applied in conventional banking are not applicable to Islamic banking (El-Hawary, Grais and Iqbal, 2007, p. 779). In other words, the credit risk management tools in Islamic banking stay behind to those used in conventional banking. In addition, unlike conventional banking, participatory mode of lending requires some other activities including prior determination of PLS sharing ratio and frequent monitoring and supervision for ensuring better governance (Sundararajan and Errico, 2002, p. 4). These additional activities may accelerate the transaction costs for Islamic banks and accordingly, the 'α' factor stated earlier, encourages them to choose low-risk assets for their portfolio.

Islamic financial service providers face severe competition stemming not only from Islamic financial institutions but also from conventional financial service providers upon Fintech. The ubiquity of the smartphone, for example, allows access to retail financial products on an unprecedented scale. Similarly, while small and medium enterprises lack access to finding via traditional channels, technology has the power to standardize due diligence and contracts in order to accelerate the provision of venture capital to them. 'Although conventional venture capital and angel investing have found a foothold in conventional (non-Islamic) finance, there are very few examples of *Shari'ah*-compliant venture capital conducted through e-platforms' (Irfan and Ahmed, 2019, pp. 26–27).

Wilson (2019, p. 33) points out that the increasing pace of technological advance has major implications for how Islamic financial services are delivered, with significant implications for staff and their clients. The effect is equally destructive for conventional financial services, with threats of closure of branch offices as clients increasingly transact their businesses online rather than face to face.

> Given the disruption resulting from technological innovation, there needs to be continuous monitoring of existing Islamic financial products by *Shari'ah* boards to ensure they do not deviate from the approved templates. Monitoring can be undertaken by internal *Shari'ah* audit staff by random

sampling of the contracts to verify compliance. It would be time consuming and costly to examine every contract.

(Wilson, 2019, p. 34)

Can Islamic finance providers earn the extra profit (Islamic bank rent) enough to cover the cost of *Shari'ah* compliance under an intense competition further intensified upon the trend of DX among Islamic financial institutions – including the so-called 'Islamic windows' of major conventional financial institutions – as well as with conventional financial providers? The answer is probably negative.

As Wilson (2019) points out, with fintech, there are high fixed costs, but low variable costs. It is considered that newly established Islamic banks face high entry costs, given client expectations regarding the necessity of technologically intensive financial services.

Economies of scale and scope are facilitated with online platforms which can serve millions of clients. There are few Islamic banks which have millions of clients however, and it is much costlier per customer to provide technological intensive financial services when there are at best thousands rather than millions of clients.

(Wilson, 2019, p. 36)

Besides, the *Shari'ah* aspect of financial transactions can be a hurdle to digitalize the process (Alam, Gupta and Zameni, 2019).

4 Is *Shari'ah*-compliance a necessary and sufficient condition for realizing the *maqasid al-Shari'ah*?

Scholars suggest that fintech-led financial intermediation would lead to better *Shari'ah* compliance and address the issue of financial inclusion as well as better financing of SMEs who have hitherto been unable to access mainstream financial market (Nisar and Farooq, 2019, p. 65). Although some studies have rightly pointed out that Islamic banking should be moral and more concerned about social issues, the literature, however, does not shed light on the issue as to how Islamic financial institutions can play more social role under the existing socio-cultural environment. An idealist view may require that Islamic financial institutions should switch completely to *Shari'ah*-based financing abandoning completely the currently practiced *Shari'ah*-complaint techniques.

One of the salient features of Islamic finance that distinguishes it from conventional financial model is that the former complies, in objectives and operations, with *Shari'ah* (Islamic law). Prohibition of *riba* (interest) is one of the major prohibitions in the *Shari'ah* principles. Qur'an (2:275–276) clearly states that dealing with *riba* – profit on loans – is 'sinful'. However, it is still difficult to get explicit Qur'anic text on the logic as to why interest is prohibited because the rationales are more implicit than explicit. Albeit, Islamic scholars, for instance,

Siddiqi (2004) analyzing the context of various Qur'anic verses summarize five broader reasons: (i) interest corrupts society, (ii) interest implies improper appropriations of other's property, (iii) interest slows down the growth of real sectors, (iv) interest demeans and diminishes human personality, and (v) interest is simply unjust. Though the Qur'an does not provide a detailed analysis of the rationale of prohibition of interest, the primary rationale regarding the prohibition of *riba* that can be sensed from the Qur'anic verse is related to 'exploitation' or 'injustice' (Suzuki and Miah, 2018a, p. 14). It is stated in the Qur'an, 'deal not unjustly (by asking more than your principal) and you shall not be dealt with unjustly' (2:279).

In general, the profit on sales has no ceiling, may be determined by the market competition or technology. If we consider *murabaha* as trade, the associated profit also should have no limit. Meanwhile, in the conventional finance, 'usury' is prohibited. Usury is referred to as a rate of interest greater than the one which the law or public opinion permits (Looft, 2014). For instance, in Japan, the law prohibits the lender operating as a business unit to form any contract to receive an annual interest of exceeding 20%. The lender which breaches the law is subject to imprisonment with work for not more than five years, a fine of not more than 10 million yen, or both. This lends us to ask: how is the Islamic lender prohibited to charge a profit margin in the *Shari'ah*-compliant *murabaha* transaction greater than the one which is equivalent to the 'usury' referred in the conventional finance? This point is understated in the academic as well as practitioner's debate in Islamic finance.

Suzuki and Miah (2021) propose to set up two benchmarks to judge whether a particular financial transaction is acceptable or not in the context of Islamic finance; '*Shari'ah*-compliant' benchmark and '*Shari'ah*-based' *raf'al-haraj* (the removal of hardship) benchmark. The former benchmark is addressed to ensuring that a transaction brings 'profits on sales', not 'profits on loans'. The latter benchmark should be addressed to ensuring that a transaction does not exploit anyone. Is *Shari'ah*-compliance a necessary and sufficient condition for realizing the *maqasid al-Shari'ah*? Perhaps, most Islamic scholars may wish to believe that these two benchmarks are identical in a sense that the *Shari'ah*-compliance would bring the desired outcome toward social justice. However, even in the *Shari'ah*-compliant *murabaha* transaction, the lender still possesses the discretion to possibly exploit the borrower by pricing upon an extraordinarily high mark-up, resulting in giving unnecessary hardship to the borrower.

The *Shari'ah*-compliant benchmark is a necessary condition but not always a sufficient condition. Financial transactions in Islamic finance should be monitored not only on the *Shari'ah*-compliant but also on the *Shari'ah*-based benchmark. Unlike conventional banks, the maxim of profit-maximization alone is unsuited to *maqasid al-Shari'ah;* but rather profit should be accompanied by justice and fairness at all levels of human interaction (Chapra, 2000). In this sense, Islamic banks must not exploit their customers *ex-ante* and *ex-post*. As Quran mentions, 'Allah has imposed no hardship (*haraj*) upon you in religion' (22:78). And again,

'Allah does not burden a soul beyond its capacity' (2:286). Quran reiterates, 'Allah desires not to inflict any hardship upon you' (5:6).

We may bring *taysir* (ease) and *raf'al-haraj* (the removal of hardship) which are identified as objectives (*maqasid*) rather than rules of specific application. Making things easier for people and removing unnecessary hardship from them are among the cardinal objectives (*maqasid*) of the *Shari'ah*, and these principles tend, in many ways, to characterize Islam itself (Kamali, 2000). This can be attributed to the fact that

> ... each is inherently dynamic and comprehensive and tends to involve a process capable of continuous application and refinement. In this sense, the two principles are as relevant to the conditions of society today as they were in the early days of Islam.
>
> *(Kamali, 2000, p. 70)*

Figure 2 shows the category of 'gray-zones' in Islamic banking upon different combinations of *Shari'ah*-compliant benchmark and *Shari'ah*-based *raf'al-haraj* benchmark. The net social benefit would be the highest in quadrant I where Islamic financiers are well-contributing to the removal of hardship in borrowers upon the *Shari'ah*-compliance. In quadrant II, Islamic financiers are complying the *Shari'ah*, but less contributing to the removal of hardship in borrowers. From the perspective of Islamic 'perfectionist' economists who respect the pure mode of PLS, the so-called '*murabaha* syndrome' could be considered to fall into this quadrant. On the other hand, from the Islamic 'pragmatist' view of emphasizing upon the element of 'wealth creation', the *Shari'ah*-compliant *murabaha*, if it is still contributing to the removal of hardship in borrowers through the function of wealth creation, can be categorized as a contract in quadrant I. Here, quadrant II suggests a gray-zone. If Islamic financiers charge a profit margin in the *Shari'ah*-compliant transaction greater than or equivalent to the usury referred in the conventional finance, the transaction with the excess rate of profit would be considered as 'usurious trade' to exploit the borrowers. Meanwhile, the opportunity of charging a high but socially permissible profit margin or less usurious trade may create a gray-zone in the quadrant of less contributing to the removal of hardship in borrowers. Then comes quadrant III as the worst contract which is

	Less contributing to *raf'al-haraj* ⟷ *Shari'ah* based contributing to *raf'al-haraj*	
Shari'ah-compliant ↕ Controversial on compliance (or non-compliance)	(II) *Shari'ah*-compliant but less contributing to the removal of hardship	(I) *Shari'ah*-compliant and contributing to improving social justice
	(III) Controversial on compliance and less contributing to the removal of hardship	(IV) Controversial on compliance but contributing to the removal of hardship

FIGURE 2 Category of Gray-Zones in Islamic Finance.
Source: Suzuki and Miah (2021).

either controversial on the *Shari'ah* compliance or non-compliance while being less contributing to the removal of hardship in borrowers. The transactions in this quadrant – most likely upon 'opportunism' – are difficult to justify, turning out to be 'black'.

This figure suggests another gray-zone in Islamic finance. In quadrant IV, the transactions or contracts Islamic financiers offer are still controversial on the *Shari'ah*-compliance, but they are contributing to the removal of hardship in borrowers through the function of wealth creation. Suzuki and Miah (2021) refer to the issue of *tawarruq* which is prohibited in Indonesia. Most scholars particularly in Indonesia believe that the transaction of *tawarruq* is not *Shari'ah*-compliant. We can say that the quadrant IV type gray-zone in Indonesia's Islamic banking seems narrower, partly undermining the profit base for Islamic banks in Indonesia. In other words, the quadrant IV type gray-zone in Malaysia can be considered to be wider to create and maintain the level-playing field between conventional and Islamic banks (see Alkhan and Hassan, 2019). The width of gray-zones might be different in each Muslim-majority country.

Upon the element of asymmetric information, fraud, no-confidence, and distrust between counterparties, a trade-party is possible to be exploited. The potential 'usurious' trade should be prohibited in the context of *raf'al-haraj* (the removal of hardship) as the cardinal objective (*maqasid*) of the *Shari'ah*. If the usurious trade is to be prohibited, the usurious pricing on the *murabaha* contract by Islamic financiers should be prohibited, too.

To what extent – rather automatically or structurally – could we expect the *Shari'ah*-compliant FinTech to help achieving the *maqasid al-Shari'ah*? The *Shari'ah* compliance is a necessary condition in the Islamic mode of finance. However, in our view, the *Shari'ah*-based *raf'al-halaj* benchmark should be considered as a complimentary condition to judge if an Islamic financial product upon FinTech would meet the *maqasid al-Shari'ah* of realizing social justice in societies and communities.

Human beings should aim to conform, in intention and action, to the truth prescribed in the *Qur'an*. However, creatures of omniscience must act, with their limited computational capacity, in an environment full of uncertainty and unknowns. It is important to scrutinize Islamic products through the lens of *shari'ah* principles. On the other hand, merely trying to meet the way of *Shari'ah* compliance without seeking for the rationale can be construed as procedural rationality. This means that we have to match the *Shari'ah* principles with the pragmatic benefits of the society under the broader objectives of social justice and equity. In parallel, we have to consider that removal of hardship or *raf'al-haraj* can be another dimension in judging if a particular transaction is acceptable or not especially when there is a doubt about *Shari'ah* compliance.

How can we avoid the 'usurious trade' which may have exploited the buyers or borrowers? Perhaps, one of the options would be to wait for a general consensus (*ijma*) on the *maslahah* (public interest) of prohibiting a margin of profit in trading greater than that which the public opinion permits. However, as Wilson

(2019) points out, there is no single 'ideal' *maslahah*, since given the diversity of Muslim-majority countries in terms of stages of development and economic fundamentals, it is inappropriate to argue that there is a universal *maslahah*.

Usury is prohibited on conventional financial institutions. Usury is referred to a rate of interest greater than the rate which the law or public opinion permits. As was mentioned earlier, in Japan, the law prohibits the lender operating as a business unit to form any contract to receive an annual interest of exceeding 20%. In theory, so far as a free and fair competitive market between Islamic and conventional financiers is being operated, no Islamic lender would charge a profit margin in the *murabaha* transaction greater than that which is equivalent to the usury referred in the conventional finance, because any higher profit margin would not at all attract their clients to sign any contract of *murabaha*. In other words, the prohibition of usury on conventional financial institutions would be influential, at least 'indirectly', on Islamic financiers as an important regulation for preventing them from exploiting their clients. For instance, in Bangladesh as one of Muslim countries, 'usurious' loans are regulated to give additional powers to Courts to deal in certain cases with usurious loans of money or in kind; The Usurious Loans Act, 1918 (Act no. X of 1918) in Bangladesh.

Even in Muslim countries, the term 'usury' is empirically used as a completely unacceptable or illegal transaction. For instance, in Indonesia, 'business based on *Shari'ah* principles' is regulated as the business which does not contain, including but not limited to, the element of *usury, maisir, gharar, haram*, and *zalim* (Article 2, Elucidation to the Act of the Republic of Indonesia Number 21 of 2008 concerning Sharia banking). Here 'usury' is defined as

> illegally obtain additional income (*batil*) among others the exchange transaction of similar types of goods but of different quality, quantity, and delivery time (*fadhl*), or in lending transaction requiring the Facility Receiving Customer to repay the fund received exceeding the principal due to the passing of time (*nasi'ah*).

The definition of usury in the regulation is still ambiguous to judge how is the Islamic lender prohibited to charge a profit margin in the *Shari'ah*-compliant *murabaha* transaction greater than that which is equivalent to the usury referred in the conventional finance.

From a Muslim viewpoint, the *Shari'ah* compliance should be a necessary and sufficient condition for realizing the *maqasid al-Shari'ah* including the mitigation of exploitation in societies. Our economic activities are subject to our bounded rationality because we are not the absolute existence with omniscience and omnipotence, but human being with the brain of limited computational capacity. In order to get closer to the *truth*, it is quite rational for the believers to pay their best effort as an exercise of *ijtihad* to understand and incarnate the logic and rationales implicit in the Qur'anic text. This exercise of *ijitihad* can be treated as being 'instrumentally' rational to get closer to the Truth. On the other hand, our behavioral pattern aims to be instrumentally rational at the beginning. However, as more complex factors are encountered, the pattern would quite often change to be limitedly instrumental, eventually become 'procedurally' rational at best.

As for a mean to the objective of mitigating the potential usurious pricing in *murabaha*, the Muslim community can utilize the regulation on the prohibition of usury over conventional financial institutions. As mentioned earlier, so far as a free and fair competitive market between Islamic and conventional financiers is being operated, any Islamic lender would not charge a profit margin in the *murabaha* transaction greater than that which is equivalent to the usury referred in the conventional finance. This suggests that the harmonious coexistence with conventional finance and the maintenance of free and fair competitive market would amount to be an important strategy for mitigating the exploitation in societies, consequently realizing the *maqasid al-Shari'ah*.

5 A policy option: Islamic fintech in merchant financing

Some scholars insist that the extent of financial exclusion is high within the Muslim community because Muslims have traditionally stayed away from the financial sector owing to Islamic prohibition of *riba, gharar,* and *maysir.* These scholars expect Fintech solutions to facilitate crowdfunding and P2P lending, consequently automating and enhancing Islamic financial inclusion (Nisar and Farooq, 2019). As discussed earlier, the precondition of capital distribution is the capital accumulation. Unless there is a substantial accumulation of capital and wealth in the community, the smooth transformation to the mode of direct finance including crowdfunding and P2P lending would be infeasible. Taking into consideration the low level of banking and financial deepening in Arab countries and Asian Muslim-majority nations, we should not too much expect Fintech solutions to facilitate the mode of direct finance. Rather, the debate on how to utilize Fintech solutions to facilitate the expansion of Islamic banking asset should be outweighed.

Some scholars expect the advanced technologies such as blockchain, distributed ledger technology (DLT), and smart contract to reduce the prevalence of moral hazard and agency problem in *mudarabah* and *musharakah* contracts. These technologies are expected to 'reduce information asymmetry and the trust gap and can help improve transparency and reporting and thus, help improve compliance and ultimately reduce cost, which can make these contracts more competitive and *Shari'ah*-compliant' (Nisar and Farooq, 2019, p. 73). This 'New-Keynesian' claim overlooks an important credit rationing or credit crunch which can be caused by other types of information problems. From the 'Post-Keynesian' perspective, the credit crunch or the volatility in credit market are stemming from lenders' 'uncertainty' in credit risk screening, which is one of the most crucial factors making their screening and monitoring activities extremely difficult and ineffective. According to this view, the credit risk involved is a subjective judgment, and this can vary across persons making the judgment based on their experience and knowledge of subtle and unquantifiable aspects of a situation. The formulation of subjective probability judgments is what Frank Knight describes as decision-making under uncertainty. Uncertainty – 'unmeasurable risk' in the Knightian term – may be more or less ignored or, alternatively, subject probabilities may be applied, together with a risk premium to cover unspecified adverse events. Since there is no precise economic theory of how decisions are made under uncertainty, agents tend to observe each other's responses and do not deviate widely from the norm regarding which factors should be taken into account and how much weight should be assigned to them (Suzuki, 2011). But 'when the crowd is wrong *ex-post*, there is the making of a financial crisis' (Davis, 1995, p. 135).

The absorption of various types of risk and uncertainty depends on each country's capacity of capital accumulation enabling to absorb and diversify the risk and uncertainty. In this sense, it would make sense to observe why the P2P lending market has developed in the United States (see the ratio of domestic credit to private sector in the United States in Table 1). Gassner and Lawrence (2019) report that 'Lendingclub' in the United States is one example, besides, the most thriving country for P2P lending is China in the context of its 'shadow banking'.

Islam is a religion born in the Arabian Desert, where trade constituted the most important, 'perhaps even the sole economic activity, favours merchants, property rights, free trade and market economy' (Çizakça, 2011, p. xv). In this context, Islam is called the religion for merchants (Ayub, 2007). The business ethics in the Islamic mode of transactions are related to the civilized urban way of life at the birth of Islam. The holy Prophet had spent half of his life working as a merchant in Mecca, where the urban culture was flourished and the values for facilitating fair transactions among the merchants in equal positions were shared (Okawa, 2008). Perhaps, the primary principles in the Islamic mode of financial intermediation including the prohibition of *riba* should be understood in the historical context that 'trade' constituted nine-tenth of the livelihood of early Muslims. In fact, of the four righteous Caliphs, Abu Bakr was a cloth merchant and Uthman was an importer of cereals (Çizakça, 2011, p. xiv).

From another perspective, we may say that Islamic financial institutions are expected to provide the necessary working capital for 'merchants'. We hypothesize that, in particular, Islamic banks as the core institutions in the Islamic mode of finance are, more or less, expected to take the role as a provider of merchant's capital. Here, the term 'merchant's capital' reminds us the Marxian tradition on the identification of the circuit of *merchant's capital* separated from the circuit of *interest-bearing capital* (see Miah, Suzuki and Uddin, 2021).

One of the salient features in the Marxian view on money is to differentiate between the circuit of *merchant's and industrial capital* and the circuit of *interest-bearing capital*. There is a definite relationship between the two functions of money in capitalism, since the exchanges of simple commodity circulation and of industrial production are ultimately connected, 'most notably when we recognize that C-M (money as capital and money as money) for one agent is M-C for another' (Fine and Saad-Filho, 2004, p. 136). Further, both the use of money as money and as capital can involve credit relations as money is lent and borrowed to facilitate the acts of exchange involved.

In a capitalist economy, commercial capital buys and sells commodities and remains entirely within the sphere of exchange. 'Commercial profits accrue through the resale of the commodities originally bought by merchants, and not through the employment and exploitation of labor power' (Itoh and Lapavitsas, 1999, p. 69). With the development of capitalist production, the acts of buying and selling become the specialized tasks of particular capitalists (for example, transport, storage, retailing, and wholesale), thereby creating a division of 'labor' among capitalists. In this case, industrial capitalists rely upon specialized merchant capitalists to undertake the realization of (surplus) value. Furthermore, certain functions arising from the commodity form of production become the specialized activity of money dealers. These include book-keeping, the calculation and safeguarding of a money reserve, and the rules of cashiers and accountants (Fine and Saad-Filho, 2004).

One of the themes running through Marx's treatment of capital in exchange is that there is a crucial distinction to be made between *money as money* and *money as capital*. Money functions as money when it acts simply as a means of exchange between two agents, hence mediating commodity exchange, irrespective of the position of those agents in the circulation of capital as a whole – whether they are capitalists engaging in production or capitalists and workers engaging in consumption. Hence, the role of money as money is understood by reference to simple commodity circulation, C – M – C. By contrast, money as capital is understood by reference to the circuit of capital, M – C...P...C' – M', where money is employed for the specific purpose of producing surplus value (Fine and Saad-Filho, 2004, pp. 135–136).

Basically, in the Marxian context, there is the division between industrial capital that produces surplus value, and merchant's capital that circulates it and facilitates the transition between the commodity and money forms of capital, which indirectly increasing the efficiency of industrial capital and consequently the mass of surplus value produced (Fine and Saad-Filho, 2004). For Marx, both commercial and banking capital as the advanced capitalist form are integral parts of the sphere of circulation in the circuit of total social capital. As capitals are integral to the circuit, they take part in the redistribution of total surplus value on the same footing as industrial capital. Interest-bearing capital, on the other hand, is continually formed outside the circuit and enters and exits the latter. By so doing, interest-bearing capital mobilizes the spare money funds present in the course of accumulation and reallocates them among the capitals, integral to the circuit (thus, also accelerating the turnover of these capitals). Consequently, interest-bearing capital also earns a share of the total surplus value, but not on the same basis as industrial, commercial, and banking capital (Itoh and Lapavitsas, 1999, p. 70). The Marxian dichotomy of money circulation has, interestingly, a compatibility with the Islamic perspective on capital.

Merchants' capital is an ancient form of capital that has always had extensive connections with interest-bearing capital in the Marx's term. In general, in the Islamic mode of financial intermediation, interest-bearing capital is prohibited. Marx attempted to show that concentration of 'idle' money is systematically generated in the course of the reproduction of total social capital. Temporarily idle profits, the depreciated funds of fixed capital, precautionary reserves, and reserves that allow the continuity of the turnover of capital as production and circulation alternate are all purely capitalist forms of money hoarding (Itoh and Lapavitsas, 1999). Needless to say, even in the Islamic mode of financial intermediation, constantly creating and mobilizing idle money in the course of capitalist reproduction as a foundation for both commercial and banking credit is a very important challenge. While following the principle of prohibition of interest-bearing capital, the Islamic banking system is expected to be a mechanism for the internal reallocation of spare funds among industrial and commercial capitalists.

As mentioned earlier, Marx observed the division between industrial capital which produces surplus value, and merchant's capital which circulates it and facilitates the transition between the commodity and money forms of capital, indirectly increasing the efficiency of industrial capital and, therefore, the mass of surplus value produced. The Marxian tradition on the identification of the circuit of merchant's capital is, in our view, suggestive for identifying and reviewing the expected role of Islamic banks. From the Islamic historical perspective, we hypothesize that Islamic banks are expected to take the role as a provider of merchant's capital. Of course, as Marx pointed out, merchant's capital is subject to mobility with industrial capital, because industrial capitalists can move into trading, and vice versa.

Miah, Suzuki and Uddin (2021) investigate the sectoral distribution of investment of various types of Bangladeshi banks by the end of December 2019. According to the data, the majority of the financing goes to trade and commerce for almost all types of banks, except for specialized and foreign banks. In the case of Islamic banks, 40.58% of the financing goes to trade and commerce, which is the highest among all types of banks. The rate is even higher than the rate of 35.35% of other private banks excluding Islamic banks. The combined proportion of working capital financing for industries and trade and commerce portrays that about two-thirds of Islamic banking sector's asset is concentrated on these two sectors. Most importantly, 41.26% and 25.63% of income for Islamic banks come from trade and commerce and working capital financing, respectively. This leads to an aggregate income from these two sectors a total of 66.89% for Islamic banks, which is the highest in the banking sector. This pattern of financing of Islamic banks conforms to the Marxian circuit of merchant's capital.

Besides, remittance is considered a major pillar for the economy of Bangladesh. Islamic banks account for more than 35% during the whole period and their share remained higher than private banks excluding Islamic banks, that is, conventional private banks. Among all banks, Islami Bank Bangladesh Limited has secured the first position by holding 19.6% of the total market share (Miah, Suzuki and Uddin, 2021).

To satisfy their major clients and customers, it would make sense for Islamic banks to pay their best effort to apply advanced technologies such as blockchain, DLT, and smart contract, first, to their business focuses of trade finance and remittance. DX in trade finance and digital remittance should be put their priority in the promotion of Fintech.

Nisar and Farooq (2019) insist that the Islamic financial institutions remain elitist and, in spirit, follow the segregation from the real economy.

> Over the years, Islamic finance has come to be known more as a conscience keeper rather than a real economic movement focusing on distancing itself from *riba*, supporting the real economy and spreading economic fruits to a wider section of the society.
>
> *(Nisar and Farooq, 2019, p. 65)*

Islamic finance scholars ask; why do Islamic banks not actively participate in equity-like financing instead of their current debt-like financing? This is a right question but wrongly directed because suggesting banks to take more risk associated with participatory finance is contrary to the long-standing practice of the banking industry. It is rational for the greater stability of a financial system that Islamic banks simply should not be encouraged to accept higher risk because the bankruptcy of a single bank can lead to a county-wide or world-wide bank run which in turn, through its ripple effect, may trigger financial and economic crisis. In the case of bankruptcy of a depositary corporation, it is usually the depositors who lose their deposit asset beyond the amount insured under the deposit insurance. On the other hand, they are ultimately the taxpayers who would pay the socio-economic cost for insurance. Even worse, once it happens, depositors lose their confidence on the financial system, which would often lead to the disintermediation of financial resources resulting in economic slowdown (Suzuki and Miah, 2018b).

Under the PLS contract, banks' function is confined merely to financial intermediaries. Ideally, they bear no risk of clients because they can transfer the risks associated with the borrowers to the depositors (for instance, investment account holders). This structure would, however, cause serious principal-agent problems between depositors (investors) and Islamic banks, which actually drain the 'risk fund' as resources that are needed for participatory financing. More importantly, the depositors of Islamic banks like their conventional counterparts are mostly small savers who are assumed to be risk averse. A wholesale transfer of risk may keep this group of depositors away from the formal financial system. The operation of Islamic banks can be seen as complementary, to a great extent, to the conventional banking model at least, in regard to financial inclusion and financial stability (Suzuki and Miah, 2018b).

Given the nature of commercial banks as depository corporations, it makes sense for Islamic banks to concentrate on the mark-up financing on their attempt to protect the welfare of depositors. The 'division of work' and 'specialization' strategy by Islamic banks would contribute to mediating more 'safety' idle money from the general risk-averse depositors who are limitedly willing to absorb risk and uncertainty, as well as meeting the still strong demand of asset-based investment, partly contributing to further economic development through the credit multiplier (Suzuki and Miah, 2018b).

In our view, Islamic banks should pay their best effort to apply the advanced technologies such as blockchain, DLT, and smart contract, first, to their business focuses of trade finance and remittance. Their division of work and specialization strategy would be the most feasible and, perhaps, the most desirable for themselves and societies, provided that (1) a certain harmonious coexistence with conventional financial institutions can be expected, because the other full range of financial products and services except trade finance and remittance should be provided for societies by conventional finance providers, and (2) a certain level of competitive edge in trade finance and remittance by Islamic banks toward conventional banks can be preserved.

Conventional banks also pay their effort to apply the advanced technologies to their business of trade finance and remittance. Under a cut-throat competition with conventional banks, Islamic banks may face the difficulties in creating a level of profits enough to maintain their franchise value as prudent providers and servicers of trade finance and remittance for their clients. In addition to the profit base, as was discussed earlier, Islamic banks need to earn an extra profit – Islamic bank rent – to cover the cost of *Shari'ah* compliance as well as *raf'al-haraj* compliance which conventional banks do not require to pay. Islamic banks may face the difficulties in surviving under an unfettered competitive market.

A certain financial support from *waqf/zakat* or Islamic multinational financial organizations or donors who have the incentives to incubate and enhance the Islamic banking industry is to be considered in the Muslim community. 'An efficient financial intermediary will mobilize funds from savers to those seeking these funds for more productive use at an affordable cost to help accelerate the growth and development of the economy' (Nisar and Farooq, 2019, p. 66). However, the Muslim community is, at the beginning, expected to consider how to incubate and develop an efficient Islamic banking and financial intermediary. While avoiding the occurrence of potential free-riding and moral hazard problems, the Islamic bank rent opportunity for improving the efficiency in dealing with trade finance and remittance to compete with conventional banks should be argued.

6 Remaining issues in the trend of FinTech

Should the lender be altruistic to the borrower? In general, the lenders as financial intermediaries are expected to pay the best effort to maximize the benefit of the stakeholders, in particular, the depositors and/or investors as fund providers to lenders. In the context of Islamic finance upon PLS, the answer may depend on how altruistic those fund providers to lenders are. In theory, if the fund providers to lenders are concerned more about 'wealth distribution' rather than 'wealth creation', the general altruism in lending behavior might be observed. What can we expect Fintech to install the general altruism in fund providers?

Altruism is a vibrant concept that may inculcate the motive to assist the poor. However, if altruism interacts with a sense of strong reciprocity, the meaning of altruism may take a different form. Bowles (2012, pp. 145–146) clarifies

> strong reciprocators wish to help those who try to make it on their own but who, for reasons beyond their own control, cannot, and they wish to punish, or withhold assistance from, those who are able but unwilling to work hard or who violate other social norms.

Bowles further points out that both *unconditional altruists* and *strong reciprocators* may support redistribution to the poor. In arguing so, Bowles refers to 'strong reciprocity' which is a propensity to co-operate and share with others similarly disposed, even at personal cost, and a willingness to punish those who violate co-operative and other social norms, even when punishing is personally costly and cannot be expected to result in net personal gains in the future (Bowles, 2012). Bowles is concerned about strong reciprocity as a driving force of making people willingly help the poor but withdraw support when they perceive that the poor may cheat or not try hard enough to be self-sufficient and morally upstanding.

> Never shall you attain the highest state of virtue unless you spend (in the cause of Allah) out of that which you love; and whatever you spend. Allah, indeed, knows it well.
>
> *(Qur'an 3:92)*

Islamic altruism appears to depend on the reciprocity backed by mutual belief in the omnipotence and omniscience of the absolute power. In the Muslim society, there is the powerful concept of Allah's ownership of all wealth and that human beings are mere 'trustees' of this wealth (Qur'an 3:180, 57:10). In contrast, it is mentioned by Nagel (1970, p. 3), in the tradition of western political philosophy, altruism itself depends on a recognition of the reality of the other persons, and on the equivalent capacity to regard oneself as merely one individual among many.

In our view, the capacity as economic and financial 'power' enabling them to make altruistic behaviors (also make necessary penalties or sanctions if necessary) should be sought and taken into consideration in Islamic independent reasoning in the *mu'alamat*. As was mentioned earlier, the lenders as financial intermediaries are expected to pay the best effort to maximize the benefit of the stakeholders, in particular, depositors and/or investors as fund providers to lenders. In reality, the 'unconditionally altruistic' fund is not ample. Therefore, the practice of PLS should be based on an effective power retained by the lender to discipline the borrower. However, we should ask if the retention of the power by the lender would not breach *maqasid al-Shari'ah*.

Wealth creation should be outweighed to realize a collaborative economy or sharing economy. Wealth in essence is *khair* or something good (Qur'an 2:215 and 2:272). According to Izutsu (2000), *khair* is a very comprehensive term, 'meaning as it does almost anything that may be considered in any respect valuable, beneficial, useful, and desirable' (Izutsu, 2000, p. 222). Mustafa and El Amri (2019) demonstrate a framework based on *maqasid al-Shari'ah* for measuring the fintech business activities in Islamic finance. Three dimensions are identified: development of *Mal* (wealth), *Shari'ah* value proposition, and socio-economic welfare. 'The dimension of the development of al-*Mal* is the means to achieve the other two dimensions, *Shari'ah* value proposition and socio-economic welfare' (Mustafa and El Amri, 2019, p. 109). Allah is the sole owner of *mal* and people are entrusted to vicegerents to utilize this wealth in a manner ordained by Allah (Qur'an 27:40). In another instance, *mal* is regarded as a test from Allah for man (Qur'an 6:165). 'In dealing with wealth, people are urged by the Qur'an to avoid negative elements such as hoarding, inequitable circulation of wealth and its concentration in a few hands' (Mustafa and El Amri, 2019: 100).

Kamali (2000) points out that the position of the *shari'ah* in the area of *mu'amalat* is predicated on the prevention of conflicts, exploitation, and injustice among people. Kamali (2000) insists that this is an important *shari'ah* principle that is sometimes neglected by those who maintain that the intellect and human reason have no place in the *shari'ah*. Many problems in the fields of Islamic economics, banking, and finance arise from this inability to understand the proper role of reason in the *shari'ah* (Kamali, 2000, p. 78).

Ijtihad (independent reasoning), according to Kamali (2000), is the main vehicle by which the *shari'ah* can be adjusted so as to accommodate social change, and it relies, to a large extent, on the proper understanding and application of *ta'lil* (ratiocination). The law concerning *mu'amalat* is generally founded on their rational, effective cause and benefit. This means that the law in this area is open to rational analysis, enquiry, and evaluation (Kamali, 2000, p. 78).

From a liberal point of view, the ratiocination in the Qur'an means that the laws of *shari'ah* outside *ibadat* are not imposed for their own sake but in order to realize certain benefits (Kamali, 2000, p. 82). This pragmatic viewpoint, in our view, can be reinforced by the reorganization of the concept of *hilm* in the context of independent reasoning in the mutual economic activities among us, that is, in the human relation – from man to man. *Hilm* is considered as calmness, balance mind, self-control, and steadiness of judgment (Izutsu, 2015, p. 211).

Izutsu insisted that *hilm* is not a passive quality, but a positive and active power of the soul that is strong enough to curb her own impetuosity that may drive the man headlong to folly and calm it down to patience and forbearance. It is a sign of the power and superiority of the mind (Izutsu, 2015, p. 213). The concept of *hilm* itself had to disappear from the stage as a basic religious attitude of man toward God. In our view, the concept of *hilm* should be resurrected in the process of independent reasoning for facilitating and monitoring commercial transactions.

Islamic economies are concerned about fulfilling the socio-economic objectives of 'social justice' in accordance with the objectives of *shari'ah*, like as the 'altruism' of the *Medinan* Muslims was praised by Allah in the Qur'an (Qur'an 59:9). In the Muslim society, there is the powerful concept of Allah's ownership of all wealth and that human beings are mere 'trustees' of this wealth (Qur'an 3:180, 57:10). As is summarized by Naqvi (2003, p. 105), what this means is that the individual's right to spend his wealth is limited in several ways: (a) he must spend it according to Divine wishes (Qur'an 57:10), (b) he cannot hoard it, especially when there are urgent social needs to be met (Qur'an 3:180), (c) he must give it to the poor not as charity but as a matter of the latter's acknowledged right in his wealth (Qur'an 70:24–25), and (d) he must spend wealth only in moderation because being spendthrift is both a social waste and a cardinal sin (Qur'an 17:26–27). Many scholars including Mawdudi (2011) and Naqvi (2003) point out that the Islamic right of the poor to receive their share in the wealth of the rich strengthens altruism significantly in running efficiently and equitably an essentially individualistic economy, and it minimizes the free-riding and assurance problems. The Holy Qur'an unambiguously states that the poor have a due share in the wealth of the rich.

We should argue that to ensure the poor's right in society, the rich man's accumulation of wealth must be a pre-requisite in a sense that no wealth distribution can be done before wealth creation. It implies that the *Muslim* individuals should be encouraged to become those who can afford to supply a part of their earnings for realizing social justice. We may say that the *Muslim* individuals should be encouraged to become *hilm* (or *halim*) toward man in the *mu'amalat*. This dimension in Islamic altruism should be more argued. Perhaps, this dimension is related to the issue of enhancing the supply of participatory finance (*musharakah*) or venture capital for entrepreneurs who face difficulties in fund-raising. As *hilm* is essentially based on the concept of 'power' (*qudrah*), economic and financial 'power' is construed as an essential force for incubating new ventures and realizing social justice.

As the scholars have generally characterized, the *Shari'ah* should be the legal system of pragmatism and convenience (Kamali, 2000, p. 70). Here, we would propose that the concept of *hilm* toward man should be argued as a supplementary value in the process of creating *ijma* (general consensus), *maslahah* (public good), and *fatwa* (juristic opinion) which often originate in the customs and living experience of the Islamic community. The application of advanced technologies is to be argued from the viewpoint of contributing to the 'wealth creation' to bring 'ease' (*taysir*) and 'the removal of hardship' (*raf'al-haraj*) in borrowers, simultaneously enhancing the economic and financial 'power' as their capacity for contributing to the 'wealth distribution' to society in the next round.

The regulators need to consider an appropriate legal framework for creating the Islamic bank rent opportunity and protecting the effective power by the lenders. The retention of effective power by the lender is less argued in designing the regulatory framework of the Islamic mode of financial intermediation. As discussed earlier, the conceptualization of resurrected *hilm* toward the other persons can be regarded as the process of seeking for a hybrid way of thinking of Islamic altruism. We propose that the practice of PLS should be based on an effective power retained by the lender to discipline the borrower. The retention of the power by the Islamic lender does not necessarily breach *maqasid al-Shari'ah*, so far as the power is well-managed and monitored upon the concept of *hilm*. The regulator is expected to take the role as the monitor to see if the economic and financial power retained by the Islamic lender contribute to the 'wealth creation' to bring 'ease' (*taysir*) and 'the removal of hardship' (*raf'al-haraj*) in borrowers.

Another issue is that the P2P mode of saving and payments would put the existing centralized (monopolized) mode of savings and payments, which has been highly regulated and monitored by the regulators under the current mode of supervising the banking industry for ensuring financial stability to an end. How will the decentralized/P2P mode of savings and payments affect the financial stability? In theory, as more commercial banks are shifting their mode of business to investment banking by diversifying credit risk, the regulators would be less concerned about the accumulation of non-performing loans which would trigger the bank run. However, the regulators may be more concerned about a liquidity shock in a respective level of diversified investors, which may trigger the chain reaction of the shortage of liquidity in diversified types of currency and money upon digitalization. How will the regulators respond to the diversified and P2P mode of savings and payments? The response is becoming an important challenge for the regulators to respond to the trend of FinTech and Digitalization of financial products and services.

7 Concluding comments

We aimed in this chapter to assess critically how FinTech and DX in financial contracts reshape the current mode of financial intermediation and Islamic mode of financial contracting. Obviously, there are positive and negative effects FinTech would bring to Islamic financial institutions. We have argued that so far as P2P lending provides less bankable individuals and MSMEs with the opportunities to raise fund, it would contribute to financial inclusion. It implies that P2P lending would not necessarily cast a threat to conventional commercial banks, because those less bankable and marginalized individuals and MSMEs are not their main clients. On the other hand, it implies that if the expansion of

P2P lending includes the bankable individual clients and firms, in particular, the secured loan backed by residential or commercial property as collateral (P2P/Marketplace Property Lending) would cast a threat to conventional commercial banks. In other words, we may say that it would give an opportunity for them to diversify the associated risk and uncertainty as well as to create a new agency/arrangement fee business by fund arrangement upon online and mobile banking platform.

Second, we have illustrated that the effect of Fintech is equally destructive or creative for both conventional and Islamic banks. The P2P mode of financial intermediation and services would make traditional commercial banks – irrespective of conventional or Islamic banks – extremely difficult to earn a sufficient profit (bank rent) to maintain their franchise value. Some innovative commercial banks may reshape their mode of business for their survival with the direction to P2P and 'direct-finance' mode of financial intermediation and services upon the technology of digitalization. We have highlighted that Islamic banks are required to earn extra profit, what we call as 'Islamic bank rent', to maintain the franchise value as prudent *Shari'ah*-compliant lenders, while competing with innovative conventional banks. In an unfettered competitive market, in theory, the survival of Islamic banks in the banking industry would be extremely difficult.

Third, the infrastructure of Islamic finance, including Islamic banking, is necessary for facilitating investment and economic transactions for Muslim depositors and investors. If the infrastructure is not available, they would have to pay more transaction costs for *Shari'ah* compliance at individual levels. If they are aware (or unsure) that the proceeds from their investment had not complied with the *Shari'ah* principles, Muslim investors would consider the need for the proceeds to be 'purified', for instance, by donating to charity or *zakat* institutions. This circumstance may discourage them from engaging in investment. In other words, the infrastructure of Islamic finance could possibly mobilize more funds from Muslim investors, which would also contribute to the national economic growth and development, consequently, not only for Muslims but also for non-Muslims (Pramono and Suzuki, 2021).

Fourth, we have identified a potential area in which FinTech can provide a competitive edge to Islamic financial institutions. We have shown that incubating the Islamic banking industry with a focus on the DX in the financial products related to 'merchant's capital' in trade finance and remittance would contribute to the national economic growth and development. Simultaneously, the Muslim-majority countries should opt for a DX of the Islamic mode of financial intermediation while keeping a harmonious coexistence with conventional financial providers under a fair and competitive condition. This argument underlies the rational that it is not always feasible for the Muslim-majority countries to automatically transform into the P2P direct-finance mode for several reasons. The argument on 'what is desirable' (wealth distribution) as a pious work might be a belief or worship from the religious perspective. Simultaneously, we propose that the Muslim community recognize that the argument on 'what is feasible' (wealth creation) is equally welfare relevant. The pragmatist view on Islamic fintech should be argued in parallel to achieve the *maqasid al-Shari'ah*.

Finally, our analysis suggests that it is not always feasible for the Muslim-majority countries to automatically transform into the P2P direct-finance mode. In our view, the Muslim-majority countries should opt for a DX of the Islamic mode of financial intermediation while keeping a harmonious coexistence with conventional financial providers under a fair and competitive condition, simultaneously, seeking a consensus in the Islamic community for incubating (providing a certain financial support) the Islamic banking industry with a focus on the DX in the financial products related to 'merchant's capital' in trade finance and remittance.

Notes

1 Technology-enabled financial transactions such as wealth management, robo-advising, peer-to-peer lending, crowdfunding, and digital payments have spawned very recently. According to Forbes, digital banking amounted to US$7.7 billion in 2019 whereas digital insurance (insurtech) recorded transactions amounting to US$6.8 billion, and the digital payment summed up US$15.1 billion at the same time.
2 The process of credit creation is also known as 'credit multiplier'. In theory, the total credit creation is determined by the amount of original deposit and the reciprocal number of 'cash reserve ratio' (1/r). If the cash reserve ratio is 10% (0.1), the credit multiplier effect would be 10 times (1/0.1).

References

Alam, N., Gupta, L. and Zameni, A. (2019) *Fintech and Islamic Finance: Digitalization, Development, and Disruption*, Cham: Springer Nature Switzerland.

Alkhan, A. M. and Hassan, M. K. (2019) 'Tawarruq: Controversial or Acceptable?', *Arab Law Quarterly*, 33(4), 307–333.

Aoki, M. (1994) 'Monitoring Characteristics of the Main Bank System: An Analytical and Developmental View', in M. Aoki and H. Patrik (eds.), *The Japanese Main Bank System: Its Relevance for Developing and Transforming Economies* (pp. 109–141), New York: Oxford University Press.

Ayub, M. (2007) *Understanding Islamic Finance*, Chichester: John Wiley & Sons.

Bakar, M. D. (2016) *Shariah Minds in Islamic Finance: An Inside Story of A Shariah Scholar*, Kuala Lumpur: Amanie Media.

Bakar, M. D. (2021) *Maqasid Shariah: The Face and Voice of Shariah Embedded with Big Data Analytics & Artificial Intelligence*, Kuala Lumpur: Amanie Media Sdn Bhd., in press.

Bowles, S. (2012) *The New Economics of Inequality and Redistribution*, New York: Cambridge University Press.

Cambridge Centre for Alternative Finance (CCAF) (2020) *The Global Covid-19 FinTech Market Rapid Assessment Study*.

Chapra, M. U. (2000) *The Future of Economics: An Islamic Perspective*, Leicester: The Islamic Foundation.

Çizakça, M. (2011) *Islamic Capitalism and Finance*, Cheltenham: Edward Elgar.

Davis, E. P. (1995) *Debt Financial Fragility and Systemic Risk*, Oxford: Clarendon Press.

De Anca, C. (2019), 'Fintech in Islamic Finance: From Collaborative Finance to Community-Based Finance', in U. A. Oseni and S. Nazim Ali (eds.), *Fintech in Islamic Finance: Theory and Practice* (pp. 47–63), New York: Routledge.

Dusuki, A. W. and Abozaid, A. (2007) 'A Critical Appraisal on the Challenges of Realizaing Maqasid Al-Shariaah in Islamic Banking and Finance', *International Journal of Economics, Management and Accounting*, 15(2), 143–165.

El-Hawary, D., Grais, W. and Iqbal, Z. (2007) 'Diversity in the Regulation of Islamic Financial Institutions', *The Quarterly Review of Economics and Finance*, 46, 778–800.

Fine, B. and Saad-Filho, A. (2004) *Marx's Capital*, London: Pluto Press.

Gassner, M. and Lawrence, J. (2019) 'Fintech in Islamic Finance: Business Models and the Need for Legal Solutions', in U. A. Oseni and S. Nazim Ali (eds.), *Fintech in Islamic Finance: Theory and Practice* (pp. 174–182), New York: Routledge.

Hazik, M. and Hassnian, A. (2019) *Blockchain, Fintech, and Islamic Finance: Building the Future in the New Islamic Digital Economy*, Berlin: Walter de Gruyter.

Hellmann, T. F., Murdock, K. C. and Stiglitz, J. E. (1997) 'Financial Restraint: Toward a New Paradigm', in M. Aoki, H.-K. Kim and M. Okuno-Fujiwara (eds.), *The Role of Government in East Asian Economic Development: Comparative Institutional Analysis* (pp. 163–207), Oxford: Clarendon Press.

Irfan, H. and Ahmed, D. (2019) 'Fintech: The Opportunity for Islamic Finance', in U. A. Oseni and S. Nazim Ali (eds.), *Fintech in Islamic Finance: Theory and Practice* (pp. 19–32), New York: Routledge.

Itoh, M. and Lapavitsas, C. (1999) 'Interest-Bearing Capital: The Distinctive Marxist Approach', in M. Itoh and C. Lapavitsas (eds.), *Political Economy of Money and Finance* (pp. 59–80), Basingstoke: Macmillan.

Izutsu, T. (2000) *The Structure of Ethical Terms in the Quran*, Chicago: ABC International Group, Inc.

Izutsu, T. (2015) [originally published in 1964] *God and Man in the Koran: Semantics of the Koranic Weltanschauung*, Tokyo: Keio University Press.

Kamali, M. H. (2000) *Islamic Commercial Law*, Cambridge: The Islamic Texts Society.

Khan, M. H. (2000) 'Rents, Efficiency and Growth', in M. H. Khan and J. K. Sundaram (eds.), *Rents, Rent-Seeking and Economic Development: Theory and Evidence in Asia* (pp. 21–69), Cambridge, UK: Cambridge University Press.

Looft, M. (2014) *Inspired Finance*, Palgrave: Macmillan, Basingstoke.

Mawdudi, S. A. A. (2011) *First Principles of Islamic Economics*, translated by Ahmad Imam Shafaq Hashemi, Leicestershire: The Islamic Foundation.

Miah, M. D., Suzuki, Y. and Uddin, S. M. S. (2021) 'The Impact of COVID-19 on Islamic Banks in Bangladesh: A Perspective of Marxian "circuit of merchant's capital"', *Journal of Islamic Accounting and Business Research*, 12(7), 1036–1054.

Mustafa, O. M. and El Amri, M. C. (2019) 'Fintech in the Light of Maqasid al-Shari'ah', in U. A. Oseni and S. Nazim Ali (eds.), *Fintech in Islamic Finance: Theory and Practice* (pp. 93–112), New York: Routledge.

Nagel, T. (1970) *The Possibility of Altruism*, Princeton, NJ: Princeton University Press.

Naqvi, S. N. H. (2003) *Perspectives on Morality and Human Well-Being*, Leicestershire: The Islamic Foundation.

Nisar, S. and Farooq, U. (2019) 'Financial Intermediation, Fintech and Shari'ah Compiance', in U. A. Oseni and S. Nazim Ali (eds.), *Fintech in Islamic Finance: Theory and Practice* (pp. 64–74), New York: Routledge.

Okawa, S. (2008) *Kaikyo Gairon*, Tokyo: Chikuma Shobo (in Japanese).

Oseni, U. A. and Nazim Ali, S. (2019) 'Fintech in Islamic Finance', in U. A. Oseni and S. Nazim Ali (eds.), *Fintech in Islamic Finance: Theory and Practice* (pp. 3–15), New York: Routledge.

Pramono, S. and Suzuki, Y. (2021) *Growth of Islamic Banking in Indonesia: Theory and Practice*, New York: Routledge.

Siddiqi, M. N. (2004) *Riba, Bank Interest and the Rationale of Its Prohibition*, Jeddah, Saudi Arabia: Islamic Research and Training Institute.

Stewart, A., Lamont, K. and Yaworsky, K. (2018) *Demystifying Digital Lending*. Available at: https://www.findevgateway.org/sites/default/files/publications/files/1123_digital_lending_r10_print_ready.pdf [Accessed July 7, 2021].

Sundararajan, V. and Errico, L. (2002) 'Islamic Financial Institutions and Products in the Global Financial System: Key Issues in Risk Management and Challenges Ahead', *IMF Working Paper IMF/02/192*, 1–27. Washington: International Monetary Fund. Available at http://kantakji.com/fiqh/Files/Markets/y144.pdf.

Suzuki, Y. (2011) *Japan's Financial Slump: Collapse of the Monitoring System under Institutional and Transition Failures*, Basingstoke: Palgrave Macmillan.

Suzuki, Y. and Miah, M. D. (2018a) 'Heterodox vs. Islamic Views on Interest and Uncertainty', in Y. Suzuki and M. D. Miah (eds.), *Dilemmas and Challenges in Islamic Finance* (pp. 11–27), New York: Routledge.

Suzuki, Y. and Miah, M. D. (2018b) 'Alternative Views Upon the "Division of Work" and "specialization" towards a New Mode of Profit-Loss Sharing', in Y. Suzuki and M. D. Miah (eds.), *Dilemmas and Challenges in Islamic Finance* (pp. 177–189), New York: Routledge.

Suzuki, Y. and Miah, M. D. (2021) 'Shari'ah-Compliant Benchmark and Shari'ah-based "raf al-haraj" Benchmark on Prohibition of Riba', *International Journal of Islamic and Middle Eastern Finance and Management*, 14(1), 151–163.

Suzuki, Y. and Uddin, S. (2014) 'Islamic Bank Rent: A Case Study of Islamic Banking in Bangladesh', *International Journal of Islamic and Middle Eastern Finance and Management*, 7(2), 170–181.

Wanniarachchige, M. K., Miah, M. D. and Suzuki, Y. (2017) 'Banks as Financial Intermediaries and Their Roles in Economic Development', in Y. Suzuki et al. (eds.), *Banking and Economic Rent in Asia* (pp. 26–37), New York: Routledge.

Wilson, R. (2019) 'Implications of Technological Advance for Financial Intermediation in Islamic Finance', in U. A. Oseni and S. Nazim Ali (eds.), *Fintech in Islamic Finance: Theory and Practice* (pp. 33–64), New York: Routledge.

World Bank (2021) 'Domestic credit (by banks) to private sector (% of GDP)', available at: https://data.worldbank.org/indicator/FS.AST.PRVT.GD.ZS (accessed on 12 November, 2021)

Zaher, T. S. and Hassan, M. K. (2001) 'A Comparative Literature Survey of Islamic Finance and Banking', *Financial Markets, Institutions & Instruments*, 10(4), 155–199.

2
A TYPOLOGY OF FINANCIAL BUSINESS MODELS ON DIGITAL TRANSFORMATION ('DX')

Expected impacts on commercial banks

Yasushi Suzuki and Mohammad Dulal Miah

1 Introduction

Digital transformation (DX) has become the most frequently used word in this last decade, though the term 'DX' has no universal definition due to its diversity. It encompasses many dimensions like digital supply chain, digitalization of services, products and so on (Hazik and Hassnian, 2019). Solis, Li, and Szymanski (2014) define DX as 'the realignment of, or new investment in, advanced technology and business models to more effectively engage digital customers at every touchpoint in the customer experience lifecycle'. Financial institutions are the pioneers in embracing the ongoing DX with an aim to harness their efficiency and performance. Moreover, the adoption of technologies is considered an essential endeavour for financial service provider to remain competitive and survive in the market. As a result, technology-enabled financial transactions such as wealth management, robo-advising, peer-to-peer lending (sometimes referred to as P2P lending or abbreviated to P2PL), crowdfunding, and digital payments have spawned recently. According to Forbes data, digital banking amounted to US$7.7 billion in 2019, whereas digital insurance (Insurtech) recorded transactions amounting to US$6.8 billion, and the digital payment summed up US$15.1 billion.

Defined broadly, Fintech encompasses advances in technology and changes in business models that have the potential to transform the provision of financial services through the development of innovative instruments, channels, and systems (CCAF, 2020, p. 24). In fact, more and more Fintech business models are proposed. A recent study [*The Global Covid-19 FinTech Market Rapid Assessment Study*] by Cambridge Centre for Alternative Finance (CCAF) developed a working taxonomy that brings together a coherent conceptualization of Fintech activities, while appreciating the sector's diversity and differentiated

DOI: 10.4324/9781003262169-4

TABLE 1 The working Fintech taxonomy and classification by CCAF

Category	Fintech vertical/ business model	Sub-verticals/business models included in each vertical
Retail facing (consumers, households and MSMEs) Number of respondents 1,122	Digital lending	P2P/Marketplace Consumer Lending, P2P/Marketplace Business Lending, P2P/Marketplace Property Lending, Balance Sheet Consumer Lending, Balance Sheet Business Lending, Balance Sheet Property Lending, Debt-based Securities, Invoice Trading, Crowd-led Microfinance, Consumer Purchase Financing/Customer Cash advance, Digital Merchant – cash Advance Solutions
	Digital capital raising	Equity-based Crowdfunding, Real Estate Crowdfunding, Revenue/Profit Share Crowdfunding, Reward-based Crowdfunding, Donation-based Crowdfunding
	Digital banking	Fully Digitally Native Bank (Retail), Fully Digitally Native Bank (MSME), Marketplace Bank (Retail), Marketplace Bank (MSME), BaaS, Agent Banking (Cash-in/Cash-out)
	Digital savings	Digital Money Market/Fund, Digital Micro Saving Solutions, Digital Savings Collective/Pool, SaaS
	Digital payments	Digital Remittances (Cross Border-P2P), Digital Remittances (Domestic-P2P), Money transfer (P2P, P2B, B2P, B2B), eMoney Issuers, Mobile Money, acquiring services providers for merchants, Points of access (PoS, mPoS, online PoS), Bulk Payment Solutions – Payroll, Grants etc., Top-ups and refill, Payment gateways, Payment aggregators, API Hubs for Payments, Settlement and clearing services providers
	Digital asset exchange	Order book, DEX relayer, Single dealer platform/OTC trading, Trading bots, HFT services, Advanced trading services, Brokerage services, Aggregation, BTM, P2P marketplaces, Clearing
	Digital custody	Software Wallet (Mobile Wallet/Tablet Wallet/Desktop Wallet), Web Wallet (eMoney Wallet), Vault services, Key management services, Hardware Wallet
	Insurtech	Usage-based, Parametric-based, On-Demand Insurance, P2P Insurance, Technical Service Provider (TSP), Digital Brokers or Agent, Comparison Portal, Customer Management, Claims & Risk Management Solutions, IoT (including telematics)
	Wealthtech	Digital Wealth Management, Social Trading, Robo-Advisors, Robo Retirement/Pension Planning, Personal Financial Management/Planning, Financial Comparison Sites

(Continued)

Category	Fintech vertical/ business model	Sub-verticals/business models included in each vertical
Market provisioning Number of respondents 306	Regtech	Profiling and due diligence, Blockchain forensics, Risk Analytics, Dynamic Compliance, Regulatory Reporting, Market Monitoring
	Alternative credit & data analytics	Alternative Credit Rating Agency, Credit Scoring, Psychometric Analytics, Sociometric Analytics, Biometric Analytics
	Digital identity	Security & Biometrics, KYC Solutions, Fraud Prevention & Risk Management
	Enterprise technology provisioning	API Management, Cloud Computing, AI/ML/NLP, Enterprise Blockchain, Financial Management and Business Intelligence, Digital Accounting, Electronic Invoicing

Created on CCAF (2020).

business models. This working taxonomy includes 13 discrete primary Fintech verticals and 103 sub-verticals. These have been further categorized into two overarching groups – *Retail Facing* (i.e., providing financial products and services with a focus on consumers, households and micro, small & medium enterprises (MSMEs), and more likely to be B2C) and *Market Provisioning* (i.e., those which enable or support the infrastructure or key functionalities of Fintech and/or Digital Financial Services markets, thus more likely to be B2B) (Table 1).

This chapter aims to review the working taxonomy by CCAF and to propose a typology of 'Fintech' business models, to provide a platform for further academic and professional debate towards predicting how the Fintech and DX in financial contracts would reshape the current mode of financial intermediation and financing contracting. In particular, we are concerned about the future of the 'commercial banking unit' which still plays a significant role under the current mode of financial intermediation and services. Commercial banks are, more or less, protected under the banking regulation for the regulatory objectives of maintaining financial stability (preventing potential bank runs) while promoting sound financial intermediation. While we identify who has a keen interest in promoting each Fintech business model, we argue how each Fintech business model would cast 'threat', 'opportunity' or 'remain neutral' to the commercial banking unit. Simultaneously, we argue what kinds of 'incentives' are held by the stakeholders for promoting each Fintech business model.

2 Analyses of working taxonomy of Fintech by CCAF

The Global Covid-19 FinTech Market Rapid Assessment Study was conducted as a joint initiative of CCAF at the University of Cambridge Judge Business School, the World Bank Group, and the World Economic Forum. Between June 15th and August 18th, 2020, the joint research team designed an online questionnaire and surveyed 1,385 unique Fintech firms operating in 169 countries. This study draws on a rapid global survey of Fintech. A major contribution of this study is further standardization towards a commonly acceptable taxonomy when discussing an array of differentiated Fintech activities both for market analysis and regulatory context. According to their working taxonomy of Fintech activities, the survey respondents were from 13 different primary verticals, and 103 sub-verticals representing both *retail-facing* and *market-provisioning* activities (CCAF, 2000, p. 16).

This working taxonomy is useful for understanding the scope of Fintech activities, however, rather too comprehensive. Here, our concern is to predict how the Fintech and DX in financial contracts would reshape the current mode of financial intermediation and financing contracting. To answer this question, we clarify who are the major stakeholders (who have a keen interest) in promoting each Fintech business model. Under the current mode of financial intermediation and services, we raise the following players: (a) *commercial banking unit,* being mainly engaged in deposit-undertaking, dealing with payment settlement, and mobilizing savings to finance bankable clients (indirect financing), (b) *investment banking unit,* being mainly engaged in underwriting & distributing securities (direct finance), fund management, private banking, and (c) *other financial units,* including microfinance institutions mobilizing the fund from donors to empowering the marginalized people, non-bank consumer finance companies, insurance companies and so on.

This section aims to argue how the Fintech business models classified into *Retail Facing* that provides financial products and services with a focus on consumers, households and MSMEs: (1) Digital lending, (2) Digital capital raising, (3) Digital banking, (4) Digital savings, (5) Digital payments, (6) Digital asset exchange, (7) Digital custody, (8) Insurtech, (9) Wealthtech, would reshape the current mode of financial intermediation and services.

2.1 Digital lending

Digital lending is the process of offering loans that are applied for, disbursed, and managed through digital channels, in which lenders use digitized data to inform credit decisions and build intelligent customer engagement (Stewart, Lamont, and Yaworsky, 2018). 'P2P/Marketplace lending' (referring to the sub-verticals of P2P/Marketplace[1] Consumer Lending, Business Lending and Property Lending) is one of the characteristic financial forms in digital lending. P2PL is a form of loan provision centred on an online marketplace forum structure. The online platform enables individuals and companies to lend and borrow money by connecting lenders with borrowers 'directly' through an online P2PL platform.

The fundamental nature of P2PL is 'direct finance' (see Figure 1 in Chapter 1). P2PL is to be backed by large and diversified investors who are willing to absorb various types of credit risks and uncertainty as well as to absorb the associated transaction cost of screening and monitoring. So far, as P2PL provides 'less bankable' individuals and MSMEs with the opportunities to raise fund, it would contribute to the so-called 'financial inclusion'. In other words, it implies that P2PL would not necessarily cast a 'threat' to conventional commercial banks, because those 'less bankable' and marginalized individuals and MSMEs are not yet their main clients of mainstream banking system.

On the other hand, it implies that if the expansion of P2PL includes the 'bankable' client individual and firms, in particular, the secured loan backed by residential or commercial property as collateral (P2P/Marketplace Property Lending), it would cast a 'threat' to mainstream commercial banks. Or, we may say that it would give an 'opportunity' for them to diversify the associated risk and uncertainty as well as to create a new agency/arrangement fee business opportunity by the fund arrangement upon online and mobile banking platforms.

In passing, we should note that the market size of P2PL is still limited. According to International Banker, Lending Club, the P2PL industry leader, arranged about 56,600 loans totalling only US$790 million in the first quarter of 2014, while the US commercial bank of JP Morgan Chase delivered consumers loans with no less than US$47 billion over the same period. The size may depend on further capital accumulation in the risk-averse investors and/or further provision of proper credit information such as debt-to-income ratio, credit history and credit profile of the candidate borrowers to shift those investors' risk preference closer to risk-neutral.

The working taxonomy refers to the sub-verticals of 'Balance Sheet' Consumer Lending, Business Lending, and Property Lending. Balance sheet lending is a loan that a lender retains on their own asset instead of selling it off to another financial institution or to individual investors (Schmidt, 2020). The fundamental nature of balance sheet lending is considered 'indirect finance' (see Figure 1 in Chapter 1). The lender in this case is the platform *per se*. In practice, balance sheet lending usually requires that the platform should obtain a banking license.

The working taxonomy refers to the sub-vertical of Debt-based Securities, which is a debt instrument such as bonds and fixed-income securities in the form of digital securities (Fernando, 2020). Perhaps, it refers to the digitalized collateralized debt obligations (CDO), which securitize debt obligations in lenders (typically in conventional commercial banks) to distribute the CDO to investors so that banks may diversify the associated credit risk and uncertainty.

The sub-vertical of Invoice Trading allows business units to sell individual invoices, in order to free up cash, to an online community of investors (Hecht, 2018). The concept takes the principle of P2PL and applies it to invoice finance. This financing form *per se* is almost the same as the traditional financing upon 'bill discounting' or 'factoring' which are dealt with by non-bank financial companies.

The sub-vertical of Crowd-led Microfinance also applies the principle of P2PL and crowdfunding (including donation) to microfinance for empowering the poor and marginalized clients.

The working taxonomy refers to Consumer Purchase Financing/Customer Cash advance. The sub-verticals also apply the principle of P2PL to the traditional financing to consumers such as auto loans and car financing/payday loans which charge exorbitantly high rates of interest. The sub-vertical of Digital Merchant-cash Advance Solution also applies the principle of P2PL to the quick but very-high–interest rate (close to 'usury') loans/promissory notes discounting to small-business units in financial trouble. The above-mentioned 'factoring' and consumer purchase financing are dealt with by non-bank financial companies under the current mode of financial intermediation and services. They are using their own balance sheet for these financings. The Fintech platform would change the nature of risk absorption from 'indirect finance' to 'direct finance' to diversify the associated risk and uncertainty, possibly giving an 'opportunity' to the commercial banking unit for the new frontier of its business. Table 2 summarizes our analyses of 'digital lending' of the working taxonomy.

TABLE 2 Expected impacts of digital lending on commercial banks

Sub-verticals	Stakeholders in the current mode	Nature of risk absorption	Impact on commercial banks	Incentives for the platform
P2PL (Property Lending, Lending to bankable clients)	Commercial banks	Direct (Indirect in Balance Sheet Lending)	Threat	Creation of alternative financial route to seek for profits
P2PL to marginalized clients, Crowd-led-microfinance	Investment banks (venture fund), Microfinance institutions	Direct	Neutral	Diversification of investors
Debt-based securities	Commercial banks/ investment banks	Direct	Opportunity	Diversification of risks/ investors
Invoice trading, consumer purchase financing	Commercial banks/ non-bank consumer finance companies	Indirect (-> Direct)	Opportunity	Diversification of risks/ investors

2.2 Digital capital raising

Digital capital raising is explained as an investment platform which employs powerful and scalable technology that connects entrepreneurs and investors, enabling companies to raise capital digitally (Businesswire, 2020). Needless to say, lending and fund raising are two sides of the same coin. The working taxonomy here focuses on 'crowdfunding'.

The history of crowdfunding can be traced back to the 1700s. The concept of displaying the names of the donors was an 'age-old' technique that was displayed by Alexander Pope back in 1713 to translate an ancient Greek poetry into English. Nearly more than half a century later, an identical attempt was done by Mozart to crowdfund his three piano concertos. At first, his proposal got rejected by the potential donors. A year later, he made another attempt and obtained grants from 176 donors. In exchange for their contributions, their names were listed in the concertos' manuscripts (Bashir and Banze, 2020). Comparably, the notion of *Zakat* and *Sadaqah* (voluntary charity) of Muslim teachings has existed in the Middle East to alleviate the less fortunate.

The original form of crowdfunding is 'donation' (Donation-based Crowdfunding). The modern form includes the P2PL (Debt Crowdfunding) or investment in the equity share in an early-stage company, which means the sub-vertical of Equity-based Crowdfunding.

The sub-vertical of Real Estate Crowdfunding refers to the one for financing a temporary liquidity problem in the process of investing in real estate projects. The sub-vertical of Revenue/Profit Share Crowdfunding is the *profit-sharing* model as a particular form of crowdfunding model in which contributors receive a share in the profits of the business or royalties of the artist (Belleflamme, 2014). The sub-verticals of Reward-based Crowdfunding is a type of small-business financing in which entrepreneurs solicit financial donations from individuals in return for a product or service (Zimmermann, 2020). Table 3 summarizes our analyses of 'digital capital raising' of the working taxonomy.

TABLE 3 Expected impacts of digital capital raising on commercial banks

Sub-verticals	Stakeholders in the current mode	Nature of risk absorption	Impact on commercial banks	Incentives for the platform
Real estate crowdfunding	Commercial banks/ non-bank financial companies	Indirect -> Direct	Opportunity/ threat	Diversification of risks
Other sub-verticals	Crowdfunding platform, NGO	Direct	Neutral	Diversification of investors

2.3 Digital banking

The term 'digital banking' essentially combines online and mobile banking services under one umbrella (Napoletano and Foreman, 2021). These sub-verticals in the working taxonomy – Fully Digitally Native Bank/Marketplace Bank – are traditional banking business models improved with the latest digital technologies to offer a better banking experience for lower cost (PwC, 2017). The sub-vertical of Agent Banking (Cash-in/Cash-out) refers to Cash-in/cash-out (CICO) networks which play a critical role in a country's transition from cash-based to fully digital financial systems such as 'mWallet'. Mobile Wallet or Wallet is also known as digital wallet or eWallet. It basically refers to a mobile technology that is used the same as a real wallet (Goyal, 2020).

The sub-vertical of Banking as a Service (BaaS) is a model in which licensed banks integrate their digital banking services directly into the products of other non-bank businesses, enabling a non-bank business to offer its customers digital banking services such as mobile bank accounts, debit cards, loans and payment services, without needing to acquire a banking license of their own[2] (Dolan, 2021). Table 4 summarizes our analyses of 'digital banking' of the working taxonomy.

2.4 Digital savings

Digital Money Market/Fund refers to digital money which is the digital representation of value. The public sector can issue digital money called central bank digital currency – essentially a digital version of cash that can be stored and transferred using an internet or mobile application. The private sector can also issue digital money. Some forms can be redeemed for cash at a fixed face value. These are fully backed with very safe and liquid assets and are usually referred to as eMoney (Adrian and Mancini-Griffoli, 2021). The most successful and widely used form of digital money is the cryptocurrency, Bitcoin.

TABLE 4 Expected impacts of digital banking on commercial banks

Sub-verticals	Stakeholders in the current mode	Nature of risk absorption	Impact on commercial banks	Incentives for the platform
Fully digitally native bank, marketplace bank, agent banking	Commercial banks	N.A.	Threat	Penetration into banking services
BaaS	N.A.	N.A.	Opportunity	Expanding the scope of business

TABLE 5 Expected impacts of digital savings on commercial banks

Sub-verticals	Stakeholders in the current mode	Nature of risk absorption	Impact on commercial banks	Incentives for the platform
Digital money market/fund	Digital money platform	N.A.	Threat	Penetration into saving/deposit taking business
Digital microsaving solutions, digital savings collective/pool	Microfinance financial institutions, NGO	N.A.	Opportunity	Expanding the scope of business
SaaS	As a service by commercial banks, investment banks	N.A.	Threat/opportunity	Penetration into private banking business (related to Wealthtech)

Digital Micro Saving Solutions is the DX of microsavings as a form of microfinance where organizations and financial institutions encourage individuals to save money (Davis, 2012). A mobile-based solution enables banks, SACCOs, or mobile wallet operators to attract the unbanked or underbanked population to open a savings account and earn interest from it (Moran, 2021). Digital Savings Collective/Pool is another service for financial inclusion where groups of 15–30 members pay into a common platform, at any time, from the 'mobile wallet' of their choice (Aga Khan Development Network, 2017). These savings are pooled for purposes of issuing loans within the group.

The sub-vertical of Savings-as-a-service (SaaS) aims to provide the level of customer services to which only the private banking client has access (Bell, 2020). Table 5 summarizes our analyses of 'digital savings' of the working taxonomy.

2.5 Digital payments

Generally speaking, the sub-verticals in Digital payments are related to a transaction that takes place via digital or online modes, with no physical exchange of money involved. For instance, the definition of digital remittance is when sending money is performed either online, via mobile, or app. The second feature of digital remittance is that the transfer does not involve the use of cash with funds usually sent from a bank account or other electronic wallet (Shubhangi, 2020).

TABLE 6 Expected impacts of digital payments on commercial banks

Sub-verticals	Stakeholders in the current mode	Nature of risk absorption	Impact on commercial banks	Incentives for the platform
All the sub-verticals except the two below	Payment processors/ service providers	N.A.	Threat	Penetration into Payment settlement business
Bulk payments, settlement and clearing service providers	Payment processors	N.A.	Neutral	Betterment of paying methods and management

Cross-border/Domestic P2P payment services such as Google Pay/Paypal's Venmo are provided.

The sub-vertical of Point of access refers to PoS (point of sale) and mPoS (Mobile PoS). It is a mobile device, smartphone or tablet that works as a cash register or traditional PoS terminal wirelessly.

The sub-verticals of Bulk Payment Solution/Top-ups and Refill/Payment Gateways/API (Application Programming Interface) and integration/Payment aggregators are also addressed to the DX of payment services. Modern payment gateways offer a robust and flexible API and strong integration capabilities with financial, accounting, tax and eCommerce platforms (Patiño, 2020). Table 6 summarizes our analyses of 'digital payments' of the working taxonomy.

2.6 Digital assets exchange

The Fintech business model of 'Digital Asset Exchange' is related to a P2P or closed/private 'exchange' of digital assets. 'Digital assets' are defined as 'digital representations of value, made possible by advances in cryptography and distributed ledger technology. They are denominated in their own units of account and can be transferred from *peer-to-peer* without an intermediary' (He, 2018). The working taxonomy refers to several types of digital asset exchange: Order book,[3] DEX relayer,[4] Single dealer platform, OTC trading,[5] Crypto trading bots,[6] Brokerage services, Aggregation, Bitcoin Teller Machines (BTM), Clearing. Table 7 summarizes our analyses of 'digital assets exchange' of the working taxonomy.

2.7 Digital custody

Custody at a digital exchange typically results in transfer of the possession of the digital assets to the exchange, which manages its own private keys in hot and cold storage. In return, a customer's account is credited for the transferred

TABLE 7 Expected impacts of digital assets exchange on commercial banks

Sub-verticals	Stakeholders in the current mode	Nature of risk absorption	Impact on commercial banks	Incentives for the platform
Order Book, DEX relayer	Brokers/traders	N. A (Exchange)	Neutral	Facilitating the origination and marketing
SDP/OTP trading, Brokerage Services	Investment banks, brokers/traders	N.A. (Exchange)	Neutral	Reducing transaction cost
Crypto trading bots/BTM	Cryptocurrency – brokers/traders	N.A. (Payment settlement)	Threat	Facilitating the origination and marketing
Aggregation	Non-bank financial institutions, microfinance institutions	N.A. (Exchange)	Opportunity	Diversification of risks/investors Facilitating the origination and marketing
Clearing	Brokers/traders	N.A. (Payment settlement)	Threat	Seeking for new profit base

digital assets (e.g. cryptocurrency). Most commonly, digital exchanges employ an omnibus model that results in comingling of customer assets across several private keys. Digital assets are an increasingly popular asset class among investors. Custodians – Key management services – are expected to fit a key role as this space matures with investors demanding a full suite of offerings inclusive of trading, lending, and staking (Walker et al., 2021).

The working taxonomy refers to Software Wallet. Wallets are distinguished by a set of supported cryptocurrencies and software platforms such as Windows, Mac and other operating systems. The taxonomy also refers to Web Wallet which is a widely used modern-day term that refers to an online wallet. There are two different versions of web wallets. One of those two types is commonly referred to as an eWallet. These are used for storing our everyday fiat currency and some of the most popular ones are *Skrill*, *PayPal* and *Neteller*. Other types of web wallets are the ones that can be used to send and receive cryptocurrencies. They're a software program that stores public and private keys and interacts with blockchain (SoftGamings, 2019).

The taxonomy also refers to Hardware Wallet. It is a key component of the blockchain ecosystem (Relay, 2019). They provide security and utility when interacting with blockchains. A hardware wallet is a type of cryptocurrency wallet. Table 8 summarizes our analyses of 'digital custody' of the working taxonomy.

TABLE 8 Expected impacts of digital custody on commercial banks

Sub-verticals	Stakeholders in the current mode	Nature of risk absorption	Impact on commercial banks	Incentives for the platform
Software wallet (mobile wallet/ tablet wallet/ desktop wallet), web wallet (eMoney wallet), hardware wallet	Custodian, operators of platform	N.A.	Threat	Enhancing the infrastructure for Fintech business models
Vault services, key management services	Custodian, operators of platform	N.A.	Neutral	Enhancing the infrastructure for Fintech business models

2.8 Insurtech

Insurtech is a combination of the words 'insurance' and 'technology' inspired by the term 'Fintech'. Insurtech is technology developed or used specifically for insurance operations applications and is mentioned more and more in industry publications (Hargrave, 2021). Insurtech is exploring avenues that large insurance firms have less incentive to exploit, such as offering ultra-customized policies, social insurance and using new streams of data from Internet-enabled devices to dynamically price premiums according to observed behaviour (Hargrave, 2021). Table 9 summarizes our analyses of 'insurtech' of the working taxonomy.

The working taxonomy refers to 'On-Demand Insurance' as a sub-vertical, which allows policies to be purchased online without directly interacting with a broker or a company representative. Customers can buy insurance using their smartphones. There are generally no long-term contracts, no lengthy forms and no need to speak to a representative over the phone, making insurance coverage literally a simple swipe on a smartphone. Premiums for these micro-duration

TABLE 9 Expected impacts of Insurtech on commercial banks

Sub-verticals	Stakeholders in the current mode	Nature of risk absorption	Impact on commercial banks	Incentives for the platform
All the sub-verticals	Conventional insurance companies	N.A.	Neutral	Facilitating the origination of new types of insurance

policies are paid in-app and claims are typically filed using a mobile chat interface (NAIC, 2021).

P2P insurance is a risk-sharing network where a group of individuals pool their premiums together to insure against a risk. P2P insurance may also be referred to as 'social insurance'. The innovative nature of P2P insurance has presented some challenges for insurance regulators who consider the P2P model different from the traditional one. Similar concerns across regulatory bodies that are seeing technology disrupt the traditional norm in the financial industry have given rise to a new group of companies called Regtech. Regtech uses innovative technology to help companies and industries partaking in digital advancements efficiently comply with industry regulators (Frankenfield, 2021).

Another sub-vertical here is the Internet of Things (IoT), which is a network of internet-connected devices transmitting, collecting, and sharing data. Among the most mature and fast-growing IoT applications involve connected vehicles using telematics, smart home devices (e.g., Amazon Alexa), and wearable devices (e.g., Fitbit) (NAIC, 2020).

IoT-connected insurance uses the data from internet-connected devices to improve the understanding of risks. Advances in IoT can improve productivity, overall profitability of the business and the risk profile of the portfolio. Through IoT, insurers can better connect with consumers adding important touch points in particularly sensitive phases, like acquisitions, and claims. Moreover, IoT advances can be realized for the full range of products and lines of business, from commercial, to life, property and casualty and health (NAIC, 2020).

2.9 Wealthtech

Wealthtech stands for *wealth* and *technology* and is one of the subsections of fintech.

> Just as fintech combines finance with technology to change the way we organize, spend, and receive our money both as individuals and as companies, wealthtech unites wealth and technology with the goal of providing digital solutions to enhance personal (and professional) wealth management and investing.
>
> *(Cheng, 2019)*

The working taxonomy of wealthtech refers to the sub-verticals of Social Trading (also known as Copy Trading),[7] Robo-Advisors,[8] Robo Retirement/Pension Planning, Personal Financial Management/Planning, Financial Comparison Sites. These sub-verticals can be categorized by their characteristics of service: platform and software service. Platform services such as Social Trading and Financial Comparison Sites, and software solutions such as Digital Wealth and Robo-Advisors both are backed by diversified individual investors who are willing to absorb risks and uncertainty. As such, the fundamental nature of wealthtech is 'private banking'.

TABLE 10 Expected impacts of Wealthtech on commercial banks

Sub-verticals	Stakeholders in the current mode	Nature of risk absorption	Impact on commercial banks	Incentives for the platform
Financial comparison sites, social trading	Investment banks Private banks Other players	N.A.	Neutral	Reducing the asymmetry of information
Digital wealth management, Robo-advisors, Robo retirement/ pension planning, Personal finance management/ planner	Investment banks Private banks	N.A.	Opportunity	Reducing the transaction cost through automation and algorithm

While the fundamental nature of those services is the same, the impact on the commercial banks is the opposite. Services that are provided in the form of the platform allow people to compare and contrast different services that various financial institutions provide. Such platforms reduce the asymmetry of information by displaying collected prices and specifications. Platform services with strong network effects grow into a big platform provider. Since commercial banks are not incentivized to provide such comparison and run the platform, the platform services come as a threat to commercial banks.

On the other hand, software services that are characterized by machine learning and artificial intelligence (AI) pose more opportunity to commercial banks. The essence of what the software service provides is diminishing transaction costs through the algorithm and automation (Deloitte, 2016). Written and automated algorithms form the software that produces insights and strategies for better decision-making to investors after understanding their behaviours by collecting decision-making patterns and preferences. Many investment banks are leveraging this technology to grow their businesses. Unlike the platform service, commercial banks are also capable of facilitating and are incentivized to implement this technology to enhance their businesses. By doing so, commercial banks can maximize the opportunity to expand their businesses by capturing investors who would prefer not to take direct risk but still want to enjoy the perks of the powerful AI tool. Table 10 summarizes our analyses of 'wealthtech' of the working taxonomy.

3 Is the trend of DX a threat or opportunity for commercial banks?

As mentioned earlier, commercial banks are, more or less, protected under the banking regulations for the regulatory objectives of maintaining financial stability (preventing potential bank runs) while promoting sound financial intermediation. So far, we argued how each Fintech business model would cast 'threat', 'opportunity' or 'remain neutral' to the commercial banking unit. Now, it is time to sum up our argument.

1 The Fintech business models/sub-verticals which would cast a 'threat' to commercial banking unit:

   P2PL (Property Lending, Lending to bankable clients) (Digital lending)
   Fully Digitally Native Bank, Marketplace Bank, Agent Banking (Digital banking)
   Digital Money Market/Fund (Digital savings)
   SaaS (Digital savings/Wealthtech)
   Most of sub-verticals in Digital payments
   Crypto trading bots/BTM (Digital asset exchanges)
   Clearing (Digital asset exchanges)
   Software Wallet (Mobile Wallet/Tablet Wallet/Desktop Wallet), Web Wallet (eMoney Wallet), Hardware Wallet (Digital custody)

2 The Fintech business models/sub-verticals which would cast a 'neutral' to commercial banking unit.

   P2PL to marginalized clients, Crowd-led-microfinance (Digital lending)
   Most of sub-verticals in Digital capital raising
   Order Book, DEX relayer (Digital asset exchanges)
   SDP/OTP trading, Brokerage Services (Digital asset exchanges)
   Vault services, Key management services (Digital custody)
   Insurtech

3 The Fintech business models/sub-verticals which would bring an 'opportunity' to commercial banking unit:

   Debt-based securities (Digital lending): Diversification of risks and investors
   Invoice Trading, Consumer Purchase Financing (Digital lending): Diversification of risks and investors
   Real Estate Crowdfunding (Digital capital raising): Diversification of risks
   BaaS (Digital banking): Expanding the scope of business
   Digital Micro Saving Solutions, Digital Savings Collective/Pool (Digital savings): Expanding the scope of business
   Aggregation (Digital asset exchanges): Diversification of risks/investors/ Facilitating the origination and marketing
   Digital Wealth Management,
   Robo-Advisors, Robo Retirement/Pension Planning, Personal finance management/planner (Wealthtech): Reducing the transaction cost through automation and algorithm

Needless to say, Fintech and digitalization would give other financial servicers a chance to penetrate into the traditional financial products and services which have been monopolized by the commercial banking unit; in particular, *deposit taking* (Digital savings), *payment settlement* (Digital payments) and *mediating financial resources from depositors to corporations* (Digital lending). Also, the services related to *money dealing* (cash and exchange) would be penetrated by the newcomers in digital banking, Digital asset exchange and digital custody. The 'P2P' financial services would erode the monopolistic/oligopolistic market in lending, payments and money dealing operated by commercial banks in the past.

On the other hand, Fintech and digitalization would give commercial banks an opportunity to expand the scope of business as well as to diversify risks and uncertainty with ultimate investors. In our view, (1) the lending business upon securitization (CDO) and crowdfunding (Digital lending and Digital capital raising) for diversifying credit risks, (2) the sale and utilization of the accumulated credit/client information to other financial service providers and platforms (Digital banking and Digital asset exchange), (3) the business related to 'Private Banking' (wealth management) upon Fintech (Wealthtech) for reducing the fund management cost would give commercial banks an opportunity to seek for a new profit base. We should note that the shift to the lending business upon securitization and crowdfunding would mean that the business of commercial banks would be shifted from 'indirect' to 'direct' finance. At the same time, the sales and utilization of credit information would bring commercial banks a 'fee' based business opportunity. In addition, we should note that the wealth management (private banking), in its nature, is a business in 'investment banking'.

Roughly speaking, the 'P2P' mode of financial intermediation and services would make traditional commercial banks face the difficulty in earning a sufficient profit (bank rent) to maintain their franchise value. Some innovative commercial banks may be able to reshape their mode of business for their survival with the direction to 'P2P' and 'direct finance' mode of financial intermediation and services upon the technology of digitalization. However, such innovative commercial banks would not be called 'commercial banks' anymore.

One of the dominant principles of Islamic finance is the prohibition of *riba* or interest, while, no doubt, interest is an essential element of finance and is embedded in our financial system. A theory of the rate of interest is still debatable. For the classical economists the rate of interest is the price at which saving out of revenue (understood as real output not consumed) becomes equal to investment. Keynes postulated that interest is the price at which the demand for money, driven by liquidity preference, is equal to a given supply of money. The process of determining the liquidity preference is, according to Keynes, reflected in 'uncertainty' and 'expectation'. On the other hand, Marx accepted that interest is a part of total profit and argued that it is also the price at which the supply of loanable capital (interest-bearing capital) equals the demand; such capital typically assumes the money form and is not equivalent to real resources saved and reinvested (Itoh and Lapavitsas, 1999, pp. 212–213). The Marxian view on the process of determining the rate of interest is based on the 'class struggle' between lenders and borrowers. In the context of the PLS mode in Islamic finance, further arguments on how reasonably (or poorly) the associated risk and uncertainty would be reflected in the expected rate of profit as well as on how appropriately (or with bias) the rate of profit would be shared between lenders and borrowers are necessary. Chapter 1 provides several points for the arguments.

So far, as a sufficient level of wealth and capital has been accumulated in the society and the sufficient number of investors are ready and willing to absorb various types of credit risk and uncertainty, the P2P mode of financial intermediation and services would be feasible and, perhaps, desirable for ultimate investors and users of financial products and services. One of the questions here is that if sufficient level of wealth and capital has not yet been accumulated, widely observed in developing countries, can we simply conclude that the trend of digitalization would be desirable? In developing countries, we may still need the role of commercial banks as financial intermediaries by mediating idle/stagnant funds held by households to the industrial sector in a considerably large scale. In theory, so far, as the sufficient level of wealth and capital has been accumulated enough to meet the financial demand in a global scale including that in developing countries, the trend of digitalization would be feasible. However, there is no guarantee of always ensuring the stable and sufficient circulation and flows of fund from an investor to a user of fund. Perhaps, the process of determining the rate of profit or the rate of interest is still supposed to be based on the 'class struggle' between lenders and borrowers.

Another question is that the P2P mode of savings and payments would put the existing centralized (monopolized) mode of savings and payments to an end, which has been highly regulated and monitored by the regulators under the current mode of supervising the banking industry for ensuring financial stability (for avoiding the potential bank runs). How will the decentralized/P2P mode of savings and payments affect the financial stability? In theory, as more commercial banks are shifting their mode of business to investment banking by diversifying credit risk, the regulators would be less concerned about the accumulation of non-performing loans which would trigger the bank run. However, the regulators may be more concerned about a liquidity shock in a respective level of diversified investors, which may trigger the chain reaction of the shortage of liquidity in diversified types of currency and money upon digitalization. How will the regulators respond to the diversified and P2P mode of savings and payments? The response is becoming an important challenge for the regulators to respond to the trend of Fintech and digitalization of financial products and services.

Acknowledgement

Yasushi would like to thank Mizuki Amagai, Yasha Athalladhira, Francisca Diandra S, Mahmudul Islam Fahim, Mahmud Hasan, John Kim and Satrio Komang for their various contributions to the data collection and discussions.

Notes

1 The terms P2P/Marketplace are often used interchangeably today, but there are technical differences between the two. Pure P2PL is applied when individuals lend to borrowers, whereas marketplace lending platform is applied when it allows institutions to loan out money alongside individuals (Friedman, 2016).
2 BaaS is also often referred to as 'white-label banking', since the banking services are delivered through the branded product of the non-bank (Dolan, 2021).
3 The transaction of 'Order-book' is a list of current buy and sell orders used by an *exchange* to fill orders on a specific market. The order book consists of both orders to buy or sell at a fixed price ('limit' orders) and orders to buy or sell at the best available price ('market' orders). But since market orders only appear in the order book momentarily, they aren't shown in the publicly viewable order book (Handa and Schwartz, 1996).
4 The main property of a decentralized exchange (DEX) is giving custodianship to users/traders of their own assets. Unlike a centralized crypto exchange (e.g. coinbase, binance) where the exchange stores a user's private key, in DEX, private keys always remain with the users, hence the user is always in control of his own asset (Agrawal, 2019). A Relayer hosts an off-chain order book. Using relayers, users can find, create, fill or cancel orders. Relayers help traders discover counter-parties and move cryptographically orders between them. A relayer can talk to other relayers and create a pool of orders to increase liquidity (Agrawal, 2019).
5 Over-the-counter (OTC) refers to the process of how securities are traded via a broker-dealer network as opposed to on a centralized exchange (Murphy, 2021).
6 Crypto trading bots are a set of programs designed to automate cryptocurrency trading.
7 Social trading is a form of dealing that enables traders or investors to copy and execute the strategies of their peers or more experienced traders. While most traders perform their own fundamental and technical analysis, there is a class of traders that prefer to observe and replicate the analysis of others. Copy trading allows traders in social networks to receive information on the success of other agents in financial markets and to directly copy their trades (Apesteguia, Oechssler and Weidenholzer, 2020).
8 Robo-advisors (also spelled robo-adviser or robo advisor) are digital platforms that provide automated, algorithm-driven financial planning services with little to no human supervision (Deloitte, 2016). Better information is available in the report.

References

Adrian, T. and Mancini-Griffoli, T. (2021) A new era of digital money. [online] *International Monetary Fund*. Available at: https://www.imf.org/external/pubs/ft/fandd/2021/06/online/digital-money-new-era-adrian-mancini-griffoli.htm [Accessed July 7, 2021].
Aga Khan Development Network (AKDN). (2017) *Digital Savings Groups: Low-Cost, Mobile*, Paperless. p. 2.
Agrawal, G. (2019) 'A beginner's guide to building A RELAYER with 0x protocol'. *Medium*. Available at: https://medium.com/crowdbotics/a-beginners-guide-to-building-a-relayer-with-0x-protocol-c725c45f0b2f [Accessed July 27, 2021].
Apesteguia, J., Oechssler, J. and Weidenholzer, S. (2020) 'Copy Trading', *Management Science*, 66(12), pp. 5608–5622.
Bashir, I. and Banze, R. (2020) *Crowdfunding: The Story of People*. Project Nile 20.
Bell, M. (2020) Fintech Raisin Launches Savings as a service software for U.S. banks and credit unions. [online] *Raisin*. Available at: https://www.raisin.com/us/press/fintech-raisin-launches-us-market/ [Accessed July 7, 2021].

Belleflamme, P. (2014) Crowdfunding: Giving rewards or sharing profits? [online] Available at: http://www.ipdigit.eu/2014/05/crowdfunding-giving-rewards-or-sharing-profits/ [Accessed July 7, 2021].

Businesswire. (2020) Digital capital raise on Netcapital platform sells out in less than 24 hours. [online] Available at: https://www.businesswire.com/news/home/20201208005274/en/Digital-Capital-Raise-on-Netcapital-Platform-Sells-Out-in-Less-Than-24-Hours/ [Accessed July 7, 2021].

CCAF [Cambridge Centre for Alternative Finance]. (2020) *The Global Covid-19 FinTech Market Rapid Assessment Study*. Cambridge Centre for Alternative Finance.

Cheng, M. (2019) The future of Wealthtech. *Forbes*. Available at: https://www.forbes.com/sites/margueritacheng/2019/02/19/the-future-of-wealthtech/?sh=315e84cf35e6 [Accessed 2 January, 2021].

Davis, D. (2012) Microsavings: Opening the door for individuals to invest in themselves. [online] *Federal Reserve Bank of St. Louis*. Available at: https://www.stlouisfed.org/publications/bridges/summer-2012/microsavings-opening-the-door-for-individuals-to-invest-in-themselves [Accessed July 7, 2021].

Deloitte. (2016) *The Expansion of Robo-Advisory in Wealth Management*. Deloitte.

Dolan, S. (2021) How the banking-as-a-service industry works and BaaS market outlook for 2021. [online] *Business Insider*. Available at: https://www.businessinsider.com/banking-as-a-service-industry?r=AU&IR=T/ [Accessed July 7, 2021].

Fernando, J. (2020) Debt security. [online] *Investopedia*. Available at: https://www.investopedia.com/terms/d/debtsecurity.asp [Accessed July 7, 2021].

Frankenfield, J. (2021) Peer-to-peer (P2P) insurance. *Investopedia*. Available at: https://www.investopedia.com/terms/p/peertopeer-p2p-insurance.asp [Accessed July 27, 2021].

Friedman, A. (2016) WTF is marketplace lending? [online] *Tearsheet*. Available at: https://tearsheet.co/wtf/what-is-marketplace-lending/ [Accessed July 7, 2021].

Goyal, S. (2020) What is mobile wallet and how does it work? [online] Available at: https://www.jagranjosh.com/general-knowledge/what-is-mobile-wallet-and-how-does-it-work-1538043252-1/ [Accessed July 7, 2021].

Handa, P. and Schwartz, R.A. (1996) 'Limit Order Trading', *Journal of Finance*. Available at: https://econpapers.repec.org/article/blajfinan/v_3a51_3ay_3a1996_3ai_3a5_3ap_3a1835-61.htm [Accessed July 27, 2021].

Hargrave, M. (2021) Will insurtech disrupt the insurance industry? [online] *Investopedia*. Available at: https://www.investopedia.com/terms/i/insurtech.asp [Accessed July 7, 2021].

Hazik, M. and Hassnian, A. (2019) *Blockchain, Fintech, and Islamic Finance*. Boston, MA: Walter de Gruyter Inc.

He, D. (2018) 'Monetary Policy in the Digital Age', *Finance & Development*, 55 (2). Available at: https://www.imf.org/external/pubs/ft/fandd/2018/06/central-bank-monetary-policy-and-cryptocurrencies/he.htm [Accessed July 27, 2021].

Hecht, J. (2018) 4 business loans that work well with invoice financing. [online] *Forbes*. Available at: https://www.forbes.com/sites/jaredhecht/2018/01/29/4-business-loans-that-work-well-with-invoice-financing/?sh=6ab196964d9a [Accessed July 13, 2021].

Itoh, M. and Lapavitsas, C. (1999) *Political Economy of Money and Finance*. Basingstoke: Palgrave Macmillan.

Moran, N. (2021) How e-money issuers may be the biggest challengers to banks yet. *Bobsguide*. Available at: https://www.bobsguide.com/articles/how-e-money-issuers-may-be-the-biggest-challengers-to-banks-yet/ [Accessed July 27, 2021].

Murphy, C.B. (2021) Over-the-counter (otc). *Investopedia*. Available at: https://www.investopedia.com/terms/o/otc.asp [Accessed July 27, 2021].

NAIC. (2020) Internet of things (iot). *National Association of Insurance Commissioners*. Available at: https://content.naic.org/cipr_topics/topic_internet_things_iot.htm [Accessed July 27, 2021].

NAIC. (2021) On-demand insurance. *National Association of Insurance Commissioners*. Available at: https://content.naic.org/cipr_topics/topic_ondemand_insurance.htm [Accessed July 27, 2021].

Napoletano, E. and Foreman, D. (2021) What is digital banking? [online] *Forbes*. Available at: https://www.forbes.com/advisor/banking/what-is-digital-banking/ [Accessed July 7, 2021]

Patiño, D. (2020) Why is digital remittance replacing traditional money transfer? *Rocket Remit*. Available at: https://www.rocketremit.com/2020/11/02/digital-remittance-is-replacing-traditional-money-transfer/ [Accessed July 27, 2021].

PwC. (2017) Bank to the future: finding the right path to digital transformation. [online] *PwC*. Available at: https://www.pwc.com/us/en/industries/financial-services/library/digital-bank-transformation.html [Accessed July 7, 2021].

Relay, R. (2019) Hardware wallets explained. *Medium*. Available at: https://medium.com/radartech/hardware-wallets-explained-da8bd93ce801 [Accessed July 27, 2021].

Schmidt, J. (2020) P2P lending explained: Business models, definitions & statistics. [online] *P2PMarketData*. Available at: https://p2pmarketdata.com/p2p-lending-explained/ [Accessed July 7, 2021]

Shubhangi, B. (2020) Digital payments: Definition and methods – razorpay payment gateway. *Razorpay Learn*. Available at: https://razorpay.com/learn/digital-payments-india-definition-methods-importance/ [Accessed July 27, 2021].

SoftGamings. (2019) Web wallet. *SoftGamings*. Available at: https://www.softgamings.com/casino-glossary/web-wallet/ [Accessed July 27, 2021].

Solis, B., Li, C. and Szymanski, J. (2014) *The 2014 State of Digital Transformation*. Altimeter Group.

Stewart, A., Lamont, K. and Yaworsky, K. (2018) Demystifying digital lending. [online] *Accion*. Available at: https://www.findevgateway.org/sites/default/files/publications/files/1123_digital_lending_r10_print_ready.pdf. [Accessed July 7, 2021].

Walker, R., et al. (2021) 'The Unique and Complex Considerations of Digital Asset Custody', *Journal of Securities Operations & Custody*, 13(2), pp. 150–162.

Zimmermann, J. (2020) Rewards-based crowdfunding: What it is, when it works. [online] *Nerdwallet*. Available at: https://www.nerdwallet.com/article/small-business/rewards-based-crowdfunding [Accessed July 7, 2021].

3
FINTECH, TECHNOMANIA, AND PERSISTENT SOCIO-CIVILIZATIONAL CHALLENGES

Mohammad Omar Farooq and Muhammad Dulal Miah

1 Introduction

Modern life is shaped and dominated by technology. While technological change has always been present as a constant in the evolution of human civilization, the pace and extent to which technology now not just shapes, but also controls our individual and collective life is unprecedented. According to Harvard sociologist Daniel Bell (1980:20), "technology like art is a soaring exercise of the human imagination. ... Technology is the instrumental ordering of human experience within a logic of efficient means, and the direction of nature to use its powers for material gain."

We are continuously pushing the frontier and, due to technological change among other things, drastically changing the way we live. The positive, expansive impact of technology is undeniable. Standard of living has phenomenally increased. The pace of life has picked up at a mind-boggling level. The art of problem-solving, in many areas, has become cutting edge and fast-paced. As part, the expansive presence of technology affecting all aspects of life, one area that also has emerged as a dominant sub-field is financial technology, Fintech, in short.

As a nascent field, it is already impacting various aspects of our financial life and is expected to touch our lives more closely as it evolves. There is a lot of excitement in the air, as Fintech, based on breakthrough technologies, such as blockchain, artificial intelligence (AI), machine learning, big data, robo-advisory, smart contracts, and so on (Arslanian and Fischer, 2019), we might be in an unchartered territory. Arvind Sankaran, a global business leader, has stated about the Fintech revolution, a creative destruction of what we know and have: "we're witnessing the creative destruction of financial services, rearranging itself around the consumer. Who does this in the most relevant, exciting way using

DOI: 10.4324/9781003262169-5

data and digital, wins!" (Haq, 2020). This is not just a change, it's being viewed as part of the fourth industrial revolution (Miller and Wendt, 2021), changing the "DNA of finance" (Phadke, 2020).

While Muslims, in general, and Islamic finance, in particular, are not part of leading technology creation and development, Islamic finance is trying to take advantage of the emerging Fintech revolution and through the relevant technology adoption and diffusion (Alam and Ali, 2020). However, as Islamic finance is mainly a prohibition-driven industry so far, it is largely disconnected from the broader, positive socioeconomic aspirations (Farooq, 2012). In this chapter, we explore some deeper socio-civilizational challenges that not only affect the humanity from socioeconomic perspective, but also some of which at the civilizational level that relate to finance as well as Islamic finance (Mihalcova et al., 2019). Therefore, the analysis presented here applies to Islamic finance as well.

The rest of the chapter is organized as follows: section two underpins the primary philosophy of Fintech. Section three discusses technological changes and the resulting technomania. Some persistent problems such as climate change, rising inequality and the resulting poverty, gender gap, etc. are affected by the advancement of technology. Chapter 4 assesses the potential impact of Fintech on these critical elements, considering the interlinked nature of those problems. The chapter also highlights how can Fintech play a decisive role in subsiding the adverse effects of Fintech on the foundation of society. This is followed by a brief conclusion.

2 Value proposition and underlying philosophy of Fintech

Fintech is poised to revolutionize the entire financial services sector, covering banks, insurance, and asset management, while addressing five key issues: improving financial inclusion; enhancing customer experience; providing targeted or customized support and guidance aided by AI and data analytics; increasing transparency; and security and compliance (KPMG, 2017). We will briefly explore these issues.

Financial inclusion is one of the major aspects of Fintech, touching the lives of a lot of people who are otherwise left out from the mainstream banking and finance. The computer, wireless technology, internet, and smartphone were crucial in laying the foundation for Fintech revolution. There are many disadvantaged people in the world, who have low education and lack computers and the relevant skills; but a good portion of them now not only use internet and smartphone for communication, but also access many modern services, including financial services. Andree Simon (2020), President and CEO of FINCA Impact Finance, identifies four key emerging trends related to Fintech and financial inclusion: (a) the gender gap is closing; (b) banking, instead of banks, is getting more attention; (c) collaboration, instead of traditional competition, between banks and tech-based firms is bringing together economic forces to facilitate greater participation; and (d) Fintech is enhancing a "human touch ... culturally, technologically, and operationally."

Educated and technology-savvy customers are already experiencing enhanced capabilities, such as chatbots, cloud computing, etc. On the transparency issue, it is undeniable that the champions of Fintech were deeply motivated by the lack of transparency in traditional banking and finance, and they desire to bring positive disruptions. However, opportunities from Fintech also come with new risks (IMF, 2019). Considering the opportunities and risks, let's consider one of the hottest areas of Fintech: cryptocurrency. A key feature of cryptocurrency is the transparency of the transactions based on blockchain; the coded data is immutable. However, transparency of transaction does not necessarily cover the identity behind the transaction, which has become a serious challenge for the regulators, and this tug of war between the pursuit of openness and the need or desire for regulation remains unresolved (Goodell and Aste, 2019).

A similar concern relates to security and compliance. While the transactions are generally secure, they are also vulnerable to fraud and hacking, as in some well-known cases cryptocurrency worth billions of dollars has been stolen. One of the largest hackings, worth one billion dollar, from banks across the globe was recorded in 2015 (Blue Water Credit, 2015). Notably, in 2016, Bitfinex cryptocurrency exchange was hacked and bitcoins worth $4.5 billion were stolen, even though a good part of it was later recovered. Indeed, security remains one of the most critical concerns, where the Fintech users expect a substantively better performance.

So far, the leading aspects of Fintech's value proposition have been faster and more efficient payments, better and friendlier customer experience, the newly discovered capacity to generate business insight using big data and data analytics and expanded financial inclusion. This value proposition is relevant for Islamic finance industry as well. The *Global Islamic Fintech Report 2021* identifies several important areas where Islamic finance industry is benefiting from and is poised for expansion and growth. However, the report does not indicate any special competitive advantage of Islamic finance industry (Dinar and Elipses, 2021). A good proportion of Muslim population avoids conventional interest-based banking. Hence, Islamic finance industry has been a valuable option for this population segment. This means that a greater degree of financial inclusion through Fintech will be possible in the future.

Notably, just like there is potential vulnerability to technomania, Muslim world also has a parallel undercurrent of technophobia. It is not surprising that even before the actual benefits and harms of cryptocurrencies, as part of Fintech revolution, are adequately assessed, there are technophobic and obscurantist religious scholars, who are pronouncing "haram" (prohibited) fatwas (Mellor, 2021).

While financial sector and Islamic finance both are expected to benefit from Fintech and deliver benefit for the society and economy, the larger picture involving technology and progress is often glossed over. Technological progress has been instrumental behind the transformation of the society. However, it is important that human society remains the master of technology than being its slave, especially in the civilizational context. Of course, "technological determinism," viewing technology as an autonomous force of change over which we have little control, paints a rather pessimistic picture of civilization (Bergandi, 2013).

3 Technological progress and technomania

One of the undeniable impacts of technology is that it has made the world much smaller, connecting people across the globe. Holdstock (2019) refers Matt Mullenberg, a social media entrepreneur, who aptly said, "technology is best when it brings people together." In general, technology now not just shapes, but also dominates, our life. Instead of being a useful servant, it seems to be emerging as, Nobel Laureate Christian Lange (Lange, 1921) puts it, a "dangerous master." Indeed, technology is being presented in civilization term. Ryan (2020) quoted Jacques Ellul "modern technology has become a total phenomenon for civilization, the defining force of a new social order in which efficiency is no longer an option but a necessity imposed on all human activity." Unfortunately, technology, instead of improving our life, seems to have become our life. While it is people who make technology possible, we seem to be losing faith in people and putting more faith in technology. Steve Jobs (2019) had sagaciously argued, "technology is nothing. What's important is that you have faith in people, that they're basically good and smart, and if you give them tools, they'll do wonderful things with them."

The ubiquitous and domineering impact of technology is aptly captured by Steven Levy (1995):

> The revolution has only just begun, but already it's starting to overwhelm us. It's outstripping our capacity to cope, antiquating our laws, transforming our mores, reshuffling our economy, reordering our priorities, redefining our workplaces, putting our Constitution to the fire, shifting our concept of reality.

Levy's observation was in 1995, based on what he observed, while the last two decades have seemed to appear as an unprecedented technological transformation, even by Levy's benchmark.

Yet, the fact remains that even though technology is a contribution from human beings, and it will continue to exert its indomitable influence on the human society as an autonomous force of change, and it makes us more efficient and bring transformational impact on the lives of people in so many ways, Ord (2020) asks: does everything have technological solutions, especially for socio-civilizational challenges that either have been persistent or gradually becoming existential ones?

There is exuberance with technology, in general, and Fintech, in particular, and there are compelling reasons to believe that more exciting solutions are forthcoming that will make things faster, cheaper, inclusive, more decentralized, more reliable (maybe), and secure (maybe). However, there are some persistent socio-civilizational problems or challenges (Truevtsev, 2016) that beg question whether those are amenable to technological solution or, in other words, if solutions to those challenges lie in technology. Also, a question remains whether financial sector, in general, or Islamic finance, in particular, can really address these existential civilizational challenges. Such concerns are relevant because ultimately if these socio-civilizational challenges are not addressed, especially the existential ones, there might not be any problem to solve.

4 Socio-civilizational, especially existential, challenges not treated as priorities

In 2017, the famous and influential scientist, Stephen Hawking, made a dire prediction that human species has about 100 years to save itself by finding another habitable planet (Zorthian, 2017). Doomsday predictions are not that uncommon, and many observers have pointed out the tendency of Hawking and other doomsday forecasters to exaggerate. Therefore, any such doomsday prediction must be taken with enormous caution. However, if we can put aside the existential challenges in doomsday terms, there are still challenges that the modern civilization finds persistent and growing. Not only their mere existence, but these challenges are worsening, pushing the concerns to an existential level.

Based on a number of works related to the study of civilization and its modern crisis (Avery, 2017), here we explore five challenges, two of which are persistent, while the other three are not just persistent but growing worse to the level of existential concerns.

4.1 Poverty

Poverty has been a persistent challenge for human civilization, where a significant segment of the population is bypassed by the economic development and progress around them. Whatever criteria are used for measuring poverty and extreme poverty, the last century's economic progress across the globe has had notable improvement in alleviating poverty. The economic development, with specific target to alleviate poverty, has been possible through the effects of education, infrastructure, and technology, which facilitated rising productivity and income.

According to various international sources, just in the last three decades, "the number of people in extreme poverty has fallen from nearly 1.9 billion in 1990 to about 650 million in 2018" (Roser and Ortiz-Ospina, 2019). Notably, these are pre-pandemic data, and, ignoring the adverse effects of the pandemic and barring any other major global mishap, if the trend of the past three decades continues until 2030, "the number of people in extreme poverty will stagnate at almost 500 million" (UNDESA, 2021). As the effects of the pandemic on global poverty are becoming clear, the progress in poverty alleviation has taken a big hit, and some of the progresses have been reversed (UNDESA, 2021). Also, noteworthy is that much of the discussion about poverty is focused on extreme poverty, with a very low threshold of US$1.90 per day. With a higher and more relevant threshold, those in poverty (not just in extreme poverty) would be a much higher in number. The definition and measurement of poverty and extreme poverty are rather highly contested areas of research. Some of the rosy pictures about the progress in poverty alleviation have been challenged by many studies (Hickel, 2019).

The father of microcredit movement, Nobel Laureate Muhammad Yunus, dreams of putting poverty in museum and many other voices also would like to see not just alleviation of poverty, but rather its elimination. Most of them see technology as a relevant but not necessarily the driving force for achieving that goal of poverty eradication. Modern technology has been one of the powerful catalysts on many fronts to enhance economic progress and alleviate poverty, but the issues related to poverty and deprivation are more complex. Despite all the progress, including the impact of technology, if the number of people in poverty and extreme poverty persist from 500 million to 1.5 billion, it should not be difficult to understand that the problem and complexity involved go beyond technology. Therefore, technology in general and Fintech in particular might bring further improvement in certain ways. Since the reason behind persistent poverty is not necessarily amenable to merely technological cure, we must be circumspect regarding any over expectation from technology-led, technology-driven, or technology-dependent model of progress and development, without concurrently focusing on other and more complex factors.

Realistically, the most promise of Fintech for poverty alleviation is through financial inclusion, especially microfinance and crowdfunding. As technology is breaking down the barrier for more and more people by making modern financial services scalable and accessible, evidence shows that consequential changes can happen in a facilitating environment. Several studies from around the world show the promise of Fintech for poverty alleviation. For instance, Appiah-Otoo and Song (2021) in the context of China, Emara and Mohieldin (2021) for data selected from Middle East and North Africa (MENA) region, and Aba and Linardy (2021) drawing evidence from Indonesia show a positive impact of Fintech on poverty alleviation. The study by Omar and Inaba (2020) concludes based on data from 116 countries that financial inclusion "… significantly reduces poverty rates and income inequality in developing countries."

As Islamic finance is already making a positive contribution to financial inclusion, better equipped with scalable Fintech services, Islamic finance can also make further contribution. A World Bank study (2020) finds solid potential for Islamic finance to utilize Fintech toward financial inclusion, which is an important aspect of poverty alleviation. However, the study also notes that there are potential risks of Fintech diffusion among people with low literacy and education, which would require "careful mitigation" and an active role of the industry stakeholders, including the regulators. As some of the Islamic finance experts, who are also working with Fintech, articulate "if Islamic fintech can demonstrate how they uphold the core values of Islamic finance, using tools like blockchain, they could be formidable force for good across financial services" (London Institute of Banking and Finance, 2020).

4.2 Inequality

Inequality and concentration of wealth have always been present in human civilization. Throughout modern periods and in different contexts, the inequality and concentration of wealth have seen better and worse periods. However, the concentration of wealth has been alarmingly worsening during the 21st century, and quite interestingly contributed by modern technologies and dominated by those who have pioneered and led the tech revolution (Summers, 2016).

Modern technologies have contributed to productivity growth, accelerated economic development, expanded access to practical information sharing, and enhanced access to basic services and amenities. Indeed, a significant decline in extreme poverty would not have been possible without the role of, among other things, modern technology. However, neither technology evenly or fairly impacts the world, nor does it improve inequality and concentration of wealth. The adverse impact of technology on inequality has been attributed to "generation of economic rents and rent-seeking behavior" (UNESCAP, 2018). From economic viewpoint, this economic rent is extracting excess income or unearned gains without contributing anything to the real economy, and often through preferential regulation. UNESCAP (2018:20) reports "… financial globalization, digitalization and the rise of frontier technologies are the enabling environments for rent-seeking that cause extreme, long-lasting, and deepening inequality." Digital economy has leveled the playing field to a great extent for the broader population by giving access to modern communication technology, but at the same time, technology has also concentrated the capacity of wealth creation in the hands of tech companies and those companies that have been directly and significantly aided by technological change.

However, it is not just accumulation of wealth by a few rich, but also their extraordinary power of regulatory capture – the ability to control the relevant regulators (Allen, 2017). Many prominent economists, including Thomas Picketty (2014), place the concentration of wealth and the resulting inequality as one of the biggest challenges facing the globe (Lohr, 2022). Contemporary world is dominated by capitalist societies, and under this system, capital owners are the masters and the story of this system revolves around capital. Unfortunately, there is no technological solution to his worsening, destabilizing problem, unless technological progress consciously pursues paths toward shared prosperity.

Reducing income inequality is a formidable challenge because while technology, especially Fintech, is helping to enhance financial inclusion, which may help alleviate poverty, inequality and concentration of wealth have a more complex systemic and structural bias. Ironically, such biases are also facilitated by modern technology, creating disproportionate wealth for those who are already rich. So far, studies (e.g., Foohey and Martin, 2021; Jones and Maynard, 2023; Petrou, 2018) connecting Fintech and wealth inequality do not indicate any significant positive impact on reducing the inequality. Notably, Global Islamic Fintech Report 2021 has no reference at all to poverty, inequality, or wealth gap.

4.3 Epidemics/pandemics

The latest epidemic is a devastating reminder that the human civilization is acutely vulnerable to non-technological factors. Our mastery of science and technology has been helpful to mitigate the impact of the pandemic and to overcome through discovery of relevant vaccines. However, scientists and experts predict that, far from this being the last time, bigger, wider, and more devastating pandemic is not only possible, but also likely and not all such possibilities have technological solutions.

As discussed about poverty and inequality, two interrelated problems, even with the biotechnological solutions to address pandemic, it is clear that the global divide between the poor and not-poor persists. The Western countries, where vaccines were developed, got the priority in the vaccine distribution, and many countries with lower resources have not been able to make the vaccines available to their own population, because vaccine is costly and many poorer countries, reeling from the devastating economic effects of pandemic, has yet been able to afford wider distribution for their people. Once again, the complexity of an interrelated world precludes purely or even primarily technology-driven solutions.

Even before we get rid of this global pandemic, experts are warning that more, and even more lethal, pandemics are very likely (Gregory and Elgot, 2021). To be fair, modern technology allows now better and wider dissemination of news and information, but that includes both useful and accurate as well as misleading and fake information. Moreover, just like technology has made this planet an interconnected village and bringing the global communities closer, the risk of spreading epidemic faster and wider has increased massively.

In several areas, Fintech has had very useful and beneficial impact during Covid 19 pandemic. One such key area has been contactless payment. While the technology has been developing for some time, the pandemic provided the impetus for aggressively developing solutions in this area. Indeed, researchers and industry observers point to the fact that this pandemic induced as well as forced many innovations. Islamic finance has not lagged in this area of adopting relevant innovations. Forbes (2021) identified 14 tech innovations that would have enduring impact on our life, especially in connection with our work. Some tech solutions related to our health, such as telehealth and mental fitness, can help people with their health aspects or innovations that may smoothen the life of many people, but they would not necessarily be directly relevant for preventing epidemic. However, that is not necessarily related to Fintech, but technology in general will have to play the desired role for better health and safety.

4.4 Wars and conflicts

One persistent scourge of human civilization has been wars and conflicts. There was hardly any era in human history when some wars or conflicts did not take place. However, modern civilization has not seen less of them. Rather, 20th century has been noted as the century of genocide, and the same century also has seen two of the worst wars of global scales, the two world wars.

If technology has brightened, enriched, and enhanced many aspects of our lives, and positively touched so many people around the world, it is also the science and technology driven by war or military pursuits that now have brought the planet to an existential threat. The human species now has built the military capacity to be able to self-destruct. As Russia invaded Ukraine, both countries part of Europe as the hotbed of two world wars, and if the global military powers and NATO did not feel restrained and behave pragmatically, such a war initiated by a nuclear superpower can easily spin out of control and turn into another existential threat.

The quest of major powers to have dominating edge over the adversaries involves no-stone-unturned approach, where they are in morbid race in biological, nuclear, chemical, and other disastrous weapons of mass destruction. Many of these wars are for vain glories of individual megalomaniacs or dominance-seeking global and regional powers. Many of these wars occur under false pretexts, and often to serve the interest of the global military weapons manufacturing industry, whose quest is not just for innovating defensive solutions, but also offensive solutions that are bought and sold like kitchen knives.

In 2015, Federation of American Scientists warned:

> while it is impossible to precisely predict all the human impacts that would result from a nuclear winter, it is relatively simple to predict those which would be most profound. That is, a nuclear winter would cause most humans and large animals to die from nuclear famine in a mass extinction event like the one that wiped out the dinosaurs.
>
> *(Starr, 2015)*

Some of these risks might be exaggerated, but if there is a nuclear war where nuclear powers get involved and deploy their weapons, beyond the deterrence, there is a potential existential threat to human civilization. At least in the context of wars and conflicts, without humanity-oriented values and empathy, technology so far has been more of bane than boon.

The most recent development of Russian invasion of Ukraine, which can escalate to a major war of the 21st century in the heartland of Europe, has placed Fintech industry into a new bind. Fintech envisions a world with "money without borders" (Webb, 2022). Under the new, globally coordinated sanction against Russia, Fintech companies are feared to face enormous restrictions on their transactions. Ukrainian allies, in particular, the European Union, UK, and USA have imposed various sanctions on Russian government and oligarchs in response to Russia's invasion in Ukraine. The sanctions include, along with other broad measures, expelling major Russian banks from the SWIFT, a communication system for international banking transactions. The key to implementing sanctions is the international banking system through which funds are transferred cross-borders. Banks put every measure to know their customers as well as the sources and purpose of funds being transferred. In such a process, banks are strictly reluctant to process financial transactions related to sanctioned individuals or entities. However, Flitter and Yaffe-Bellany (2022) put it in this way "… if banks are the eyes and ears of governments in this space, the explosion of digital currencies is blinding them."

The primary motto of cryptocurrency is to maintain its neutrality which means that no regulatory entity including the government can prevent its use. Unlike banks which require formal approval from the respective central bank for processing major transactions, the exchange of cryptocurrency aims to bypass such procedures. In effect, no regularity entity can effectively prevent parties to exchange cryptocurrency because the exchange takes place between peers without involving any intermediary. Some countries including North Korea, Iran, and Venezuela have used the loopholes of cryptocurrency to ease the pressure of Western sanctions. North Korea is a notorious example which has occasionally used hacking techniques, using ransomware, to steal cryptocurrency from different parts of the world worth billions of dollars (Kim, 2022). In 2020, about 74% of global ransomware revenues valued US$400 million worth of cryptocurrency were captured by entities that are most likely linked to Russia (Flitter and Yaffe-Bellany, 2022). Hence, it is highly likely that Russia would leave no stone unturned to use cryptocurrency to ease the ongoing sanctions.

Abundance supply of energy has provided Russian miners with a competitive edge to mine crypto in the country. Russia ranks third in the world in mining bitcoin, the capstone among all the cryptocurrencies (Makhlouf and Selmi, 2022). Although Kazakhstan ranks second following only the USA, it is believed that Russia has an upper hand in bitcoin mining in Kazakhstan. According to Bloomberg estimation, Russia is a home to at least $214 billion worth of cryptocurrency (Fortune, 2022). Such a mounting possession of crypto would enable Russia to use crypto for buying goods and services which are currently under sanctioned. It is believed that Russia may develop a network of complicit exchange services to evade sanctions. For instance, Russia is on the verge to develop some new tools that can help mask the origin of such transactions that would allow businesses to trade with Russian entities without the risk of being detected. In addition, there are some cryptocurrencies such as Moreno, which apply private distributed ledger with a feature of privacy-enhancing technology that aims to conceal transactions. Russia can also resort to dark web marketplace such as Hydra, powered by cryptocurrency, to accomplish obscured transactions. Strict regulations and their compliance requirement enable such platforms to remain outside of researchers and regulator's focus. Besides Hydra, other money-laundering techniques, such as "nesting," are also used for anonymous transactions. Nesting and other such techniques can hide themselves within a larger, legitimate structure to avoid regulatory purview.

Moreover, the Russian government plans to develop its own digital currency, digital ruble, so that the country can use it with partner countries without first converting to dollars. China, which has already initiated digital currency, is highly likely to partner with Russia. Moreover, it is still possible that some illicit trades are happening under the radar because exchanges and cryptocurrency compliance firms do not necessarily know about all the wallets controlled by proxies of an individual on a sanction list. In such a case, sanctions against Russia wouldn't achieve the intended purpose. This proves that while Fintech aims to facilitate transactions with ease and lower transaction cost, its use can also create a loophole for violating international orders and legitimacy.

4.5 Climate crisis

Of all the potential challenges to human civilization, none is more existential in nature than the climate crisis. From the time of industrial revolution, the unprecedented economic and material progress of human society, technology has been a primary mover, but due to human factor where the people with economic and political power have put material progress before human welfare, economic development has occurred in ways that paid little attention to the welfare of the planet that sustains us. Even today, technology is helping to reverse or slow down the climate crisis, but scientists and experts also are forewarning that it might be too late, too slow, or too little actions to save the planet. According to a climate change report, human civilization has a potential reckoning by 2050 (Pascus, 2019).

While addressing climate crisis requires a more holistic approach and strategy, technology in general will play a pivotal role and within that role Fintech can also make relevant contribution. Working with the Bank for International Settlements and major global financial institutions, Global Government Fintech highlights "the potential for technology to tackle challenges in green and sustainable finance" (Hall, 2022). Banks and financial services as a leading sector have a pivotal role to play, and many of them are gearing up for leveraging Fintech through niche area of Fintech: "Climate fintech – where the tech innovation is used to address both sustainability and financial needs" (Mercado, 2021).

Global financial powerhouse like Citibank is taking aggressive interest in engaging Fintech to fight climate change, especially through effective utilization of big data and AI (Zec and Brunet, 2021).

Parallel to these positive developments and potentials in climate-related technology and Fintech, there is also negative impact and further potential risk, if Fintech, as a subset of tech sector, does not change drastically its dependence on fossil fuel and its mammoth generation of e-waste. Experts identify five relevant areas where Fintech needs to adapt substantively: (a) dependence on and complacency with fossil fuel; (b) extravagant consumption of energy; (c) finance industry's lack of transparency regarding carbon footprints; (d) electronic waste, commonly known as e-waste, which has become one of the fastest growing sources of waste in the world; and (e) the potential of expanded financial inclusion, accompanied by promotion of debt culture, to lead to another major tranche of consumerism (Cag, 2022).

5 Conclusion

Technology has been an indispensable driver of human civilization and, in modern times, the phenomenal rise in standard of living and quality of life are testimony to it. Technology as a whole will remain such indispensable in future too. However, technology in general or Fintech in particular must not succumb to technomania, where we are deluded in thinking that everything has a technological solution because human beings must remain at the core of civilization's problem, and it is they who will drive and reign in technological progress. As long as we remain excited about the positive and human-welfare-enhancing potentials of technology, and seek its benefit in a responsible, ethical, and wise manner, technology will continue to play the role it should. These observations apply equally from Islamic perspective in general and in the context of Islamic finance in particular.

In this chapter, we have mentioned the limitations of technology showing some existential problems human beings face today. The challenges mentioned above are not exhaustive and each of these separately might appear less ominous than they actually seem to be. However, they are not isolated; rather, interlinked and thus, pose a level of complexity that often obscures the nature and extent of the challenges.

Considering the value proposition of Fintech, which is slated to reshape our life in the financial services arena, there is much to be excited. However, the use of technology should be without being entrapped by technomania and seeking solutions to all problems through technology. Because of the interconnections of the challenges, several aspects deserve our collective attention. (a) The humankind should explore new ways to fulfill our needs and wants within the framework of the finite capacity of this planet; (b) establishing and practicing authentic democracies, where the commitment to human welfare can ensure accountable and empathic leadership; (c) reverse or substantively reduce economic inequality and extreme concentration of wealth and promote shared prosperity; (d) transition from non-renewable fossil fuels to renewable energies, especially in the framework of cutting-edge thoughts like circular economy; (e) bringing global population to a level that can be supported by sustainable agriculture, which is important because agriculture is an existential need for the humanity; (f) wars and conflicts need to be managed in ways where they are treated as uncivilized before modern weapons of mass destruction wreak irreversible havoc on the planet; and (g) develop a mature and sensitive ethical system to match our evolving technological capabilities (Avery, 2017).

Achieving the above-mentioned suggestions still require new and adapted technology to address these challenges. However, that requires a system and environment where technology is at the service of the humanity and human civilization, not the master of it.

It is heartening to see that in a more decentralized environment, inventors and problem-solvers are coming forward to harness the power of technology to make positive difference in many of the several civilizational challenges identified earlier. Ultimately, it will take all the stakeholders, especially those who hold the political and economic power to lead and facilitate the quest for solutions to those challenges. Much of the problems that human civilization faces require the human beings becoming better human beings, building institutions are genuinely pro-people, and pursuing an economy and society that embraces shared prosperity, where every human being can live and let live with fundamental human dignity. It is possible, because just like technologies are domains of possibilities, the real source of all possibilities in this world are anchored in human beings as trustees of our Creators.

References

Aba, Fransiskus and Linardy, Denise (2021). "Financial Technology in Financial Inclusions and its Implications on Poverty from Indonesia," https://www.preprints.org/manuscript/202111.0061/v1/download

Alam, Nafis and Ali, Syed Nazim (2020). *Fintech, Digital Currency and the Future of Islamic Finance: Strategic, Regulatory and Adoption Issues in the Gulf Cooperation Council* (Cham, Switzerland: Palgrave Macmillan).

Allen, Jonathan (2017). *Technology and Inequality: Concentrated Wealth in a Digital World* (Cham, Switzerland: Palgrave-Macmillan).

Appiah-Otoo, Isaac and Song, Na (2021). "The Impact of Fintech on Poverty Reduction: Evidence from China," *Sustainability*, Vol. 13, No. 9, 1–13.

Arslanian, Henri and Fischer, Fabrice (2019). *The Future of Finance: The Impact of FinTech, AI, and Crypto on Financial Services* (Cham, Switzerland: Palgrave Macmillan).

Avery, John Scales (2017). *Civilization's Crisis: A Set of Linked Challenges* (Singapore: World Scientific).

Bell, Daniel (1980). *The Winding Passage: Essays and Sociological Journeys, 1960–1980* (New Brunswick, NJ: Transaction Publishers), p. 20.

Bergandi, Donato (2013). "Ecology, Evolution, Ethics: In search of a Meta-paradigm – An Introduction," in Bergandy, Donato (Ed.), *The Structural Links between Ecology, Evolution and Ethics: The Virtuous Epistemic Circle* (New York, NY: Springer), pp. 1–28.

Socio-civilizational challenges **77**

Blue Water Credit (2015). "The Top 10 Bank Heists of All Time," *Blue Water Credit*, https://bluewatercredit.com/top-10-bank-heists-time/.
Cag, Derin (2022), "Top 5 Causes of Climate Change Related to the Fintech Sector," *Fintech Magazine*, January 13, https://fintechmagazine.com/sustainability/top-5-causes-climate-change-related-fintech-sector.
Dinar Standard and Elipses (2021). *Global Islamic Fintech Report 2021*, https://www.capitalmarketsmalaysia.com/wp-content/uploads/2021/06/Global-Islamic-Fintech-Report-2021.pdf.
Emara, Noha and Mohieldin, Mahmoud (2021). "Beyond the Digital Dividends: Fintech and Extreme Poverty in the Middle East and Africa," *Topics in Middle Eastern and African Economies Proceedings of Middle East Economic Association*, Vol. 3, No. 2, 41–73.
Farooq, Mohammad Omar (2012). "Exploitation, Profit and the Riba-Interest Reductionism," *International Journal of Islamic and Middle Eastern Finance and Management*, Vol. 5, No. 4, 292–320.
Flitter, E. and Yaffe-Bellany, D. (2022). "Russia Could Use Cryptocurrency to Blunt the Force of U.S. Sanctions," *New York Times*, February 24, 2022.
Foohey, Pamela and Martin, Nathalie (2021). "Fintech's Role in Exacerbating or Reducing the Wealth Gap," *University of Illinois Law Review*, 460–504, https://papers.ssrn.com/sol3/Papers.cfm?abstract_id=3551469#.
Forbes (2021). "14 Pandemic-Driven Tech Innovations That Will Continue to Impact the World," June 4, https://www.forbes.com/sites/forbestechcouncil/2021/06/04/14-pandemic-driven-tech-innovations-that-will-continue-to-impact-the-world/?sh=7f0666bc6a23.
Fortune (2022). "Russia Nears Plans to Regulate Its Local Crypto Valued at $214 Billion," March 30, 2022, https://fortune.com/2022/02/01/russia-local-crypto-214-billion-regulation/.
Goodell, G. and Aste, T. (2019). "Can Cryptocurrencies Preserve Privacy and Comply With Regulations?" *Frontiers in Blockchain*, Vol. 2, No. 4, 1–14.
Gregory, Andrew and Elgot, Jessica (2021). "Covid Not Over and Next Pandemic Could Be More Lethal, Says Oxford Jab Creator," *The Guardian*, December 6, https://www.theguardian.com/world/2021/dec/06/covid-not-over-next-pandemic-could-be-more-lethal-oxford-jab-creator.
Hall, Ian (2022). "Going Green: Government Look to Fintech to Help Combat Climate Crisis," *Global Government Forum*, February 17, https://www.globalgovernmentforum.com/going-green-governments-look-to-fintech-to-help-combat-climate-crisis/.
Haq, Rashed (2020). *Enterprise Artificial Intelligence Transformation* (Hoboken, NJ: John Wiley), p. 67.
Hickel, Jason (2019). "A Letter to Steven Pinker about Global Poverty," *Resilience.org*, February 4, https://www.resilience.org/stories/2019-02-04/a-letter-to-steven-pinker-about-global-poverty/.
Holdstock, David (2019). *Smart Geospatial Practices and Applications in Local Government: An Altogether Different Language* (Boca Raton, FL: CRC Press), p. 77.
International Monetary Fund (IMF) (2019). *Fintech: The Experience So Far* (Washington, DC: World Bank).
Jobs, Steve (2019). "Technology Is Nothing," October 5, https://www.cnbc.com/2019/10/05/apple-ceo-steve-jobs-technology-is-nothing-heres-what-it-takes-to-achieve-great-success.html.
Jones, Lindsay and Maynard, Goldburn (2023). "Unfulfilled Promises of the FinTech Revolution," *California Law Review*, Vol. 111, https://papers.ssrn.com/sol3/papers.cfm?abstract_id=4031044.

Kim, M. H. (2022). "North Korea's Cyber Capabilities and Their Implications for International Security," *Sustainability*, Vol. 14, No. 3, 1744.

KPMG (2017). "Value of Fintech," https://assets.kpmg/content/dam/kpmg/uk/pdf/2017/10/value-of-fintech.pdf.

Lange, Christian (1921). "Nobel Lecture," https://www.nobelprize.org/prizes/peace/1921/lange/lecture/.

Levy, Steven (1995). "Technomania," *Newsweek*, February 26, https://www.newsweek.com/technomania-185328.

Lohr, Steve (2022). "Economists Pin More Blame on Tech for Rising Inequality," *New York Times*, January 11, https://www.nytimes.com/2022/01/11/technology/income-inequality-technology.html

Picketty, Thomas (2014). *Capital in the Twenty-First Century* (Cambridge, MA: Harvard University Press).

London Institute of Banking and Finance (2020). "Islamic Fintech as a Force for Good," *LIBF*, https://mena.libf.ac.uk/2020/11/02/islamic-fintech-as-a-force-for-good/.

Makhlouf, F., and Selmi, R. (2022). "Do Sanctions Work in a Crypto World? The Impact of the Removal of Russian Banks from SWIFT on Remittances," hal-03599089, last access on April 02, 2022 from https://hal.archives-ouvertes.fr/hal-03599089/document.

Mellor, Sohpie (2021). "Muslim Can't Trade Crypto, Says the Head of the Shariah Compliance in the World's Largest Islamic Country," *Yahoo Finance*, November 11, https://finance.yahoo.com/news/muslims-t-trade-crypto-says-114358155.html.

Mercado, Angely (2021). "How Banks Are Using Technology to Fight Climate Change," *Popular Science*, December 13, https://www.popsci.com/environment/climate-fintech/.

Mihalcova, B., Szaryszova, P., Stofova, L., Pruzinsky, M. and Gontkovicova, B. (Eds.) (2019). *Production Management and Business Development: Proceedings of the 6th Annual International Scientific Conference on Marketing Management, Trade, Financial and Social Aspects of Business*, May 17–19, 2018, Slovakia and Ukraine (London, UK: Taylor & Francis).

Miller, Katharina and Wendt, Karen (Eds.) (2021). *The Fourth Industrial Revolution and its Impact on Ethics: Solving the challenges of the Agenda 2030* (Cham, Switzerland: Springer).

Omar, Md Abdullah and Inaba, Kazuo (2020). "Does Financial Inclusion Reduce Poverty and Income Inequality in Developing Countries? A Panel Data Analysis," *Journal of Economic Structures*, Vol. 9, https://doi.org/10.1186/s40008-020-00214-4.

Ord, Toby (2020). *The Precipice: Existential Risk and the Future of Humanity* (New York, NY: Hachette Books).

Pascus, Brian (2019). "Human Civilization Faces 'Existential Risk' by 2050 According to New Australian Climate Change Report," *cbsnews.com*, https://www.cbsnews.com/news/new-climate-change-report-human-civilization-at-risk-extinction-by-2050-new-australian-climate/.

Petrou, K. (2018). "The Crisis Next Time: The Risk of New-Age Fintech and the Last-Crisis Financial Regulation," *Federal Financial Analytics Research Report*, https://fedfin.com/wp-content/uploads/2018/09/FedFin-Policy-Paper-on-The-Risk-of-New-Age-Fintech-and-Last-Crisis-Financial-Regulation.pdf.

Phadke, Sanjay (2020). *Fintech Future: Changing the DNA of Finance* (London, UK: Sage Publications).

Roser, Max and Ortiz-Ospina, Esteban (2019). "Global Extreme Poverty," *Our World in Data*, https://ourworldindata.org/extreme-poverty.

Ryan, Donna (2020). *Equipped to Tell the Next Generation* (Eugene, Oregon: WipF and Stock Publishers).
Simon, Andree (2020). "Four Fintech & Financial Inclusion Trends for 2020," *Responsible finance Forum*, https://responsiblefinanceforum.org/four-fintech-financial-inclusion-trends-2020/.
Starr, Steven (2015). "Nuclear War, Nuclear Winter, and Human Extinction," *Federation of American Scientists*, https://fas.org/pir-pubs/nuclear-war-nuclear-winter-and-human-extinction/.
Summers, Chris (2016). "Rise of the Self-Made Billionaires: How Technology Created a New Generation of Super-Rich in America," *dailymail*, May 17, https://www.dailymail.co.uk/news/article-3594283/Rise-self-billionaires-technology-created-super-rich-generation.html.
Truevtsev, Konstantin (2016). "Globalization as a Political Process," *Journal of Globalization Studies*, Vol. 7, No. 1, 66–86.
UNDESA (2021). "Sustainable Development Report Shows Devastating Impact of COVID, Ahead of 'Critical' New Phase," July 6, https://www.un.org/africarenewal/news/sustainable-development-report-shows-devastating-impact-covid-ahead-%E2%80%98critical%E2%80%99-new-phase.
UNESCAP (2018). *Inequality in Asia and Pacific in the Era of the 2030 Agenda for Sustainable Development*, 70, https://www.unescap.org/publications/inequality-asia-and-pacific-era-2030-agenda-sustainable-development.
Webb, Alexander (2022). "Ukraine Invasion Upends the Fintech World," *Observer*, March 4, https://observer.com/2022/03/ukraine-invasion-upends-the-fintech-world/.
World Bank Group (2020). *Leveraging Islamic Fintech to Improve Financial Inclusion* (Washington, DC: World Bank), https://openknowledge.worldbank.org/handle/10986/34520?locale-attribute=es.
Zec, Jelena and Brunet, Alix (2021). "Climate Fintech: Using Data and AI to Fight Climate Change and Create Business Opportunities," https://www.citi.com/ventures/perspectives/opinion/climate-fintech.html.
Zorthian, Julia (2017). "Stephen Hawking Says Humans Have 100 Years to Move to Another Planet," https://time.com/4767595/stephen-hawking-100-years-new-planet/.

PART II
Empirical studies

4
BUSINESS RISK MITIGATION THROUGH "VALUE-CHAIN INTEGRATED" FINANCING IN ISLAMIC PEER-TO-PEER LENDING IN INDONESIA

PT Qazwa Mitra Hasanah's experience

Sigit Pramono, Dikry Paren, M. Iqbal Ramadhan and Muhammad Razikun

1 Introduction

This chapter provides an overview of the recent progress of Islamic peer-to-peer (P2P) lending platform for supporting micro, small, and medium enterprises (MSMEs) in Indonesia. P2P has emerged as a potential alternative to mainstream financing which eliminates the need for intermediation. The popularity of P2P can be attributed to quick processing, low cost, and ease of management. It is worth noting that the financial and banking industry will face massive digital disruption with the emergence of financial technology (fintech). Consequently, this will also affect the Islamic finance and banking sector. Fintech will encourage the acceleration of collaboration between banking business and P2P.

Some studies show that the P2P business model has the potential to efficiently carry out financial intermediation process and change financing modes of financial institutions to the business segments (Huang et al., 2020; Linawati et al., 2019; Yoshino and Taghizadeh-Hesary, 2017). Moreover, it is projected that P2P will contribute to the development of the MSMEs sector.

This fintech start-up shares a vision to achieve equity and justice in the society through economic development facilitated by Islamic financial technology. Since fintech empowers small start-ups, this case is believed to unfold important information about P2P financing and the accompanied opportunities and challenges. Regulators can take this information into account for accelerating the pace of fintech revolution.

This chapter brings practical experience from PT Qazwa Mitra Hasanah (Qazwa), an Indonesian Islamic P2P company. In specific, this chapter presents an interesting finding from the risk management practice implemented by

DOI: 10.4324/9781003262169-7

Qazwa in terms of business risk mitigation through the "value-chain integrated" financing model to help MSMEs.

Recognizably, MSMEs sector relatively has higher business risk and complicated risk management practices. As an Islamic P2P, Qazwa is considered as a pioneer in implementing "value-chain integrated" financing strategy in which financing to MSMEs business is carried out by promoting an integrated business ecosystem approach. The basic concept of "value-chain integrated" financing relies on the understanding that all "players" in the MSMEs business ecosystem have mutual relationship and contribute to each other in providing "economic value-added" for their business counterparts. Thus, by "connecting and maintaining" relationship and "economic value-added" contribution of each economic player in the MSMEs business ecosystem, it is expected that this financing strategy will facilitate risk mitigation of MSMEs business financing.

In principle, "value-chain integrated" financing applied by Qazwa is "working capital" financing in relation to the "supply-chain" cooperation in MSMEs business operation. With this financing-mode, it is designed that the level of business failure of MSMEs can be reduced since business dealings under this circumstance usually are based on good recognition and close relation between "suppliers-buyers" in MSMEs business ecosystem. Moreover, Qazwa's "value-chain integrated" financing will disburse its financing directly to MSMEs in the form of working capital (inventory, raw material, factoring facilities, etc.) or "capital goods" (i.e., fixed assets, equipment, etc.). This particular mode of financing will avoid spending in "cash financing". It is supposed that this mode of financing will prevent moral hazard attitudes as financing received by MSMEs in cash has potential to be misused for non-business purposes as proposed in the financing proposal.

This chapter is organized as follows: Section 2 discusses an overview of fintech development in Indonesia. Section 3 highlights issues on digital disruption in Indonesian Islamic finance and banking industry. Section 4 presents current development of P2P in Indonesia. Section 5 presents an analysis of business risk mitigation through "value-chain integrated" financing model to MSMEs. This is followed by a concluding comment in Section 6.

2 Fintech development in Indonesia

Based on the projection analysis report published by PricewaterhouseCoopers entitled *"The World in 2050, The long view: how will the global economic order change"* by 2050? (PwC, 2017), Indonesia has the potential to become one of the world's economic magnets by having an economy that will be the world's fifth largest (at US$5.424 trillion) in 2030 and in the top four in the world (worth US$10.502 trillion) in 2050.

In terms of the demographic profile, based on the 2020 Population Census, Indonesia is the fourth most populous country in the world with 270.2 million population (BPS, 2020). The proportion of the working-age population (aged 15–64 years) out of the population reaches 70.7%. The 2020 Population Census also shows that Generation Z (born 1997–2012) at 27.9% and the Millennial Generation at 25.8% (born 1981–1996) dominate the demographic structure of Indonesia. Therefore, it is believed that Indonesia will receive benefits from the peak of demographic bonuses by 2030.

Meanwhile, according to the report *"Digital 2021: the latest insights into the 'state of digital'"* (Kemp, 2021), as of January 2021, the internet penetration rate in Indonesia stands at 74%. In which, there are 202.6 million people (73.7% of the total population) internet users and 170 million (61.8% of the total population) are active social media users, and there are 345.3 million (125.6% of the total population) who are connected and become users of mobile phones. This data shows that currently there has been a rapid growth in internet access penetration which is very promising in Indonesia.

Nevertheless, it is worth noting that there are two fundamental problems in Indonesia's financial sector that need to be taken into account. Firstly, low level of financial inclusion in the economy. Secondly, large financing gap for MSMEs. According to the World Bank Group Global Findex Database in 2018, only 48.9% of Indonesian adults (15+ years) had bank accounts (World Bank, 2018). This 48.9% of the banked Indonesian population is still substantially behind the world average of 69%. Primary barriers to financial inclusion include and are not limited to the lack of personal documents and credit history, poor financial infrastructure, logistics and delivery challenges, restrictive regulations, and financial products offered by banks that are more suitable for urban population (UOB, 2017).

The emergence of financial technology (fintech) has created massive digital disruption for the financial and banking industry. Fintech is trusted to bring increased convenience for consumers in using digital financial services. Fintech will make it easier for customers in making payment transactions, accessing various financial services, and doing financial investments online.

Indonesia's fintech companies are growing and evolving continuously as shown by the increasing number of licensed firms in the industry. As of May 2019, there were 250 fintech companies across the business model, from deposit, lending, payment gateway, and capital funding (Batunanggar, 2019). P2P and e-payments are the top of two fastest-growing business model among other fintech business models. Consecutively, P2P and e-payments took 43% and 26% of Indonesia's fintech landscape compositions, respectively (Figure 1).

Association for Digital Financial Innovations players in Indonesia (AFTECH), which was appointed by the Financial Services Authority (FSA, Otoritas Jasa Keuangan/OJK) based on POJK No. 13/2018, reported that AFTECH members (which represent 80% of licensed fintech start-up in Indonesia) have increased by 54% (YoY) in 2019. By the end of Q2 2020, the growth is 56.7% (YoY) with the total number of 362 fintech start-up members registered (Asosiasi Fintech Indonesia, 2021) (Figure 2).

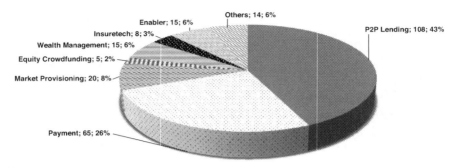

FIGURE 1 Indonesia's Fintech compositions by business model.
Source: Batunanggar (2019), created by the authors.

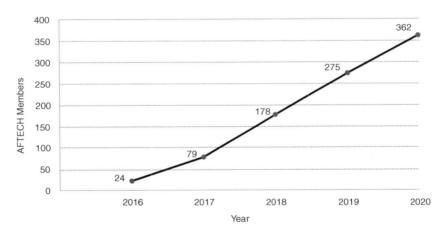

FIGURE 2 AFTECH members from 2016 to Q2 2020.
Source: Asosiasi Fintech Indonesia (2021), created by the authors.

In accordance with the growth of the P2P and e-Payment, FSA recorded an accumulation of 259.6% increase in loan disbursement from January to December 2019 (Asosiasi Fintech Indonesia, 2021). Total loan amount of IDR 81.5 trillion was disbursed from 605,935 lenders to 18.5 million of borrower's accounts. In addition, FSA also recorded IDR 113.46 trillion of total loan disbursement from 659,186 lenders to 25.7 million of borrower accounts in January–June 2020 cumulatively; whereas, Bank Indonesia (BI) noted 53% increase in e-money transaction value from January to December 2019 (Asosiasi Fintech Indonesia, 2021). The cumulative transaction value is IDR 47 trillion in 2018 and reached IDR 145 trillion in December 2019. The transaction value is expected to further increase in 2020 and reached a total of IDR 93 trillion in June 2020.

Government regulations play a crucial role in the development of fintech industry. Fintech industry in Indonesia is regulated by BI and the Financial

Service Authority (Otoritas Jasa Keuangan/OJK). Each regulator plays a different role in regulating the Indonesia's fintech industry, in which BI conducts monetary policy and supervises payment ecosystem, whereas FSA performs supervision on financial services provided by P2P, crowdfunding, digital banking, etc. In addition, FSA also regulates financial data security, technology security, and financial services consumer protection (DailySocial.id, 2021; OJK, 2020; OJK, 2021; OJK 2022). In terms of supporting fintech development in Indonesia, both BI and OJK have developed specific division in their organization with the responsibility to periodically manage coordination and evaluation performance of the fintech market players in order to optimize the development of fintech industry.

In summary, Indonesia's government has rolled out 11 regulations for financial technology sector, comprise of six regulations issued by OJK, four regulations issued by BI, and one regulation issued by the Members of the Board of Governors of BI (Table 1).

In Indonesia, the digitalization in financial sector shows rapid progress with variety of innovation in financial technology in the range of payment system to digital banking. Information technology and internet development play an important role to support this progress of financial technology. Financial service users are enthusiastic for such financial innovation, and this situation boost fintech company to creatively offer innovations that comfort customers' life and make business transactions easy. Obviously, the development of fintech not only

TABLE 1 List of Indonesia's Fintech regulations

Sector	Regulation	Government entity
Lending	FSA Regulation (POJK) No. 77/POJK.01/2016	OJK
Equity Crowdfunding	FSA Regulation (POJK) No. 37/POJK.04/2018	OJK
Digital Financial Innovation	FSA Regulation (POJK) No. 13/POJK.02/2018	OJK
Investment Platform	FSA Regulation (POJK) No. 31/POJK.04/2018, FSA Regulation (POJK) No. 30/POJK.04/2017, FSA Regulation (POJK) No. 13/POJK.02/2018	OJK
Digital Wallet	BI Regulation (PBI) No. 20/6/PBI/2018	BI
Payment System	BI Regulation (PBI) No. 19/12/PBI/2017	BI
Remittance	BI Regulation (PBI) No. 14/23/PBI/2012	BI
Electronic Money	BI Regulation (PBI) No. 20/6/PBI/2018	BI
Regulation Sandbox (Bank Indonesia)	Board of Governor (PADG) No. 19/14/PADG/2017	BI

Source: Daily Social Innovate Fintech Report 2021.

creates technological disruption in the financial sector, but also about financial inclusion in the economy (Chapra, 2017; PwC Indonesia, 2019).

3 Digital disruption and Indonesian Islamic finance and banking industry

Some studies underline that although Islamic banking and finance in Indonesia have enormous potential, the economic reality shows that the Islamic finance sector has not played its role optimally in the national economy (Ismal, 2014, 2011; Pramono and Suzuki, 2021; Sukmana and Kuswanto, 2015).

Based on the Indonesian Islamic Finance Development Report 2021 (OJK, 2022), at the end of December 2021, Indonesia's total Islamic financial assets reached Rp. 2,050.44 trillion (around US$143.70 billions). Indonesia's total Islamic financial assets have grown by 13.82% (YoY) from the previous year of Rp. 1,801.40 trillion. In detail, we note that the Islamic Capital Market has the largest portion of Islamic financial assets (60.27%). The Islamic capital market has experienced the highest growth among other sectors at a rate of 14.83% (YoY). Meanwhile, Islamic banking with a share of 33.83% of total Islamic financial assets has grown by 13.94% (YoY). On the other hand, non-bank Islamic Financial Institutions (IFI) which have a share of 5.90% of total Islamic financial assets experienced a growth of 3.90% (YoY).

It is worth noting that Indonesia's total Islamic financial assets have only reached 10.16% of the total assets of the national financial industry. In particular, we note that the market share of Islamic banking in Indonesia has only reached 6.74% of the national banking industry. Therefore, technology disruption through fintech in the Islamic finance and banking industry is believed to become a new trigger for the development of Islamic banking and finance in Indonesia as well to increase financial services inclusion in the economy.

In 2020, the FSA/OJK has prepared the Indonesia Islamic Banking Development Roadmap 2020–2025. The Indonesia Islamic Banking Development Roadmap 2020–2025 is a strategic policy of the FSA in aligning the direction of Islamic finance development in Indonesia, especially in the Islamic financial services industry sector as a guidance of catalyst and accelerating Islamic finance and banking development in Indonesia. Comprehensively, this roadmap includes three pillars of development direction, which consist of *Strengthening Islamic Banking Identity*, *Encouraging Synergy within Islamic Economy Ecosystem*, and *Strengthening Licensing, Regulation, and Supervision*.

In these three pillars, there are several strategic initiatives which are in line with efforts to encourage the growth of fintech in the Islamic finance and banking industry in Indonesia. *First*, in the pillar of *Strengthening Islamic Banking Identity*, FSA has stated that one of the strategic initiatives is "Accelerating Islamic banking digitalization". FSA underlined that digitalization of the banking sector will enable banking infrastructure to ensure faster, better, and more convenient services to the customers. Also, digitalization will become a significant value-added for financial products offered by Islamic banking and finance.

Obviously, banking and finance industry is required to have features which deliver service excellence for the customers and create efficient business processes in financial services. Financial sector disruption and fintech progress will have a significant impact and accelerate digital transformation process in the banking and financial industry. Hence, in this situation of immense business environment changes, if the Islamic banking and finance industry fails to carry out its digital transformation, they will have less competitive advantage in the industry. Meanwhile, we witnessed that the Covid-19 pandemic has also encouraged innovation to reduce negative impact of the pandemic and accelerate the digital transformation of Islamic financial products and services.

Second, in the pillar of *Encouraging Synergy within the Islamic Economy Ecosystem*, the strategic initiative in the form of "Synergy amongst Islamic Financial Institutions" is based on the awareness that synergy and integration within the ecosystem is key factor to take advantage of opportunities for rapid information technology development in expanding access to Islamic financial and banking services. For example, the Islamic bank can synergize with non-bank financial institutions in which Islamic fintech offers collaborative opportunities for Islamic banks through P2P lending by providing lender account services and financing coverage for its potential customers. Obviously, the policy direction of the Islamic banking and financial authorities will focus attention on the development of fintech for the Islamic finance and banking industry to respond to disruption in this financial sector.

4 Islamic P2P Lending and MSMEs in Indonesia

One of the financial technology innovations which is believed will play an important role in developing Islamic finance industry is P2P lending platform. FSA (Otoritas Jasa Keuangan/OJK) in Indonesia has issued regulation (Peraturan Otoritas Jasa Keuangan/POJK) No. 77/POJK.01/2016 related to P2P lending, to respond to the establishment of start-up companies offering P2P lending financial services. P2P lending platform, according to FSA Regulation (POJK) No. 77 of 2016, is defined as "Information Technology-Based Lending and Borrowing Services". Thus, P2P can be interpreted as providing financial services to bring together lenders and loan recipients in entering lending and borrowing agreements directly through the system electronically using the internet platform.

FSA regulation No. 77/ POJK.01/2016 regulates the company to have a registration as a P2P company from FSA before offering its service to the public legally. This P2P business scheme can be described in Figure 3 below.

The development of P2P financial services has gained its momentum and grew fast after the enactment of FSA regulation No. 77/ POJK.01/2016. The growth of P2P companies peaked in 2020 with the 164 fintech companies which were successfully recorded as registered P2P companies by FSA. However, until

FIGURE 3 P2P lending business scheme.

TABLE 2 Fintech lending company overview

Description	Number of companies (units)	Total assets (IDR billion)	Total liabilities (IDR billion)	Total equities (IDR billion)	Outstanding financing (IDR billion)	Financing accumulation (IDR billion)
1. Conventional company	96	3,986.22	1,554.35	2,431.88	28.61	10.3
2. Syariah-based companies	7	74.13	45.92	28.22	1.27	3.28
Total	103	4,060.35	1,600.27	2,460.10	29.88	13.58

Source: FSA (2021).

the end of 2021 only, 103 P2P companies succeeded to meet the requirements to obtain a license from FSA.

Currently, P2P companies have contributed to disburse loans of IDR 272.4 trillion (equivalent to US$19.4 billion) since 2016, and 71.8 million accounts have been registered as lenders and borrowers up to the end of 2021. These facts show significant role of P2P lending in financing demand and increasing financial access for the public.

With the rapid growth of P2P in Indonesia, Islamic finance industry in Indonesia should also be able to utilize this digital innovation to increase market share and accelerate Islamic finance services to the public. However, as shown in Table 2 below, there is a lack of Islamic P2P potentials.

At the end of 2021, as shown in Table 2, there were only 7 companies of Islamic P2P lending compared to 96 companies of conventional P2P lending. It should be a concern to the main stakeholders of the Islamic financial and banking industry, considering that P2P has the potential to fill the vast financing gap in financing the Indonesian business sector, especially financing for the MSMEs sector. In fact, according to ILO (2019), the SME Finance Forum reported that financing gap in Indonesia's MSMEs is about $165.8 billion and credit to MSMEs sector from banking industry reach only about 16% of total banking credit. It is a very unfortunate circumstance, considering the financing potential that can be served by P2P to business sectors who have not yet accessed the services of formal financial institutions.

Recognizably, MSMEs have played an important role in the Indonesian economy. The MSMEs sector accounts for approximately 99% of the total number of business units in the economy. This sector has also contributed no less than 90% in absorbing the country's workforce (Linawati et al., 2019; Tambunan, 2011; Yoshino and Taghizadeh-Hesary, 2017).

The most fundamental problem relates to MSMEs in financial inclusion policies is the low access and acceptability of the MSMEs sector to formal financial institutions and the risk of confined MSMEs in shark-loan trap. In 2014, BI released data that of the 56.4 million MSMEs in Indonesia, only about 30% were able to gain access to financing from formal financial institutions (LPPI and BI, 2015; OECD, 2015).

In particular, we note that in practice, MSMEs in Indonesia face difficulties in accessing banking financing, due to inappropriate business operations, reporting and collateral requirements, and also higher cost of service compared to corporate loans (Linawati et al., 2019).

In this context, we realize that financial technology in the form of P2P has advantages because it can operate with the support of information technology that allows financial institutions to operate immensely efficient, charge cost of fund with lower margins, and cut non-substantive intermediary and administrative activities in the financing process. In short, P2P can be expected to be a crucial alternative to provide a faster, cheaper, and easier way in financing MSMEs (Capri, 2019; Linawati et al., 2019; OJK and Boston Consulting Group, 2020).

In carrying out the financial intermediary function, financial institution will concern on obtaining and analyzing information of the customers (borrower) as crucial factor in making decision of credit (financing) to its customer (Boyd and Prescott, 1986; Diamond, 1984; Huang et al., 2020). The favorable analysis results from the information related to the borrowers will determine decision on allocation and arrangement credit between financial institution and the customer (Boyd and Prescott, 1986).

In providing financial services to the MSMEs sector, financial institutions often have difficulties in analyzing information related to MSMEs business due to lack of reliable financial information and its nature of informal business. Accordingly, it is MSMEs' preference to access business financing from financial institution which can accommodate its informal business institution, i.e., non-bank financial institutions or micro finance institutions (Behr, Entzian, and Guttler, 2011).

P2P is being expected to become a new vehicle to finance MSMEs business. P2P is projected to simplify the intermediary function of the financial industry as it bases its operation on fintech innovation. At the end, it is believed that financial technology carried out through P2P can reduce MSMEs business risks because it can monitor costs more efficiently and prevent credit rationing from the conventional banking operation (PwC Indonesia, 2019).

5 Business risk mitigation through "Value-Chain Integrated" financing model to MSMEs: PT Qazwa Mitra Hasanah's experience

PT Qazwa Mitra Hasanah (Qazwa) is a licensed Shari'ah-based fintech P2P lending company in Indonesia. As a shariah-compliant P2P lending company in Indonesia, Qazwa has been registered by OJK in 2019 and has obtained a full license according to OJK's Member of Board of Commissioners Decree No. KEP-80/D.05/2021 dated 24 August 2021. Qazwa implements a prudent business process, particularly in financing activities for MSMEs. The company conducts financing risk mitigation that fits to its market segment. Although Qazwa's business size and contribution are relatively small in this industry segment, it is interesting to discuss risk management practices carried out by Qazwa in mitigating MSMEs' business risks. Qazwa tries to harmonize standard principles of risk management in the financial sector with adequate consideration to the specific characteristics of risk profile faced by MSMEs.

Qazwa has concerns on credit rating (scoring) as an important procedure in P2P business operations, which serves to measure risk mitigation in every possible occurrence of "undesirable conditions" (known as probability of default). Essentially, implementation of credit ratings in the financial and banking industry is an important element in risk management practice. In Indonesia, credit rating in the process of credit (financing) disbursement officially uses Financial Information Service System (Sistem Layanan Informasi Keuangan/SLIK) issued by FSA or information and document from credit rating agency, such as PEFINDO Credit Bureau.

It is worth noting that credit rating applied in process of MSMEs business financing should take into account the informal business character of MSMEs. In particular, non-bank financial institutions, including P2P, must modify their credit scoring variables and mechanisms when providing financing to MSMEs. In this case, credit scoring is designed to be more adaptive in preventing business failure and default payments that occur in the MSMEs business, but at the same time credit rating should be in line with business strategy of financial institutions to achieve the company's goal (Wendel and Harvey, 2006).

In preparing a reliable financing scoring, Qazwa management will enrich updated data related to economics and business conditions for MSMEs. Besides, the scoring process includes an assessment of future prospects of the MSMEs business to determine eligibility in financing their businesses. In addition, the purpose of the analysis carried out is to minimize potential losses that will be borne by lenders if Qazwa makes inappropriate financing assessments of the applicants.

In developing its credit scoring, Qazwa manages that entrepreneur profile (borrower) conforms to Qazwa's financing segment of micro and small-scale business with criteria based on Indonesia's business regulations (i.e., maximum turnover in a year is Rp. 2,500,000,000 about US$174,000). In this sense, as suggested by Hyytinen and Pajarinen (2008), Qazwa could not merely look at the financial statements of MSMEs with the consideration that these potential borrowers have "information opacity" conditions. With information opacity underpinning, financial information of MSMEs could present unreliable data, thus make a credit scoring model based solely on financial statement will make scoring instrument generates misleading results.

McEvoy (2014) proposes various alternative data that can be used in performing financing analysis, such as prepaid mobile phone data, social media data, and e-commerce data. However, based on Qazwa's experience, using this personal financial data is not feasible to be implemented in MSMEs financing as insufficient reliable financial and operating data could not be gathered easily (Abbasi, Wang, and Alsakarneh, 2018; Liu et al., 2021; Wendel and Harvey, 2006). One main reason for this condition is that the application of a single identity number in Indonesia has not yet been fully implemented for citizens.

Even though the management of Qazwa has implemented a comprehensive analysis and risk measurement system (i.e., legal document fulfillment, credit rating, and site visit), there is still a possibility of business failure of MSMEs. In general, potential business risk is caused by two main problems. First, because of the unfavorable economic conditions and business environment. Second, caused by the potential for fraudulence, where MSMEs commit fraudulent actions in doing business, for instance providing incorrect information or not conducting business with sound manner.

Recognizing the potential of business failure conditions that may be faced in financing this sector of MSMEs, Qazwa performs a breakthrough by providing supply-chain–financing scheme. Qazwa is considered as an Islamic P2P pioneer in implementing "value-chain integrated" financing strategy in which financing to MSMEs business is carried out by promoting an integrated business ecosystem approach. The basic concept of "value-chain integrated" financing relies on all "players" in the MSMEs business ecosystem that have mutual relationship and contribute to each other in providing "economic value-added" for their business counterparts (Pfohl and Gomm, 2009; Söderberg and Bengtsson, 2010; Yang et al., 2021). Thus, by "connecting and maintaining" relationship and contribution of each economic player in the MSMEs business ecosystem, it will facilitate risk mitigation of MSMEs business financing.

In principle, "value-chain integrated" financing applied by Qazwa is "working capital" financing in relation to the "supply-chain" cooperation in MSMEs business operation. With this financing-mode, it is designed that the level of business failure of MSMEs can be reduced since business dealings under this circumstance usually are based on good recognition and close relation between "suppliers-buyers" in MSMEs business ecosystem. Moreover, "value-chain integrated" financing will disburse the financing directly to MSMEs in form of working capital (inventory, raw material, factoring facilities, etc.) or "capital goods" (i.e., fixed assets, equipment, etc.) and not in "cash financing". It is supposed that this mode of financing will prevent moral hazard attitudes as financing received by MSMEs has the potential to be misused for non-business purposes as proposed in the financing proposal.

This "value-chain integrated" financing aims to provide significant risk mitigation in MSMEs' project financing. Therefore, this financing strategy needs supporting data from "supply-chain transactions", which can be the basis for Qazwa to develop a financing mitigation model. One of which is information related to the relationship between buyers and suppliers in MSMEs business (Abbasi, Wang, and Alsakarneh, 2018; Edwards, Delbridge, and Munday 2005). Hence, the data used by Qazwa's credit scoring practice also be equipped with these complementary data.

For instance, if Qazwa provides financing to MSMEs in the form of purchasing inventory or invoice financing, then Qazwa management must obtain information about patterns and track records between suppliers and potential borrowers. This information is important to analyze the ability to pay of the borrower and the possibility of business failure. Information about how the "buyer-supplier" relationship and the creation of economic value-added in the business ecosystem become important concern of Qazwa in financing decision and measuring the level of financing risk.

Thus, this "value-chain integrated" financing strategy is expected to contribute to mitigating MSMEs business risks since it aims at maintaining economic value-added in the MSMEs business ecosystem, preventing decoupling between financial sector and risk sector in the economy, and build cohesiveness among MSMEs business stakeholders. Figure 3 below presents Qazwa's "Value-Chain Integrated" financing approach to MSMEs.

Following is an explanation of the supply-chain–financing data that will be processed when there is a financing application (Figure 4).

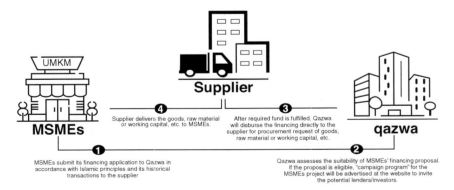

FIGURE 4 Qazwa's "value-chain integrated" financing approach.

5.1 Supply-chain variable

Supply-chain variable is data taken from MSMEs' business process to understand and analyze business character of MSMEs in the supply chain. This is important because Qazwa will only facilitate financing which is allocated for procurement of working capital and capital goods; therefore, performance and prospect of MSMEs in the supply chain should be understood precisely.

5.2 Demand risk data

Demand risk data is data obtained through interviews with MSMEs related to potential risk that may rise from sales activities to the customers. This is to find out whether MSMEs have a contingency plan if they face the risk and how they manage it to maintain their business activities. This data highlights some issues:

Variable	Data resource	Credit risk relationship
Failed to pay	Interview	If there are customers experienced default, it will increase the risk of repaying the loan
Change of season demand	Interview	If the sale of products is affected by the season, it will increase the risk of non-repayment
Late payment	Interview	If there are customers who have possibility of late payment, it will increase the risk of repaying the loan
Specific types of goods for certain market	Interview	If the type of goods sold is too specific for a particular market, it has the potential that the goods are not well absorbed into the market, thus increasing the risk of non-repayment
Unable to complete customer's order	Interview	If MSMEs cannot complete its customer order, it will increase the risk of repaying the loan

5.3 Supply risk data

This data contributes to determine the risks faced by MSMEs in terms of the availability of such products to be sold. A smooth supply flow of products with good quality indicates stable and sustainable MSMEs business. Supply risk data is obtained through interviews with MSMEs and suppliers of the products. This data includes these issues (Figure 5):

Variable	Data resource	Credit risk relationship
Short supply of products	Interview	If MSMEs has lack of supply for the products from suppliers, it will hamper production process and increase the risk of default
Delay in items availability	Interview	If suppliers are not able to provide goods on time, it will hamper the production process and increase the risk of default
Items do not match	Interview	If the ordered goods from the supplier are not suitable to the provisions, it will hamper the production process and increase the risk of default
Number of suppliers subscribed	Interview	If MSMEs only have one supplier, it will increase risk of not being able to fulfill the demand
Product return from supplier	Interview	If the supplier does not provide product return for rejected or damage goods, it will hamper the production process and increase the risk of default

The following is the supply chain–financing workflow carried out by Qazwa:

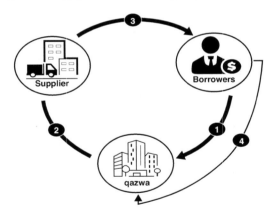

FIGURE 5 Supply chain–financing model workflow.

1. Prospective borrower submits a financing proposal to Qazwa, and credit scoring will be carried out by Qazwa regarding the proposed financing proposal.
2. If the financing proposal is approved, Qazwa will coordinate, arrange business dealing and perform transaction with the supplier to be able to supply the requested products of the borrower
3. Delivery goods from the suppliers to the borrower, this goods delivery mechanism is to avoid misuse of fund by the borrower.
4. The borrower will repay its financing bill through Qazwa.

In the context of risk management practice, it is worth noting to highlight experiences and challenges faced by Qazwa in implementing this pertaining "value-chain integrated" financing, as follows:

Qazwa has put forward a breakthrough to implement "a business incubator" in supporting MSMEs business through formatting business dealings under this circumstance usually based on good recognition and close relation between "suppliers-buyers" in MSMEs business ecosystem. In turn, this strategy is expected also to optimize mutual relationship and contribution from all players in MSMEs business ecosystem under "value-chain integrated" framework to "support each other" in generating "economic value-added" from their business counterparts.

Meanwhile, this Qazwa's strategic financing approach, basically aims to utilize "interlock mutual good relation and cooperation" among all players of "suppliers-buyers" in MSMEs business ecosystem to reduce level of business failure of MSMEs since Qazwa's financing will be disbursed only to the MSMEs which have good credential and reputation in this ecosystem business dealing.

In fact, from the perspective of Shari'ah compliance issues apply to good corporate governance practice in Islamic mode of financing, Qazwa is concentrating and conducting only to financing MSMEs directly in the form of working capital (inventory, raw material, factoring facilities, etc.) or "capital goods" (i.e., fixed assets, equipment, etc.) and not in "cash financing". This mode of financing intends to prevent moral hazard attitudes as financing received by MSMEs has potential to be misused for non-business purposes as proposed in their financing proposal. In this sense, as practicing in Indonesian IFI refers to Fatwa (Syariah Opinion) DSN-MUI Nomor 4/DSN-MUI/IV/2000 about *Murabahah* and Fatwa (Syariah Opinion) DSN-MUI Nomor 113/DSN-MUI/IX/2017 about *Akad Wakalah bi Al-Ujrah* (the granting of authority/mandate with rewards); in Murabahah financing, the IFI/Islamic bank can grant authority to the customer/borrower to buy specific goods as their propose for financing on behalf of IFI/Islamic banks as financier. Thus, IFI/Islamic bank just simply give "cash financing" to the customer/borrower. In many cases, unfortunately, this typical of financing has the possibility to bring negative/contra productive impacts as the customer/borrower has opportunity to use the money with fraud (i.e. misused the money for non-business purposes or not in accordance with the agreement). Consequently, this condition will impact in increasing business failure and payment default occurrences.

6 Concluding comments

Islamic P2P Lending is a promising alternative for financing Indonesian MSMEs business. Yet, this potential fintech needs a robust policy direction from government and FSA. Moreover, this strategic breakthrough to solve financing gap to the MSMEs should be supported by all the stakeholders of Islamic finance and banking industries.

There are crucial challenges to bring successful Islamic P2P in doing their business, including but not limited to: a strong regulation from the FSA to drive IFI to collaborate with others financial institution (especially banking sector) in financing MSMEs business; conducive innovation and collaboration of IFI widely, and improvement of business innovation and good government practice of the practices Islamic P2P Lending.

Meanwhile, we recognize that P2P is a fintech mode of financing to MSMEs sector that should be prioritized by the financial sector as a business trust and avoiding incidences of frauds. Thus, Qazwa's "value-chain integrated" financing scheme is considered as a smart practice to provide significant risk mitigation in MSMEs' project financing. This "value-chain integrated" financing strategy is expected to realize conducive condition in maintaining economic value-added in the MSMEs business ecosystem, prevent decoupling between financial sector and risk sector in the economy, and build cohesiveness among MSMEs business stakeholders.

References

Abbasi, W. A., Wang, Z., and Alsakarneh, A. (2018). Overcoming SMEs Financing and Supply Chain Obstacles by Introducing Supply Chain Finance. *International Journal of Business and Management*, 13(6), 1–9. https://doi.org/10.5539/ijbm.v13n6p165

Asosiasi Fintech Indonesia. (2021). *Annual Members Survey* 2019/2020. Indonesia: AFTECH. Retrieved from: https://fintech.id/storage/files/shares/

Badan Pusat Statistik (BPS). (2020). *Hasil Sensus Penduduk 2020 (The 2020 Population Census)*. Retrieved from: https://www.bps.go.id/pressrelease/2021/01/21/1854/hasil-sensus-penduduk-2020.html

Batunanggar, S. (2019). Fintech Development and Regulatory Frameworks in Indonesia. *ADBI Working Paper 1014*. Tokyo: Asian Development Bank Institute. Retrieved from: https://www.adb.org/publications/fintech-development-regulatory-frameworks-indonesia

Behr, P., Entzian, A., and Guttler, A. (2011). How Do Lending Relationship Affect Access to Credit and Loan Conditions in Microlending? *Journal of Banking and Finance*, 35, 2169–2178.

Boyd, J. and Prescott, E. (1986). Financial Intermediary-Coalitions. *Journal of Economic Theory*, 38, 211–232.

Capri, Alex. (2019). *Micro and Small Businesses in Indonesia's Digital Economy: Keys to Developing New Skills and Human Capital*. Canada: Asia Pacific Foundation of Canada.

Chapra, A. (2017). *How FinTech Startups Are Transforming the Way Banks Function in Indonesia*. Retrieved from: https://inc42.com/features/fintech-indonesia-banks-startups/

DailySocial.id. (2021). *Fintech Report 2021: The Convergence of (Digital) Financial Services*. Retrieved from: https://dailysocial.id/research/fintech-report-2021

Diamond, D.W. (1984). Financial Intermediation and Delegated Monitoring. *The Review of Economic Studies*, 51(3), 393–414.

Edwards, T., Delbridge, R., and Munday, M. (2005). Understanding innovation in small and medium-sized enterprises: a process manifest. *Technovation*, 25, 1119–1127.

Huang, Y., Zhang, L., Li, Z., Qiu, H., Sun, T., and Wang, X. (2020). Fintech Credit Risk Assessment for SMEs: Evidence from China. *IMF Working Paper No. 2020/193*.

Retrieved from: https://www.imf.org/en/Publications/WP/Issues/2020/09/25/Fintech-Credit-Risk-Assessment-for-SMEs-Evidence-from-China-49742

Hyytinen, A. and Pajarinen, M. (2008). Opacity of young businesses: Evidence from rating disagreements. *Journal of Banking and Finance,* 32(7), 1234–1241.

International Labour Organization (ILO). (2019). *Financing Small Businesses in Indonesia: Challenges and Opportunities.* Jakarta: ILO. Retrieved from: https://www.ilo.org/publns

Ismal, R. (2011). Islamic Banking in Indonesia: Lessons Learnt. *Paper presented at Multi-year Expert Meeting on Services, Development, and Trade: The Regulatory and Institutional Dimension,* Geneva, 6–8 April 2011.

Ismal, R. (2014). Indonesia, The Resilience and Prospects of Islamic Banking, in S. Thiagaraja et al. (Eds.), *The Islamic Finance Handbook: A Practitioner's Guide to the Global Market,* Singapore: John Wiley and Sons, pp. 155–173.

Kemp, S. (2021). *Digital 2021: The Latest Insights Into the State of Digital.* Retrieved from: https://wearesocial.com/uk/blog/2021/01/digital-2021-the-latest-insights-into-the-state-of-digital/

Lembaga Pengembangan Perbankan Indonesia (LPPI) and Bank Indonesia (BI). (2015). *Profil Bisnis Usaha, Mikro, Kecil dan Menengah (UMKM).* Jakarta: LPPI and BI.

Linawati, N., Moeljadi, M., Djumahir, D., and Aisjah, S. (2019). The Role of Peer to Peer Lending in Increaing Funding Micro, Small, and Medium Enterprises. *The 1st International Conference on Social Sciences and Humanities (ICSH 2019).*

Liu, F., Fang, M., Park, K, and Chen, X. (2021). Supply Chain Finance, Performance and Risk: How Do SMEs Adjust Their Buyer-Supplier Relationship for Competitiveness? *Journal of Competitiveness,* 13(4), 78–95. https://doi.org/10.7441/joc.2021.04.05

McEvoy, M. J. (2014). *Enabling Financing Inclusion through "Alternative Data".* Bentonville, AR: Mastercard Advisors.

OECD. (2015). *New Approaches to SME and Entrepreneurship Financing: Broadening the Range of Instruments.* Istanbul: OECD.

Otoritas Jasa Keuangan. (2020). *Indonesia Islamic Banking Development Roadmap 2020–2025.* Jakarta: Otoritas Jasa Keuangan.

Otoritas Jasa Keuangan. (2021). *Laporan Perkembangan Keuangan Syariah Indonesia 2020: Ketahanan dan Daya Saing Keuangan Syariah di Masa Pandemi.* Jakarta: Otoritas Jasa Keuangan.

Otoritas Jasa Keuangan. (2022). *Laporan Perkembangan Keuangan Syariah Indonesia 2021: Menjaga Ketahanan Keuangan Syariah dalam Momentum Pemulihan Ekonomi.* Jakarta: Otoritas Jasa Keuangan.

Otoritas Jasa Keuangan and Boston Consulting Group. (2020). *Bagaimana UMKM dan Perbankan dapat Sukses di Era Ekonomi dan Digital.* Jakarta: OJK – BCG Joint Research.

Pfohl, H.C., and Gomm, M. (2009). Supply Chain Finance: Optimizing Financial Flows in Supply Chains. *Logistics Research,* 1, 149–161. https://doi.org/10.1007/s12159-009-0020-y

Pramono, S., and Suzuki, Y. (2021). *The Growth of Islamic Banking in Indonesia: Theory and Practice.* London: Routledge.

PricewaterhouseCooper (PwC). (2017). *The World in 2050: How Will the Global Economic Order Change?* Retrieved from: https://www.pwc.com/gx/en/world-2050/assets/pwc-world-in-2050-summary-report-feb-2017.pdf

PricewaterhouseCooper (PwC) Indonesia. (2019). Indonesia's Fintech Lending: Driving Economic Growth through Financial Inclusion. *PwC Indonesia - Fintech Series.* Retrieved from: https://www.pwc.com/id/fintech-lending

Sukmana, R., and Kuswanto, H. (2015). Assessment on the Islamic banking market share projection by Bank Indonesia and proposed methods. *Journal of Islamic Monetary Economics and Finance*, 1(1), 107–133.

Söderberg, L., and Bengtsson, L. (2010). Supply chain management maturity and performance in SMEs. *Operations Management Research*, 3, 90–97.

Tambunan, Tulus T. H. (2011). Development of Micro, Small and Medium Enterprises and Their Constraints: A Story from Indonesia. *Gadjah Mada International Journal of Business*, 13, 21–43.

United Overseas Bank (UOB). (2017). *State of FinTech in ASEAN*. Retrieved from: https://www.uobgroup.com/techecosystem/news-insights-fintech-in-asean-2017.html

Wendel, B., and Harvey, M. (2006). SME Credit Scoring: Key Initiatives, Opportunities, and Issues. *Access Finance*, March 2006, Issue No. 10. The WorldBank Group. Retrieved from: https://documents1.worldbank.org/curated/en/221231468339556964/pdf/389550AF101Wendel1article

World Bank. (2018) *The Little Data Book on Financial Inclusion*. Washington: World Bank Group. Retrieved from: https://openknowledge.worldbank.org/handle/10986/29654

Yang, Y., Chu, X., Pang, R., Liu, F., and Yang, P. (2021). Identifying and Predicting the Credit Risk of Small and Medium-Sized Enterprises in Sustainable Supply Chain Finance: Evidence from China. *Sustainability*, 13(5714), 1–19. https://doi.org/10.3390/su13105714

Yoshino, N, and Taghizadeh-Hesary, F. (2017). Solutions for Mitigating SMEs' Difficulties in Accessing Finance: Asian Experiences. *ADBI Working Paper 768*. Tokyo: Asian Development Bank Institute. Retrieved from: https://www.adb.org/publications/solutions-smesdifficulties-accessing-finance-asian-experiences

5
PROSPECTS AND OPPORTUNITIES OF ISLAMIC CROWDFUNDING IN BANGLADESH

S. M. Sohrab Uddin, Rima Akter and Md Imran Hossain Anik

1 Introduction

Bangladesh is a developing country with huge potentials to grow in the near future. The development depends on certain factors and one of the key factors here is the roles and activities of the financial intermediary, which assists in capital formation, investment and savings. It plays a vital role in a well-developing economy (Salehi, 2008). But the current financial institutions have certain limitations and problems that don't allow the start-ups to grow smoothly, an activity that is highly essential in a developing economy. Not only do the developed countries have the opportunity to implement the frameworks related to crowdfunding, but for the simplicities in its structure and the ease of process which enables people from every sector to connect with it via mobile and online platforms, the developing countries are also considering crowdfunding as an important tool in capital formation and investment. In fact, by 2025, the market potential of crowdfunding for developing countries is estimated to be $96 billion per year.

At present, Bangladesh has also initiated to emphasize this sector. Having crowdfunding as their core operational activity, some small and medium start-ups have initiated some projects that are not yet running at full pace. The government is looking to bring this sector under a regulatory framework so that the people can find it reliable to invest in the crowdfunding platform (CFP).

Bangladesh has the vision to be a developed country by adapting the latest technologies and transforming traditional activities into digital. Hence, the implementation of fintech has become an important concern. Crowdfunding is a wing of fintech that works with the collection of funds through blockchain technology. This can bring a revolution in the financial sector of Bangladesh where small businesses can collect their funds efficiently; poverty can be reduced through donation-based funding and alternative sources of finance will boost the economy.

There has been some research on the future potential of crowdfunding in Bangladesh on a general basis that mainly included interest-based financing. But a country like Bangladesh with the majority of its population being Muslim has more opportunity to flourish the economy by replacing interest-based financing with profit-based financing platforms that are compliant with the Shari'ah. Considering the growth of Islamic Banking, at the end of March 2021, Bangladesh's 10 full-fledged Islamic banks have been operating with 1,558 branches out of a total of 10,767 branches of the whole banking sector. In addition, 19 Islamic banking branches of 8 conventional commercial banks and 178 Islamic banking windows of 11 conventional commercial banks are also providing Islamic financial services in Bangladesh (Hasin & Alamin, 2021). This implies the need for a framework in all financial institutions and types including the sector of crowdfunding. But here a research gap has been seen which implies questions like What will be the Islamic crowdfunding scenario in Bangladesh? What will be its type? What will be the framework compared with other Islamic developing countries? Considering these issues, this research paper aims to find answers.

The paper has high significance because crowdfunding itself is an emerging sector with huge potential in Bangladesh and blending it with Islamic mechanisms, it will portray some valuable insights about its different characteristics, possibilities and mechanisms that comply with the Shari'ah law.

2 Literature review

Crowdfunding is said to be the modern and digitalized form of the traditional fund collection (Wahjono et al., 2015). Bottiglia and Pichler (2016) have defined three attributes that are a must for crowdfunding, and they are – (i) the existence of a business project that requires funding; (ii) the presence of several investors who are likely to associate with the project and (iii) the investors and entrepreneur have to be connected via internet. According to several pieces of research, four forms of crowdfunding have been in practice till now – donation-based crowdfunding, reward-based crowdfunding, equity-based crowdfunding (ECF), and peer-to-peer lending (Hagedorn & Pinkwart, 2016; Harrison & Mason, 1992; Mohd Thas Thaker, 2018).

The global volume of crowdfunding in 2012 was $2.7 billion in which donations and reward-based crowdfunding represented an amount of 51.4%, followed by lending-based crowdfunding which was about 44.2% and ECF was only 4.2% of the total volume (Massolutions, 2013). This difference is caused due to the variation in the complexity and uncertainty range of the different models.

Donation-based crowdfunding comes with the least risk and uncertainty as the donor doesn't provide fund in exchange of any investment or return, whereas ECF has the highest amount of risk and uncertainty as the return on their investment depends on the company's actions and they have to bear loss if the company cannot make profit. So, the regulatory framework of equity-based models would be more complex (Athlers & Cumming, 2012). Since equity holders don't rip the fruits of profit only but also bear the losses with the companies so this model is more coherent with the idea of Islamic crowdfunding.

The concept of crowdfunding can bring a revolution in the field of Islamic finance as it opts for the socio-economic development of the community by bringing investors, entrepreneurs, and donors under the same platform. So, it is important to ensure that the crowdfunding components are Shari'ah-compliant. Since Islamic finance aims to support projects which are labelled halal according to Islamic laws so Islamic crowdfunding should support the same and thus gambling and speculations (Maysir), uncertainty (Gharar) and interest rate (Riba) are prohibited in the platform (Aizah Ibrahim et al., 2018). Crowdfunding based on reward is closely related to Bai Salam as it rewards the investors through specific products or services in exchange for the money they invested. The model is appropriate according to the Islamic Shari'ah as the entity unable to produce a product due to shortage of finance can produce it by getting the money from the investors as a pre-payment for the product. And once the product gets created, the manufacturer can deliver the product to the investor as a reward for their investment (Chowdhury & Shil, 2017). One of the largest CFPs based on reward exists in Malaysia known as Mystartr (Mahadi et al., 2018). Many donation-based CFPs around the world support education and health expenses and new entrepreneurs by seeking a small number of donations from the general public through platforms like GoFundMe, YouCaring.com, GiveForward, FirstGiving, Skolafund and BitGiving. Thus, both reward and donation-based crowdfunding align with the Shari'ah. ECF can also be aligned according to Islamic laws by implementing certain changes. The closest Islamic finance model to this type is Mudarabah where one party bears the capital, and the other parties give their skill, effort and time. ECF comes up with the highest amount of risk as only the Mudarib (the capital provider) is entitled to bear the monetary loss. The Shari'ah-based sale and investment instruments like Murabaha (mark-up sale), Salam (advanced sale), Istisna (manufacturer's advanced sale), Musharakah (partnership) and Mudarabah can be brought under the CFP to digitalize the Islamic financial practices (Muneeza et al., 2018). In the present scenario, where there exists an absolute lack of trust between investors and entrepreneurs and a lack of experience of the small business entrepreneurs, ECF is becoming more complicated. But bringing this idea under Shari'ah rules would reduce the risks to some extent as the operations will be limited to halal projects and products that are compliant with Shari'ah.

The main distinction between traditional crowdfunding and Islamic crowdfunding is the latter's adoption of Islamic precepts. The Maqasid-Shari'ah, or Shari'ah purposes, has traditionally been the criterion for determining whether Islamic products or enterprises are compatible with Shari'ah standards. Necessities, needs and luxuries are the three levels of the Maqasid-Shari'ah order. In supplement to the three parties engaged in traditional crowdfunding, the Shari'ah committee is an essential aspect in Islamic crowdfunding. That is, four parties take part in Islamic crowdfunding. The fund pursuer, the investor, the portal operator, and the Shari'ah committee are the four parties involved (Nordin & Zainuddin, 2021).

If considered peer-to-peer or P2P crowdfunding, then we will see that Islamic P2P crowdfunding follows the identical framework and operating procedures as traditional P2P. It must, nevertheless, be devoid of any interest-based contracts in order to be Shari'ah-compliant. Alternatively, it uses a profit-sharing deal, which allows investors to enjoy a pre-determined amount of the earnings from the ventures they fund.

Mudharabah and Murabahah are two famous Islamic peer-to-peer structures. The advent of Islamic crowdfunding provides halal investment alternatives for investors wanting a Shari'ah-compliant commodity while participating in crowdsourcing. Due to the strict principles of Islam, which prevent purposely dangerous and detrimental acts, Islamic crowdfunding guarantees higher protection to investors compared to ordinary crowdfunding. It gives investors a larger selection of Islamic commodities to decide from while also helping individuals in need of money by redirecting funds to productive projects.

Islamic crowdfunding, unlike certain other Shari'ah-compliant commodities, is not restricted to Muslims. It is open to all investors, and they can contribute depending on the product's profitability and risk sensitivity.

There is a high potential in Musharakah to be adopted as a practice of ECF where the investors would be able to gain a return as Shari'ah-compliant arrangement of profit sharing. The need for a third-party guarantor would be substituted by the crowdfunding site in exchange for a certain amount of fee. To unleash the full potential of Mudarabah and Musharakah with the use of fintech, a Mudarabah crowdfunding model based on blockchain technology has been proposed by Muneeza et al. (2018). The use of blockchain would mitigate the probable privacy risks, eliminate the need for third parties and promote transparency in the projects that need investment.

But in developing countries like Bangladesh where there is an acute lack of digital literacy, implementation of such a high-tech platform is challenging (Ishak & Rahman, 2021). Slowly but gradually the country is shifting towards the adaptation of technology in many of its financial services. In recent times, the country has seen a revolutionary rise in the usage of fintech. More and more customers are now inclining towards fintech media like bKash, Rocket, mCash, Ucash, UPay, and Nagad (Tanjib Rubaiyat, 2020). These media provides both banking and non-banking services like sending money, depositing money, paying bill, recharge, online payment and many more.

3 Research methodology

The research has been conducted with both qualitative and quantitative analysis to portray the prospects and opportunities of Islamic crowdfunding in Bangladesh that is in both numerical and descriptive manner. For secondary research, different articles, research papers and journals that have focused on crowdfunding have been evaluated. The sources will be used to justify the concepts and analysis that will bring insights about the particulars. This mixed approach uses previous sources but there will be a gap regarding primary data which can be taken as a consideration for future research.

4 History and current situation of crowdfunding in Bangladesh

Bangladesh has had some attempts in creating CFPs but hasn't been able to make a big impact until now. The microfinancing concept in Bangladesh came from the Noble Laureate Dr. Mohammad Younus, where he had the idea of facilitating people who are in poverty by lending a small amount of money and providing it to a large number of people. 'Somiti' in Bangladesh is another type of crowdfunding where the members save a portion of their salary and later the sum is invested in the business where the members divide the profit among themselves. But none of these matches with the centralized tech-based crowdfunding system.

The first web-based CFP in Bangladesh that has been created including a centralized online system was Projekt.co which is a reward-based platform with industries related to music, arts, and technology. This platform had intended to help the people related to the creative industries, entrepreneurs, and makers to make their ideas come to life. The website was founded by Waiz Rahim who mainly got the idea to do such kind of thing from Kickstarter. But this CFP's journey came to an end in 2017 because people in Bangladesh weren't used to crowdfunding and the popularity was very low. Ultimately the project became a failure. In 2015, another CFP was launched with the name GoRiseMe. They have accommodated 33 campaigns until now but they are to achieve a successful campaign. Their vision was to reshape the global e-trade and build a community based on trust, privacy, and secure real-time business with integrity (Suresh et al., 2020).

Oporajoy.org was launched in 2018 which is a donation-based crowdfunding site. Oporajoy has completed a campaign where they raised $150 through the platform that was to assist a student with the admission fee of the University of Dhaka. The founder of Oporajoy is Monjurul Islam who got the idea of Oporajay while doing his post-graduation program in the US. He saw that in the US, people even collect funds for their pet's birthdays, so he had the question of why he can't use the same type of platform in Bangladesh where people are hungry and living in poverty. Thus, he created the donation-based CFP Oporajoy for this reason. Another platform was launched in 2018 called GoFundsMe which is an equity-based platform. This platform is partially funded by the Department of the International Labor Department of the UK. This platform has bought some projects to fund for equity but hasn't still been able to complete a project (Table 1).

TABLE 1 CFPs in Bangladesh

Platform	Type	Established year	Percentage of commission
Projekt	Reward-based	2015	–
GoRiseMe	Donation-based	2015	3%, for PayPal 3.4% + €0.35 per donation
Fundsme	Equity-based	2018	Upfront fee on the funding purpose
Oporajoy	Donation-based	2018	5%

Source: Suresh et al. (2020).

Ekdesh is a recent CFP that was launched by Access to Information (a2i). a2i is the signature program of the Digital Bangladesh movement of the government of Bangladesh. Ekdesh is the first CFP that is based on raising funds from the public which will be later distributed among the poor people as Zakat or Financial Aid. This platform allows the people to donate to the Prime Minister's relief fund, Islamic foundation or other NGOs. Along with helping the poor people, the platform gives an opportunity to help the small businesses that were hit in the time of the Corona pandemic. The platform has both website and mobile app and organizations like BRAC, Bidyanondo, and Centre for Zakat Management have joined the program.

As of now, there is no centralized platform in Bangladesh working on Shari'ah-based crowdfunding. The few that are operating are focused on donation only. But Islamic crowdfunding is a more diverse field that can bring substantial profit for the country if implemented and monitored with the right regulations.

Hence, it is seen that there are some attempts made in crowdfunding, but the success hasn't been observed vastly. It is still in a growing phase and if the potentials are implemented in the right manner, crowdfunding can be a major source of funding in Bangladesh.

So, by analysing the essentials, the problems that are seen from the previous experiences are listed below:

- The people are not still used to the term 'Crowdfunding'. They do not have an idea of its mechanism and how it will serve a benefit to them. The gap of knowledge has become a core issue of the failure of crowdfunding in Bangladesh until now. Trust has become a vital issue in the crowdfunding sector as many MLM companies have cheated people with new terminologies and investment opportunities. So, people are afraid of trying out a new thing as the previous experiences have made them more risk-averse in this case.
- There are still no formal regulations regarding crowdfunding in Bangladesh, so it is not getting the desired structure for all the stakeholders included. The development of structure, rules and regulations is highly needed so that the activities in this sector get a legal body and authority.

- If there is any investor wanting to invest in an Islamic CFP, there is no opportunity for them, as the current CFPs are not built complying with that mechanism (in terms of equity and debt-based CFPs).
- There is a strong resistance to change in the mentality of Bangladeshi people. They are more likely to embrace certainty and what is known. This is indeed a reason for the hindrance of growth, especially in the technological sector in Bangladesh.

5 Comparison of economic infrastructures of Bangladesh with other developing countries

Crowdfunding has been established successfully in many of the developed countries with guided rules and regulations. The countries dominating the crowdfunding industry mainly include the USA, UK and China. China has more than 80% of the market share in the crowdfunding industry. But our concern is how effective it is for the developing nations and if it is feasible to implement crowdfunding models (particularly Islamic crowdfunding) in Bangladesh.

Bangladesh has been one of the fastest developing nations in the world over the last decade and made remarkable progress in sustainable economic growth. The country reached a lower-middle-income status in 2015 and currently, the government aims to target to be a developed nation through the implementation of technological infrastructure and building a Digital Bangladesh. Hence, crowdfunding can be a source of development for three reasons. First, crowdfunding itself is a wing of fintech that supports the Digital Bangladesh vision of the government. Second, crowdfunding can be a source of alternative finance that will radically decrease the problems regarding investment and boost infrastructural development. Third, donation-based crowdfunding can be a source of bringing income equality and social development in Bangladesh.

Considering Bangladesh's neighbours, India is a developing country that has implemented all four forms of crowdfunding to a greater extent (Suresh et al., 2020). ECF and lending-based crowdfunding have got a good market now in India. In fact, P2P is said to be one of the fastest-growing markets in India where the current market size is around 2 billion INR and 40–50 platforms under the P2P umbrella (Saleem, 2018). Hence, Bangladesh has not yet shown any promise regarding the P2P platform. In case, if Bangladesh wants to implement such a kind of crowdfunding, following the general model will not satisfy the rules of Shari'ah. That is why if Bangladesh wants to bring a P2P lending platform like India, it should be modified under the rules and regulations of Islam to comply with the Islamic financial system, which is the main concern of this research. Hence, banks like IBBL can make a major contribution here.

One point to be noted here is that India doesn't have bespoke regulations regarding reward and donation-based crowdfunding but has strong regulations under authority regarding lending and ECF. This is because lending and ECF need an essence of trust, clarity and if gone out of control, there is a huge possibility of misuse and fraud. Thus, in terms of Bangladesh, we can see that the lack of regulations is a vital reason why equity and lending-based crowdfunding still hasn't got the confidence of the stakeholders related to it.

If considered the list of countries that successfully executed the idea of Islamic crowdfunding, then Malaysia would be one of the top choices. It is the fourth largest economic power in Southeast Asia. For the technological transformation and adoption, the labour productivity is significantly higher in Malaysia. The Global Competitiveness Report of 2019 had declared Malaysia as the 27th most competitive country in the world. The country has adopted an infrastructure according to the guidance of Islamic Shari'ah, which has made Malaysia a central hub for Islamic fintech. 'Ethis' is a CFP based in Malaysia that is playing a leading role in Malaysia's growth. This platform has collected more than $15 million and completed 16,000+ transactions. It is regulated under the crowdfunding licenses of Malaysia and Indonesia that approve it as Shari'ah. This P2P platform can be a benchmark for Bangladesh in case of establishing an Islamic CFP. Thus, compared with Malaysia, certain measures can be taken in case of developing economic infrastructure and harnessing the power of Islamic fintech effectively. First, the regulatory framework regarding CFPs should be developed quickly. Second, the literacy rate should be increased and effectiveness in learning should be included so that people can understand the concepts of fintech and have confidence about utilizing the power of digital economy platforms. Third, the platforms should be made easy to use with availability to all.

Finally, it can be said that by understanding the trends of other developing countries and comparing them with Bangladesh's condition, there is a huge potential of crowdfunding in Bangladesh that needs some regulatory and awareness concerns.

6 Opportunities of Islamic crowdfunding in Bangladesh

The World Bank has valued the South Asian market of crowdfunding to be worth US$5 billion. The societal, cultural, and religious norms of the countries of this region (Bangladesh, India, Sri Lanka, and Pakistan) encourages helping each other through donations and loans during their extreme necessities like medical emergency, education finances or starting a business. So, these societal and religious traits are very similar to the crowdfunding principles. But despite having such potential the alternative finance activity in the South Asian region amounted to only US$269 million where more than 95% of the value was contributed by India alone.

The volume of alternative finance in Bangladesh is only US$10,272 as exhibited in Table 2, whereas even countries like Nepal and Pakistan that are similar to the infrastructure and size of Bangladesh have a volume of US$1,014,850 and

TABLE 2 Volume of alternative finance in South Asian countries

Country	Population (million)	The volume of finance (US$)
Bangladesh	161	10,272
Bhutan	0.8	10,000
Nepal	28	1,014,850
India	1352	268,579,820
Pakistan	212	8,571,762
Srilanka	21	38,926

Source: The World Bank Database (2013).

US$8,571,762 respectively. Thus, there exists a greater portion of the unutilized potential of crowdfunding finance in Bangladesh.

As of 2020, Bangladesh recorded the highest unemployment rate of 5.30% in its history. The youth of the country are more interested in government jobs. But the government itself can't arrange job opportunities for such a vast population. So, the government has been encouraging the youth towards entrepreneurship. One of the main barriers for young entrepreneurs is securing capital for their businesses. The financial needs of the entrepreneurs are basically met by three sets of financial intermediaries in Bangladesh. The first one is the commercial bank including all the financial institutions that are operated under the direct control of Bangladesh Bank (the central bank of Bangladesh). The second financial intermediary is the stock market and the third one includes some of the NGOs that operate in the rural economy. But the small firms and start-ups are the last things that come to their mind while investing.

Over the last 10 years, the small firms and enterprises did not even receive 1% of the total loans disbursed by the scheduled banks of the country. One of the prime reasons behind this is the credit management policy of these banks that depend excessively on a codified system of assessing the risk that is responsible to generate a 'credit crunch' for the small firms specifically (Adhikary et al., 2018). Another reason for small firms not getting enough credit extension would be low profits and high NPLs of the scheduled commercial banks (SCB) and Development Financial Institutions (DFI) that collectively hold 31.5% of the total industry assets and 30.3% of the total industry deposits. This imposes a significant impact on the ROA of the banks which is shown in Table 3.

Second, the two stock markets of Bangladesh – the Dhaka Stock Exchange and Chittagong Stock Exchange – have financed a very limited number of companies in the last 10 years. Moreover, they exhibited poor performance in financing the productive sectors and even to the established companies (Kumar Adhikary & Kutsuna, 2015). Many countries in the world have a separate market for financing start-ups and young entrepreneurs like Japan has 'Mothers', China has 'ChiNext' and Korea has 'Kosdaq' unlike Bangladesh.

TABLE 3 NPL and ROA of different banks

Year	NPL (% of total loan)					ROA (%)				
	SCB	PCB	FCB	DFI	All banks	SCB	PCB	FCB	DFI	All banks
2003	29	12.4	2.7	47.4	22.1	0.1	1.1	2.8	0.7	0.7
2004	25.3	8.5	1.3	42.8	17.6	−0.1	0.8	2.4	0.3	0.5
2005	21.35	5.62	1.26	34.87	13.56	−0.1	0.7	2.6	0	0.5
2006	22.94	5.45	0.81	33.68	13.15	0	1.2	3.2	−0.2	0.7
2007	29.87	5.01	1.43	28.58	13.23	0	1.1	3.1	−0.1	0.6
2008	25.4	4.4	1.9	25.5	10.8	0.7	1.1	2.2	−0.2	0.8
2009	21.4	3.9	2.3	25.9	9.2	1	1.3	3.1	−0.3	0.9
2010	15.7	3.2	3	24.2	7.3	1.1	1.4	2.9	−0.6	1.2
2011	11.3	2.9	3	24.6	6.1	1.3	1.6	3.2	0.4	1.4
2012	23.9	4.6	3.5	26.8	10	−0.6	2.1	2.9	0.2	1.8

Source: Annual Report of Bangladesh Bank (Bangladesh Bank, 2012).

And the last financial intermediary consists of the NGOs that mainly work with the underprivileged and marginalized communities like women, farmers, and rural artisans. So, all of the three financial intermediaries have their separate target market where the small firms and start-ups are not a part of it.

Thus, the country is losing the potential of the entrepreneurs and their innovative ideas which contributes to the country's economy the most. In this scenario, crowdfunding can play a pivotal role in mitigating this gap between entrepreneurs and financial intermediaries. Integrating the Shari'ah rules will make crowdfunding a trustable and efficient platform for both investors and entrepreneurs. Since Islamic crowdfunding promotes risk-sharing by both parties, so no parties can be held responsible to bear the losses.

7 A convenient framework of crowdfunding for Bangladesh

As said earlier, there are quite a few platforms in the country that exhibit the practice of informal crowdfunding specially donation-based crowdfunding for example GoRiseMe, Oporajoy where the platform posts the stories of the people who are in need, to motivate the audience to donate. Both the platforms take a small percentage of the amount collected as their commission. Apart from these, there is Project.co which is a reward-based CFP, and Fundsme which is an equity-based CFP. Yet, there has not been much success gained in any of these platforms. Also, no CFP has been introduced in Bangladesh that permits Shari'ah-based investments. In this situation, it is ECF and reward-based crowdfunding can be utilized to get hold of the potential of Islamic crowdfunding in Bangladesh as these two models are closely related to the Islamic Shari'ah-based business models such as Bai Salam and Musharakah.

7.1 Reward-based crowdfunding platform

Here, the buyers and sellers would be able to connect through the crowdfunding website. The seller would portray his products and services, the detailed description of it including the dimensions, materials, uses and proper costing of the products. The website will host this information along with the seller's profile. Then, the interested buyers will choose their desired products from that and have to pay the cost of the product in advance which portrays the essence of the practice of Bai Salam. Then, the seller will deliver the product at an agreed-upon date in the future. Being the intermediary between the buyers and seller, the website will charge a specific percentage of the cost which will have to be not more than 5% (Figure 1).

7.2 ECF platform

Equity-based CFP goes with the Shari'ah-mentioned rules and regulations the most. Many Islamic countries like Malaysia, Indonesia, United Arab Emirates have already established crowdfunding websites that follow the equity model according to the Shari'ah-based rules of profit and risk-sharing. Since Bangladesh is a country with a majority of its population being Muslim, this platform can easily grab both the investors' and borrowers' attention. And if the platform is introduced by an already existing trustworthy enterprise for example a reputed bank like Islamic Bank Bangladesh Limited or any other financial institution, then it will add more value to the branding of the platform. bKash which is the leading mobile financial service provider of Bangladesh was also launched by the BRAC bank as a subsidiary which helped the platform gain the trust of the market as an initiator of a new service. The small firms or entrepreneurs will present their idea, the equity that they are ready to offer, the investments required for the implementation and how far the idea reached in the Islamic crowdfunding website (ICFW). The ICFW will then play the role of the investment generator by marketing the campaign in their social and personal networks. The interested individuals can invest in the campaigns directly using the ICFW and they will

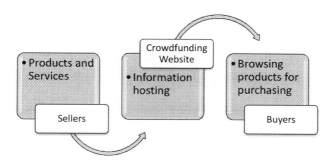

FIGURE 1   Reward-based crowdfunding model.

become equity stakeholders for which they will receive dividends in exchange for their investment. The website will also be the medium of communication between the investors and entrepreneurs where the investors can have direct queries from the entrepreneur. This would increase the transparency between them which will help both parties to make rational decisions. The ICFW are entitled to receive a fixed fee from the firms that collect their capital through the website (Figure 2).

This model is extremely suitable for start-up companies as they do not receive necessary firms from other financial intermediaries. Through the proper exhibition of the potential of their idea and a realistic business model, start-up companies will be able to collect their required capital in a short span of time without getting involved in a time-consuming and uncertain traditional loan processing system. Since the function of ICFW is similar to the stock exchange so the implementation of this platform has to be regulated by the security laws of the country so that the investors are protected from fraud contracts (Suresh et al., 2020). The role of the Central Shari'ah Board for Islamic Banks of Bangladesh (CSBIB) is also significant in this aspect to monitor if the website is following the Shari'ah rules in real or just applying this as a marketing strategy.

7.3 Regulations for crowdfunding platforms in Bangladesh

While crowdfunding is still a new concept to the Muslim countries or the South Asian countries, it has been practised in western countries much before that. So, they have already created proper policies and regulatory frameworks for running the CFPs.

As it can be seen in Table 4, the CFPs of the USA and Australia are regulated by the Securities and Exchange Commission (SEC), and in the UK and

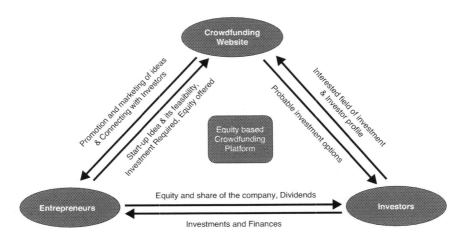

FIGURE 2 ECF model.

TABLE 4 Crowdfunding regulatory policies of different countries

Country	UK	USA	Canada	New Zealand	Australia
Raise limit/1 year	€8 million	US$1 million	CA$1.5 million	NZ$2 million	AU$5 million
Open to ordinary investors	Yes	Yes	Yes	Yes	Yes
Investment limit per ordinary investor	Under 10% of net total assets	US$2,000 per offer or, 5% income per offer if income is less than US$100,000	CA$2,500 per offer (some provinces have additional limits for total crowdfunding)	None	AU$10,000 per offer
Investment limit per accredited investor	None	US$100,000 or 10% lesser income/net worth greater than US$100,000	CA$25,000 per offer (some provinces have additional limits for total crowdfunding)	None	None
Regulator	Financial conduct authority	SEC	Province-by-province regulation	Financial markets authority	Australian securities and investment commission
Others	Very lucrative tax exemption (SEIS/EIS)	Explicit 'no exemption' of platform and intermediary liability	Various levels of crowdfunding exemptions	Not specifically restricted to small businesses	Restricted to public and proprietary limited companies

Source: Planetcompliance.com (2022)

New Zealand, they are regulated by the financial market's authority. The SEC of the United States has set regulatory standards on crowdfunding that include four basic points: the amount of money that can be raised, the financial history of investors, the role of intermediaries, and investor eligibility. Meanwhile, in emerging nations such as Indonesia, the policy on crowdfunding or fintech looks to be harsher, with the Financial Service Authority Regulation 2016 No. 77 proposing ten points. The Securities Commission of Malaysia has overseen Islamic crowdfunding under the Guidelines on Recognised Markets, which specifies that all Islamic financial services must conform with IFSA 2013 (Uluyol et al., 2018). At present, the registered platforms include Leet Capital, Ata Plus, Pitchin, Ethis Ventures, Fundnel and so on.

In Bangladesh, crowdfunding is still quite far from the proper exhibition for which there are no regulations introduced till now by the Bangladesh Bank. The deputy governor of the bank said in an interview that there is no regulation about crowdfunding in Bangladesh. He also added that the event is a timely initiative to create awareness among the citizens of the country. Even if it is implemented in the near future, the main regulator should be Bangladesh SEC or the central bank. For Islamic crowdfunding one of the main regulators would include the CSBIB too.

8 Problems related to the implementation of Islamic crowdfunding in Bangladesh

Bangladesh has enormous opportunities in terms of economic development by using crowdfunding, but certain limitations need to be addressed. The first and foremost problem is the bureaucracy in creating rules and regulations. It takes years in Bangladesh to enact and implement a valid policy, but the current competitive and dynamic situation demands Bangladesh to create a regulatory framework regarding crowdfunding within the least time possible. Dr. Habib, a professor and director of the Bangladesh Institute of Bank Management, has portrayed the fact that due to the lack of policy and regulatory framework, it has been difficult for Bangladesh to explore the potentials of crowdfunding. Hence, there should be a framework regarding Islamic crowdfunding so that it becomes possible for the institutions to approve their platforms under the Islamic Shari'ah.

Again, there is a need for awareness and training for the people as most of the people aren't still familiar with the concept of crowdfunding in Bangladesh (Suresh et al., 2020). In a survey, it was seen that, among the respondents who were small business owners, only 5% had heard about the term crowdfunding (Kumar Adhikary & Kutsuna, 2015). Here, the government can play the biggest role by creating awareness programs about crowdfunding, assisting the new platforms in their growth and providing monetary help. This is aligned with the accordance of government's vision of revolutionizing the country with fintech for boosting economic growth and removing poverty.

Furthermore, one of the core challenges is to build trust among the people. As mentioned by Islam and Khan (2021), the success of crowdfunding depends on the engagement of the end-users. People in Bangladesh has been facing fraud through online medium and transactions. The past issues regarding Evaly, Dhamaka and E-orange where the customers have lost their trust and money have made it tougher for the new online platforms to acquire new customers. This will ultimately hurt the crowdfunding sector too and this implies the need for close monitoring, building regulatory framework and creating an environment of trust and clarity. Islamic crowdfunding needs clarification of Shari'ah compliance as the religious-minded people who will be interested to invest in the platforms would want to be sure about the ethical and Shari'ah aspects of both the systems and the platforms.

Finally, there is a challenge to implement a successful business model that will be profitable for all the stakeholders (Gooch et al., 2020). There is an amount that the platform charges for providing the benefits and to bear the costs associated with the platform. Again, no matter what type of CFP it is, the stakeholders will look to gain their interest and because of that reason, the whole model should be built to meet those interests that will assist in making the platforms successful, trusted and sustainable. Hence, by tackling the challenges, Bangladesh has huge potential in this industry and gain economic benefits in the long term.

9 Conclusion

For the Bangladeshi financial market, crowdfunding is still in its infant stage. It is a blessing for small enterprises and entrepreneurs who are mostly ignored by microcredit organizations and commercial banks. The country has already experienced a technological boom in its financial sector through the increasing use of mobile financial services. This has resulted in an extreme rise in the mobile banking sector as well. So, it is no doubt that the people are ready to some extent for the upcoming revolution in the fintech industry. The integration of Islamic Shari'ah in the fintech sector would give the platforms like crowdfunding an extra edge to reach the customers as the majority of the country's population are Muslims. The greatest challenge right now for the implementation of Islamic crowdfunding is the lack of digital infrastructure, lack of digitally skilled employees and no regulation has still been set up for such platforms. So, the policymakers must set up strict rules so that the investors' money can be protected from incurring losses due to the lack of efficient risk management techniques. Also, there is a huge risk for CFPs to be under cyber-attacks and other digital crimes for which people tend to restrict themselves from online financial services. So, the CFPs and the cyber security regulator of the country must work together to make this highly anticipated platform safe and secure from such mishaps. When dealing online or on the internet, another major challenge for CFPs would be gaining the trust of the people. In this case, being the subsidiary of already existing reputed financial institutions will make the platforms have their back. The Islamic Banks of the country can be the initiator of this service in Bangladesh. As a whole, successful implementation of Islamic crowdfunding would require the coordination of factors like digital literacy, Shari'ah literacy, an encouraging environment for technological innovation, proper regulatory framework and effective online markets. The image of the Bangladeshi online market has been damaged severely due to increasing scams and frauds on such platforms. This image has to be immediately restored to enjoy the fruits of the potential of Islamic crowdfunding in the future.

References

Adhikary, B. K., Kutsuna, K., & Hoda, T. (2018). Crowdfunding Potential in Developing Countries—A Case of Bangladesh. In Adhikary, B., Kutsuna, K., & Hoda, T. (eds.) 'Crowdfunding: Lessons from Japan's Approach (pp. 77–94), Springer, Singapore. https://doi.org/10.1007/978-981-13-1522-0_6

Aizah Ibrahim, S., Nurhidayah Mohd Roslen, S., Aizah binti Ibrahim, S., bt Mohamad Salleh, N., Soon Theam, T., Yeen Lai, K., & Tunku Abdul Rahman Malaysia, U. (2018). Islamic Microfinancing: Crowd-funding as a Drive to Improve Financial Inclusion in Malaysia. International Journal of Engineering & Technology, 7, 18–20. https://www.researchgate.net/publication/332140862

Athlers, G., & Cumming, D. (2012). Signaling in crowdfunding. SSRN Working Paper.

Bangladesh Bank. (2012). Annual Report 2012.

Bottiglia, R., & Pichler, F. (2016). Introduction. In Crowdfunding for SMEs. https://doi.org/10.1057/978-1-137-56021-6_1

Chowdhury, A., & Shil, N. C. (2017). Public Sector Reforms and New Public Management: Exploratory Evidence from Australian Public Sector. Asian Development Policy Review, 5(1). https://doi.org/10.18488/journal.107/2017.5.1/107.1.1.16

Crowdfunding's Potential for the Developing World CONFERENCE VERSION. (2013).

Gooch, D., Kelly, R. M., Stiver, A., van der Linden, J., Petre, M., Richards, M., Klis-Davies, A., Mackinnon, J., Macpherson, R., & Walton, C. (2020). The Benefits and Challenges of Using Crowdfunding to Facilitate Community-led Projects in the Context of Digital Civics. International Journal of Human-Computer Studies, 134, 33–43. https://doi.org/10.1016/j.ijhcs.2019.10.005

Hagedorn, A., & Pinkwart, A. (2016). The Financing Process of Equity-Based Crowdfunding: An Empirical Analysis. In FGF Studies in Small Business and Entrepreneurship. https://doi.org/10.1007/978-3-319-18017-5_5

Harrison, R. T., & Mason, C. M. (1992). International Perspectives on the Supply of Informal Venture Capital. Journal of Business Venturing, 7(6). https://doi.org/10.1016/0883-9026(92)90020-R

Hasin, Z., & Alamin, M. (2021). Developments of Islamic Banking in Bangladesh January–March 2021. Islamic Banking Cell, Research Department, Bangladesh Bank.

Ishak, M. S. I., & Rahman, M. H. (2021). Equity-based Islamic Crowdfunding in Malaysia: A Potential Application for Mudharabah. Qualitative Research in Financial Markets, 13(2), 183–198. https://doi.org/10.1108/QRFM-03-2020-0024

Islam, M. T., & Khan, M. T. A. (2021). Factors Influencing the Adoption of Crowdfunding in Bangladesh: A Study of Start-Up Entrepreneurs. Information Development, 37(1), 72–89. https://doi.org/10.1177/0266666919895554

Kumar Adhikary, B., & Kutsuna, K. (2015). Small Business Finance in Bangladesh: Can "Crowdfunding" Be an Alternative? *Review of Integrative Business and Economics Research*, 4(4), 1–21. www.sibresearch.org

Mahadi, R., Sariman, N. K., Noordin, R., Mail, R., & Fatah, N. S. A. (2018). Corporate Governance Structure of State Islamic Religious Councils in Malaysia. *International Journal of Asian Social Science*, 8(7). https://doi.org/10.18488/journal.1.2018.87.388.395

Massolutions. (2013). *Crowdfunding Industry Report*.

Mohd Thas Thaker, M. A. bin. (2018). Factors influencing the adoption of the crowdfunding-waqf model (CWM) in the waqf land development. *Journal of Islamic Marketing*, 9(3). https://doi.org/10.1108/JIMA-05-2016-0043

Muneeza, A., Arshad, N. A., & Arifin, A. T. (2018). The Application of Blockchain Technology in Crowdfunding: Towards Financial Inclusion via Technology. *International Journal of Management and Applied Research*, 5(2). https://doi.org/10.18646/2056.52.18-007

Nordin, N., & Zainuddin, Z. (2021, August). Islamic Crowdfunding: A Shariah-Compliant Investment Alternative. *The Halal Journal*. https://ethis.co/blog/islamic-crowdfunding-shariah-compliant-investment-alternative/#:~:text=The%20key%20difference%20between%20conventional,or%20businesses%20with%20Shariah%20principles.

Planetcompliance.com. (2022). The Impact of Equity Crowdfunding Regulations – Planet Compliance. https://www.planetcompliance.com/the-impact-of-equity-crowdfunding-regulations/ [Accessed 8 October 2022].

Salehi, M. (2008). The Role of Financial Intermediaries in Capital Market. *Zagreb International Review of Economics & Business*, 11(1), 97–109.

Saleem, Shaikh Zoaib. (2018). *Lessons for P2P Lending in India*. https://www.livemint.com/Money/tuI4wvfqdbVH9nQVYC1M5I/Lessons-for-P2P-lending-in-India.html

Suresh, K., Øyna, S., & Munim, Z. H. (2020). Crowdfunding Prospects in New Emerging Markets: The Cases of India and Bangladesh. In *Advances in Crowdfunding*. https://doi.org/10.1007/978-3-030-46309-0_13

Tanjib Rubaiyat. (2020). Future of Fintech in Bangladesh. *Daily Sun*, 2(April).

Uluyol, B., Musito, M. H., & Yücel, E. (2018). Islamic Crowdfunding: Fundamentals, Developments and Challenges. *The Islamic Quarterly*, 62, 469–484. https://www.researchgate.net/publication/324593863

Wahjono, S. I., Marina, A., & Widayat. (2015). Islamic Crowdfunding : Alternative Funding Solution. *1st World Islamic Social Science Congress*, December.

6
EMPIRICAL ASSESSMENT ON DIGITAL TRANSFORMATION IN ISLAMIC BANKING[1]

Abideen Adeyemi Adewale and Rifki Ismal

1 Background

Digital transformation in the Islamic banking industry is building momentum and increasingly transforming the financial products offered and services rendered. This development is crucial in order to sustain the growth momentum of the industry by reinvigorating its current outreach and radically exploring new horizons, identifying untapped potentials and unlocking opportunities. What is required to achieving this is a radical departure from the traditional sales and product inclination banking model to collaborative or competition-induced innovative ways of service delivery. Such innovative banking model should align with the high expectations of today's tech-savvy and convenience-driven customers (PWC, 2019).

Digitalising Islamic banking will bring about a myriad of opportunities for growth. For instance, it will help the Islamic banks (IBs) to respond to changing customer structure and expectations, as well as the consequential disintermediation due to competition from new-entrant non-bank financial services providers. Digitalising Islamic banking will also impact positively on financial inclusion, assist small and medium enterprises, and enhance value-based intermediation among many other benefits.

Notwithstanding, digitalisation may also create exposure to potential risks that have implications for financial stability and integrity of the Islamic banking industry. For instance, digitalisation may also expose IBs to cyber-security risk, money laundering and financing terrorism (ML/FT) risk cloud-concentration risk, and Sharia non-compliance risks. Consumers and investors may also be exposed to protection issues.

Across jurisdictions, IBs and the Regulatory and Supervisory Authorities (RSAs) are in different stages of the development and implementation of digital

DOI: 10.4324/9781003262169-9

Islamic banking. Some IBs are already deploying technology in their operation via the use of software applications, especially for payments and transaction services.

Other IBs are adopting robotics process automation, machine learning and Artificial Intelligence (AI) technology for repeatable transactional tasks. Predictive analytics based on big data, cloud computing and the Internet of Things (IoT) are also being deployed to better anticipate customer needs. Similarly, unbundling of services and data sharing in open banking applications are also being implemented via Application Programming Interfaces (APIs) (Thomson Reuters and DinarStandard, 2019).

Arising from both the benefits and risks of digitalisation, there are also both operational and regulatory implications of its implementation for the financial stability of Islamic banking. The first derives from how the incumbent IBs respond to the challenges arising from both market structure dynamics and transformation to digital Islamic banking. IBs face stiff competition from FinTechs and BigTechs and increased possibility for new disruptors to enter the market, thus heightening competition and contestability (Financial Stability Board, 2019). Moreover, on the management front, there would be the need to attract new staff with, or train existing staff on requisite skills, innovative and agile mind-set.

The second derives from RSAs' response to finding a balance between encouraging technology-based financial innovation while protecting consumers, supporting business operations, and promoting financial inclusion. This should be done without infringing on the fundamental premise of Sharia upon which Islamic banking is built. In this regard, RSAs have also been issuing guiding framework and regulations, promoting regulatory sandboxes and establishment of digital banking institutions including for IBs (Elipses and Salaam Gateway, 2019).

The specific objectives of this study include to investigate (i) what is the current status of the digital transformation of Islamic banking, (ii) what are the peculiar impediments or challenges to its implementation in various Islamic Financial Services Board (IFSB) jurisdictions, (iii) what prudential risks may crystallise from digitalisation of Islamic banking, (iv) what needs to be done to support the digital transformation process in Islamic banking. The data used are collected via questionnaire survey distributed online to some countries having Islamic finance industry between the period September and October 2020. Mainly, it gathered data and information from 90 IBs and analysed with descriptive analysis based on simple percentage, frequency and, in a few instances, weighted mean scores to show relative importance.

2 Research method

The research adopts a quantitative method which is a survey questionnaire; particularly, the data analysed in this study were collected via questionnaire survey distributed online. The survey was addressed to IBs via the RSAs in various IFSB member jurisdictions between September and October 2020. The survey comprised mainly closed-ended questions with codes to indicate options a respondent IB might wish to select. In some other instances, open-ended questions were also included for the respondents' IBs to freely express their opinion on related matters beyond the closed-ended options provided. The cooperation of the responding IBs was sought especially in terms of ensuring that the responding officer was the person with the relevant responsibility to do so and that the permission of relevant superiors or authorities was obtained where necessary. The responses provided by an institution are assumed to reflect its perspectives on the issues raised. Owing to the exploratory nature of the research, data elicited from 80 IBs cutting across 21 IFSB member jurisdictions 18 were subjected to descriptive data analysis only, mainly based on simple percentage, frequency and, in one instance, weighted mean scores to show relative importance.

3 Digitalisation in Islamic banking industry

3.1 Islamic banking perception about digitalisation

IBs view digitalisation of their operations from the perspective of (i) what Islamic banking products and services they offer and (ii) the various channels or platforms through which such services are offered to their customers. Some IBs also view digitalisation of their Islamic banking activities as enhancements to their operational efficiency, data security, regulatory compliance and customer experience in its entire ramification via technology.

Regardless of the perspective, a notable common statement among the respondent IBs is that Sharia-compliance must nonetheless be ensured. Though digitalisation universally reflects the application of new technology to improve the process, products and business models in rendering of financial services, Islamic banking digitalisation would require something more for it to be conceptually, practically and justifiably different.

3.2 Rationale for Islamic banking digitalisation

The next question in the survey sought the responding IBs' rationale for embarking or proposing to embark on digital transformation. Based on the literature reviewed, 12 possible reasons why IBs should engage in digital transformation were listed in the survey questionnaire. Responses obtained from the IBs that participated in the survey indicate that all reasons stated are considered pertinent. In order to find out the relative importance of each of these stated reasons, a weighted mean analysis was conducted, and the outcome is depicted in Figure 1. The mean-weighted distribution of responses indicated results in an average of 1.51 for all 12 reasons stated therein.

Empirical assessment on Digital transformation in Islamic banking   **121**

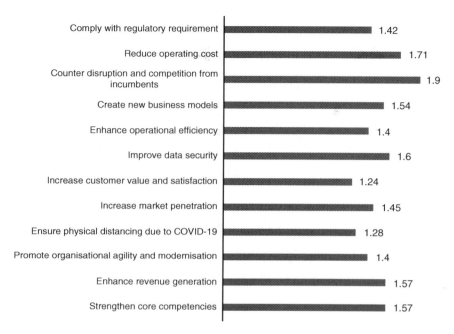

FIGURE 1   Reasons why IBs engage in digital transformation.

With a weighted mean score of 1.9, the IBs generally consider countering disruption by new entrants and competition from other incumbent IBs as a very pertinent justification for embarking on digital transformation. Both competition and competitors are changing, and IBs will need to respond accordingly. Competitive differentiation and contestability of the IBs will largely depend on to what extent they can digitalise their workplaces. This is crucial to enhance operational efficiency through optimal combination of both front-office and back-office technology, as well as to attract the right talents with the specific requisite human capital.

Competition and contestability are envisaged to further increase as new players come on board and regulators respond to finding a balance between encouraging innovation, protecting consumers, and ensuring financial stability (Vives, 2019). The responses obtained, therefore, may be more of a pre-emptive justification than contingent reaction to threat from both FinTechs and BigTechs. This is because, at the moment, both large and small IBs consider competition from the novel and technology-enabled business model of the new entrants as being moderate at most (General Council for Islamic Banks and Financial Institutions, 2019). This view is similar to the responses obtained in this current study. As shown in Figure 2, only 32% of the respondent IBs 'strongly agree' that competition from new entrants when considered in isolation, is a reason for their digitalisation process. The responding IBs also indicate the need to reduce

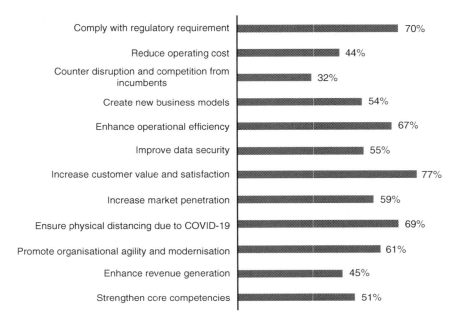

FIGURE 2 Proportion of IBs that 'Strongly Agree' with Reasons for Digitalisation.

operating costs with a weighted mean score of 1.71. It has become inevitable for IBs to replace legacy infrastructures to enhance their competitiveness during and post-COVID-19. As shown in Figure 2, 44% of the IBs 'strongly agree' that cost reduction is a reason to embark on digital transformation.

Customer satisfaction as an important reason for digitalisation recorded a weighted mean score of 1.24 as shown in Figure 1, with 77% of the respondent IBs also indicating that they 'strongly agree' with this view as shown in Figure 2. Customer satisfaction is a very important rationale for IBs' engaging in digital transformation in today's customer-centric financial market. The future outlook of the financial system revolves around the repository, availability, and access to accurate yet comprehensive digitalised data about a customer. Such data are expected to be processed in real-time based on algorithms to arrive at credit worthiness, insurance or investment preferences of customers.

Simplification of banking processes and added convenience via technology have resulted in customer satisfaction with positive implication for economic bottom line of banks. Changing customer demand particularly from increasing number of millennials that have grown up in a digitally connected world and do not have the same loyalty to banks is adduced as one of the factors driving the prominence of digitalisation. While some consumers, particularly corporates, remain loyal to banks, changing retail consumer expectations are exerting pressure on banks to adopt various forms of technology to improve their services. This has brought about value given that customers now have more access to hitherto restricted assets, more control on their choices, and more visibility in product development.

3.3 COVID-19 and digital transformation in IBs

The need to ensure physical distancing due to COVID-19 recorded a weighted mean score of 1.24 as shown in Figure 1. Arguably, the outbreak of COVID-19 and the consequential need for physical distancing and efficient disbursement of funds to the needy have amplified the indispensability of digitalisation of banking services. Figure 2 indicates that 69% of the respondent IBs 'strongly agree' that the pandemic is one of the important reasons for their digitalisation process.

As a strategy to reduce infection rate, contactless digital payments between persons as well as for purchases in stores have been greatly encouraged since the outbreak of the pandemic. Incentives to use digital payments have also been provided in some instances, especially in developing countries (Agur, Peria, & Rochon, 2020). The increased experience with online banking due to the restrictions on movement, especially during the first wave of the pandemic, does not favour the physical service delivery that bank branches are meant to provide.

Prior to the COVID-19 pandemic, 42% of the responding IBs did not implement the work from home (WFH). The pandemic has necessitated that 34% of the IBs implement a rotational WFH–work-from-office (WFO) policy in which case staff come to the office on alternate days of the week. Almost 20% apiece among the responding IBs indicate that they have implemented a blend of 25% WFH or 25% WFO policy depending on the stringency and duration of the lockdown in their respective jurisdictions. The IBs need to get used to this new normal of staff working from home by enhancing their teleworking and remote access capabilities without compromising on the integrity of their technology network.

In response to how effective the WFH policy has been, 42% of the respondent IBs stated that the nature of banking operations would require that some technical and administrative matters can only be conducted at the office. Although 19% stated that with the requisite supporting digital infrastructure, WFH can be applied for most types of activities, 32% noted that adopting WFH makes them more susceptible to cyber risk.

3.4 Status of Islamic banking digitalisation

Three questions were further asked to know the current state of digital transformation. These specifically relate to the proportion of digital operation, as well as proportion of the most recent budget spent on the digital transformation process respectively among the responding IBs. As shown in Figure 3, most IBs (77%) are at various stages of their digital transformation process, while only 3% are planning to commence, another 4% of the IBs are not having any related digital transformation plan at the moment. Of the remaining IBs, 13% indicate that

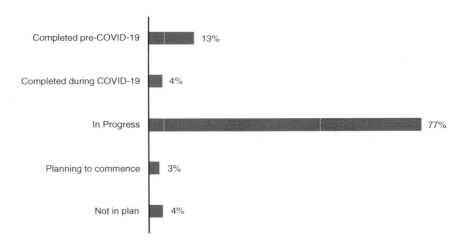

FIGURE 3 Status of IBs Implementation of Digital Transformation.

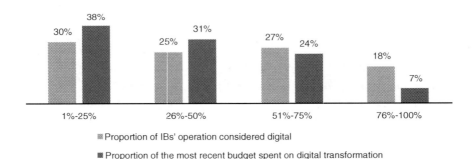

FIGURE 4 Proportion of IBs digital operation and most recent IT budget spent.

they have already completed necessary related processes prior to the outbreak of COVID-19. Only 4% completed their digital transformation process during the pandemic.

The specific status of IBs that indicate that their digital transformation process is in progress is unknown. However, the fact that a process is promising. This is because the swift change in technological advancement implies that the proliferation of disruptive financial technology and the rate of adoption by IBs will not only be unprecedented but also likely un-abating anytime soon.

As shown in Figure 4, the proportion of the digital operation of the IBs as well as the proportion of the most recent IT budget spent on digital transformation activities are classified into four. As indicated, while 30% of the IBs indicate that up to 25% of their operations are digitalised, 38% indicate that they spent up to 25% of their most recent IT budgets on digital transformation. For the 25% of the IBs whose proportion of digital operations is between 26% and 50%, their corresponding proportion of IT budget spent is 31%. In both classifications, the proportion of digital activities is greater than the proportion of IT budget spent.

Furthermore, while 27% of the IBs indicate that between 51% and 75% of their operations are digitalised, 24% indicate that they spent a similar proportion of their most recent IT budgets on digital transformation. Perhaps due to overhaul of legacy infrastructure, 7% of the IBs indicate that at least 76% of their operations are digitalised while 18% of their IT budget is spent on digital transformation. At such a relatively higher level of digital operation, it is likely that huge sums of money would have been spent on an outright overhaul of legacy infrastructures for information sharing among stakeholders as well as to strengthen cyber-security units with the requisite human talents, especially domain specialists.

4 Important issues in Islamic banking digitalisation

4.1 Technological advances adopted in digital transformation of IBs

Responses to the question on various technological advances being adopted by the IBs indicate that related digital banking activities are already taking place in the Islamic banking industry. As indicated in Figure 5, the three most adopted technologies are mobile and digital wallets (93%), API (91%) and biometric authentication (87%). The three least used technologies are robo-advisory (27%), distributed ledger technology and smart contract (26%), and IoT (23%).

Numerous IBs have introduced various mobile banking apps and digital wallets, which are among the most popularly deployed technologies – especially for deliveries and e-hailing services. Their usefulness especially for financial inclusion through payment services and financing is well noted in jurisdictions with a low penetration of bank accounts ownership but a high rate of access to mobile smartphones, especially among millennials.

Mobile wallets are also very useful for flattening the curve of the spread of COVID-19 because they allow users to make contactless payments based on a near-field communication (NFC) technology in which case a mobile device is held within a short distance from a point-of-sale terminal. This offers a lot of benefits to users including convenience of not needing to carry physical cards or remembering PINs. Another IB also introduced Chat Banking via the WhatsApp platform. This is to further enhance the experience and engagement of the patrons of its digital banking channels who will be able to perform a myriad of financial transactions in a secure and confidential manner over the platform.

API is also very much adopted by the IBs. This also reflects the increased use of APIs within the global financial ecosystem from 1 in 2005 to 17,000 in 2017 (Financial Stability Board, 2019). It connects software programmes and allows them to communicate based on programming code bringing about efficient and reliable interactions among computerised systems. APIs allow for secured data

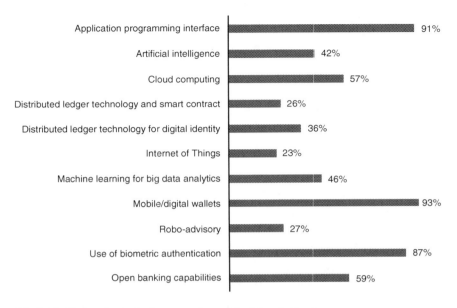

FIGURE 5   Technological advances adopted by Islamic Banks.

sharing and analytics among disparate systems and separate financial institutions especially in open banking applications (Dubai Islamic Economy Development Centre, 2019).

Nonetheless, if not properly secured, adopting APIs can lead to market structure fragility as well as trigger network instability with contagion effects in the event of a breakdown. APIs may also influence customer switching behaviour with a significant impact on deposits as a source of funding for financial institutions (World Bank, 2019).

The widespread use of biometric authentication by IBs as indicated by responses provided to the survey could be due to its benefits especially streamlining of authentication processes. It also provides additional security benefits through the use of a stable and unique biometric features, for instance fingerprints, voice, face, iris patterns or some other internal features recognition. Some jurisdictions also use biometric verification number which is unique to every bank customer regardless of the number of accounts operated with same or different banks within a jurisdiction. The use of this technology extends beyond biometric identification which answers the question of 'who are you?' because authentication requires a proof of who the user is prior to gaining access to a desired financial service.

Biometric authentication via smartphones with pre-installed fingerprint scanners has increased the use of this technology. Typically, it is used for limited services like checking account balance or transfer of a limited amount between pre-registered and verified accounts via mobile banking application.

This technology is less susceptible to theft, spoofing, and online phishing which are quite common with password authentication. In a scenario like that of the current COVID-19 pandemic, this technology could also help with remote customer on-boarding without infringing on the customer due diligence process. This may not only result in increased market penetration as indicated by 59% of the IBs as per Figure 2 but also reduced operating costs on call centres for password reset for instance.

Cloud computing has also been very much deployed especially for unbundling of services as well as for data sharing in open banking applications. More than half (57%) of the respondent IBs indicate that they adopt cloud technology. This perhaps reflects a gradual shift among IBs from an on-premises data service to a public cloud-based data service. The possibility of technology externalisation due to the proliferation of technology vendors and platforms that offer cloud services would significantly reduce IBs' infrastructure and human resource requirement costs. However, IBs may have to contend with providing financial services on platforms they neither own nor have control over. This may have implication for financial stability in the event of a breach or cyber-attack on the part of the cloud service provider.

The use of software applications, especially for payments and transaction services, is becoming fundamental to IBs' operations due to increasing contestability and competition. Robotics process automation, machine learning and AI technology are now pervasive. For instance, an IB, as part of its innovation and digital transformation process to enhance customer experience and convenience, unveiled its digital virtual employee called 'Dana'. Dana will digitally provide FinTech tips and insights as well as information on the Islamic bank's products and services (Wanbaba, 2019). IBs are expected to use these technologies more for repeatable transactional tasks, as well as predictive analytics based on big data, cloud computing and the IoT to better anticipate customer needs.

Based on the alignment of its operational principles with Sharia principles such as trust, transparency, traceability, fairness and equality, IBs have also applied blockchain technology in their various operations. Specifically, 36% of the respondent IBs as shown in Figure 5 indicate they apply this technology. When combined with AI and complemented with cloud computing, IBs operational resilience and regulatory compliance can be enhanced through facilitation of customer due diligence and prevention of fraud and irregularities. Although still at a very early stage, blockchain technology in Islamic finance is mainly in cryptocurrency which has attracted variety of rulings among Sharia scholars but seems to be gaining traction (Alam, Gupta, & Zameni, 2019). Some FinTech firms have obtained certification for the Sharia compliance of their digital currencies in their respective jurisdictions.

As indicated by 26% of the respondent IBs, blockchain technology is also increasingly being used for the operation of smart contracts in Islamic banking. In this case, programmable applications have been employed to self-verify and self-execute Sharia-compliant financial transactions. For instance, while appearing virtually to all network users, automatic change of ownership or adjustment to financial flow in a contractual transaction can be triggered due to the occurrence of specified events in the contractual clause (Zaina, Alib, Adewale, & Hamizah, 2019). Some IBs have also used blockchain in their cheque-based payment process as well as for *ṣukūk* issuance to authenticate transactions and mitigate potential for fraud.

With the support of multilateral organisations like the Islamic Corporation for the Development of the Private Sector, further options are still being explored by start-ups to deploy blockchain technology for Sharia-compliant liquidity management, interbank relations and commodity transactions. Other areas being explored include the use of smart contracts based on blockchain technology to automate the entire contractual process of institutions offering Islamic financial services (i-Fikr, 2019).

4.2 Types of technology on which IBs are currently investing

In addition, the IBs were asked to indicate which among the listed variants of technology they are presently investing in as part of their digital transformation process. As shown in Figure 6, the distribution also reflects that observed earlier in Figure 5. Most IBs, specifically, 82% currently expend on mobile application technology. This is followed by expenditure on biometric authentication techniques indicated by 68% as per Figure 6.

Regarding other technologies, 59% of the IBs are currently investing on security and privacy technologies, while 59% are also investing on NFC, QR codes and SMS technology (59%). Furthermore, 59% indicate they currently expend on business intelligence, data and analytics. This reflects the fact that even though customer convenience, preference and experience are being prioritised, it is not at the expense of data and privacy protection. Smart contract via blockchain technology currently receives relatively lower investment among IBs as indicated by 15%.

The cloud computing service model receiving the most investment is Software-as-a-Service as indicated by 27% of the respondent IBs. This perhaps may be due to its relatively lower costs, reduced time to benefit, scalability and integration, ease of use, and upgrades possibility (IBM, 2020). Infrastructure-as-a-Service (IaaS), which is considered the most relevant level of cloud service to financial institutions for processing core banking systems and storing critical data in the cloud is being invested on by 21% of the responding IBs (World Bank, 2019). IaaS allows the users to access cloud service on a pay-as-you-go basis. Apparently, in response to the new normal of staff working from home due to COVID-19, 34% of the responding IBs indicate they are also expending on requisite workforce enablement software towards enhancing their teleworking and remote access capabilities.

In response to the question on what aspects the IBs' digital transformation is most costly, 44% indicated it is on providing and investing in online platforms and security system. While 35% stated that investing on digital banking

Empirical assessment on Digital transformation in Islamic banking **129**

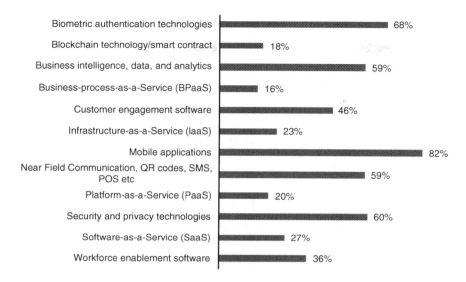

FIGURE 6 Technological advancement being currently expended on as part of IBs' digital transformation process.

infrastructure is the costliest, 11% indicated that it is the cost of maintaining existing digital system. Staff training is considered the least costly aspect of digital transformation as indicated by 11% of the IBs. This distribution also reflects the response of the IBs to the questions relating to the challenges to implementing digitalisation in which legacy infrastructure and lack of requisite human capital are considered among the top issues.

4.3 Prudential risks faced by IBs in their digitalisation process

Technological adoption has not only brought about new possibilities and enhancement to the operational efficiency of IBs but also potential risks. Responses obtained from the IBs that participated in the survey indicate that risks relating to cyber security, technology, third-party/outsourcing, and data integrity risks are on the front burner. The distribution of responses provided by the IBs is shown in Figure 7.

Cyber-security risk seems to be the main prudential risk facing the IBs in their digital Islamic operation. This risk is indicated by 76% of the IBs. The swift changes in technological advancement make the legacy infrastructure of many IBs highly susceptible to cyber risk. In fact, the CIBAFI Islamic Global Bankers' Survey 2019 ranked cyber risk as the number one risk facing IBs.

High susceptibility to cyber-security risk may also create reputational risk for an IBs' digital operation as highlighted by 41% of the respondents. Given the implications of cyber-risk occurrence for financial stability, the focus of IBs

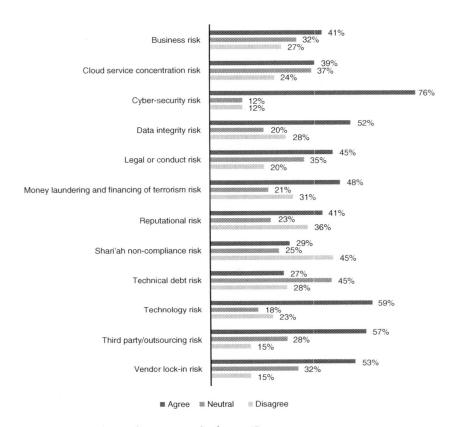

FIGURE 7 Digital transformation risks facing IBs.

should, therefore, transcend cyber-risk prevention. Such focus should also cover response, recovery and adaptation, given that such risks are difficult to pre-empt yet evolve and transform swiftly with no trace of perpetrators.

The FSB already notes the financial stability implications of such, especially in the event of a cyber-attack on or an operational failure of cloud services. In a case where quite a number of IBs rely on a few dominant cloud service suppliers, this may pose a systemic risk triggered by 'cloud-concentration' risk due to operational centrality of computing services (Harmon, 2019). This risk is also indicated by 39% of the respondent IBs. The effects of such failures on perceptions of data integrity may also have implications for public confidence in the technology thus creating reputational risk.

In terms of data security risk, the manifestation depends on the type of technology deployed. There could be issues arising from dependency on, for instance, mobile device manufacturers or third-party wallet. The proliferation of viruses and malwares as well as the danger of lost or stolen mobile devices could also heighten the risk of unauthorised payments (European Banking Authority, 2018). Reliance on third-party smartphone manufacturers and the pre-installed biometric authentication technology in the devices also means financial institutions have no direct control on a technology crucial to their operational efficiency. This exposes them to third-party risk which is indicated by 59% of the responding IBs. In addition to the fact that unlike password, a fingerprint cannot be changed if accessed without consent, a potential data security risk may result from residual attacks due to possibility of collecting fingerprints from various objects touched by a customer or even fingerprint sensors.

Vendor lock-in risk is indicated by 53% of the responding IBs as having prudential implication arising from digitalisation of their banking operations. This risk would arise where an IB is dependent on a particular service provider, for instance, for cloud services, and cannot switch to a different vendor without incurring significant costs, facing legal actions or suffering technical incompatibilities. This raises concerns for movement of data in and out from the cloud, data ownership and confidentiality and susceptibility to cyber breaches with implications for business operations. The intensity of the IBs to this risk would depend on the extent to which they retain flexibility to switch to other providers as and when required (Opara-Martins, Sahandi, & Tian, 2016).

Although 59% of the respondent IBs strongly agree that technology risks have prudential implications for the digitalisation of their banking operations, a lower percentage, 29%, indicate that technical debt is a concern. The former risk occurs when either unsuitable or outdated technology is deployed for the daily operations of the bank such as reconciliation of books of accounts. The latter occurs where avoidable additional costs would have to be incurred later by adopting and investing in a cheaper technology now as a short-term fix at the expense of more expensive, efficient, and effective alternative.

As indicated in Figure 7, almost half (48%) of the respondent IBs indicate they strongly agree that ML and FT risk might have prudential implication arising from digitalising their operations. This concern is not peculiar to the IBs given that perpetrating such crime is driven more by opportunity and convenience rather than by an institution or transaction follow Islamic banking. Nonetheless, the proliferation of innovative financial products and processes due to financial technology should not make IBs more susceptible to ML/FT activities in such a way that money launderers might use the sophisticated methods employed by financial institutions to launder illicit funds (Mamun, Adewale, Mwis, & Youssef, 2019).

From a prudential risk perspective, Sharia non-compliance risk could crystallise from the use of mobile wallets, for instance. This could also potentially impact the risk profile of an IB as indicated by 29%. Such risk could result from concerns that bother on the non-specificity of the contracts upon which such mobile wallets are offered as well as the modus operandi involved. Are funds in these wallets based on *qarḍ* or *wadī'ah*? Are the promised rewards which are based on luck and guaranteed in some instances, a form of *hibah* or returns? Can this be applicable if the funds placed in the wallets are based on *qarḍ*? Can the funds be based on equity-based contracts like *muḍārabah* and *mushārakah* given that the deposits are guaranteed? Prior to being used by depositors, are the wallet funds used for Sharia-compliant purposes by the digital wallet providers? These and related questions raise the needs for Sharia considerations in digital products and financial apps development in response to perceived 'Sharia neutrality' of technology and financial apps (Islamic Bankers Resource Centre, 2019).

5 Challenges and regulatory approaches

5.1 Challenges to digital transformation in IBs

IBs were also asked about factors that impede their digital transformation process. A list of such factors drawn from various publications was provided against options indicating the level of agreement or otherwise on a scale of ranging from 'strongly agree' to 'strongly disagree'. Responses obtained as shown in Figure 8 indicate that factors relating to legacy infrastructure, lack of open banking initiatives, budgeting constraint and lack of requisite human capital are front-burning. Issues relating to regulatory uncertainty and lack of top management support are among the least cited impediments to digital transformation process in IBs.

Based on responses obtained, 74% of the IBs indicated that legacy infrastructure and technologies impede their response to changing market dynamics and competition driven by technology. Perhaps, there are concerns for IBs relating to mitigating operational risks that may crystallise from using legacy technology infrastructure to cope with the rate and speed of technological transformation today. There will even be more pressure where the IBs still rely on obsolete legacy infrastructure, outdated applications, siloed data platforms, overextended branch network, disparate data sources and rigid internal operations and culture. Not only would these hinder the IBs' usage of the huge data at their disposal, but it also makes them highly susceptible to, for instance, cyber risks.

As shown in Figure 8, 57% of the IBs strongly agree that lack of the requisite human capital needed for digitalised banking like data analysts may be an impediment. Human capital development is a fundamentally important pillar for innovation to be successful. The digital transformation process requires highly specialised human capital and domain experts. For instance, as automation of most banking operation becomes the new norm, a new competency model would also become pertinent in the human capital strategy of the IBs.

Providers of digital Islamic financial services will, therefore, need to retrain and reskill existing talent even as they make efforts to attract new ones that fit the imminent digital workforce transformation of the banking workforce. This process may not be as straight-forward as presented for a number of reasons. For instance, attracting and recruiting the right talent may involve looking beyond the financial service industry or even beyond a particular jurisdiction. This is added to the fact that most of these potential talents are likely to be millennials whose expectations and preferences in terms of remuneration, work flexibility in

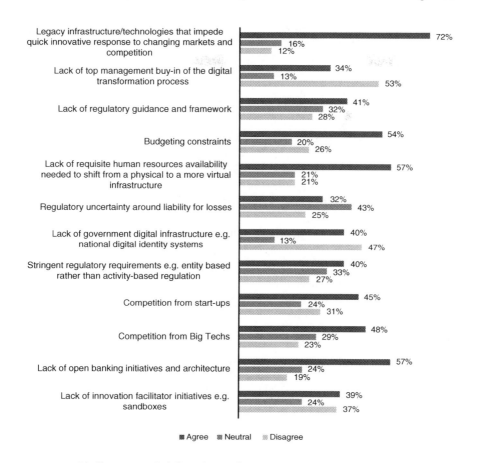

FIGURE 8 Challenges to IBs' digital transformation.

terms of location and time, as well as opportunities for development would suit competitors such as FinTechs and BigTechs better than the IBs.

Budgeting constraints are also indicated as an impediment to digitalising Islamic banking operations by 57% of the respondents. The need to replace legacy infrastructures to enhance their competitiveness co and post-COVID-19 will further strengthen the effect of budgeting constraint on implementing distal transformation. As shown in Figure 8, 70% of the responding IBs spend less than 50% of their most recent budget on IT, and 45% indicated more than 50% of their operation is digitalised. This may imply that IBs have hitherto not been spending much on technology but may have to do so now for so many reasons earlier stated. However, while these may yield favourable outcome in the future as IBs leverage on technology, it will put immediate pressure on their capital expenditure.

Lack of open banking initiatives and architecture is indicated by 57%, while lack of innovation facilitator initiatives such as regulatory sandboxes is indicated by 39% of the responding IBs. Although quite a number of the jurisdictions where Islamic banking is operated have provided such requisite infrastructure and initiatives, there are still challenges. For instance, regulatory sandboxes still need to thoroughly assess the relevance and benefit of their solutions to the domestic banking market. Similarly, IBs' resistance due to infrastructure setback and lack of technical standards have also impeded implementation of open banking in some jurisdictions. Such regulatory uncertainty and lack of regulatory guidance have been indicated by 32% and 34% of the respondent IBs respectively.

Competition from both start-ups and BigTechs has been indicated by 45% and 48% of the respondent IBs respectively as some of the digitalisation challenges confronting them. The effect of the BigTechs may be discerning especially if they chose to obtain digital Islamic banking license. FinTechs on the other hand are envisaged to continue to have an increasing influence on customers' experience and expectations. For now, such influence may not be severe due to various factors. These include regulatory barriers to entry, inertia to switch among many old customers, and the possibility of the incumbents using their financial capability to either replicate or absorb the FinTech firm outright.

Nonetheless, the FinTechs have expanded the scope of their services beyond digital payments and e-wallets. They now offer Sharia compliant P2P financing and equity crowd funding which are considered top growth sectors for the Islamic FinTechs in 2020 (Elipses and Salaam Gateway, 2019). This may exert pressure on the incumbent IBs' profitability and ability to weather future business cycles (Financial Stability Board, 2019).

5.2 Regulation of Islamic digital banking

Technological advancement also presents new regulatory and supervisory challenges for the financial sector regulators. Most jurisdictions where Islamic banking is operated have one form of regulation, policy document, rule-book etc. or the other that guides the application of these various technologies. As stated by most of the respondent IBs in response to a related question in the survey, most of these regulations are available on the websites of their respective RSAs.

About two-thirds (77%) of the IBs also responded that there are no specific or different digital banking regulations for IBs separate from the conventional banks. This is generally expected given that various forms of technology being applied are meant to aid delivery of Islamic banking products and services without infringing on the tenets of the applicable Sharia injunctions. It is the extra emphasis placed on this consideration that is adduced as the reason why the remaining 23% stated otherwise. IBs were asked to describe the regulatory approach prevalent in their jurisdiction vis-à-vis digital transformation process and developments. As shown in Figure 9, in most jurisdictions, there are various regulatory approaches that are adopted in this regard. Based on responses

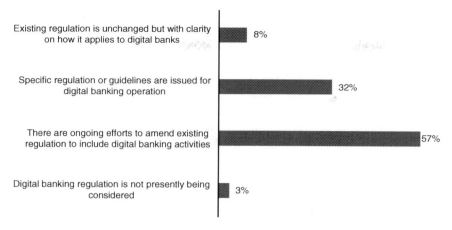

FIGURE 9 Regulatory approaches to digital transformation.

obtained, 8% of the IBs indicate that although existing regulation remains unchanged, further clarity has been provided on how such regulation applies to digital banking operation.

RSAs have been generally cautious about ensuring that a favourable disposition towards technological financial innovation does not infringe on financial market integrity and stability. In this regard, 32% of the respondent IBs indicate that specific digital banking regulations have been issued in their jurisdiction. Most respondent IBs, specifically 53% indicated that there are ongoing efforts to amend existing regulation in their jurisdiction to cater for the peculiarities of digital banking operations. The remaining 3% of the respondent IBs indicate that digital banking regulation is not presently being considered in their jurisdiction.

6 Implication of digitalisation in Islamic banking financial stability

Without prejudice to the numerous benefits that digital banking offers, it has resulted in increasing activities of the non-bank financial institutions, as well as increasing cyber-security risks among other operational issues (General Council for Islamic Banks and Financial Institutions, 2019). Technological adoption has brought about a new regulatory and supervisory challenge for the financial sector regulators as new risks are introduced – for instance, safeguarding data privacy, cyber-security, consumer protection, consumer financial health, compliance with anti-money laundering/combating the financing of terrorism (AML/CFT) regulations and so on. All these are some of the manifestations of the financial stability implications of digitalising banking operations.

In terms of financial stability implications of digitalisation of the operation of IBs, 78% of the IBs indicated that positive competition would be heightened due to the entrants of disruptors. This would reduce concentration in the

Islamic banking industry especially if there are regulatory guidance and requisite infrastructure that allows new entrants to leverage on technology to unbundle financial services as well as increase contestability.

Perhaps new entrants, in a bid to avoid regulation and compliance costs, would not opt to become licensed Islamic digital banks, so would not be able to venture into activities such as accepting deposits (Dubai Islamic Economy Development Centre, 2018). The fact that the new entrants do not perform liquidity transformation means that as per e-money regulations clients' funds at their disposal would have to be placed for instance as deposits in the IBs. This presents a competitive advantage to incumbent IBs due to the opportunity it provides for them to get stable and cost-efficient funding.

If properly executed, digital transformation holds opportunities for IBs to boost their revenues (The Malaysian Reserve, 2019). Nonetheless, the new entrants are envisaged to continue to have an increasing influence on customers' experience and expectations. This may exert pressure on the incumbent IBs' profitability especially in profitable lines like payments thus constraining their ability to weather future business cycles (Financial Stability Board, 2019). This view is agreed by 61% of the IB respondents that also state that in a bid to sail through, the incumbents may resort to increased risk taking to make up for the shortfall in margins.

In order to curb excessive risk taking at the individual bank level and systemic risks at a macro level, prudential requirements have often been imposed on incumbents. For instance, to complement the Basel III accords, there are equivalent IFSB standards on capital adequacy and liquidity requirements for IBs that have been implemented in numerous jurisdictions. However, by imposing prudential regulations, the impetus for shadow banking activities may increase, as has been observed in conventional banking. Shadow banks as financial service disruptors have been said to prosper in areas and activities where compliance with regulatory requirements has been considered a burden by traditional deposit-taking banks (Buchak, Matvos, Piskorski, & Seru, 2018).

Sixty-five per cent of the respondents supported the view that the regulatory challenge in balancing the objectives of facilitating innovation while ensuring financial stability inhibits the provision of a clear policy guideline. Moreover, a lack of, or unequal application of regulation on, for instance, prudential requirements may encourage regulatory arbitrage and higher risk taking by new-entrant disruptors. The inertia that inhibits provision of a clear policy guideline in this regard could also magnify the threat to financial stability. This view is supported by 88% of the respondent IBs.

The fact that these new entrants help to mobilise a substantial amount of funds, which they do not retain, may heighten their susceptibility to moral hazards and adverse selection due to information asymmetry. There are also arguments that the new entrants in a bid to increase financing volume to boost revenue may result in a lower-quality financing assessment process (Vives, 2019). This view is supported by 58% of the respondents' IBs.

In the medium to long term, however, these new entrants, and other non-bank players such as TechFins, are expected to be the pivot around which the changing landscape of the financial ecosystem including IFSI rotates. A widely held view is that the future of financial services will be shaped by how much control customers have over the data held about them by financial institutions and how much access third parties have to this data. In this case, Islamic FinTechs are also expected to accelerate their entry into prominence in the Islamic banking and financial ecosystems.

The gradual shift among financial institutions from an on-premises data service to a public-cloud-based data service makes subscribing to an external third-party cloud service provider inevitable. The potential is high for a systemic risk to be triggered by cloud concentration risk due to the operational centrality of computing services.

7 Conclusions and recommendations

7.1 Conclusion

Emerging technology is expected to further revolutionise the financial sector, enhance financial accessibility, convenience, and efficiency. The inevitability of the digital transformation process as a new normal in the banking industry has been strengthened by the movement restriction order and physical distancing instructions as measures to curb the spread of COVID-19. IBs that commenced their digital transformation process prior to the outbreak of COVID-19 may find it relatively easier than those that would have to react due to the inevitability of such transformation as a crucial co and post-COVID-19 economic recovery reality.

The adoption of innovative technologies and business models is a prominent emerging trend that is fast changing the ecosystem of the IFSI, and IBs are not immune to these developments. In order to enhance their competitiveness and contestability in the IFSI via operational efficiency and modernisation of their business model, IBs must leverage on technological innovation. However, this should be done without infringing on the fundamentals of the Sharia.

Both competitors and competition are changing and the IBs need to respond accordingly through technology. The rationale for IBs' digital transformation drive is informed by a plethora of reasons. This is mainly in response to the disruption of financial services rendering by new-entrant FinTech start-ups as well as competition from incumbent IBs. This would entail that the IBs leverage on technology to increase customer value and satisfaction, reduce operational cost, enhance revenue generation, strengthen core competences, and improve data security among other considerations.

The COVID-19 outbreak and the consequential movement restrictions and physical distancing as measures to flatten the curve of its spread have added to the need for digitalising financial services including those offered by the IIFS.

For instance, most of the IBs have also adopted the WFH policy which requires remote access and strengthening of the security of their technology network.

More than two-thirds of the IBs are at various stages of their digital transformation process. While the specific status of their implementation varies, it is promising to know that they have commenced. However, most of the IBs in this category are also those that expended less than 25% of their most recent budget on IT-related activities. For the few IBs that have commenced earlier and have completed implementation either pre or during the COVID-19 pandemic, they would have an edge in coping with the new normal of digital banking operations.

Mobile technology/digital wallets and the use of biometric authentication are the most adopted technologies by the IBs. Plausible reasons could be their usefulness especially for financial inclusion through payment services and financing especially during COVID-19. Moreover, both technologies can be applied via smartphones which are quite common among IBs' customers. These two technologies in addition to security and privacy technologies are those on which a larger chunk of IBs' IT budgets is expended.

APIs are also very common among the IBs due to their data sharing and analytics possibilities. Cloud computing has also been very much deployed especially for unbundling of services as well as for data sharing in open banking applications. The adoption of robo-advisory and blockchain technology for smart contract are, however, still in their very early stages of adoption. Cyber security is the main prudential risk facing IBs in their digital transformation activities. Also notable are technology risk, data integrity risk, third-party outsourcing risk and vendor lock-in risk. Although the IBs are faced with issues of legacy infrastructure, technical debt risk is not a front burner. Also, Sharia-compliant risk from digital Islamic banking operation is not considered a direct risk. However, susceptibility to such risk through, for instance, system error is duly noted.

In most jurisdictions where Islamic banking is practised, there are no specific or different digital Islamic banking regulations. However, most jurisdictions have issued one form of regulation, policy document, rule-book etc. or the other that guides the application of these various technologies. There are also ongoing efforts in most jurisdictions to amend their existing regulations in line with technological developments. The COVID-19 pandemic and the resulting lockdown revealed a lot of room for operational and supervisory improvements. For example, real-time monitoring of IBs is essential when a crisis unfolds rapidly. Digital tools could help in that respect. Similarly, supervision is to some extent still paper-based. This can be an issue for supervisors that are currently working remotely. The crisis has shown the need to set up systems so that future supervision can be carried out paperless.

Legacy infrastructure that impedes quick innovative response to changing market needs is the main impediment to IBs' digital transformation. Budgeting constraints as well as lack of human capital especially domain specialist may slow the pace of digital transformation of Islamic banking. It is important to note that in most jurisdictions, the government continues to provide requisite supports and infrastructures like technology hubs, national identity, and APIs which are crucial for open banking initiatives and architecture.

The digitalisation of the operations of IBs has implications for the financial stability of the IFSI. This is arising from how the incumbents respond to the digital transformation process and its consequential increased possibility for new disruptors to enter the market, thus heightening competition. Such response would also reflect on related issues such as cyber security, consumer protection, consumer financial health, compliance with AML/CFT regulations and so on.

7.2 Recommendations

Regulators in jurisdictions where Islamic banking is practised have and are continuing to roll out requisite policy guidance and framework, as well as promoting regulatory sandboxes etc. Nonetheless, as events unfold further consideration needs to be explored on how technological innovation can be pursued without adversely impacting financial stability and achieving support for financial inclusion and real-economic growth. It is essential to ensure that technology-led operations duly comply with Sharia governance requirements to ensure best practices while protecting consumer rights. An effective Sharia governance system for maintaining Sharia compliance is the core of the Islamic banking business that differentiates it from conventional banking regardless of the platform through which products and services are provided.

As new risks are introduced, safeguarding data privacy, cyber security, consumer protection, consumer financial health, compliance with AML/CFT and so on would require that regulations are up to speed. In order to strengthen regulatory oversight on financial technology, RSAs may consider monitoring the implications of third-party relationships that exist among various IBs and their FinTech partners, perhaps to mitigate against step-in risk that may arise outside of, but connected to, the Islamic banking industry (Vives, 2019).

RSAs need to be cognisant of the potential new risks that digital Islamic banking poses as they coordinate prudential regulation and competition policy. Developing a 'fit-for-purpose' regulatory and supervisory regime is imperative, notwithstanding the formidable challenge it presents in balancing the objectives of facilitating innovation while ensuring effective risk management, financial stability. In this regard, regulators are expected to increase the frequency of simulation exercises on emerging technology risks and to strengthen the focus on internal cyber-security activities by requesting data on cyber threats.

Human capital development is a fundamentally important pillar for innovation to be successful. The digital transformation process requires highly specialised human capital and domain experts. Therefore, providers of digital Islamic financial services will need to retrain and reskill existing talent even as they make efforts to attract new ones that fit the imminent digital workforce transformation of the digital banking workforce.

Note

1 Modification of the authors' working paper titled Financial Stability Implications of Operational and Regulatory Digital Transformation in Islamic Banking, published by IFSB.

References

Agur, I., Peria, S. M., & Rochon, C. (2020). *Digital Financial Services and the Pandemic: Opportunities and Risks for Emerging and Developing Economies.* International Monetary Fund. Retrieved from https://www.imf.org/~/media/Files/Publications/covid19-special-notes/en-special-series-on-covid-19-digital-financial-services-and-the-pandemic.ashx

Alam, N., Gupta, L., & Zameni, A. (2019). *Fintech and Islamic Finance.* Cham: Palgrave Macmillan. https://doi.org/10.1007/978-3-030-24666-2

Buchak, G., Matvos, G., Piskorski, T., & Seru, A. (2018). Fintech, Regulatory Arbitrage, and the Rise of Shadow Banks. *Journal of Financial Economics, 130*(3), 17–39.

Dubai Islamic Economy Development Centre. (2018). *Islamic Fintech Report 2018.* Dubai: Dubai Islamic Economy Development Centre.

Dubai Islamic Economy Development Centre. (2019). *State of the Global Islamic Economy Report 2018/2019.* Dubai: Dubai Islamic Economy Development Centre. Retrieved from https://islamicbankers.files.wordpress.com/2019/02/thomson-reuters-difc-state-of-the-islamic-economy-report-2018.pdf

Elipses and Salaam Gateway. (2019). *The Global Islamic Fintech Report 2019.* London: Elipses and Salaam Gateway. Retrieved from https://ceif.iba.edu.pk/pdf/IslamicFinTechReport19.pdf

European Banking Authority. (2018). *EBA Report on the Prudential Risks and Opportunities Arising for Institutions from Fintech.* London: European Banking Authority.

Financial Stability Board. (2019). *FinTech and Market Structure in Financial Services: Market Developments and Potential Financial Stability Implications.* Basel: Financial Stability Board. Retrieved from https://www.fsb.org/wp-content/uploads/P140219.pdf

General Council for Islamic Banks and Financial Institutions. (2019). *Global Islamic Bankers' Survey 2019.* Bahrain: General Council for Islamic Banks and Financial Institutions. Retrieved from https://cibafi.org/images/FI153-CI1809-GIBS%20 2019%20Report_English%20Summary_for%20printing.pdf

Harmon, R. L. (2019). *Cloud Concentration Risk: Will This be our Next Systematic Risk Event?* Atlanta, GA: Cloudera

IBM. (2020, September 18). *IBM Blog.* Retrieved from IBM Blog: https://www.ibm.com/cloud/blog/top-5-advantages-of-software-as-a-service

i-Fikr. (2019, January 2). *i-Fikr.* Retrieved from i-Fikr ISRA: https://ifikr.isra.my/news/post/blockchain-is-making-its-way-into-islamic-finance

Islamic Bankers Resource Centre. (2019, January 15). *Islamic Bankers Resource Centre.* Retrieved from E-Wallets: Did You Forget Us Again?: https://islamicbankers.me/2019/01/15/e-wallets-did-you-forget-us-again/

Mamun, M. S., Adewale, A. A., Mwis, G. A., & Youssef, N. (2019). *Joint IFSB–AMF Working Paper on Money Laundering and Financing of Terrorism (ML/FT) Risks in Islamic Banking*. Kuala Lumpur: IFSB–AMF. Retrieved from https://www.ifsb.org/download.php?id=5509&lang=English&pg=/index.php

Opara-Martins, J., Sahandi, R., & Tian, F. (2016). Critical Analysis of Vendor Lock-in and Its Impact on Cloud Computing Migration: A Business Perspective. *Journal of Cloud Computing: Advances, Systems and Applications, 5*(4), 1–18.

PWC. (2019). *Virtual Banking: Malaysian Customers Take Charge*. Kuala Lumpur: PWC. Retrieved from https://www.pwc.com/my/en/assets/workshops/2019/virtual-banking-malaysian-customers-take-charge-report.pdf

The Malaysian Reserve. (2019, 8 July). *Business*. Retrieved from Digitising to Drive Growth of Islamic Banks: https://themalaysianreserve.com/2019/07/08/digitising-to-drive-growth-of-islamic-banks/

Thomson Reuters and DinarStandard. (2019). *State of the Global Islamic Economy Report 2018/19*. Dubai: Thomson Reuters and DinarStandard. Retrieved from https://islamicbankers.files.wordpress.com/2019/02/thomson-reuters-difc-state-of-the-islamic-economy-report-2018.pdf

Vives, X. (2019). *Digital Disruption in Banking*. Barcelona: Annual Review Connects. https://doi.org/10.1146/annurev-financial-100719-

Wanbaba. (2019, May 28). *Wanbaba Blog*. Retrieved from Wanbaba Blog: https://wanbabablog.com/2019/05/28/bahrain-islamic-bank-unveils-its-first-virtual-employee/

World Bank. (2019). *Prudential Regulatory and Supervisory Practices for Fintech: Payments, Credit and Deposits*. Washington: World Bank. Retrieved from https://documents1.worldbank.org/curated/en/954851578602363164/pdf/Prudential-Regulatory-and-Supervisory-Practices-for-Fintech-Payments-Credit-and-Deposits.pdf

Zaina, N. R., Alib, E. R., Adewale, A., & Hamizah, A. (2019). Smart Contract in Blockchain: An Exploration of Legal Framework in Malaysia. *Intellectual Discourse, 27*(2), 595–618.

7
FINTECH IN ISLAMIC BANKING IN BANGLADESH

Opportunities and threats

Md. Joynal Abedin, Syed Mahbubur Rahman and Riyashad Ahmed

1 Introduction

Fintech is about using a wide array of technologies to ensure the smooth delivery of financial services (Arner et al., 2018). It is considered as one of the most promising sectors in view of the solutions it extends to the financial systems (Chishti and Barberis, 2016). While Fintech in the traditional interest-based banking application has attracted substantial number of researchers across the world, specialized mode of financing like Shariah-based Islamic banking has yet to draw attention of the researchers, particularly from the developing South, targeting Fintech. A substantiated recent review revealed a negligible concentration of Fintech's association with Islamic banking (Tarique and Ahmed, 2021), which urges for further inquiry about the implementation of Fintech from Islamic banking perspective.

Fintech has been growing. It has been argued that the use of Fintech is likely to assist Islamic banks in serving their customers, eventually resulting in higher market share (Todorof, 2018). For instance, Indonesians are more fascinated to invest in Fintech peer-to-peer lending (Dewi, 2018); and the contribution of Fintech was £7 billion with around 60,000 employments in Britain's economy in 2017 (Williams-Grut, 2017). The most active Fintech countries globally are the USA, the UK, and Israel, while Singapore, Australia, and China are from the other side (Findexable, 2021). The global Fintech contribution in 2020 was $105 billion, in which the contribution of the USA was $76 billion, Europe, Middle East, and Africa (EMEA) region's contribution was $14.4 billion, and the Asia-Pacific region's contribution was $11.6 billion (KPMG, 2020). In contrast, the market size of Islamic Fintech was $49 billion in 2020, and it is expected to grow at 21% compound annual growth rate to $128 billion by 2025 (Ahmed et al., 2021).

Considering the unavailability of market information related to Fintech, it may be argued that the presence of Fintech particularly in Islamic banking is substantially low. The use of technology is growing rapidly, mainly in the banking industry in Bangladesh. Although Fintech is still in its primary stage, the Islami Bank Bangladesh Limited, the first of its kind, has already announced that it will use Islamic Fintech in all its operations in the near future, which will serve as a new milestone for the growth of the Islamic finance in Bangladesh. Al Arafah Islami Bank recently introduced its mobile application "Islamic Wallet" but has not yet been able to reach many customers. Some other banks have recently restructured from conventional banking to full-fledged Islamic banking, for instance, National Bank Limited. It has been observed that only a limited number of Islamic banks are more concerned with the application of Fintech. In this backdrop, this research aims to investigate the opportunities and threats Islamic banks in Bangladesh may face in embracing Fintech in their operations.

There is a dearth of literature about Fintech in Islamic banking system in Bangladesh. Besides, previous and very recent literature about Fintech in Bangladesh has conducted some quantitative analyses based on survey conducted among a specific group of users or consumers, for instance, mobile phone users (Ayoungman et al., 2021). Few of the studies are based on surveys of executives from the financial sectors (Islam et al., 2021a, 2021b). In contrast, this research has taken a qualitative stand keeping both regulator and regulatee in the sample of respondents. This chapter contributed to the existing literature in two ways. First, it combines the responses of both regulator and regulatees, which has not been observed in previous studies. Second, instead of focusing on a particular tool, like mobile applications or mobile app-based limited financial transactions, this research discusses Fintech in a wider context.

2 Literature review

Islamic finance is based on the concepts of Islamic Shariah and public interest. Compared with the traditional financial system, Islamic finance must comply with the principles of sharia law that promote competition and sustainability. It must also comply with sharia law to avoid prohibited issues such as interest, gambling, speculation, and ambiguity. In Islamic banks, interest on traditional loans is altered into financial income through risk as well as profit and loss sharing between the bank and its trading partners. Start-up business and business with innovative ideas require factors of production to climb the ladder, and one of the key rudimentary factors is capital (Gompers and Lerner, 2004). Najaf et al. (2021) demonstrated that the appropriate nexus between banking financial institutions and Fintech can be beneficial and sustainable when they work together to mitigate excessive underlying cybersecurity risks.

Darussalam et al. (2019) investigated consumer perception about the impact of Fintech on Islamic banking system of Indonesia, which is poor in infrastructure.

However, it is anticipated that Fintech would facilitate the financial inclusion of the underprivileged Muslims around the world (Tarique and Ahmed, 2021; Todorof, 2018). Besides, in the Fintech era, digitalization offers various accessibilities in conducting financial transactions efficiently (Tarique and Ahmed, 2021).

According to Murinde et al. (2022), banking is changing because of the various financial crunches and Fintech is playing a significant role in this transformation of banking financial institutions. They also revealed that Fintech lenders are unlikely to replace banks, perhaps banks are uninterruptedly developing their own Fintech platforms or collaborating with Fintech startups. Fintechs have extensively increased competitive pressure through uninterrupted communication with consumers. The battle for "customer ownership" will be fierce, as in most industries the links in the value chain closest to the customer generate the highest margins. (Petralia, 2019). The current regulatory dilemma is to create a balance between maximizing the benefits of Fintech innovation and protecting the financial system and clients from the possible rudimentary uncertainties that these revolutions convey (Appaya and Gradstein, 2020).

Fintech innovations are causing economically significant changes in the production of financial services with implications for industrial finance structure. Improvements in connectivity and data processing can help improve efficiency and competition. In many cases, financial services have experienced an unbundling of different products and services. At the same time, the financial frictions and forces that drove the need for financial intermediaries in the first place have increased again (Feyen et al. 2021).

Recent research about Islamic banking in Bangladesh has concentrated on the evaluation and assessment of financial performance (Akter et al., 2021), comparing performance with the conventional banks (Ullah et al., 2021), risk disclosure in comparison to conventional banks (Nahar et al., 2021), corporate social responsibility (Bhuiyan et al., 2022; Islam et al., 2021a, 2021b), and roles and responsibilities of the Shariah Board (Alam et al., 2021; Islam et al., 2021a, 2021b). Many operations and impacts of both conventional and Islamic banking systems have attracted numerous researchers across the globe, Fintech, particularly in Islamic banking, focusing on Bangladesh is an underexplored area of research. However, recent studies about Fintech in Bangladesh have elaborated the role of Fintech during COVID (Ahmed et al., 2022), factors impacting the adoption of Fintech in finance and investment companies (Islam et al., 2021a, 2021b), users' perspective in adopting Fintech (Ayoungman et al., 2021; Chowdhury and Hussain, 2022; Hasan, 2021), and problems and opportunities of Fintech (Taher and Tsuji, 2022). Among the studies, a wider discussion about situation analysis and opportunities is prevalent.

Rahman et al. (2021), based on quantitative analysis, have identified that Fintech has been growing with a significant opportunity for further growth in Bangladesh local market and has the potential to impact the financial sector. However, the study also identified some barriers toward the growth of Fintech.

The authors have also found that website-based growth is more likely in future compared to that with mobile application. Blockchain has been identified as the most popular emerging technology followed by biometric authentication and artificial intelligence. Among the sectors, banking is more likely to enjoy automation, followed by securities and among the banking activities, consumer banking (Rahman et al., 2021). At the same time, Islam et al. (2021a, 2021b) have also found the factors of Fintech adoption in Bangladesh market, which are ease of convenient task accomplishment, knowledge about how to operate, frequency of use, and adaptability. Accordingly, Chowdhury and Hussain (2022) have suggested that government and Fintech service providers should initiate knowledge and awareness-raising programs for low-income and less-education customer segments for higher adoption of Fintech.

Ayoungman et al. (2021) surveyed among mobile users in Bangladesh and come to conclusion that perceived trust, usefulness, compatibility, cost efficiency, risk, and attitude impacts the use of Fintech among consumers. Ahmed et al. (2022) added another dimension on Fintech research with respect to Bangladesh, the gender issue. The authors investigated the Fintech situation during COVID in three different communities. The study found gap between digitally disconnected communities, which is rational, and suggested some measures for inclusive Fintech implications in the Bangladesh market.

3 The Bangladesh context

Bangladesh celebrated the 50th anniversary of its independence in the year 2021. After the birth in 1971, Henry Kissinger, the then US national security advisor, derisively affirmed the country as a "basket case." Despite the awful beliefs and several natural disasters, Bangladesh has in fact made a huge evolution in decreasing poverty and in stimulating economic growth. The country's economy raised by an average of 6.9% from 2011 to 2019 and in the face of COVID-19 pandemic grew by an approximate 5.2% in the year 2020. The country secured lower middle-income grade in 2015 and congregated the United Nations entitlement principles to proceed from the least developed country position in March 2018 with validation to be operative in 2026. Bangladesh has made great strides in economic growth, with its gross domestic product (GDP) increasing from $5.7 billion in 1972 to $329.12 billion in 2020 (World Bank national accounts data). International Monetary Fund, in its World Economic Outlook, April 2021 has ranked Bangladesh the 41st largest economy in the world in terms of GDP (nominal) and ranked 31st in terms of GDP (PPP) based on the data of 2020. Readymade garment industry plays a vital role in both export volume and employment. In 2020, remittances sent by Bangladeshi expatriates totaled $21.75 billion, a rise of 18.40% from the year 2019, which also forms a strong pillar of the country's economy (KNOMAD, 2021). At the end of June 2021, the foreign exchange reserves stood at $46.39 billion. Bangladesh is among the top 20 foreign direct investment (FDI) recipients (UNCTAD, 2017), a record

$2.65 billion of FDI inflow was observed in 2019. The real per capita income stands at $1,968.79 in 2020.

To survive in the era of globalization, a nation needs to focus on information technology (IT). Without the development of IT, it is almost impossible to keep up with the pace of today's world. Digital Bangladesh, although a political motivation, is the first initiative in building a science-based country. Digitization of public services is the fundamental goal of digital Bangladesh initiative. Prominent digital services employed and currently at hand are e-banking, e-book, e-commerce, e-education, e-filing, e-health service, e-mutation, e-paper e-voting, online registration, online income tax return, online public exam result, and transportation tickets. An e-book platform was launched to spread the light of education. To strengthen the IT sector, the country's first high-tech park was built on an area of 202 acres in Gazipur. Internet services are becoming more accessible today with the addition of submarine cables. Currently, more than 101.20 million people are using internet (Digital Bangladesh, Vision 2021). Union digital center has been set up in each union, the smallest rural administrative units in Bangladesh, to ensure online government services. During COVID-19 pandemic, Bangladesh government has distributed Bangladesh taka (BDT) 2,500 each to five million helpless families through mobile banking. More than one million readymade garments workers have been receiving their wages through mobile banking. There has been a revolution in banking services, and now people can conduct their banking services online. Mobile banking like bKash, Nagad, and Rocket has made people's life easy. This has prevented people from exposing themselves to contamination from the deadly coronavirus. The growth in internet access has contributed to a significant increase in the number of mobile phone subscribers. Currently, 171,854 million people are using mobile phones in the country (Bangladesh Telecommunication Regulatory Commission (BTRC) report end of January 2021). The growth of transactions of e-commerce is much higher than before, especially during COVID-19.

The position of Islamic banks in Bangladesh is stronger than before, because one third of all banking activities are conducted through Islamic banks, which accounts for 25.04% of total deposits, circulates 24.93% of total investments, and holds 27.20% of total remittances (IFN Annual Guide-2021). Despite COVID-19 pandemic, Islami Bank Bangladesh Limited recorded a milestone of $11.54 billion in deposits during the year 2020, for the first time in the history of commercial banks in Bangladesh (IFN, 2021). By the end of December 2020, eight full-fledged Islamic banks operated with 1,311 branches. In addition, 19 Islamic banking branches of nine conventional banks and 198 Islamic banking windows of 14 conventional banks are also serving Islamic financial services. The number of Islamic banking branches including Islamic branches/windows of conventional banks reached at 1,528 at the end of December 2020 which was 1,380 in 2019. Total employment in the Islamic banking sector stood at 38,784 as of December 2020 which was 35,906 in 2019 (Bangladesh Bank, 2020). At the end of Decembe 2020, total deposits of Islamic banking reached BDT 3,269 billion, which increased by 16.66% and total investment stood at BDT 2,941 billion, which went up by 8.09% compared to December 2019. Surplus liquidity of Islamic banking stood at BDT 293 billion in December 2020. Total remittances mobilized through Islamic banking stood at BDT 214 billion during October–December 2020. Islamic banks have accounted for 40.51% share of remittances mobilized by the entire banking industry during the last quarter of 2020 (Bangladesh Bank, 2020).

4 Research method

4.1 Research design and respondents

As an underexplored area of research, particularly in the context of Bangladesh, this research is drawn on a qualitative approach including in-depth interviews of the key informants from the Islamic banking sector and Bangladesh Bank, the central bank. Qualitative approach has been implemented for identifying Fintech's opportunity for instance by Darussalam et al. (2019). Trotter (2012) suggested a range of 15–25 informants for survey; hence, this research is drawn on 22 interviews of professionals working in the banking sector including the regulator and the regulatee. The respondents were selected using snowball sampling, since specialized knowledge about Fintech was required. Table 1 provides the profile of the respondents.

Respondents from the Bangladesh Bank are engaged in various capacities in different departments. Few of them have PhD in economics or related fields. One of them was a PhD candidate during the interview. One former Governor of Bangladesh Bank was also interviewed. It is to note that, although the Governor has retired, for this study, we considered the Governor as a respondent from the regulator side. The employees from various Islamic banks were found to have a postgraduate degree with more than six years of experience in various departments and branches.

Due to the COVID situation, interviews were conducted online. Most of the interviewees declined to let the interviewer record the session, while very few agreed for a recorded session. Sufficient notes were taken during interviewees. The duration of the interviews ranges from around 40 minutes to more than 60 minutes. Since the information generation saturated during the 19th interview, three more interviews were conducted to assess the quality of information.

TABLE 1 Profile of the respondents

Status	Mid-level	Top management	Total
Regulator	3	4	7
Regulatee	12	3	15
Total	15	7	22

4.2 Analysis

Thematic content analysis was implemented to evaluate the data. After the interviewees, the research team carefully coded the information from the notes taken during the interview. Data were read and systematically analyzed by the investigators to identify the themes related to the research objectives (Creswell and Creswell, 2017). The responses have been analyzed in terms of awareness about Fintech, expertise and ability to promote Fintech, pressure from the central bank and market, opportunities, and challenges.

5 Results and discussions

5.1 Awareness about Fintech

Respondents were found aware of the Fintech services Islamic banking sector provides, while one respondent with research background raised concern about the vague definition of Fintech. The respondent explained,

> Fintech does not have a universally accepted definition yet, making it difficult to explain the level of understanding.
>
> *(Translated from Bengali)*

The awareness about overall Fintech, however, was confined to mobile banking services provided by many banking and non-banking (non)financial institutions. Among them, commonly uttered names were Rocket, bKash, M-cash, and Upay which allow consumers to access various banking services in limited form 24×7. Internet banking and SMS banking were also mentioned, along with the ATMs instant cash deposit services. Informed about Fintech, respondents also mentioned the necessity of adopting the application of artificial intelligence, cloud computing, crowdfunding for funding a project or venture, blockchain, and robo-advice in their services. A handful number of respondents answered to operate technologies such as Real-Time Gross Settlement, Bangladesh Electronic Funds Transfer Network, Electronic Funds Transfer, and the Society for Worldwide Interbank Financial Telecommunication to make the banking experience prompt and customer-friendly. A few banks provide POS services, Bangladesh Automated Clearing House services, cash recycling machines, QR code transactions, Core banking software, and automated batch processing software to make the daily life of a customer easier. Coming to the technologies yet to be adopted, a more significant number of respondents shared that the specialized Islamic banking software in service is not adequate to fulfil a variety of customer demand. It was sensed from discussions that the Shariah-based banks were lagging behind compared to the conventional banks in terms of availability and application of Fintech in day-to-day operation.

The finding of this research is well-aligned with the previous studies conducted by Islam et al. (2021a, 2021b) and Chowdhury and Hussain (2022), in which the authors identified lack of awareness among mass people and hence suggested Fintech awareness training programs. Ahmed et al. (2022) also found a knowledge gap between digitally connected and not-connected communities. Connectivity may also be a reason for low awareness.

5.2 Capability of Islamic banks in bringing and promoting Fintech

This study was done to figure out the organization's ability to bring or promote Fintech to the customers. It was found that a considerable portion of the existing staff are unaware of Fintech innovations in the global market. This phenomenon was more experienced with the senior employees, while comparatively younger staff are more aware of the latest technologies available elsewhere. Since senior managers are less informed about the latest technologies, it remains a barrier in bringing innovative tools in the service or promoting it to the customers. The lack in technical expertise has also been identified by the respondents in promoting new Fintech to local market. One respondent explained,

> The employees who have been working in remote or rural branches for substantially longer time, they are less aware of latest technologies, while employees in branches located in big cities or head office are more informed.
> *(Translated from Bengali)*

When such employees are promoted to higher positions and posted at head office or given responsibilities for any specific units, they remain less capable to plan or suggest for innovations including launching new Fintech. To overcome this limitation, continual training and development has been suggested to make them understand the technology. Although Islamic banks in Bangladesh enjoy a comparable IT infrastructure as installed in the conventional banks, in terms of availability of services based on technology and individual skill and expertise, Islamic banks are little behind.

In line with our study, Darussalam et al. (2019) have also observed poor infrastructure in Indonesian context; however, it is claimed that Fintech has the potential to improve Islamic banking services. Besides, digital connectivity as suggested by Ahmed et al. (2022) has also been a factor for the promotion of Fintech in Islamic banks in Bangladesh.

5.3 External pressure in innovating and launching Fintech in Islamic banks

This study was done to recognize the pressures from market and the central bank in developing tools using Fintech. The majority of the respondents disagreed with having pressure from the central bank in developing Fintech tools. Instead, they agreed to get full support from the central bank in adopting the technologies. However, Islamic banks experience market pressure from the informed customers. A substantial part of the respondents refers to having intensive pressure from the customers' side for adapting continuous change in the services. Though the market leaders have already started artificial intelligence, blockchain, and cloud computing to provide efficient financial services, the customers are asking for faster innovation. They are asking for full-fledged mobile banking and more web-based services and demanding to outnumber the ATMs. It provides massive pressure to the banks that the customer may leave if they fail. In several instances, respondents mentioned about intense competition in adapting the innovative tools because every player in this sector is stepping into innovation and becoming more focused on serving the customers. In that case, if any of the providers adopt one, the others face immense pressure from their customers to adapt the service right away, and if the institution fails to do so, it may be dropped from the race instantly. This happens for the big cities only. Customers of the urban branches are better informed about Fintech, and they raise the issues with the executives working in urban branches. Besides, customers compare other banks, including both conventional and Islamic, with the host bank about newer technologies available. Hence, the pressure in innovating Fintech come more from the customer and competitors than the central bank. The central bank encourages the banks to implement Fintech and supports them full-fledged to this journey. Some discrete issues like real-time payment settlement have been identified by few. Therefore, this research has added one more dimension as identified by Ayoungman et al. (2021) which includes trust, usefulness, compatibility, cost efficiency, risk, and attitude, for the adoption of Fintech.

5.4 Fintech opportunities for Islamic banks in Bangladesh

Most of the respondents suggested for acquisition of more young employees and young customers. As the world evolves toward technology, the young generation may find it very handy and show their interest in this. It could help Islamic banks to provide services more smoothly than the previously applied one, which can eventually make their work more effective, saving time, and at the same time it can lower the costs as well. The study found that the use of Fintech will help Islamic banks to provide better service and thus increase market share. Adapting technology can drastically minimize operational costs as it will lower the number of employees. Thereby, by cutting down the costs and time, banks can maximize the profit significantly. All respondents agreed that many non-resident Bangladeshi customers would be acquired if Fintech was adapted to the banking system. The finding of this research also supports the arguments made by Taher and Tsuji (2022) about the opportunities of Fintech.

5.5 Challenges for innovating and implementing Fintech in Islamic banks

The majority of the respondents mentioned about less workforce with sound knowledge as the primary challenge. A small number of people refer to security issues as there is always a cyber-security risk as it takes place now and then. Without having competency about this can lead them to a massive loss. In line with our study, despite the concern about cybercrime, Tarique and Ahmed (2021) have predicted newer wings of opportunities through the use of Fintech. In our study, few of the responses raised not having any specific guidelines toward this from the Islamic banking to adapt the technology. A handful of people bring up the issue of whether it will be sustainable or not for the customers or not having any prior experience, and software efficacy is one of the fundamental reasons behind it. In a few instances, it is raised that it requires a handsome amount of budget to achieve this change, and even after implementing it, it requires a vast amount of cost to train and develop the human resources. Ultimately, the top management is found to be not interested about this, and the reason behind this might be the insufficiency in knowledge about the change as they are used to the core banking system or the fear of losing their job in case the adjustment fails. Respondents also stated to include two or more IT personnel in decision-making team. It will help and guide the top management to implement appropriate technology in their organization and hence maximize the profit.

6 Conclusion

Artificial intelligence, Robo services, Blockchain, and other latest financial technologies have gradually found some space in the Islamic banking industry, though it is not up to the mark in Bangladesh. With ever-changing technology and pace of globalization, Islamic banks around the world and particularly in Bangladesh have to focus on Fintech to ensure sustainable business. This study investigated the current status of Fintech in Islamic banks in Bangladesh as well as the opportunities and threats. This research was drawn on in-depth interviews of employees with adequate experiences in IT working in Bangladesh. The study also found that Fintech has potential influences on the brighter future of Islamic banking in Bangladesh. Through our interactive conversations with bankers, we also found that Fintech can minimize operation costs, target more young customers, compete with international banks, and eliminate unnecessary intermediaries from its operations in Islamic banking sector in Bangladesh. Apart from these findings our study also found some challenges and threats for implementing Fintech in Islamic banking industry due to insufficient budgets, skilled workforce, and appropriate IT people in decision-making. There are massive opportunities for researchers for further studies in implementing Fintech in Islamic banking sector, especially in the field of AI, Blockchain, and Cloud Computing.

References

Ahmed T., Basit, A. H., Shikoh, R. (2021). *Global Fintech Report 2021.* New York, Dubai, DinarStandard.

Ahmed, N., Rony, R. J., Khan, S. S., Ahmed, M. D., Sinha, A., Saha, A., ... & Sarcar, S. (2022). Resilience during COVID Pandemic: Role of Fintech in the Perspective of Bangladesh. http://doi.org/10.2139/ssrn.4009497

Akter, S., Rahman, M. M., Subat, A., & Rahman, M. R. (2021). Assessing the Performance of Selected Islamic Banks: Evidence from Bangladesh. *International Business Education Journal*, *14*(2), 101–123.

Alam, M. K., Ab Rahman, S., Tabash, M. I., Thakur, O. A., & Hosen, S. (2021). Shariah Supervisory Boards of Islamic Banks in Bangladesh: Expected Duties and Performed Roles and Functions. *Journal of Islamic Accounting and Business Research*, *12*(2), 258–275.

Appaya, M. S., & Gradstein, H. L. (2020). How Regulators Respond to Fintech: Evaluating the Different Approaches–Sandboxes and Beyond. In *FinTech Note* (No. 4). Washington, DC, The World Bank.

Arner, D. W., Barberis, J., & Buckley, R. P. (2018). RegTech: Building a Better Financial System. In *Handbook of Blockchain, Digital Finance, and Inclusion* (Vol. 1, pp. 359–373). New York, Academic Press.

Ayoungman, F. Z., Chowdhury, N. H., Hussain, N., & Tanchangya, P. (2021). User Attitude and Intentions Towards FinTech in Bangladesh. *International Journal of Asian Business and Information Management (IJABIM)*, *12*(3), 1–19.

Banglaesh Bank. (2020). Development of Islamic Banking in Bangladesh, Islamic Banking Cell. Dhaka.

Bhuiyan, M. A. H., Darda, M. A., & Hossain, M. B. (2022). Corporate Social Responsibility (CSR) Practices in Islamic Banks of Bangladesh. *Social Responsibility Journal*, *18*(5), 968–983.

Chishti, S., & Barberis, J. (2016). *The Fintech Book: The Financial Technology Handbook for Investors, Entrepreneurs and Visionaries*. West Sussex, John Wiley & Sons.

Chowdhury, N. H., & Hussain, N. (2022). Using Technology Acceptance Model for Acceptance of FinTech in Bangladesh. *International Journal of Internet Technology and Secured Transactions*, *12*(3), 250–264.

Creswell, J. W., & Creswell, J. D. (2017). *Research Design: Qualitative, Quantitative, and Mixed Methods Approaches*. Thousand Oaks, CA, Sage Publications.

Darussalam, A. Z., Tutuko, B., Dahlan, A., Hudaifah, A., & Tajang, A. D. (2019). Islamic Financial Technology towards the Advancement of Islamic Banking in Indonesia. *Nisbah: Jurnal Perbankan Syariah*, *4*(2), 171–181.

Dewi, T. R. (2018). The Paradoxical Case Against Interest Rate Caps for Microfinance—And: How Fintech and RegTech Resolve The Dilemma. University of Luxembourg Law Research Paper Series 2018-003, Luxembourg.

Feyen, E., Frost, J., Gambacorta, L., Natarajan, H., & Saal, M. (2021). Fintech and the Digital Transformation of Financial Services: Implications for Market Structure and Public Policy. In *BIS Papers. No 117*.

Findexable. (2021). Global Fintech Index 2021. London, Findexable.

Gompers, P. A., & Lerner, J. (2004). *The Venture Capital Cycle*. Cambridge: MIT Press.

Hasan, R. (2021). Factors Affecting Adoption of Fintech in Bangladesh. *International Journal of Science and Business*, *5*(9), 156–164.

Islam, K. M., Sadekin, M. S., Rahman, M., Chowdhury, M., & Haque, A. (2021a). The Impact of Shariah Supervisory Board and Shariah Audit Committee on CSR Adoption at Islamic Banks. *Journal of Asian Finance, Economics and Business (JAFEB)*, *8*(3), 479–485.

Islam, N., Mubassira, Q. N., Huda, R. B., & Fuad, M. A. (2021b). Adoption of FinTech by Financial and Investment Companies of Bangladesh. In *16th South Asian Management Forum 2021*, 16–18 December, Dhaka, Bangladesh.

KNOMAD. (2021). Regional trends in Migration and Remittance Flows. *Migration and Development Brief 34*, https://www.knomad.org/publication/migration-and-development-brief-34

KPMG. (2020). *Pulse of Fintech H2'20*, KPMG International, https://home.kpmg/xx/en/home/insights/2021/02/pulse-of-fintech-h2-20-global.html

Murinde, V., Rizopoulos, E., & Zachariadis, M. (2022). The Impact of the FinTech Revolution on the Future of Banking: Opportunities and Risks. *International Review of Financial Analysis*, 81, 102103.

Nahar, S., Azim, M. I., Islam, M. N., & Bepari, M. K. (2021). Corporate Risk Disclosure: A Conventional and Islamic Bank Perspective. *Accountancy Business and the Public Interest*, 184–213.

Najaf, K., Mostafiz, M. I., & Najaf, R. (2021). Fintech Firms and Banks Sustainability: Why Cybersecurity Risk Matters? *International Journal of Financial Engineering*, 8(02), 2150019. https://doi.org/10.1142/S2424786321500195

Petralia, K., Philippon, T., Rice, T., & Veron, N. (2019). Banking Disrupted? Financial Intermediation in an Era of Transformational Technology. *Geneva Reports on the World Economy*, 22.

Rahman, B., Ahmed, O., & Shakil, S. (2021). Fintech in Bangladesh: Ecosystem, Opportunities and Challenges. *International Journal of Business and Technopreneurship*, 11, 73–90.

Taher, S. A., & Tsuji, M. (2022). An Overview of FinTech in Bangladesh: Problems and Prospects. In: A. S. Al-Mudimigh, et al. (Eds.), *FinTech Development for Financial Inclusiveness*, 82–95. Hershey, PA, IGI Global.

Tarique K. M., & Ahmed M. U. (2021). The Direction of Future Research on i-FinTech. In: M. M. Billah (Eds.), *Islamic FinTech*. Cham: Palgrave Macmillan. https://doi.org/10.1007/978-3-030-45827-0_24

Todorof, M. (2018, August). Shariah-Compliant FinTech in the Banking Industry. In *ERA Forum* (Vol. 19, No. 1, pp. 1–17). Berlin, Heidelberg: Springer.

Trotter, R. T. II. (2012) Qualitative Research Sample Design and Sample Size: Revolving and Unresolved Issues and Inferential Imperatives. *Preventive Medicine*, 55(5), 398–400.

Ullah, M. H., Kamruzzaman, A. S. M., & Rahman, S. M. (2021). Performance Evaluation of Conventional and Islamic Banks in Bangladesh. *Business Studies Journal*, 12(3), 16–29.

UNCTAD (2017). World Investment Report 2017: United Nations Conference on Trade and Development. https://worldinvestmentreport.unctad.org/world-investment-report-2017/

Williams-Grut, O. (2017). Fintech Is Now Worth £7 Billion to Britain's Economy and Employs 60,000 People. *Business Insider UK*.

8
EXPLORING DIGITAL BANKING PATRONAGE IN THE NETHERLANDS

Muhammad Ashfaq, Abdul Rauf, Mai Tran and Rashedul Hasan

1 Introduction

The expansion of internet-based services across service industries has become one of the most rapidly growing trends in the world. The internet proliferates in almost every field and positively contributes to the comprehensive development of society in general. The banking industry also takes advantage of internet-based technologies to launch a new service which is digital banking (Alsayed & Bilgrami, 2017). Digital banking is a fusion of traditional banking and web-based technology. It is difficult to differentiate between online banking, web-based banking, internet banking, e-banking, mobile banking, and digital banking. Kaur *et al.* (2021:2) define digital banking as one that "goes beyond other banking models and requires a comprehensive re-engineering of a bank's internal systems. Digital banking involves the digitization of every program and activity carried out by financial institutions and their customers".

Digital banking has benefited not only the banking sector but also their customers. In short, by using digital banking, banks are able to reduce their operational expenses owing to the decline of physical facilities involving human resources and paperwork. On the other hand, by conducting transactions through digital banking, customers can access diversified financial activities as most services are available around the clock. For example, Citibank and Nations Bank have integrated the use of the internet into their traditional banking system and provide their clients with the comfort and convenience of using digital banking services leading to the contribution to the development of the banks and the popularity of digital banking (Alsayed & Bilgrami, 2017).

Data are objects with the ability to store, retrieve, and develop through a software procedure and communicate through a network. Data quality refers to completeness, accuracy, timeliness, consistency, and accessibility. Data are considered to meet the characteristic of completeness when they meet the expectations of comprehensiveness. Accuracy of data means both the correctness and reliability of data. Timeliness of data mentions the availability of data when it is needed. Consistency refers to the presentation of the same format and the compatibility with previous data. Accessibility refers how simply and rapidly data are available and retrieved. Reliable data enables the banking sector to optimize efficiency, predict constant customers' expectations and demands through advanced analytics, and make use of artificial intelligence to build new business possibilities.

Data governance is a procedure of controlling the availability, ease of use, entirety, and security of data in a company's system. Data governance comprises policies, procedures, and organizational structure helping companies manage data. Data governance focuses on data quality facilitating the sustainable development of a firm's data quality. However, the implementation of effective data governance is not easy because of the factors highlighted above and their complexity.

Since the features of digital banking are different from traditional banking, customers' experience of using digital banking is also diversified. Apart from the advantages of digital banking, there are some factors influencing customers' digital banking usage, especially data breaches (Makarevic, 2016). Customers' perceptions of data and cybersecurity in digital banking play an important role in affecting their confidence in digital banking adoption (Alwan & Al-Zu'bi, 2016; Jibril et al., 2019; Szopiński, 2016). For instance, according to Milosavljević and Njagojević (2019), there are only a limited number of research studying customers' perceptions of information security regarding illegal manipulation, access, and storage of their personal information. According to Uddin et al. (2020) cybersecurity is concerned mainly with protecting systems, networks, and programs from unauthorized access by external and internal parties. Data security becomes vulnerable because of a lack of dedicated control systems to ensure appropriate technologies, tools, training, and best approaches applied by the relevant institutions and organizations protect networks, devices, programs, and data from any attack or unauthorized access. Cybersecurity and data security risks are changing the dynamics of financial and banking industry digital operations, rapidly thus making such investigations significant.

In the Netherlands, according to the Dutch Data Protection Authority (Autoriteit Persoonsgegevens, 2019), there were around 27,000 data breaches in 2019, a rise of 29% compared to the previous year. They also reveal that most of the leaks occur in the financial sector, around 30%. A great number of data breaches are mainly caused by hacking, phishing, or malware (Autoriteit Persoonsgegevens, 2019). This points to the ever-increasing awareness and concerns for cybersecurity measures taken by the service firms providing a good range of online services to their customers. Thus, it is meaningful to investigate whether the customers in the Netherlands are as aware of cyber security risks as other customers in different parts of the world. This research focuses on exploring the factors impacting digital banking patronage in the Netherlands.

This research expects to provide useful information to the banks and their stakeholders in terms of customers' perceptions of data protection quality level in digital banking services. Subsequently, the findings of this paper could allow regulators formulate proper policies that may improve organizations' performance and increase the customers' confidence in digital banking adoption, especially during the COVID-19 outbreak. This study expects to assist two key stakeholders in the banking industry, the bankers and the regulators, with greater insight into their customers' perceptions regarding data protection of digital banking services in the Netherlands. This can be useful to top management in the banking industry to develop more effective data management and protection strategies to improve the confidence of existing customers along with potential customers' adoption and trust in digital banking services.

2 Overview of the banking system in the Netherlands

The Netherlands is a country located in Western Europe bordering Germany, Belgium, and the North Sea. The Dutch economy is known as one of the most developed economies in Western Europe (Frost, Haan & Horen, 2017). From the middle of the 19th century, the Netherlands, as well as some other European countries, experienced substantial development in the formal provision of personal finance. During this period, a diversity of new financial institutions emerged throughout the country intending to offer innovative banking services, such as savings and loan solutions, particularly to low- and middle-class clients (Colvin, Henderson & Turner, 2018).

De Nederlandsche Bank (DNB) was established by King William I in 1814 to contribute to the revival of the Dutch economy after the severe crisis during the French period (Westerhuis & Zanden, 2018). In the 20th century, DNB grew from a private lender into a part of the European System of central banks and the Dutch prudential supervisor of the entire financial sector. DNB operates as an independent financial institution with three major functions including monetary policy aimed at price stability, smooth functioning of the payment system, and stability of the financial sector (Westerhuis & Zanden, 2018). More than ten banks are operating in the country and three players, i.e. Rabobank, ING (Internationale Nederlanden Groep), and ABN (Algemene Bank Nederland) Amro, are dominating the banking sector. In short, these three banks control more than 80% of the markets for financial transactions in retail banking, mortgages, and business loans (Statista, 2020).

The Dutch banking sector contributes to GDP and plays a vital role in the economy (Frost, Haan & Horen, 2017). In 2019, banking sector assets reached over 2 trillion euros, which was more than four times the size of the Dutch GDP. However, with the development of the internet in the late 20th century, digital banking in the country has gained a certain success to meet diverse customer

Exploring digital banking patronage in the Netherlands   **157**

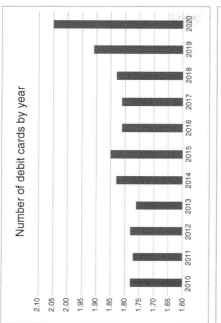

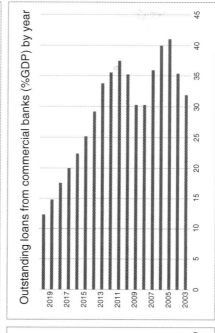

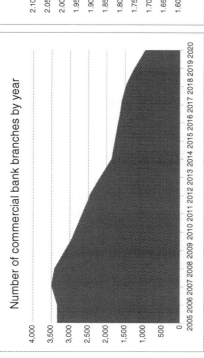

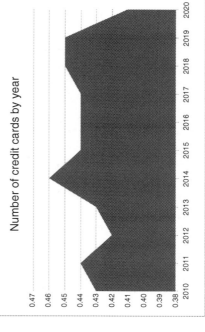

FIGURE 1 Trends in the Dutch banking sector.

expectations and demands in the provision of diversified banking services. In the Netherlands, digital banking is well developed, providing full-scale digital banking services to banking customers. In 2019, it is stated that the internet user penetration rate in the Netherlands accounted for roughly 93% of the Dutch population. Indeed, the penetration rate of digital banking users in the country constituted a considerable proportion in the same year. Specifically, individuals aged 18–25 years and 25–35 years made up the largest percentage of Dutch digital banking users, 97.8% and 96.1% respectively. In contrast, more than 40% of people aged over 70 years used digital banking services during that period (Europa, 2020). Figure 1 indicates the development of the Dutch banking sector in terms of the number of branches, credit and debit cards issued, and outstanding loans from customers. The national and international regulations play an important role in data management and security. The next section provides insights on the importance role of general data protection regulation for the banking sector.

3 General data protection regulation in the European Union

Since the potential threats to personal data security are the possible disadvantages of using digital banking, promulgating data protection regulation is the most important action to secure users' data in this regard. Understanding the importance of this issue, the European Union (EU) prescribed the General Data Protection Regulation (GDPR) in 2018 to reduce any violation or data breaches regarding personal data or personal information of European citizens (Stepenko, Dreval, Chernov, & Shestak, 2021).

In 1950, the European Convention on Human Rights was established in which the right to privacy was one of the integral parts of this convention. During the 2000s, in light of the rapid development of digital banking services throughout the world, the EU updated the 1995 European Data Protection Directive to comprehensively protect individual data over digital operations. The GDPR was introduced in 2018 after being approved by the European Parliament (Voigt & Bussche, 2017).

GDPR is a confidentiality and security regulation drafted and approved by the EU. This regulation enforces firms globally to comply with data privacy and protection legislation if they collect personal information or data of citizens living in the EU. Through GDPR, the EU has affirmed its solid viewpoint on protecting the confidentiality of personal data in Europe. However, the regulation is relatively large and extensive, making GDPR observance more difficult (IT Governance Privacy Team, 2017).

According to Voigt and Bussche (2017) and Chinn, Hannigan and London (2020), the GDPR outlines six data protection principles including:

1 *Lawfulness, fairness and transparency*—Organizations ensure that their data collection activities are lawful and transparent to data subjects. In short,

data subjects should receive information regarding the type of data the organizations collect and the purposes of processing data.
2 *Purpose limitation*—Personal data are only collected for specific, plain, and legitimate purposes. The processing of data for public interest, scientific or historical research, or statistical purposes is allowed as they are compatible with initial purposes.
3 *Data minimization*—Organizations should only process personal data which is completely necessary for specific processing purposes.
4 *Accuracy*—Organizations should ensure the accuracy of personal data. They are also required to delete or rectify personal data that is inaccurate or incomplete.
5 *Storage limitation*—Personal data must be deleted when the organizations do not use it any longer. The timescales for data storage depend on the business circumstances of organizations and the purpose of data collection.
6 *Security*—The appropriate security of personal data should be ensured while processing data. Organizations should protect the data against unauthorized or unlawful processing, accidental loss, and damage by using data security measures including encryption and so on.

Apart from complying with those data protection principles, organizations are held responsible and accountable for personal data handling. Accountability requires business subjects to demonstrate what they did to prove that they are GDPR compliant. Besides, they should conduct appropriate technical and organizational measures to protect relevant data. The measures may include maintaining a detailed file of collected data, appointing data protection officers, creating data processing agreement contracts with third parties for data processing, and others (Preece, 2018).

4 Digital banking patronage in the Netherlands

Customer confidence refers to the degree of optimism and trust that customers feel about certain products or services offered by sellers. High customer confidence in certain services reflects the credibility of the service provided by the firm, resulting in an increase in customers' purchase of the services (Meylano, Respati & Firdiansjah, 2020). The recent development in the internet of things (IoT) has influenced digital banking services provisions. IoT and data are fundamental in providing effective and high-quality banking services, as IoT will serve as the backbone for service provision in digital banking (Ramalingam & Venkatesan, 2019). Some researchers have investigated customers' confidence and trust in digital banking adoption in different parts of the world (Oertzen & Odekerken-Schröder, 2019; Singhal, 2017). Using some relevant models, such as the Technology Acceptance Model and Theory of Innovation Diffusion, they explored several factors influencing customers in digital banking adoption. Among other factors, customers' demographic factors are also taken into account

Account, female (% age 15+) and Account, male (% age 15+) by Year

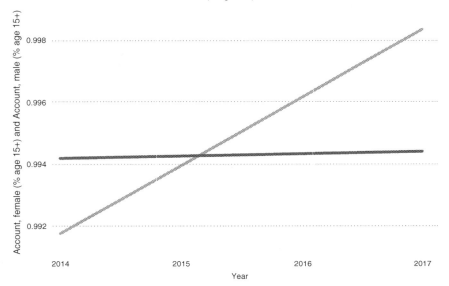

FIGURE 2 Digital banking account holders across gender.

(Gianniotis, 2018; Richard, 2020; Salem, Baidoun & Walsh, 2019). Customers' demographic factors, such as gender, age, and technical knowledge background, also play an important role in influencing customers' data security perceptions; consequently, this impacts their decisions in digital banking adoption (Alwan & Al-Zu'bi, 2016; Jibril et al., 2019; Milosavljević & Njagojević, 2019). Figure 2 indicates digital banking adoption among male and female consumers in the Netherlands. Evidence suggests an increase in the digital banking patronage among female consumers, while male consumer adoption of digital banking remains unchanged.

4.1 Gender

The first demographic factor which is one of the potential elements affecting the perception of customers toward data protection in digital banking is gender. There are some studies investigating how gender affects customers' perception of data security. It is stated that gender-based differences are found for data security perceptions in digital banking (Schomakers et al., 2019; Villarejo-Ramos et al., 2015). For example, female users tend to be more concerned about data privacy and security issues in digital banking than male users. However, they do not feel more vulnerable despite their data technology skills (McGill & Thompson, 2018). Conversely, another research indicates that men account for a higher proportion

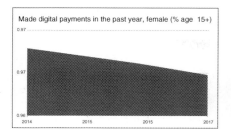 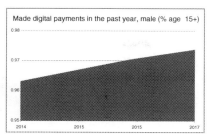

FIGURE 3 Digital payments by gender.

in information security familiarity and digital banking risk familiarity affecting their decision of digital banking adoption (Milosavljević & Njagojević, 2019).

Nevertheless, the research has also presented some contradictory findings. For instance, some studies have not found considerable gender differences in terms of data security concerns (Yang et al., 2009). While previous studies indicate that data security perceptions play an instrumental role in determining digital banking adoption more for males than for females (Milosavljević & Njagojević, 2019), other studies do not find considerable gender differences in such relationships (Alwan & Al-Zu'bi, 2016). Figure 3 shows opposite patterns for digital payment usage between male and female customers.

4.2 Age

In terms of age, some studies reveal that there is no direct impact of customers' age on data security perceptions in digital banking. Most young age groups are in harmony with older people in terms of data privacy and security. There are no statistically considerable differences between young people and older people on issues of data security (Markos et al., 2017). However, most researchers find that age-based differences are found for data security perceptions. For instance, younger age groups are less aware of data security although they share their information more on online platforms. The users aged under 25 years show less engagement in data security practices when they use digital banking than older users. This can be explained by the fact that young users rely more on technology in their daily lives, which might lead to less attention to data security. On the other hand, older customers feel less secure and would refuse to provide their personal information more than young customers (Agami & Du, 2017; Kaiser, 2016). In contrast, other researchers indicate that young people have further data security perception in digital banking compared to older people resulting in higher satisfaction in using digital banking services. Therefore, younger customers are likely to use digital banking more than older people (Oertzen & Odekerken-Schröder, 2019). Figure 4 indicates a consistent increase in digital banking among young banking consumers.

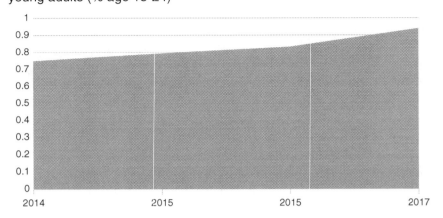

FIGURE 4 Digital payments by age.

4.3 Technical knowledge

Regarding technical knowledge, some studies state that while digital banking users' level of perception about data security is relatively high; their level of technical knowledge does not necessarily match. Irrespective of customers' degree of technological knowledge, their perceptions of security in digital banking still play an important role in affecting their adoption of digital banking. In addition, it is reported that although women have a lower level of technical knowledge and information security training, their perception of data security is still higher than their male counterparts (McGill & Thompson, 2018; Moscato & Altschuller, 2012).

Nevertheless, other studies found that there is a relationship between customers' technological knowledge and their perceptions of data security in digital banking. When customers have insufficient technical knowledge about the data security of digital banking, they do not fully understand the importance of tangible features for data protection while conducting their digital banking transactions (Jibril et al., 2019; Singhal, 2017). It also suggests that a higher educational level can improve clients' technical knowledge of data security issues in digital banking. The potential of data security policies to create customers' confidence in using digital banking might greatly depend on customers' abilities to completely understand such policies (George and Mallery, 2019).

Most studies have found that customers' awareness of data security in digital banking positively impacts them on using digital banking (Aboobucker & Bao, 2018; Al-Sharafi et al., 2016). The vast majority of banking services are provided through diverse online platforms accessed through smart devices; thus users are highly concerned about how well their data are secured by the banks.

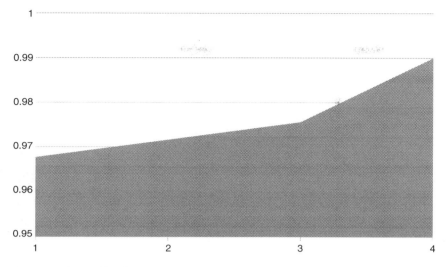

FIGURE 5 Digital banking patronage among consumers with technological expertise.

It is reported that when customers perceive the importance of data and cybersecurity and the high quality of tangible data protection policies from the banks, this might improve their confidence in continuous intention to use digital banking (Baabdullah et al., 2019; Normalini & Ramayah, 2017). For example, when clients recognize that the digital platform and interface have higher quality regarding transparent security policies, they are likely to have positive perceptions of data security of such a platform leading to an increase in digital banking services usage.

Besides, it is stated that most of the customers are increasingly concerned regarding the level of data security when they are in the process of digital banking usage. As a result, customers tend to pay more attention to tools and systems that can safely protect their data while conducting financial transactions using IoT technologies. Thus, financial institutions should emphasize their security features to enhance their customers' data security perceptions (Patel & Patel, 2018). Then, a question raised is whether the customers' awareness of the quality level of data security in their banks in the Netherlands is also the key factor significantly affecting customers' confidence in using digital banking. Figure 5 shows a steady increase in digital banking patronage among customers who have the technological expertise of mobile banking.

5 Challenges of digital banking development in the Netherlands

Cybercrime has significantly increased since the COVID-19 crisis resulting in more concerns for cybersecurity. Online hackers strive to obtain personal data, financial gains, or access to secured systems by deceiving legitimate users

(Naidoo, 2020). Organizations have increasingly recognized phishing campaigns through emails containing malware that represent medical and other charitable organizations. Email scammers have impacted executives to transfer funds to make payments to vendors' operations. Additionally, cybercriminals are attacking websites with weak security measures and protection to deliver malware. Several malware applications launch ransomware attacks, which lock the systems of users until the users pay a given amount of money to the hackers (Boehm et al., 2020).

Based on a report by Interpol, over 900,000 spam messages, 700 malware attacks, and more than 40,000 malicious domains were found from January to April of 2020 in the UK alone. The UK fraud prevention organization CIFAS (Credit Industry Fraud Avoidance System) explores online fraud in the form of a quiz testing users' understanding of the coronavirus that tries to collect users' information linked to their digital banking transactions. In Europe, the EU Agency for Cyber Security (Enisa) also warns that the attackers tend to target new digital banking users and use the outbreak as a means to force users to install fake applications or access fake websites masquerading as their reputable banks (Espinoza, 2020). According to Google, there were more than 200 million COVID-related spam messages delivered in April 2021. The number of hacking attack cases also rose to six times compared to the figure in March 2021. In addition, COVID-19 phishing messages also went up by over 600% in recent times. Apart from that, there is some malware masquerading as COVID-19 relief payments to ask for financial relief from internet users and steal their data (Mathews, 2020).

Such cybersecurity threats are equally detrimental to the development of both the conventional and Islamic fintech sectors in the Netherlands. Due to the identical nature of cyber threats to the finance industry, we witness the similar level of cyber protection mechanisms applied to both conventional and Islamic financial institutions around the world. With numerous online frauds regarding personal data, the banking industry (including conventional and Islamic) has taken effective measures to protect its customers from the diverse types of cyber frauds during the COVID-19 outbreak. In their best practices to protect customers' data effectively, banks encourage their employees to buy approved and safe hardware and software by providing the necessary funds when they work from home during the COVID-19 pandemic. Such practices are identical for both conventional and Islamic financial institutions in the Netherlands. In addition, security teams in the banks also increasingly prepared staff with up-to-date information and instructions to avoid being deceived. Furthermore, high-risk employees who frequently work with confidential data are identified and supervised for their behavior, including downloads of business data to prevent potential security breaches (Boehm *et al.*, 2020).

The Network and Information Systems Act (WBNI) provides clear guidance for the banking sector to ensure efficient cyber protection. The WBNI replaced the Data processing and Notification Requirement Act (WGCM) and strengthens the resilience of the Dutch financial sector against various cyber threats. However, the guidelines and frameworks suggested under WBNI are generic and do not necessarily provide any unique guidance for the growing Islamic fintech sector in the Netherlands. While still a draft bill, the WBNI act recommends the appointment of the Ministry of Economic Affairs and Climate policy as the National Cybersecurity certification authority.

Both Islamic and conventional banks cooperate with third parties such as contractors and external vendors. Since the banks integrate IT systems and share their data with third parties, they have made efforts to ensure that these third parties can proactively conduct adequate security controls and processes to secure customers' data in case unpredictable breaches might occur (Boehm et al., 2020; Kędzior, 2020).

Concerning the technology, the banks in the US have enhanced multi-layer protection for digital banking, such as Secure Socket Layer (SSL) encryption – an internet security protocol based on encryption to ensure the security of an internet connection and sensitive data; antivirus and anti-malware programming – programs or software (such as Kaspersky, McAfee Live) that protect data from virus or malware; multi-factor authentication – customers are required to provide their password or biometric verification to legally log into their accounts. In Europe, banks have also improved and developed their security technology to protect customers' data from online financial crimes. For example, fingerprint and facial recognition biometric technology is used to ensure only banks' customers can access their accounts; 3D Secure is an authentication step asking customers to authorize online payments through digital banking apps; the secure inbox feature ensures that only customers can read and reply to an important notification from the banks through the in-app mailbox (Lake, 2020).

6 Discussion

Not surprisingly, the penetration rate of digital banking is more than 96%, which is relatively high compared to the internet user penetration rate in the Netherlands. This can be explained by the fact that digital banking provides users with the comfort and convenience of using it. At this point, we do not differentiate between the digital services provided by both Islamic and conventional banks in the Netherlands, considering the size of the Islamic financial institutions. However, our results provide a positive note on the overall demand for fintech among consumers in the Netherlands. Digital banking customers of both conventional and Islamic banks can conduct most of the banking transactions, including bill payments, fund transfers, and account summary requirements, without physically visiting the bank. In other words, customers can immediately access diversified financial activities in their banks at the click of a mouse. According to frequency analysis, the majority of respondents believe that ease of use is the most important factor to them when they choose a bank's digital banking services. Most of them are satisfied with the quality level of data protection in their banks. They also reveal that their banks have greatly improved and developed data protection measures to protect their data. As such, Islamic financial institutions could benefit from such findings and can attract customers by ensuring flexibility in their digital services.

Regarding the impact of customers' demographic factors on their perception of data protection quality level in digital banking, this study finds that technical knowledge of customers influences their perception while gender and age do not. In particular, there is no positive impact of gender on customers' perceptions of data protection quality level in banks. Prior studies, however, found that either females or males were concerned about data security issues in digital banking affecting their decision of digital banking adoption (McGill & Thompson, 2018). This can be explained by the fact that both female and male respondents in this research have a high educational level, thus they properly understand the importance of data protection quality in their banks.

In terms of age, this study finds that there are no age-based differences in data security perceptions. In other words, there is no positive impact of age on customers' perceptions of data protection quality level in banks, which is also contradictory to other studies. Other researchers found that young people depended more on technology in their daily life leading to less attention to data security than older people (Agami & Du, 2017; Kaiser, 2016). One of the reasons why this research's finding is different from others might be that most respondents believe their banks have improved certain data protection measures as well as timely updated information regarding data protection. Thus, both young and older age groups show similar percentages of the perceptions of data protection quality levels in their banks. Regarding technical knowledge, through correlation testing, technical knowledge significantly correlates with data protection quality level. In short, technical knowledge positively impacts customers' perceptions of data protection quality in digital banking in the Netherlands.

This finding is aligned with previous studies (Jibril et al., 2019; Singhal, 2017) and can be explained by the fact that the majority of respondents attain a high educational level, which improves their technical knowledge of data protection issues in digital banking. Additionally, with the popularity of data security information through social media, banking apps, or emails, customers can also obtain adequate knowledge about the issue. Therefore, they can completely understand the importance of data protection features when they conduct digital banking transactions. Overall, this study explores that customers' perceptions of data protection quality level positively influence their confidence in digital banking adoption. This finding is also aligned with other findings (Alabdan, 2017).

Customers tend to use digital banking rather than traditional banking to avoid direct human–human interaction as much as possible according to social distancing measures. For instance, they use digital banking as a contactless payment to conduct transactions such as digital shopping. This finding is also aligned with previous findings in other countries (Droesch, 2020). With digital banking users, they indicate that COVID-19 does not greatly impact their regularity of using digital banking during the pandemic. This can be explained by the fact that whether COVID-19 prevails or not, digital banking is still the main banking service channel to them rather than other channels.

The COVID-19 pandemic positively impacts digital banking frauds in the Netherlands. This finding is also aligned with other findings (Mathews, 2020; Naidoo, 2020). The reason might be that these respondents may experience the frequency of fraudulent activities themselves. In simple terms, they might be one of the victims of crimes, including COVID-related spam messages or COVID-19 phishing messages since the pandemic occurred; consequently, they can recognize how these crimes change over time. Such threats are identical for both Islamic and conventional fintech organizations and could have a detrimental impact on their growth.

Regarding data protection measures in digital banking, this study finds that more than 50% of respondents believe that COVID-19 positively impacts data protection measures in their banks. This result is also aligned with other studies (Boehm et al., 2020; Kędzior, 2020; Lake, 2020) and could be because banks in the Netherlands might actively enhance current measures as well as develop new measures to protect customers' data during the pandemic. The respondents might be frequently notified by their banks regarding the measures that are being used to secure their data. Besides, they may also recognize how the measures have changed during the pandemic through the steps of accessing their digital banking accounts or other banking services.

7 Conclusion

This study examines the impact of customers' demographic factors on their perception regarding the quality of data protection and measures to tackle cybersecurity in digital banking. Technical knowledge is a positive factor impacting customers' perception of data protection quality. Once the customers have certain technical knowledge, they are able to understand how well their banks protect their data, resulting in the possible increase in customers' trust in using digital banking services. However, gender and age do not show any positive relationship with data protection quality level. This study concludes that there are no gender differences in the familiarity of data security perceptions in digital banking among male and female respondents. In addition, age is not considered as a factor affecting the perception of data protection. Whether young or older people, they occupy a similar proportion in the familiarity of data security in digital banking operations. In general, the banks in the Netherlands might provide adequate information regarding data protection at the service touch points to all customers so that every customer can be aware of it regardless of their age.

The evidence suggests that ease of use, less time-consuming, and high data protection/security are the most important elements affecting customers' digital banking adoption. Thus, it is correct to say that any bank in the Netherlands ensuring these features in their digital banking services can retain existing customers as well as attract more potential customers. This study also finds that customers feel more confident in using digital banking services when they are aware of the quality of data protection in their banks. With the diverse development and concerns of data breaches globally, the better the banks protect their customers' data, the more the customers trust their service providers, which can certainly lead to more adoption and trust in digital banking services. In addition, the evidence confirms that the majority of digital banking users feel satisfied with the quality of data protection in their banks. That probably explains why most customers are confident in adopting digital banking in the Netherlands.

In terms of the influence of the COVID-19 pandemic on digital banking fraud attempts, this research finds that COVID-19 has positively affected digital banking frauds in the Netherlands. Since most people use digital banking more frequently during the COVID-19 pandemic, cybercriminals take advantage of this circumstance to steal users' data. As a result, the respondents believe that there was an increase in digital banking fraud attempts in 2020 compared to the years before the COVID-19 outbreak in the Netherlands. It is undeniable that digital banking users are more vulnerable to attack, as their financial information is greatly attractive to hackers. With a rise in the number of COVID-related fraudulent activities, the appropriate action taken by the banks can reassure customers' concerns about data breaches and make them more comfortable using digital banking.

Concerning the influence of COVID-19 on data protection measures in digital banking, this study finds that the data protection measures in the banks are positively affected during the outbreak in the Netherlands. According to most of the respondents, there is an increase in the intensification of data protection measures in digital banking during the COVID-19 outbreak. In other words, banks have enhanced current data protection measures to greatly protect their data. Since there is a growth of data breaches over the pandemic, the intensification and development of existing as well as new measures are indispensable steps of the banks to ensure the security of their customer's data. Understanding the importance of data protection measures, close cooperation between banks and customers is essential to reduce unexpected losses caused by the COVID-19 crisis.

Among the respondents in this survey, more than 3% of them do not use digital banking services. The main reason is the concern over security and identity theft, representing 80%. Furthermore, in terms of the intention of using digital banking, around 30% of the respondents are strongly willing to adopt digital banking in the future, while 70% of them retain neutral attitudes and refuse to use it. Therefore, banks should create appropriate strategies regarding data security to gain more potential customers. Besides existing data protection measures, banks should improve and develop multi-layer protection for digital banking, such as firewalls, multi-factor authentication, and others. Moreover, the cooperation of the customers against cyber criminals also plays an important role in considerably protecting their data. In short, banks should constantly and timely update the latest information regarding new data breaches to the customers. As a consequence, the customers can be aware of the current situation and cooperate well with the banks to reduce unexpected harm to customers' data. Thus, the loyalty of customers to digital banking will be higher.

References

Aboobucker, I. and Bao, Y. (2018) What obstruct customer acceptance of internet banking? Security and privacy, risk, trust and website usability and the role of moderators, *The Journal of High Technology Management Research*, 29(1), pp. 109–123.

Agami, A. and Du, T. (2017) *Examining Young Users' Security Perceptions of Mobile Banking*. Master Thesis. Umeå School of Business and Economics.

Alabdan, R. (2017) The adoption of online banking with saudi arabian banks: a Saudi female perspective, *Journal of Internet Banking and Commerce*, Special issue: 8(37), pp. 1–18.

Alsayed, A.O. and Bilgrami, A.L. (2017) E-banking security: Internet hacking, phishing attacks, analysis and prevention of fraudulent activities, *International Journal of Emerging Technology and Advanced Engineering*, 7(1), pp. 109–115

Al-Sharafi, M.A., et al. (2016) The effect of security and privacy perceptions on customers' trust to accept internet banking services: An extension of TAM, *Journal of Engineering and Applied Sciences*, 11(3), pp. 545–552. doi: 10.3923/jeasci.2016.545.552

Alwan, H.A. and Al-Zu'bi, A.I. (2016) Determinants of internet banking adoption among customers of commercial banks: An empirical study in the Jordanian banking sector, *International Journal of Business and Management*, 11(3), pp. 95–104.

Autoriteit Persoonsgegevens (2019) *Cijfers Datalekken 2019*. Available at: https://autoriteitpersoonsgegevens.nl/nl/onderwerpen/beveiliging/meldplicht-datalekken/overzichten-datalekken/cijfers-datalekken-2019 (Accessed: 21 September 2020)

Baabdullah, A.M., et al. (2019) An integrated model for m-banking adoption in Saudi Arabia, *International Journal of Bank Marketing*, 37(2), pp. 452–478.

Boehm, J., Kaplan, J.M., Merrath, P., Poppensieker, T. and Stähle, T. (2020) Enhanced cyberrisk reporting: Opening doors to risk-based cybersecurity, *Cybersecurity in a Digital Era*, 9, pp. 25–33.

Colvin, C.L., Henderson, S. and Turner, J.D. (2018) The origins of the (cooperative) species: Raiffeisen banking in the Netherlands, 1898–1909, *QUCEH Working Paper Series*, pp. 1–37.

Chinn, D., Hannigan, R. and London, S. (2020) Defense of the cyber realm: How organizations can thwart cyberattacks, *Cybersecurity in a Digital Era*, pp. 89–99.

Droesch, B. (2020) *Coronavirus Boosts Online Banking, Payments Usage in the US*. Available at: https://www.emarketer.com/content/coronavirus-boosts-online-banking-payments-usage-in-the-us (Accessed: 11 December 2020)

Europa (2020) *Digital Economy and Society Statistics – Households and Individuals*. Available at: https://ec.europa.eu/eurostat/ (Accessed: 25 September 2020).

Frost, J., Haan, J. and Horen, N. (2017) International banking and cross-border effects of regulation: Lessons from the Netherlands, *International Journal of Central Banking*, 13(S1), pp. 293–313. doi:10.2139/ssrn.2839791

George, D. and Mallery, P. (2019) *IBM SPSS Statistics 26 Step by Step: A Simple Guide and Reference*. 16th edn. New York: Routledge.

Gianniotis, K. (2018) *Factors Affecting E-Banking Adoption by Greek Consumers*. Master Thesis. International Hellenic University. Available at: https://repository.ihu.edu.gr/xmlui/bitstream/handle/11544 (Accessed: 20 September 2020).

IT Governance Privacy Team (2017) *EU General Data Protection Regulation (GDPR): An Implementation and Compliance Guide.* 2nd edn. United Kingdom: IT Governance Publishing. Available at: https: www.jstor.org/stable/j.ctt1trkk7x (Accessed: 25 June 2020).

Jibril, A., et al. (2019) Customers' constraints towards online banking transaction: A literature review, *Journal of Sustainable Development*, 9(23), pp. 29–43.

Kaiser, A.F. (2016) *Privacy and Security Perceptions between Different Age Groups While Searching Online.* Bachelor Thesis. University of Twente.

Kaur, B., Kiran, S., Grima, S., & Rupeika-Apoga, R. (2021) Digital banking in Northern India: The risks on customer satisfaction, *Risks*, 9(11), p. 209.

Kędzior, M. (2020) The right to data protection and the COVID-19 pandemic: The European approach, *ERA Forum*, 21, pp. 533–543. doi:10.1007/s12027-020-00644-4

Lake, R. (2020) *Mobile and Online Banking Security During COVID-19: What You Need To Know.* Available at: https://www.forbes.com/sites/advisor/2020/06/16/mobile-and-online-banking-security-during-covid-19-what-you-need-to-know/?sh=4328379b206c (Accessed: 11 December 2020).

Makarevic, N. (2016) Perceptions towards IT security in online banking: Croatian clients vs. clients of Bosnia and Herzegovina, *International Journal of Finance & Banking Studies*, 5(1), pp. 1–15. doi:10.20525/ijfbs.v5i1.51

Markos, E., Milne, G.R. and Peltier, J.W. (2017) Information sensitivity and willingness to provide continua: A comparative privacy study of the United States and Brazil, *Journal of Public Policy & Marketing*, 36(1), pp. 79–96.

Mathews, L. (2020) *Criminals Resurrect A Banking Trojan to Push COVID-19 Relief Payment Scam.* Available at: https://www.forbes.com/sites/leemathews/2020/03/31/criminals-resurrect-a-banking-trojan-to-push-covid-19-relief-payment-scam/?sh=55dc81e75f38 (Accessed: 11 December 2020).

McGill, T. and Thompson, N. (2018) Gender differences in information security perceptions and behaviour, *Australasian Conference on Information Systems 2018*, pp. 1–11. doi:10.5130/acis2018.co

Meylano, N.H., Respati, H. and Firdiansjah, A. (2020) The effect of confidence through emotional branding Honda motorcycle customer satisfaction: A case study of Maumere, Indonesia, *International Journal of Advances in Scientific Research and Engineering*, 6(2), pp. 113–118. doi:10.31695/IJASRE.2020.33720

Milosavljević, N. and Njagojević, S. (2019) Customers' perception of information security in internet banking, *Proceedings of the 5th IPMA SENET Project Management Conference (SENET 2019)*, 108, pp. 272–277.

Moscato, D.R. and Altschuller, S. (2012) International perceptions of online banking security concerns, *Communications of the IIMA*, 12(3), 51–64.

Naidoo, R. (2020) A multi-level influence model of COVID-19 themed cybercrime, *European Journal of Information Systems*, 29(3), pp. 306–321. doi:10.1080/0960085X.2020.1771222

Normalini, M.K. and Ramayah, T. (2017) Trust in internet banking in Malaysia and the moderating influence of perceived effectiveness of biometrics technology on perceived privacy and security, *Journal of Management Sciences*, 4(1), pp. 3–26. doi:10.20547/jms.2014.1704101

Oertzen, A. and Odekerken-Schröder, G. (2019) Achieving continued usage in online banking: A post-adoption study, *International Journal of Bank Marketing*, 37(6), pp. 1394–1418. doi:10.1108/ijbm-09-2018-0239

Patel, K. and Patel, H. (2018) Adoption of internet banking services in Gujarat, *International Journal of Bank Marketing*, 36(1), pp. 147–169. doi:10.1108/IJBM-08-2016-0104

Preece, R. (2018) The GDPR accountability principle and the use of scenario workshops in the digital age, *Journal of Data Protection & Privacy*, 2(1), pp. 34–40.

Ramalingam, H. and Venkatesan, V.P. (2019) Conceptual analysis of Internet of Things use cases in Banking domain. In *TENCON 2019-2019 IEEE Region 10 Conference (TENCON)* (pp. 2034–2039). IEEE.

Richard, M.O. (2020) User adoption of online banking in Kenya: A qualitative study, *The IUP Journal of Bank Management*, 19(2), pp.7–23

Salem, M.Z., Baidoun, S. and Walsh, G. (2019) Factors affecting Palestinian customers' use of online banking services, *International Journal of Bank Marketing*, 37(2), pp. 426–451. doi:10.1108/IJBM-08-2018-0210

Schomakers, E., *et al.* (2019) Internet users' perceptions of information sensitivity – insights from Germany, *International Journal of Information Management*, 46, pp. 142–150. doi:10.1016/j.ijinfomgt.2018.11.018

Singhal, S. (2017) Demonetisation and e-banking in India, *International Journal of New Technology and Research (IJNTR)*, 3(1), pp. 20–25.

Statista (2020) *Share of Individuals Who Use Online Banking in the Netherlands from 2012 to 2019, by Age Group*. Available at: https://www.statista.com/statistics/575490/ (Accessed: 21 September 2020).

Stepenko, V., Dreval, L., Chernov, S. and Shestak, V. (2021) EU personal data protection standards and regulatory framework, *Journal of Applied Security Research*, 17(2), pp. 1–14.

Szopiński, T.S. (2016) Factors affecting the adoption of online banking in Poland, *Journal of Business Research*, 69(11), pp. 1–6. doi:10.1016/j.jbusres.2016.04.027

Uddin, M., Ali, M., and Hassan, M. K. (2020) Cybersecurity hazards and financial system vulnerability: A synthesis of literature, *Risk Management*, 22(4), pp. 239–309.

Villarejo-Ramos, A.F., *et al.* (2015) Gender differences among elderly in the use of Internet banking services, *Technology Information and Science Management of Journal International*, Special Issue: 2014, pp. 45–52

Voigt, P. and Bussche, A. (2017) *The EU General Data Protection Regulation (GDPR)*, New York: Springer.

Westerhuis, G. and Zanden, J.L. (2018) *Four Hundred Years of Central Banking in the Netherlands, 1609–2016*. United Kingdom: Cambridge University Press.

Yang, S., Ji, S. and Beyah, R. (2018) DPPG: A dynamic password policy generation system, *IEEE Transactions on Information Forensics and Security*, 13(3), pp. 545–558.

9
CAN ISLAMIC FINTECH BEST SERVE THE MIGRANTS' INTEREST IN REMITTANCE SERVICES? THE SOUTH AND SOUTHEAST ASIAN PERSPECTIVE

S. M. Sohrab Uddin and Tasfika Khanam

1 Introduction

People used to wait for a longer period of time to perform any financial transaction; but with the passage of time, there is a radical improvement in this trend. With a single click, a myriad of financial transactions, from ordering food to sending money abroad, can be performed within the blink of eyes. Modern technology has a greater contribution toward this magical transformation. Financial Technology (FinTech), an evolution of the 21st century, has made financial transactions facile with its easier approach. It is an innovation where finance and technology are blended or providing financial services to the clients in a convenient way.

Further, one of the belongings of FinTech is blockchain, a breakthrough technology based on a distributed database or public ledger of all transactions. Here, every transaction is verified by the majority of participants in the system and information entered once cannot be removed. In order to ensure the information security, cryptography is used where each block contains its own cryptographic hash and reflects the hash of the previous block. By this way, a link is established between the blocks. Hence, a blockchain is formed (Antonopoulos, 2014). However, blockchain technology has started working in a wide range of applications in both financial and non-financial sectors. Among all, the cross-border transfer payment is a mind-blowing opportunity for migrants. By using blockchain technology with the support of cryptocurrency, migrants' can remit their hard-earned money with a low-cost and transparent medium.

The periodic crisis faced by the conventional financial system since the world had bitter experiences of economic depressions under the conventional financial system, Islamic finance got the opportunity to keep its door open for all and expand service opportunities. In recent times, Islamic finance has adopted

DOI: 10.4324/9781003262169-12

FinTech in its services. Islamic FinTech, basically, represents the use of modern and innovative technologies by financial institutions based on Islamic *Shari'ah*. The success of Islamic FinTech depends on the number of financial service areas where FinTech can be linked to those areas such as cryptocurrencies, blockchain, and cross-border payments (Gomber et al., 2018; Michalopoulos & Tsermenidis, 2018).

South and Southeast Asia, a rising hub of Islamic finance, are taken into consideration in this regard since most of the remittance receiving countries are under this region. As the countries under this region have desire to flourish in Islamic finance, Islamic FinTech is a trump card for them. Some countries already have started to use Islamic FinTech in their financial services. Above all, the potential for blockchain-based remittance under Islamic FinTech is promising in this region. Thus, this chapter aims to identify whether the adoption of blockchain technology in cross-border transfer payments under Islamic FinTech can protect migrants' income.

The later part of this chapter is divided into four segments. The following section takes into account the overview of FinTech, Islamic FinTech, and blockchain-based remittance transfer. Section 3 deals with the comprehensive literature review. Section 4 represents key findings based on the scenario of remittance collection and the use of Islamic finance as well as FinTech in Asian & Southeast Asian countries. Section 5 includes drawbacks of traditional system of remittance transfer, emergency of blockchain-based remittance transfer, and essentiality of remittance under Islamic FinTech. Finally, Section 6 concludes the chapter with some policy recommendations.

2 FinTech, Islamic FinTech and blockchain-based remittance: an overview

2.1 FinTech and Islamic FinTech

Financial Technology, popularly known as FinTech worldwide, simply refers to the use of modern technologies in various financial activities. As a new concept of the 21st century, FinTech has received a great recognition from users. The essential reason behind this acceptance includes ensuring higher security to the investors with lower transaction costs. Thus, FinTech can be considered as the fusion of information technology and finance in order to provide the financial services at an affordable cost with a seamless user experience (Rabbani, Khan, & Thalassinos, 2020).

On the other hand, Islamic FinTech implies the situation when modern and innovative technologies are used by financial institutions based on Islamic *Shari'ah*. After the financial crisis of 2008, people lost their confidence in conventional finance and tend to move toward Islamic finance. Because of its inherent nature of avoiding riba (interest), maysir (uncertainty), and gharar (ambiguity), it is less prone to any financial crisis. Therefore, as a part of Islamic finance, Islamic

FinTech has huge opportunities to flourish. Islamic FinTech has made Islamic finance attract more customers and thus become more competitive against conventional finance with enhanced efficiency, reduced costs, and a wide range of products (Qatar Financial Centre, 2018). Besides, transparency, accessibility, and easiness to use are the major advantages of Islamic FinTech (Laldin, 2018; Wintermeyer, 2017). The success of Islamic FinTech depends on the number of financial service areas where FinTech can be linked to those areas such as cryptocurrencies, blockchain, and cross-border payments (Gomber et al., 2018; Michalopoulos & Tsermenidis, 2018). According to IFN FinTech, *Shari'ah*-compliant products are being offered by 116 FinTech companies including 21 in Malaysia, 18 in Britain, 15 in Indonesia, and 14 in the United States. Among them, around two-thirds are providing financial services like payments, remittance, and crowdfunding (Qatar Financial Centre, 2018).

2.2 Blockchain

Blockchain, a breakthrough innovation of modern technology under FinTech arena, is essentially a distributed database, or public ledger of all transactions or digital events that already have been executed and shared among participating members. Every transaction is verified by the majority of participants in the system and once information is entered, cannot be removed. In order to ensure the information security, cryptography is used in blockchain. Each block contains its own cryptographic hash, and each block reflects the hash of the previous block. By this way, a link is established between the blocks, and a blockchain is formed (Antonopoulos, 2014). However, blockchain technology has started work in a wide range of applications in both financial and non-financial world. It can be designed for public or private use. Public blockchains allow anyone to access the network, view transaction flow, submit their own records, and participate in the consensus process (Buterin, 2015). On the contrary, private blockchains, also known as permissioned blockchains, are used only by certain institutions like banks and other institutions to provide services and it's getting popular day by day. Bitcoin, Ripple, and so on are examples of digital currencies or cryptocurrencies used in blockchain technology. Two Islamic viewpoints do exist in using cryptocurrencies. According to the first viewpoint, cryptocurrency is *haram* since it can be used in illegal and fraudulent activities. Contrarily, the second viewpoint claims cryptocurrency is permissible in principle because such currency fulfills the conditions of being money- treated as a valuable thing, as a medium of exchange by all or substantial group, as a measure of value, and as unit of accounts, and possess no clear contradiction to *Shari'ah* (Bakar, 2017).

2.3 Blockchain-based Remittance

Remittance, simply, refers to the portion of migrants' earnings sent back from abroad to home countries. This is also known as transfer payments or cross-border payments which is one of the driving forces of the world economy. Moreover, a significant amount of remittances is being channelized through informal way, such as physical transportation of cash or *hawala*, from developed countries to developing countries and thus ultimately creating a barrier toward financial inclusion. In order to widen the arena of financial inclusion, formalized channels, such as banks, post-offices, non-bank financial intermediaries, and money transfer organizations (MTO), are encouraged through the utilization of modern technologies. Interestingly, blockchain technology can be used in a variety of financial arena such as financial services provided by different institutions and banks and among all uses, the cross-border payments are regarded as the most promising by the scholars because of its timeliness, transparency, and cost-effective features (Crosby et al., 2016; Qiu, Zhang, and Gao, 2019).

The study of Qiu, Zhang, and Gao (2019) suggests that in the long run the use of cryptocurrencies such as Ripple, blockchain can ease the medium of money transfer for migrants. These technologies deem to be better than the traditional system including Society for Worldwide Interbank Financial Telecommunications (SWIFT) because SWIFT is time-consuming and costly compared to FinTech-based technology. Ripple system for remittance includes blockchain technology to construct a Peer-to-Peer (P2P) network where Ripple acts as both the messaging network and settlement network. Besides, when remittance sender enters remittance request P2P network takes immediate action. It keeps the flow of transaction information and settles the payments simultaneously. This is why remittance time is near real-time and transaction cost is low in blockchain technology. The messenger, the inter-ledger protocol (ILP), the FX ticker, and the validator; these four key components exist in the process flow of Ripple. The task of messenger is to connect both the sender bank and receiver bank through a bidirectional message which contains relevant information such as risk details, foreign exchange rate, payment details, process cost, and estimated completion time. The ILP acts as a sub-ledger in order to keep track of credit, debit, and liquidity status across the transacting parties. Whether the process will fail or settle instantly, is decided by ILP. The exchange rate quote is examined by the FX ticker. Finally, the validator ensures the transaction's success or failure at the receiver bank through cryptography which removes settlement risk and reduces delay as well.

3 Literature review

Although it is relatively a new concept, there are a good number of studies on FinTech; but only a few studies in Islamic FinTech were conducted till date. A comprehensive review on Islamic FinTech was done by Rabbani, Khan, and Thalassinos (2020) in which Islamic FinTech was classified into three broad categories – Islamic FinTech opportunities and challenges, Cryptocurrency/Blockchain *Shari'ah* compliance, and law/regulation. The study finds blockchain technology in Islamic FinTech as a more secure and innovative way of doing business where the transactions under blockchain are more transparent and visible to all. They suggest Islamic Financial Institutions to be the partners of the FinTech companies in order to increase efficiency, transparency, and customer satisfaction. By doing firm-based analysis, Firmansyah and Anwar (2018) show study profiles, prospects, and challenges of the *Shari'ah*-compliant six financial technology firms headquartered in Indonesia and Singapore. The study reveals there is a bright prospect of Islamic FinTech and suggests fair government regulations in this regard. Crosby et al. (2016) explain blockchain fundamentals and its specific uses in both financial and non-financial areas. They claim that the advantages of blockchain technology outweigh the regulatory issues and technical challenges.

Some studies concentrate on how digital currencies can be incorporated in Islamic FinTech. The study by Bakar (2017) shows two different viewpoints on Bitcoin, cryptocurrency, and blockchain in which the first view considers cryptocurrency as *haram* whereas the second view claims that cryptocurrency is permissible in principle. Interestingly, the author agrees with the second view as cryptocurrency is acting as money and can be used in transfer payment through blockchain technology. Alzubaidi and Abdullah (2017) focus on introducing an Islamic digital currency in their study on blockchain and digital currencies. According to them, the proposed digital currency can fulfill the Islamic law, functions of money, and provides a more stable currency than fiat money.

Side by side, some studies shed light on the use of blockchain technology in migrants' remittances. In order to signify the payment infrastructures, Rella (2019) connects remittances, blockchain technologies, and correspondent banking. The study finds blockchain technologies are being used in remittance formalization as well as being incorporated into existing infrastructures, business models, and regulatory structures. The author argues that the main focus of blockchain-based remittances is on profits, risks, costs, interoperability, trapped liquidity, and idle capital in correspondent banking accounts, rather than on financial inclusion. Qiu, Zhang, and Gao (2019) focus on the Strengths, Weaknesses, Opportunities and Threats (SWOT) analysis of blockchain-based Ripple and traditional SWIFT system in remittance. The study expresses SWIFT can lead remittance market for the short term due to the economy of scale while Ripple has a greater prospect in the long run because of its extra benefits in transfer payments.

It is evident that Islamic FinTech can ensure financial inclusion. Muneeza and Mustapha (2021) focus on how financial inclusion can be ensured by Islamic FinTech. The study identifies some Islamic FinTech key drivers such as digitally native Muslim demographic, government initiatives toward Islamic FinTech, and FinTech startups for financial inclusion. They suggest government and regulatory bodies to play a decisive role in governance and regulation in FinTech to avail limitless opportunities inherent in Islamic finance. El Amri, Mohammed and Bakr (2021) investigate how FinTech-based payment system, such as M-Pesa in Kenya and Orange Money in 13 African countries, is contributing to financial inclusion. It is found that such payment system reduces transaction cost which is effective in increasing financial inclusion. The study includes some challenges like insufficient number of rural branches, lack of understanding culture and needs, legal risk, and trust deficit to this payment system.

Above all, Ahmad and Mamun (2020) figure out the possibilities of Islamic FinTech in Bangladesh and Turkey. By using qualitative method, the study finds many opportunities such as opening startups, promoting digital efficiency, offering business diversity, generating financial security, and addressing financial inclusion for both countries.

Therefore, the existing literature focuses on comprehensive review, financial inclusion, prospects and challenges of Islamic FinTech, incorporation of digital currency and blockchain in FinTech, and comparison between SWIFT and Ripple in remittance; and thus shows no concrete study on blockchain-based remittance incorporating Islamic FinTech. That's why the aim of this chapter is to identify whether the adoption of blockchain technology in remittance under Islamic FinTech is able to protect migrants' income.

4 Remittance collection scenario and current practice of Islamic finance as well as FinTech in South and Southeast Asian countries

4.1 South Asia

As a part of the world economy, South Asia is known as a remittance-based economy. Many migrant workers of this region are working abroad and thriving for the economic development of both self and nation. There is tremendous growth in inward remittance corresponding to the growth of the number of migrant workers. Therefore, the total inward remittance to South Asia rose by 5.2% to $147 billion in 2020 (World Bank, 2021). The amount will be higher if all of them could be channeled through formal channel; unfortunately, a large portion of transfer payments is made through informal channel. Consequently, mass people are out of the reach of financial intermediaries and antisocial activities can be done by these unauthorized money. Therefore, government and other concerned authorities try to make formal channels more attractive and friendlier to the migrants both in conventional and Islamic ways along with the inclusion of new technology. In Table 1, it is evident that the inward remittances in South Asian countries such as Bangladesh and Pakistan have increased by 42% and 35%, respectively from year 2015 to year 2020. Moreover, Table 2 shows the Gross Domestic Product (GDP) percentage of remittance of each country where a significant portion of South Asian countries' GDP comes from remittances.

4.1.1 Bangladesh

Bangladesh, proudly considered as a 'Rising Tiger' in South Asia with $21.74 billion inward remittance, has become the third and eighth highest remittance

TABLE 1 Year-wise remittance collection through formal sector from year 2015 to year 2020.

Country/Year	2015	2016	2017	2018	2019	2020
Bangladesh	15.30	13.57	13.50	15.57	18.36	21.75
Pakistan	19.31	19.82	19.86	21.19	22.25	26.11
Indonesia	9.66	8.91	8.99	11.22	11.67	9.65
Malaysia	1.64	1.60	1.65	1.69	1.64	1.45

Source: Constructed by the authors based on World Bank (Various Years) Data. Amounts are in US$ billion.

TABLE 2 Country-wise inward remittance and remittance percentage of GDP at the end of 2020

Particulars/Year	Bangladesh	Pakistan	Indonesia	Malaysia
Amount of remittance (in USD billion)	21.75	26.11	9.65	1.45
% of GDP	6.7	9.9	0.91	0.4

Source: Constructed by the authors based on the World Bank Data 2020.

recipient country in South Asia and the world, respectively, in 2020. Inward remittance is the second largest source of foreign currency earning followed by readymade garments (RMG) in Bangladesh. Moreover, through the creation of scope for unemployed people, alleviation of extreme poverty, improvement of living standard, growth of foreign exchange reserves, and counter balance of the current account deficit with the growing trend of migrants' remittance, the economy is moving forward. About 6.7% of the GDP of Bangladesh came from migrants' income at the end of 2020.

In Bangladesh, a huge amount of remittance is transferred through a legal channel such as banks. The highest amount of remittances, among all commercial banks, have been collected by Private Commercial Banks (PCBs) followed by the State-owned Commercial Banks (SCBs), Specialized Banks (SBs) and Foreign Commercial Banks (FCBs). From October to December 2020, about $4,577.23 million remittances (73.45 percentage of total) have been collected by PCBs. However, the highest amount of remittance with $1,922.96 million (30.86 percentage of total), among all PCBs, have been received by Islami Bank Bangladesh Limited (IBBL) (Bangladesh Bank, 2020a). In addition, Islamic banks in Bangladesh are responsible for 40.51% of remittances received by the whole banking sector at the same period (Bangladesh Bank, 2020b). This scenario shows that the appeal for the transfer payments through Islamic banks is rising in Bangladesh during the pandemic. The reasons behind include executing financial stimulus package as per the direction by the Bangladesh Bank (BB); the central bank of Bangladesh, extending the time for loan repayment; delivering remittances on time; undertaking safety measures for staffs as well as emphasizing online banking; virtual meeting and training.

Apart from this, the government of Bangladesh recently has taken several fruitful initiatives in order to promote the remittance inflow through the legal channel such as banks. In the first place, the maximum time limit for remittance disbursement becomes 48 hours instead of 72 hours. The facilities for Commercially Important Person (CIP) and special citizen among Bangladeshi expatriates have been extended. In order to facilitate medical check-up services to migrant workers, Authorized Dealers (ADs) with the request from approved medical centers can remit the fee to the beneficiaries' bank account where check-up details and applicable tax deductions are specified in invoice. With a view to facilitating house financing to the Non-Resident Bangladeshis (NRBs), the maximum debt-equity ratio has been set at 75:25 rather than previous 50:50. Besides, 2.5% cash incentives have been provided for inward foreign remittance remitting via banking channel. Again, to make the procedure of receiving cash incentive simple BB has also given specific directions.

According to the concerned authority, to perform financial transactions in a more efficient way, increase of *Shari'ah*-compliant FinTech application is essential for Islamic banking sector of Bangladesh. Consequently, this will ensure the efficient transfer of migrants' income. Being a Muslim-majority country, Bangladesh has tremendous potential for Islamic FinTech. Around 28% of market shares are held by Islamic banks among the entire banking industry in Bangladesh (Bangladesh Bank, 2021). It represents that many customers will be involved if Islamic banks can provide FinTech-based services. Acknowledging the great scope of Islamic FinTech, the country's largest PCB, IBBL has planned to convert into FinTech-based global standard bank soon (Islam, 2020).

4.1.2 Pakistan

Pakistan has become the second largest in foreign remittance earnings with $26.11 billion which is a contribution of 9.9% to the nation's GDP in 2020. This shows the level of importance of remittance in the economic development of Pakistan. In Table 1, it's seen that there is a rising trend in the remittance collection. The major reasons behind this ceaseless growth include the upward trend of digitalization, restrictions upon money transfer through Hundi and Hawala along with the limited transfer of cash in person because of traveling restrictions. In addition, the use of digital means by banks has lessened the cost of money transfer by the migrants. The report of remittance price worldwide database by World Bank has expressed the average cost of remitting $200 dropped to 4.1% in 2020 in Pakistan.

The government of Pakistan along with the central bank, the State Bank of Pakistan, has taken some major initiatives recently to boost the remittance flow through formal channels. These include starting performance-based incentive scheme for Home Remittances scheme marketing which will encourage large players to increase their efforts to transfer inward remittances, initiating massive public marketing campaign on remittance collection through banks, following a flat rate of SAR 20/- for all transactions of USD 100/- and above to support small remitters, and collaborating with the Ministry of Overseas Pakistanis and Human Resource Development (MOP & HRD) in order to initiate rule for intended emigrant worker as well as at least one of his/her family member to maintain an active bank account (State Bank of Pakistan, 2020a).

With 22 Islamic banks including 5 full-fledged Islamic banks along with 17 conventional banks with the branches and windows of Islamic banking; a total of 3,456 branches and 1,638 windows exist in Pakistan as of December 2020. Islamic banking sector's assets valued Rs. 4,269 billion whereas the deposit base is Rs. 3,389 billion at the same time. Both assets and deposits show the highest growth, 30% and 27.8% respectively, which indicates a promising transition for the banking sector of Pakistan (State Bank of Pakistan, 2020b). Moreover, on January 13, 2021, State Bank of Pakistan has been announced as the best central bank in promoting Islamic finance which is based on a poll conducted by Islamic Finance News, REDmoney Group, Malaysia. Furthermore, the Securities and Exchange Commission of Pakistan has urged to develop *Shari'ah* FinTech market.

Apart from this, Telenor Microfinance Bank in Pakistan made a partnership with Alipay in order to provide blockchain-powered remittance service between Pakistan and Malaysia in March 2018. The blockchain technology can transfer cross-border payments between Malaysia and Pakistan faster and with higher efficiency along with highly secured and transparent manner (Business Wire, 2019).

4.2 Southeast Asia

Two countries – Indonesia and Malaysia, in Southeast Asia have been considered as a sample in this section. Table 1 depicts the yearly inward remittances in Southeast Asian countries where remittances in Indonesia increased by 20% from year 2015 to year 2019. Moreover, Malaysia holds a stable position in remittance collection as its main focus is to disburse remittance rather than collect.

4.2.1 Indonesia

Being the largest economy in Southeast Asia, Indonesia is blessed with a large amount of inward remittance, amounting to $9.65 billion at the end of year 2020. This amount is responsible for almost 1% of the country's GDP. Most of the migrants of Indonesia reside in Malaysia and send their remittances to the home country by using more informal channels. A study by International Organization for Migration (IOM) reveals that there is a lack of knowledge among some segments of the migrant population on how to choose a Remittance Service Provider (RSP) wisely for earning benefit.

To encourage the formalization of the remittance flows, the Bank Indonesia (BI) has therefore taken a number of initiatives. These include making it mandatory for all migrants to open a bank account as well as for BI to train migrants on financial literacy sessions on banking and remittance procedures before their departure, establishing banking networks and initiating dialogue with destination countries. Besides, BI has been encouraging non-bank agents to conduct remittance transfers (International Organization for Migration, 2010).

Apart from this, Project Greenback 2.0 has been initiated by the World Bank so that there will be an enriched remittance market and a better remittance impact in Indonesia. All sorts of digital payments as well as the activities related to government's social assistance programs associated with cash transfers will be facilitated by the project. Moreover, the project will work for assuring the advancement of payment service network under private sector. Therefore, long-run goal of the project is to stimulate economic growth through the conversion of remittances into productive investments and creation of job opportunities against unemployment so that remittance senders can choose safer options.

Indonesia, being the world's largest Muslim country, is regarded as an organized nation to be the focal point of Islamic Fintech worldwide. According to the Financial Service Authority of the Republic of Indonesia (Otoritas Jasa Keuangan – OJK), there are 64 registered FinTech firms in which three of them including PT Ammana Fintek Syariah (Ammana), PT Dana Syariah Indonesia (Dana Syariah), and PT Investree Radhika Jaya (Investree) are the Islamic FinTech P2P lending firms (Aldila, 2018).

Based on 2019 data from OJK, it is observed that around 189 Islamic banks exist in Indonesia; among them, 14 *Shari'ah* Commercial Banks (Bank Umum Syariah – BUS), 20 Shari'ah Business Units (Unit Usaha Syariah – UUS), and 164 *Shari'ah* Rural Banks (Bank Pembiayaan Rakyat Syariah – BPRS) are working (Otoritas Jasa Keuangan, 2019). In 2018, a report on Islamic FinTech by Dinar Standard, a research firm, reckoned that among 93 Islamic FinTech start-ups in the world, 31 are Indonesian firms (The Jakarta Post, 2020).

Above all, sufficient financial literacy is crucial in Islamic banking since there remains a knowledge gap among Indonesian individuals about Islamic banks' services which, ultimately, results in impeding the prospect of developing Islamic banking in Indonesia (Sudarsono, Tumewang, & Kholid, 2021).

4.2.2 Malaysia

Malaysia, a Southeast Asian hub for remittance provider, receives a little amount of remittance of $1.45 billion which is only 0.4% of GDP. Basically, migrants come to Malaysia from neighboring countries such as Bangladesh, Indonesia, India, Nepal, Myanmar, Vietnam, and China.

Bank Negara Malaysia, the central bank of Malaysia, is concerned about the use of technology in financial services. Consequently, there is a significant growth in e-remittance services as the total value of transactions becomes more than double to RM6.6 billion (25 percentage of total outward remittances) at the end of 2020 (Bank Negara Malaysia, 2020).

Since most of the migrants are connected with their family via smart phones, it seems very comfortable to use technology. By considering this issue, financial institutions have opted to provide technology-driven innovative remittance services. For example, 'MyCash Online,' an online financial service provider with six languages, is serving migrant workers in Malaysia. In order to transfer international remittances with more convenient way and low cost, MyCash Online makes partnership with a licensed RSP named Metro Exchange. It's undoubtedly a great initiative to make easier and low-cost transfer services for migrants (Pathak, Garg and Gupta, 2018).

In order to strengthen the financial inclusion, Malaysia, with a dual banking system, has leveraged both Islamic and conventional financial instruments. In order to increase the number of digital payment users, the MoF in Malaysia has launched the 'e-Tunairakyat' (e-Cash people) initiative in which RM30 will be given to the participants using any of three e-Wallets (*Touch 'n Go, Boost, and GrabPay*). Apart from this, conditional cash transfers can also be possible and can be used as an international money transfer tool to improve social welfare and reduce poverty.

5 Problems in traditional remittance transfer

For so many years remittance is being transferred traditionally by both formal channel including banks and MTOs; and informal channel such as hawala (Ozaki, 2012), whereas the later one attracts migrants more due to the lack of financial literacy and higher costs involved with the former one. Evidence shows that South Asian migrants remit a larger portion of their hard-earned money through informal channel which has no effective linkage to capital generation in financial system of the economy as households, most of the time, spend on consumption with little productive investment (Ozaki, 2018).

SWIFT, a traditional medium of remittance transfer is nothing but simply a messaging platform providing details of the cross-border transactions. By using a standardized code, known as SWIFT code consisting of institution code, country code, location code, and bank branch code, as well as transactions details message is prepared. Moreover, this system only transfers messages whereas payment settlement is accomplished by ongoing banking system. Almost five parties – originating bank, originating bank's correspondent, the central bank, beneficiary bank's correspondent, and beneficiary banks – are involved within the process in order to reach money from originator (sender) to beneficiary (receiver). Thus, the overall SWIFT transaction process can be divided into two parts – delivering messages and settling payments as well.

Although SWIFT system is being used traditionally in remittance transfer under the banking platform, it has some inherent drawbacks such as time-consuming, costly, and settlement risk. The reason behind this is, basically, the transaction structure of the system. In most of SWIFT transactions, corresponding bank, an

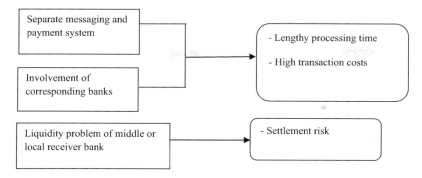

FIGURE 1 Drawbacks of SWIFT system.

intermediary between domestic and foreign bank, plays a subsidiary role in payment settlement. In brief, after receiving money from originating bank, corresponding bank of originator transfer it to the central bank of migrants' home country in order to conduct the exchange of currency and further deliver it to the corresponding bank of beneficiary; after that finally reach to the beneficiary (Chen, 2018). Thus, the whole process becomes lengthy and time-consuming for the 21st century. Sometimes, 3–5 days can be required to remit money to some region under SWIFT transaction system (Qiu, Zhang, & Gao, 2019). Apart from this, the system employs two types of service charge or fee for remitting money derived from corresponding banks and respective banks (Horton, 2021). Moreover, payment delivery is charged by both corresponding banks making remittance transfer costly for migrants. In addition, fee includes initial SWIFT messaging cost, corresponding bank fee and exchange rate fee as well. In this way, traditional SWIFT system generates higher cost in cross-border remittance. Furthermore, settlement risk can arise if any middle bank or local receiving bank faces sudden shortfall in liquidity. In such a situation, transaction will be stopped eventually and make further delay in payment settlement (Qiu, Zhang, & Gao, 2019) (Figure 1).

5.1 How does blockchain-based remittance transfer reduce the drawbacks of traditional SWIFT system?

Blockchain-powered remittance technology has the ability to overcome the shortcomings inherent in traditional SWIFT system. For instance, Ripple system by constructing P2P network acts as both the messaging network and settlement network. In this system, when migrant enters remittance request through bank P2P network takes immediate action as well as keeps the flow of transaction information and settles the payments simultaneously (Qiu, Zhang, & Gao, 2019).

Moreover, blockchain-enabled remittance eliminates multiple intermediaries such as the corresponding bank of originator and corresponding bank of beneficiary. Consequently, money is directly transferred through blockchain from originating bank to destination bank and thus reduces the transaction cost

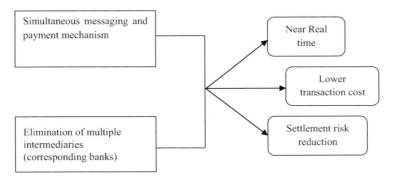

FIGURE 2 Blockchain based remittance transfer reducing the drawbacks of traditional SWIFT system.

of remittance transfer (Rahman & Yadlapalli, 2021) and making the process shortened (Shumsky, 2020). Therefore, remittance time is near real time and transaction cost is low under blockchain technology.

Apart from this, the whole process of blockchain includes some components which ensures on time message deliberation and payment settlement. For instance, the messenger, the ILP, the FX ticker, and the validator; these four key components exist in the process flow of Ripple. The task of messenger is to connect both the sender bank and receiver bank through a bidirectional message which contains relevant information such as risk details, foreign exchange rate, payment details, process cost, and estimated completion time. The ILP acts as a sub-ledger in order to keep track of credit, debit, and liquidity status across the transacting parties. Side by side, whether the process will fail or settle instantly, is decided by ILP. The exchange rate quote is examined by the FX ticker. Finally, the validator ensures the transaction's success or failure at the receiver bank through cryptography which removes settlement risk (Qiu, Zhang, & Gao, 2019). However, the system under blockchain can easily inform relevant parties about any missing document or information before the starting of transaction (Overdahl, 2019) which generally reduces settlement risk (Figure 2).

5.2 Loopholes in conventional blockchain-based remittance transfer

In order to attract migrants to use the formal channel in transferring remittance, the government, central banks, commercial banks, and other related organizations have taken different laudable steps where the inclusion of modern technology such as the use of blockchain under FinTech is praiseworthy. Since blockchain-based remittance is in its initial stage with the specific advantages of lower transaction costs, near real-time transaction, and reduction of settlement risk; some unavoidable challenges also remain. In the first place, lack of centralization and no strict regulation have created a challenge in acceptance of blockchain-based remittance transfer by all. This can create fraudulent activities (Crosby et al., 2016) even after using digital payment system and thus may create trust deficit among participants. Moreover, many people are unwilling to go with this new technology as it does not maintain any direct link with the Islamic *Shari'ah* (Islamic law). Thus, the above issues are creating room for an alternative to conventional blockchain-based remittance.

5.3 Contribution of Islamic FinTech in transferring remittance under blockchain

Since Islamic FinTech is thriving, it has potential to include blockchain technology in transfer payments. By using *Shari'ah*-compliant cryptocurrency, the task can be performed easily. Moreover, blockchain technology in Islamic FinTech gives a more secured and innovative way of doing business where the transactions under blockchain ensure more transparency to all the users (Rabbani, Khan, & Thalassinos, 2020). Since *Shari'ah* law is followed in Islamic finance, it's enclosed with strict regulation which can ensure the fairness of each transaction in remittance.

Furthermore, fraudulent activities can be prevented through mutual monitoring by relevant participants such as SSB, government, regulatory authorities, and so on. However, Islamic banks already have structured SSBs, who are responsible for monitoring and ensuring *Shari'ah* compliance of Islamic product, in their banking model; and they are opted to add technical expertise to adopt Islamic FinTech appropriately. When Islamic banks along with other stakeholders work together in monitoring and supervising, it will be easier to prevent fraudulency in remittance transfer using blockchain technology.

Apart from this, the blockchain-enabled remittance transfer under Islamic FinTech has great potential to create a new avenue for both Muslim and non-Muslim migrants. Besides, due to the expansion of access of a large number of people, Islamic FinTech enables reducing the cost of transactions remarkably (Muneeza & Mustapha, 2021). In addition, it is expected that the growth of the Muslim population will reach 3 billion by 2060 (Cooper, 2018). Hence, Islamic FinTech has opened a new horizon for financial inclusion of the Muslim community most of whom were reluctant to be a part of conventional FinTech (Muneeza & Mustapha, 2021). With the passage of time, engagement of more clients will reduce the cost of transaction although initially monetary assistance and technical cooperation from government and regulatory bodies such as Islamic Financial Services Board (IFSB) and other stakeholders are required for dealing with the costs borne by Islamic banks in order to compete with its conventional counterpart in blockchain-powered remittance. Thus, through the reduction of informal transfer payments and the enhancement of financial inclusion, Islamic FinTech-based blockchain remittance can increase the money supply in the economy and create more investment opportunities (Figure 3).

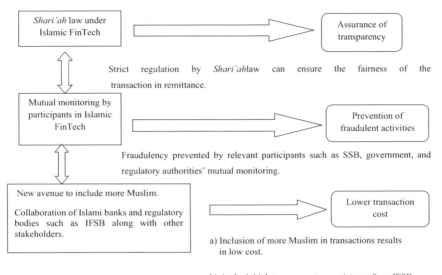

FIGURE 3 Contribution of Islamic FinTech in Transferring Remittance under Blockchain.

5.4 Challenges in blockchain-based remittance transfer under Islamic FinTech

South and Southeast Asia, being a focal zone of remittance collection along with a rising hub for Islamic finance, have a great potential for blockchain-powered remittance under Islamic FinTech. Some countries have already started financial activities by using FinTech in order to ensure smooth transactions and avail advantages as well.

With tremendous advantages, a few challenges are also waiting for blockchain-based remittance under Islamic FinTech. In the first place, lack of trained human capital (Rusydiana, 2018) and appropriate regulation can be the major impediments for developing countries. Further, people normally think financial services under Islamic finance are more complex than conventional finance.

5.5 Ways to overcome challenges in blockchain-based remittance transfer under Islamic FinTech

Proper training facilities including FinTech and blockchain need to be ensured in order to create skilled human capital in this field. Further, country-wise regulation must not be too much flexible or rigid; a proper balance is required along with timely review and monitoring. However, more studies are needed about how easily Islamic FinTech can express the process of blockchain-enabled remittance to migrants.

6 Conclusion

Since people of the 21st century are more indulged in using modern technology and most of the financial services are provided using different technologies, it creates a great opportunity for Islamic banks and other institutions to incorporate FinTech into their services. With strong potential, blockchain-powered cross-border money transfer can be included in order to ease the payment system of migrants. Mainly, some South and Southeast Asian countries – Bangladesh, Pakistan, Indonesia, and Malaysia – are taken as sample in this regard. The goal of this chapter was to identify whether the adoption of blockchain technology in remittance transfer under Islamic FinTech is able to protect migrants' income. From the findings, it is evident that some of the countries such as Pakistan and Malaysia have already started blockchain-based transfer payment under Islamic FinTech in order to avail the advantages including cost, time, and work efficiency; trust enhancement; productive investments and job creation; and financial inclusion.

Moreover, since there is a knowledge gap on blockchain-based remittance among migrants and other stakeholders, sufficient concentration and practical training are required in order to make the whole process easier and popular. Besides, central government and regulatory bodies along with SSBs need to play a vital role in this case.

Indeed, further research opportunities lie in examining the viability of the use of blockchain-based transfer payment under Islamic FinTech in non-Muslim countries and how easily Islamic FinTech can express blockchain-enabled remittance to migrants.

References

Ahmad, S. M., & Mamun, A. A. (2020). Opportunities of Islamic FinTech: The Case of Bangladesh and Turkey. *CenRaPS Journal of Social Sciences,* 2 (3), 412–426.

Aldila, N. (2018). "Indonesia Negara Paling SiapKembangkan 'Fintech' Syariah." *FinansialBisnis.* Retrieved from http://finansial.bisnis.com/read/20180707/89/813959/indonesia-negara-paling-siap-kembangkan-fintech-syariah

Alzubaidi, I. B., & Abdullah, A. (2017). Developing a Digital Currency from an Islamic Perspective: Case of Blockchain Technology. *International Business Research,* 10 (11), 79.

Antonopoulos A. M. (2014). *Mastering Bitcoin: Unlocking Digital Cryptocurrencies,* 1st ed. Sebastopol, CA: O'Reilly Media, Inc.

Bakar, M. A. (2017). Shari'ahh Analysis of Bitcoin, Cryptocurrency, and Blockchain. *Blossom Finance.* Retrieved from https://blossomfinance.com/posts/shariah-analysis-of-bitcoin-cryptocurrency-and-blockchain

Bangladesh Bank. (2020a). Developments of Islamic Banking in Bangladesh, October–December 2020. *Islamic Banking Cell Research Department Bangladesh Bank.*

Bangladesh Bank. (2020b). Quarterly Report on Remittance Inflows in Bangladesh, October–December 2020. *Bangladesh Bank Research Department External Economics Division*.

Bangladesh Bank. (2021). Developments of Islamic Banking in Bangladesh, April-June 2021. *Islamic Banking Cell Research Department Bangladesh Bank*.

Bank Negara Malaysia. (2020). *Annual Report 2020*. Annual Publication. Retrieved from https://www.bnm.gov.my/documents/20124/3026128/ar2020_en_ch1e_payments.pdf

Business Wire. (2019). Blockchain Technology Backed Home Remittances from Malaysia to Pakistan Made Possible to Promote Financial Inclusion. Retrieved from https://www.businesswire.com/news/home/20190108005651/en/Blockchain-Technology-Backed-Home-Remittances-from-Malaysia-to-Pakistan-Made-Possible-to-Promote-Financial-Inclusion.

Buterin, V. (2015). On Public and Private Blockchains. Retrieved from https://blog.ethereum.org/2015/08/07/on-public-and-private-blockchains

Chen, P. (2018). Ripple, the Disruptor to the Forty Years Old Cross-Border Payment System. *Digital Initiative*. Retrieved from https://digital.hbs.edu/platform-digit/submission/ripple-the-disruptor-to-the-forty-years-old-cross-border-payment-system/

Cooper, T. (2018). The Race to Become the World's Leading Leading Islamic Fintech Hub. *Raconteur*. Retrieved from https://www.raconteur.net/finance/race-become-worldsleading- leading-islamic-fintech-hub.

Crosby, M., Nachiappan, P. P., Verma, S., & Kalyanaraman, V. (2016). BlockChain Technology: Beyond Bitcoin. *Applied Innovation Review*, 2, 7–17. Retrieved from https://www.appliedinnovationinstitute.org/blockchain-technology-beyond-bitcoin/

El Amri, M. C., Mohammed, M. O., & Bakr, A. M. (2021). Enhancing Financial Inclusion Using FinTech-Based Payment System. In: Billah, M.M. (eds.), *Islamic FinTech*. Palgrave Macmillan, Cham, 191-207. doi: 10.1007/978-3-030-45827-0_11

Firmansyah, E. A., & Anwar, M. (2018). Islamic Financial Technology (Fintech): Its Challenges and Prospect. *Advances in Social Science, Education and Humanities Research (ASSEHR)*, 216.

Gomber, P., Kauffman, R. J., Parker, C., & Weber, B. W. (2018). On the Fintech Revolution: Interpreting the Forces of Innovation, Disruption, and Transformation in Financial Services. *Journal of Management Information Systems*, 35(1), 220–265.

Horton, C. (2021). What is Correspondent Bank? *The Balance*. Retrieved from https://www.thebalance.com/correspondent-bank-5198871

International Organization for Migration. (2010). *International Migration and Migrant Workers' Remittances in Indonesia*. Publication. Retrieved from https://publications.iom.int/books/international-migration-and-migrant-workers-remittances-indonesia

Islam, S. (2020). IBBL to Launch Global Standard FinTech Banking. Retrieved from https://thefinancialexpress.com.bd/stock/bangladesh/ibbl-to-launch-global-standard-fintech-banking-1596084333

Laldin, M. A. (2018). FinTech and Islamic Finance. *IFN Islamic Finance News*, 15, 67.

Michalopoulos, G., & Tsermenidis, K. (2018). Country Risk on the Bank Borrowing Cost Dispersion within the Euro Area during the Financial and Debt Crises. *International Journal of Economics and Business Administration*, 6(4), 76–92.

Muneeza, A., & Mustapha, Z. (2021). Islamic FinTech and Financial Inclusion. In: Billah, M.M. (eds.), *Islamic FinTech*. Palgrave Macmillan, Cham, 173–190. doi: 10.1007/978-3-030-45827-0_10

Otoritas Jasa Keuangan. (2019). Indonesia's National Financial Literacy Strategy. Retrieved from https://www.ojk.go.id/id/berita-dan-kegiatan/publikasi/Pages/Strategi-Nasional-Literasi-Keuangan-Indonesia-.aspx

Overdahl, S. (2019). How Blockchain Could Lower the Cost of Remittances. *The National News*. Retrieved from https://www.thenationalnews.com/business/money/how-blockchain-could-lower-the-cost-of-remittances-1.945431

Ozaki, M. (2012). Worker Migration and Remittances in South Asia. *ADB South Asia Working Paper Series*, 12.

Ozaki, M. (2018).Channeling Remittances and Diaspora Savings for Investments. *Migration and Remittances for Development in Asia*, Chapter 6.

Pathak, A., Garg, P., & Gupta, S. (2018). The Potential for Technology-backed Remittance Solutions in Malaysia. *MicroSave Consulting*. Retrieved from https://www.microsave.net/2018/05/25/the-potential-for-technology-backed-remittance-solutions-in-malaysia/

Qatar Financial Centre. (2018). Fintech, a Global Boost for Islamic Finance? Retrieved from https://www.reuters.com/article/idUSWAOAPHREBLWW18A3

Qiu, T., Zhang, R., & Gao, Y. (2019). Ripple vs. SWIFT: Transforming Cross Border Remittance Using Blockchain Technology. *Procedia Computer Science*, 147, 428–434.

Rabbani, M. R., Khan, S., & Thalassinos, E. I. (2020). FinTech, Blockchain and Islamic Finance: An Extensive Literature Review. *International Journal of Economics and Business Administration*, VII (2), 65–86.

Rahman, S., & Yadlapalli, A. (2021). Can Blockchain Boost Remittance Inflow? *The Financial Express*. Retrieved from https://www.thefinancialexpress.com.bd/views/views/can-blockchain-boost-remittance-inflow-1611588849

Rella, L. (2019). Blockchain Technologies and Remittances: From Financial Inclusion to Correspondent Banking. *Frontiers in Blockchain*, 2 (14), 1–2. doi: 10.3389/fbloc.2019.00014

Rusydiana, S. A. (2018). Developing Islamic Financial Technology in Indonesia. *Hasanuddin Economics and Business Review*, 2 (2), 143–152. doi:10.26487/hebr.v2i2.1550

Shumsky, P. (2020). How Blockchain Is Going to Change the Remittance in 2020. Retrieved from https://www.finextra.com/blogposting/18367/how-blockchain-is-going-to-change-the-remittance-in-2020

State Bank of Pakistan. (2020a). *Annual Report*. Annual Publication. Retrieved from https://www.sbp.org.pk/reports/annual/arFY20/Vol-1/annual-index-eng.htm

State Bank of Pakistan. (2020b). *Islamic Banking Bulletin*. Quarterly Publication. Retrieved from https://www.sbp.org.pk/ibd/Bulletin/Bulletin-1.asp

Sudarsono, H., Tumewan, Y. K., & Kholid, M. N. (2021). Customer Adoption of Islamic Banking Services: Empirical Evidence from Indonesia. *Journal of Asian Finance, Economics and Business*, 8 (3), 1193–1204.

The Jakarta Post. (2020).Traceable: Stakeholders Work to Promote Digital Shari'ahh Economy. https://www.thejakartapost.com/news/2020/11/30/traceable-stakeholders-work-to-promote-digital-Shari'ah-economy.html

Wintermeyer, L. (2017). The Future of Islamic FinTech is Bright. Retrieved from https://www.forbes.com/sites/lawrencewintermeyer/2017/12/08/the-future-ofislamic-fintech-is-bright/#684952e465fa.

World Bank. (2020). *Personal Remittances received (% of GDP)*. Data. Retrieved from https://data.worldbank.org/indicator/BX.TRF.PWKR.DT.GD.ZS

World Bank (2021). Defying Predictions, Remittance Flows Remain Strong During COVID-19 Crisis. News. Retrieved from https://www.worldbank.org/en/news/press-release/2021/05/12/defying-predictions-remittance-flows-remain-strong-during-covid-19-crisis

World Bank. (Various Years). *Personal Remittances received (Current US$)*. Data. Retrieved from https://data.worldbank.org/indicator/BX.TRF.PWKR.CD.DT. Accessed: June 12, 2022.

10
THE IMPACT OF CENTRAL BANK DIGITAL CURRENCY (CBDC) ON THE OPERATIONS OF ISLAMIC BANKS

A.K.M. Kamrul Hasan

1 Introduction

Globally accepted current forms of money are bank notes, bank deposits and central bank reserves (i.e., commercial banks' deposits at central bank). Besides, due to rapid innovation in Fintech and payment settlement system, private digital currency (Token-based money-like IC Card) is also popular around the world. On the other hand, with the growing popularity of cryptocurrencies (or crypto assets) and Distributed Ledger Technology (DLT), central banks around the world have been searching for the concept and design of digital currencies. Indeed, Central Bank Digital Currency (CBDC) has created a contemporary debate on academic circle as well as in the practitioners in last decade. The debate mainly gets momentum due to two reasons. First, several private owned digital currencies are used to settle the consumer payment, second, several central banks around the world step ahead to take pilot project to introduce a CBDC. The academic research on CBDC is still on going and central banks in the advanced economies have already stepped up to explore the opportunities of issuing CBDC and engaged in experimental work (BIS, 2020, 2021). For instance, the bank of Japan has initially aimed to start a Proof of Concept (PoC) phase 1 on CBDC as an alternative payment instrument in 2021 in responses to global demands and smooth the payment and settlement systems in the Japanese society (BOJ, 2020). In the United States, an initiative namely 'Digital Dollar project' for introducing pilot programmes for CBDC has been taken (US Senate Committee, 2021). Besides, Central Bank of the Republic of Turkey (CBRT) announced that the bank is going to examine the digital Turkish Lira currency as a potential payment settlement instrument (CBRT, 2021). Overall, the central banks around the world including China and Europe have initiated the CBDC projects to improve the payment settlement system and fend off threat from crypto

DOI: 10.4324/9781003262169-13

assets. However, there is little discussion in contemporary study on the potential impact of CBDC on Islamic banking context. To explore this, in this chapter we broadly focus on the definition and features of CBDC and its impact on Islamic baking operations specially liquidity management. The structure of the chapter is as follows. Section 2 describes the definition, trends and features of CBDC. Section 3 illustrates the architecture of CBDC. Section 4 briefly discusses about the *gharar*, CBDC and liquidity in Islamic banks whereas, Section 5 focuses on a shariah-compliant CBDC and its road map. Section 6 concludes the chapter.

2 CBDC: definition, features and trends

CBDC is considered as a new form of electronic money. 'A CBDC is a digital payment instrument, dominated in the national unit of account, that is a direct liability of the central bank' (BIS, 2020). One of the main rationales for introducing CBDC is to provide a safe central bank instrument where we observe a significant declining trend to use of cash (BIS, 2018). Scholars are very enthusiastic about the future of CBDC. For instance, 'CBDC is a global innovation which will revolutionize the international payments in the way that the first Atlantic Cable did for capital flows and international payment in 1866' (Bordo, 2021). In short, we can term CBDC as 'digital money' (Brunnermier et al., 2019, Bank of England, 2020). The major difference between cryptocurrencies (or crypto assets) and CBDC is, the former one is privately issued and not backed by any central party whereas the latter one is backed by central bank.

CBDC could be an interest bearing and a non-interest bearing. Interest-bearing CBDC would likely to increase financial inclusion and CBDC does not need to have a negative impact on bank lending operations if the central bank follows an interest rate policy rule (Andolfatto, 2018). Although till now, there is no exact physical existence of a CBDC, the Bank for International Settlement (BIS) attempts to harmonize few core features of CBDC. BIS (2020) refers that a CBDC should have three foundational principles, such as (i) 'do no harm' to central bank mandate on monetary and financial stability, (ii) it should be coexisted with the existing central bank money (cash, reserve or settlement accounts) and (iii) innovation and efficiency – it should be supportive to safe, efficient and accessible payment system. In addition, the Bank for International Settlements has described 14 core features of CBDC from three categories to fulfil the three foundational principles. The core features of CBDC that advocates in BIS (2020) are shown in Table 1.

Indeed, we have to recognize that CBDC remains a young field with limited pilot studies and testing. However, there are some potential opportunities and risks involved with CBDC. The potential opportunities include (i) it could be a useful tool for central banks to pursue their policy objectives, (ii) it continues providing safe and widely accessible central bank money, (iii) supporting a more resilient and diverse domestic payment system and (iv) it may offer opportunities

TABLE 1 Core features of CBDC

Sl no	Categories of features	Features
1	Instrumental features	Convertible, Convenient, Accepted and available, Low cost
2	System features	Secure, Instant, Resilient, Available, Throughout, Scalable, Interoperable, Flexible and adaptable
3	Institutional features	Robust legal framework, Standards

See details in BIS (2020).

that are not possible with cash (BIS, 2020). The potential risks that may arise from CBDC are as follows: (i) it could have financial stability implications that would need to assess and managed carefully, (ii) increase the potential for digital bank runs in times of stress and (iii) it could have longer-term consequences for bank funding by eroding banks; retail deposits, resulting in a less stable funding mix (BIS, 2020). However, research finds that the risk can be avoided by introducing two-tier CBDC system (Bindseil, 2020).

In a broad sense, there are three factors that are important to use CBDC as a means of payment instrument. These are widespread merchant acceptance, sufficient distribution of CBDC and demand from the consumers to pay with CBDC (Bindseil et al., 2021). Moreover, some scholars argue that allowing unrestricted access to a CBDC in to the cross-border use of CBDCs to cross-currency payments between CBDCs, there have three potential risks. For instance, (a) increase the risk of digital currency substitutions – impairing the effectiveness of domestic monetary policy and raising financial stability risk specially for emerging markets and less developed economies that have unstable currencies and weak fundamentals, (b) global spillovers – issuing a CBDC could magnify the cross-border transmission of shocks and increase exchange rate volatility and alter capital flow dynamics and (c) broader international demand for a CBDC may cause the exchange rate appreciate since cost of cross-border payment might falls by using a CBDCs as international currencies (Panetta, 2021). International cooperation among central banks could minimize the risk.

In Islamic finance and banking literature the concept of 'crypto currency' is almost similar to the traditional concept of CBDC (as we summarized in the above discussion) in terms of utilizing DLT and utility perspective. However, scholars' concern on the price volatility of crypto assets which make them reluctant to accept a CBDC as a fully shariah-compliant instrument. Once this issue has been successfully addressed, no point of differences will be existed to issue an Islamic CBDC, we believe. Next section, we summarize the architectural foundation of CBDC before moving to our core discussion.

3 Architecture of CBDC

BIS has opined that 'issuance of CBDC is not a mandatory rather a national choice and if the societies want it central banks come forward to fulfil the demand' (Carstens, 2021). A careful architectural design for CBDC is required so that the monetary policy implementation and financial stability will not be jeopardized (Carstens, 2021). Auer and Böhme (2021, 2020) mentioned three types of CBDC while architecture a retail CBDC for operation. These are 'direct' CBDC, 'hybrid and intermediated' CBDC and 'indirect' CBDC. 'Direct' CBDC refers direct claim on the central bank, which also handles all payments in real time and thus keeps a record of all retail holdings. Hybrid CBDC incorporates a two-tier structure with direct claims on the central bank while real-time payments are handled by intermediaries. In the case of indirect CBDC, a CBDC is issued and redeemed only by the central bank, but this is done indirectly to intermediaries. Intermediaries, in turn, issue a claim to consumers. The intermediary is required to fully back each claim with a CBDC holding at the central bank and the central bank operates the wholesale payment system only (Auer and Böhme, 2021, p. 10). Most recently, the Central Bank of Nigeria (CBN) has launched eNaira, a CBDC, in October 2021 which is based on a two-tier system and direct one (CBN, 2021a,b). In our view, Islamic CBDC (see in Section 6.5) should be two-tier CBDC and direct one instead of indirect CBDC. The rationale is explained in the following section.

4 *Gharar*, CBDC and Islamic banks liquidity

The term *gharar* (uncertainty) originates from the Arabic verb *gharra*, which means to deceive. Forms of *gharar* (uncertainty) include pure speculation where the outcome depends on chance or gambling, uncertain outcome where the counter-value is uncertain or not realized, inexactitude of object and unknown future of object (Paldi, 2014). Most scholars agree that the issue of speculation is related to *gharar*. Speculation according to Kamali (2000, p. 147) is the purchase and sale of an asset in the expectation of a gain from changes in the price of that asset. Some scholars consider the prohibition of *gharar* in terms of speculation have multiple dimensions. For instance, Suzuki (2013, p. 208) mentioned that

> the prohibition of *Gharar* in speculation is considered as the wisdom for minimizing the potential periodic financial disaster. In parallel, under the prohibition of Gharar (also the profit-loss sharing) framework, it may have created a dilemma of the so-called 'Murabaha syndrome' leading to the financial disintermediation (particularly the dry-up of long-term funds) in the potentials in the agricultural and industrial sector. Long-term growth may suffer as a result.

Al-Saati (2003) summarizes the concept of *gharar* from Islamic jurisprudence into three headings. These are (a) a state where it is unknown whether something will take place or not (i.e. uncertainty of existence of the subject matter of sale), (b) ignorance of the purchaser of what he has bought and the seller does not know what he has sold and (c) a state of transaction where consequences are concealed. Al-Saati (2003) also classifies the *gharar* into four types in terms of degree of its permissibility in Islamic transaction. These include (i) prohibited *gharar* – a kind of uncertainty which is taken voluntarily and transfer of money/goods with no value creation or created from the transaction, (ii) permissible *gharar* – if there is no general agreement among the school of jurisprudence to prohibit and invalid the contract that involves such kind of *gharar*. For instance, two sales in one contract, option sale, conditional sale, etc., (iii) acceptable *gharar* – if the *gharar* sources are either endogenous or exogenous uncertainty, it is permissible in shariah. For example, exogenous uncertainty are changes in consumer's taste, firms' technologies and weather conditions and of endogenous uncertainty, the buyer's uncertainty about the suitability of the seller he meets, or the quality of commodity he buys, or the term of the trade that will take place and (iv) mandatory *gharar* – the uncertainty that goes with the transaction and which can't be avoided. The musharakah, ijarah and mudarabah contracts are well examples of mandatory contract. In short, we can say that in commercial contract we cannot totally eliminate the uncertainty and there are always some elements of *gharar* (Aldohni, 2015; Hassan and Lewis, 2017) and a commercial transaction is permissible in shariah context when all the contracting parties in the transaction share the same level of acceptable risk (Balala, 2014). It is worth to refer Alvia (2020) who summarizes the definition and scope of *gharar* in Islamic finance in the following way:

> Gharar in Islamic finance is not without issues, primarily because there is no universal agreement among Muslim jurists as to what degree of legal uncertainty is acceptable in commercial transactions. *Gharar* is therefore a matter of interpretation, which in itself can cause issues (Nehad and Khanfar, 2016). In an attempt to counter such issues, learned scholars are generally relied upon to distinguish between contracts containing minor *gharar* (allowed) and contracts containing substantial *gharar* (forbidden and therefore void) (Balala, 2014).

As we discussed in Section 2 that CBDC is kind of virtual currency that is issued by central bank. We should note that the fundamental features of CBDC are identical to that of bank notes because both currencies are issued and backed by central authority. However, there exists a couple of differences between CBDC and bank notes from a utility perspective. For instance, financial transactions with the CBDC are more secure as it uses the blockchain and DLT to record transactions. Besides, CBDC has a flexibility to issue either in tier one (i.e., issuing CBDC directly from central bank to merchant and person) or tier two (i.e., through regulated and supervised financial institutions) whereas bank notes are always issued by central banks under tier two system. We should note that introducing tier one type CBDC requires a more technological and stronger regulatory framework. Ward and Rochemont (2019) refer to a few unique features of CBDC compared to bank notes. As the central bank directly guarantees the at-par convertibility of CBDC into cash and/or reserves, it would not provide lending facilities for holders of the digital currency (Ward and Rochemont, 2019). The World Economic Forum (WEF, 2019) has also described a few pros of CBDC over bank notes. These are (i) reducing frictions and costs associated with physical cash storage, transport and management within the banking system, (ii) providing alternative to private sector digital payments technologies, to counter operational risk or monopolistic control by those providers if they become dominant and to serve as a government-issued alternative for cash if it becomes scarce in the future, (iii) improves payment system resilience to cyber-attacks, operational failures and hardware faults relative to centralized data storage and processing, which has less data redundancy and, therefore, may be less robust (WEF, 2019). As we have referred earlier that if we consider fiat money and CBDC in terms of central authority, there is no basic difference however in terms of circulation or impact on bank money supply there are differences. Besides, the fluctuations of nominal value (since there are no fixed assets/gold behind issuance of CBDC) in the case of CBDC might be higher which might increase the inflation in turn enhance financial instability (Abubakar et al. 2019). Abubakar et al. (2019) also refer that the empirical study of Abdullah (2015) shows that high-value currency (the cause) means low prices (the effect) over the long term, or a low-value currency would involve high prices; thus, in order to obtain price stability, monetary authorities should pay attention to a stable value of money rather than focusing on the quantity of money, or interest rate, or even target prices. Considering this, we can say that the price fluctuations in CBDC could create chaos in the financial system. Now let's examine how CBDC has an impact on Islamic financial institutions (IFIs) operation, especially liquidity management.

First, let us discuss, how traditional IFIs are managing the liquidity at operational level. Conventional commercial banks are investing their surplus liquidity in call money market instruments and in governmental treasury bills and bonds. As both are interest-bearing instruments, IFIs could not participate in such short-term money market. Rizkiah (2018) documented that several Islamic liquidity management instruments are used across the countries in which Malaysia has much more diversified instruments and sukuk might be most familiar instrument treated as liquidity management tools (see details in Rizkiah, 2018p. 139). Global and domestic sukuk are issued with short-term and long-term maturity. Short-term sukuk with maturity of 1 year or less are indispensable in particular meeting liquidity management requirements of IFIs (IIFM, 2021). Total global short-term sukuk issuance since the inception of the sukuk market stands at USD 502.05 billion, whereas during 2020, short-term sukuk issuance was USD 56.741 billion against 2019 issuance of USD 40.00 billion which translates into an increase of around 41.84% p.a. of short-term sukuk issuances (IIFM, 2021).

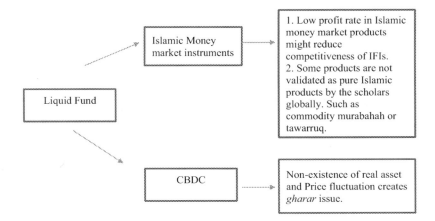

FIGURE 1 Liquidity management dilemma for IFIs.

Malaysia's share of the short-term sukuk market including International Islamic Liquidity Management remains dominant with the total market share of around 52.60% during 2020 (IIFM, 2021). However, the main obstacles for managing IFIs liquidity through short-term sukuk has the debate among the Islamic scholars regarding its *shairah* legitimacy as there are different opinions exists in Islamic schools of jurisprudence especially on *tawarruq*-type issue (Sarker, 2019).

Besides, in countries where the Islamic banking market share is not dominant, the profit rate of liquidity instruments is low because of their low demand and roll out. For example, Bangladesh Bank (BB), the central bank of the country has introduced Bangladesh Government Islamic Investment Bond (BGIIB) in 2004 with the objective to develop a sound foundation for the Islamic bond market and to convert excess liquidity into investment through Islamic bonds, however fund return is very low compared to other deposit products (BB, 2021; Sarker, 2019). In turn, BGIIB became an unattractive instrument to the Islamic banks in Bangladesh. In addition to BGIIB, BB has formed an Islamic inter-bank fund market (IIFM) in 2011, a new platform for Islamic *Sharia'h*-based scheduled banking companies and financial institutions and Islamic banking branches of scheduled conventional banking companies to conduct transactions into IIFM (Sarker, 2019). IIFM has been established in resemblance with the call money market for conventional banks to eliminate temporary and short-term liquidity crisis of Islamic banks; however, Islamic banks are not participating in this market due to lower yield rates (Sarker., 2019). To sum up, existing Islamic money market instruments face dilemmas with its legitimacy and profit rates and IFIs are struggling to manage surplus/deficit liquidity management.

On the other hand, CBDC could be a better option for IFIs for managing surplus/deficit liquidity pressure. As discussed, CBDC is a central bank instrument and can be issued with interest or interest-free. One feasible option of IFIs is to hold CBDC if it is interest-free, but profit can be loaded in CBDC like *sukuk* pay the yields to its holders. However, the crux question at this point is the price stability of CBDC and its underlying assets. In fact, the massive price fluctuations in the crypto assets link to *gharar* and if CBDC contains such price fluctuations as typical cryptocurrencies have, IFIs will face new dilemmas with the CBDC. The summary of the above discussion can be shown in Figure 1.

5 Roads towards a Shariah-compliant CBDC

We could recall that Bitcoin, the largest cryptocurrency by market value, was more volatile and proved just choppy as any other during 2021. While observing the price fluctuation of cryptocurrencies in the past decade, one of a leading bankers termed Bitcoin as 'it's a speculative asset' (Hajric, 2021). Probably this would be a real reason to issue a shariah-compliant CBDC. We should note that scholars are concerned about the features of an Islamic currency from several point of views. For instance, Hanif (2020) states that an Islamic currency should consist of eight features such as acceptability, measure and store of value, durability, desirability, stability, transferability, flexibility and security. As discussed, a CBDC's features meet all criteria (see Table 1) for being it an Islamic currency except concern on *gharar* that raised mainly from the fear of price fluctuations. Once a *shariah*-compliant CBDC is introduced, IFIs could easily be tapped on it and optimize the CBDC to tackle their liquidity management dilemma as we showed in Figure 1. In the next two sub-sections, we proposed two theoretical approaches to issue a shariah-complaint CBDC by which *gharar* could be resolved since there will be a very little possibility for price fluctuations in these two options.

5.1 Precious-metal–backed cryptocurrency (PMBC)

Ajouz et al. (2020) advocate for shariah-compliant PMBC in lieu of traditional one. However, the main limitation of this concept is the scarcity of precious metals and political compromise with the rich Muslim majority countries statesmen and rest of world powers. Another option is the issuance of only gold-based CBDC. Aliyu et al. (2020) documented that there are five *shariah*-compliant private digital currencies/cryptocurrencies in operation of which two (namely, OneGram and Bayan Token) are based on assets. OneGram is completely based on gold whereas Bayan Token is based on cloud server service. Following the development of private *shariah*-based cryptocurrencies, central banks could take initiative to introduce gold back CBDC instead of following traditional blockchain technology. However, again there is an issue of how to reconcile the supply of gold to issue a huge amount of CBDC. Few rich Muslim states might be controlling the supply of CBDC in such a gold-backed CBDC and the price fluctuation might be higher if demand goes up.

5.2 Asset-backed CBDC (ABCBDC)

A recent study conducted by the BIS reveals that most of the central banks in the emerging market and developing economies (EMDEs) prefer retail CBDC instead of wholesale CBDC (see details in Alfonso et al. (2022). EMDEs main motivation to issue retail CBDC is to national use only and place the greatest weight on financial inclusion, efficiency of the domestic payments system and safety of the payments system (Alfonso et al., 2022). Most of the Muslim majority countries are in EMDEs category and having such a reality, we could consider issuing ABCBDC instead of PMBC or Gold-backed CBDC. To issue ABCBDC long-term *sukuk* structure could be applied. There is a thin difference between asset-based *sukuk* and asset-backed *sukuk*, i.e., asset-based *sukuk* return considers as traditional income from bond whereas the asset-backed sukuk return as income from equity. Scholars argue that the latter one much more shariah compliant than the former one (see details in Herzi, 2016). Therefore, central bank could create a Special Purpose Vehicle for the issuance of ABCBDC. It can be backed by any strategic state-owned assets like minerals and natural oil field, gold mine, etc. However, it would be difficult for developing Muslim countries to issue either ABCBDC or asset-based CBDC due to resource constraint.

Overall, we argue that if there is specific asset underlying the CBDC the *gharar* issue could be resolved. Table 2 shows the implication of *shariah*-based CBDC (based on our proposed two options) on various aspects.

In our theoretical discussion on proposed Islamic CBDC, we argue to issue a CBDC on asset-backed type which might create a differentiation with its counterpart bank notes and conventional CBDC. Currently, IFIs are to some extent tap on the conventional call money market to borrow funds however they could not participate in the call money market as a lender (due to association with interest). On the other hand, the profit rate in Islamic call money markets is too low to attract the IFIs to invest their funds. Having such a reality, we suggest that

TABLE 2 Implication of Shariah-based CBDC

Details	PMBC	ABCBDC
Is it possible to make production in large volume?	Somewhat difficult due to scarcity of precious metals	Not difficult, however, developing Muslim majority countries might face resource constraint
Is there any *gharar* issue involved?	No	No
Will it be supportive to manage IFIs' liquidity issue?	Yes	Yes
Any chance to price fluctuations?	May be	May not

if CBDC is issued under asset-backed, the conventional financial institutions as well as IFIs would invest their funds in it. Either the case of high/low demand for CBDCs or the competition among CBDCs issued by multiple central banks may not fluctuate the price of ABCBDC. This will differentiate between typical CBDC, bank notes and ABCBDC. We assume that since the market participants are now larger, the return will be attractive. In turn, IFIs have an incentive to invest and manage the liquidity through the CBDC marketplace. We presume that, in such a way, circulation of CBDC could ease the liquidity management dilemma in case of IFIs. Finally, we should note that, most of the virtual currencies including CBDC will facilitate the 'peer-to-peer' settlements and decentralized manner (no intermediary). A retail CBDC acts as a substitute or complement for cash and an alternative to traditional bank deposits. Obviously, it depends on the rule of necessity (*darurah*) and the state of a country's current payment system. For instance, The Central Bank of Denmark expressed a doubt of the potential role of retail CBDC, in a report published in 2017 in the Denmark financial system, 'in a country like Denmark, with a secure and effective payment system, it is difficult to see what CBDC would contribute that is not already covered by the existing payment solutions' (DNB, 2017, p. 21). Hence, we can presume that the emerging economies where the payment system is not developed as par with the developed economies, may have most to gain to introduce CBDC and it would play a key role in 'peer-to-peer' settlements. If so, circulation of CBDC could create uncertainty/*gharar* to some extent in emerging economies. It is true for both conventional and Islamic financial systems.

6 Conclusion

In this chapter, we attempt to discuss the core concept of CBDC and its architecture of Islamic CBDC. We discuss how IFIs are facing dilemma in managing surplus or deficit in liquidity management. We advocate that although there are several financial instruments currently used in managing such dilemma, due to low-profit rate, the liquidity management products are not so attractive to the IFIs. We believe that to solve this issue if Islamic CBDC is introduced by the national regulator, IFIs will be interested to invest on it to manage their surplus or deficit liquidity problem. At this point, the price fluctuation in CBDC may be a *shariah* concern for IFIs due to *gharar*. To resolve the *gharar* issue in CBDC, we presume that ABCBDC could be a feasible solution. However, as there are a few live CBDC exists till date and most of the advanced economies and emerging economies adopt 'wait and see' approach to launch fully operational CBDC, we have little operational experience and few empirical academic research on a functional CBDC. The theoretical discussion in this chapter on the initiation of Islamic CBDC and operational concept of managing the liquidity problem in IFIs through Islamic CBDC obviously demand further research along with their conventional pair.

References

Abdullah, A. (2015). Economic security requires monetary and price stability: Analysis of Malaysian macroeconomic and credit data. *Al-Shajarah: Journal of the International Institute of Islamic Thought and Civilization (ISTAC)*, 205–247.

Abubakar, M., Hassan, M. K. and Haruna, M. A. (2019). Cryptocurrency Tide and Islamic Finance Development: Any Issue? In Choi, J.J. and Ozkan, B. (Eds.), *Disruptive Innovation in Business and Finance in the Digital World (International Finance Review*, Vol. 20, pp. 189–200). Bingley: Emerald Publishing Limited. https://doi.org/10.1108/S1569-376720190000020019

Ajouz, M., Abdullah, A. and Kassim, S. (2020). Developing a Shari'ah-compliant precious metal backed cryptocurrency. *JKAU: Islamic Economics*, 33 (1), 3–20.

Aldohni, A. K. (2015). The quest for a better legal and regulatory framework for Islamic banking. *Ecclesiastic Law Journal*, 17, 15–35.

Alfonso, V., Kamin, S. and Zampolli, F. (2022). Central bank digital currencies (CBDCs) in Latin America and the Caribbean. *BIS Working Papers No 989*. BIS Representative Office for the Americas, Monetary and Economic Department.

Aliyu, A., Abu Bakar, K., Matsuda, G., Darwish, T. S. J., Abdullah, A. H., Ismail, A. S., Radzi, R. Z. R. M., Yusof, A. F., Mohamad, M. M., Idris, M. Y., Ismail, Z., Yaacob, A. C. and Herman. (2020). Review of Some Existing Shariah-Compliant Cryptocurrency. *Journal of Contemporary Islamic Studies*, 6 (1), 22–43.

Al-Saati, A. R. (2003). The Permissible Gharar (Risk) in Classical Islamic Jurisprudence. *Journal of King Abdulaziz University: Islamic Economics*, 16 (2), 3–19.

Alvia, D. D. (2020). Risk, uncertainty and the market: a rethinking of Islamic and Western finance. *International Journal of Law in Context*, 16, 339–352. doi:10.1017/S1744552320000154

Andolfatto, D. (2018). Assessing the Impact of Central Bank Digital Currency on Private Banks. *Working Papers 2018-026*. Federal Reserve Bank of St. Louis, revised 22 April 2020.

Auer, R. and Böhme, R. (2020). The technology of retail central bank digital currency. *BIS Quarterly Review*, March 2020, 85–100.

Auer, R. and Böhme, R. (2021). Central bank digital currency: the quest for minimally invasive technology. *BIS Working papers: No 948*. Monetary and Economic Department, BIS.

Balala, M. H. (2014). *Islamic Finance and Law: Theory and Practice in a Globalized World*. New York: I.B. Tauris & Co Ltd.

Bangladesh Bank (2021). *Developments of Islamic Banking in Bangladesh (July-September 2021)*. Dhaka: Research Department, Head Office, Bangladesh Bank.

Bank for International Settlements (2018). *Central Bank Digital Currencies. Technical Report*. Basel Committee on Payments and Market Infrastructures. Basel: Switzerland.

Bank for International Settlements (2020). *Central Bank Digital Currencies: Foundational Principles and Core Features: Report 1 in a Series of Collaborations from a Group of Central Banks*. Basel: Switzerland.

Bank for International Settlements (2021). *BIS Papers no. 114: Ready, Steady, Go? – Results of the Third BIS Survey on Central Bank Digital Currency*. Basel: Switzerland.

Bank of England (2020). *Discussion Paper: Central Bank Digital Currency Opportunities, Challenges and Design*. London: United Kingdom.

Bank of Japan (2020). *The Bank of Japan's Approach of Central Bank Digital Currency*. Tokyo: Japan.

Bindseil, U. (2020). Tiered CBDC and the Financial System. *Occasional Paper Series, 2351*, ECB, Frankfurt am Main, January.

Bindseil, U., Panetta, F. and Terol, I. (2021). Central Bank Digital Currency: Functional Scope, Pricing and Controls. *Occasional Paper Series, No. 286*. ECB, Frankfurt am Main, December.

Bordo, M. D. (2021). Central Bank Digital Currency in Historical Perspective: Another Crossroad in Monetary History. *NBER Working Paper No. 29171*, August 2021.

Brunnermier, M., James, H. and Landau, J. P. (2019). The Digitalization of Money. *NBER Working Paper 26300*, September 2019.

Carstens, A. (2021). Digital Currencies and the Future of the Monetary System. *BIS*, January 2021 (https://www.bis.org/speeches/sp210127).

Central Bank of Nigeria (CBN) (2021a). *Design Paper for the eNaira*. Retrieved from https://www.enaira.gov.ng/about/design

Central Bank of Nigeria (CBN) (2021b). *Central Bank of Nigeria Press Release: President Buhari to Unveil eNaira on Monday, 25 October 2021*. Retrieved from https://www.cbn.gov.ng/Out/2021/CCD/eNaira%20Launch%20Press%20release%20%20231021.pdf

Central Bank of the Republic of Turkey (CBRT) (2021). *Press Release on Central Bank Digital Turkish Lira R&D Project*. Central Bank of the Republic of Turkey, Head Office, Ankara.

Danmarks National Bank (2017). Central bank digital currency in Denmark? *Analysis*, (28), 1–23.

Hajric, V. (2021, December 31). Bitcoin closes lucrative year with a whimper. Al Jazeera. Retrieved from https://www.aljazeera.com/economy/2021/12/31/bitcoin-closes-lucrative-year-with-a-whimper

Hanif, M. (2020). Developing a fair currency system. *ISRA International Journal of Islamic Finance*, 12 (3), 325–345.

Hassan, K. and Lewis, M. K. (2007). *Handbook of Islamic Finance*. London: Edward Elgar.

Herzi, A. A. (2016). A Comparative study of asset based and asset backed sukuk from the shariah compliance perspective. *JMFIR*, 13 (1), 25–34.

International Islamic Financial Market (IIFM) (2021). *Sukuk Report: A Comprehensive study of the global sukuk market (10th Edition)*. Manama, Kingdom of Bahrain: International Islamic Financial Market.

Kamali, M. H. (2000). *Actualization (Taf'il) of the Higher Purposes (Maqasid) of Shariah*. Herndon, VA: International Institute of Islamic Thought.

Nehad, A. and Khanfar, A. (2016). A critical analysis of the concept of Gharar in Islamic financial contracts: different perspective. *Journal of Economic Cooperation and Development*, 37, 1–24.

Paldi, C. (2014). Understanding Riba and Gharar in Islamic Finance. *Journal of Islamic Banking and Finance*, 2(1), 249–259.

Panetta, F. (2021). *"Hic sunt leones" – open research questions on the international dimension of central bank digital currencies*. Speech by Mr Fabio Panetta, Member of the Executive Board of the European Central Bank, at the ECB- Central Bank Research Association (CEBRA) conference on international aspects of digital currencies and fintech, Frankfurt am Main, 19 October 2021. Retrieved from https://www.bis.org/review/r211118c.htm

Rizkiah, S. K. (2018). Liquidity management in Islamic banking: Issues and challenges. *Tazkia Islamic Finance and Business Review*, 12(2), 132–152.

Sarker, M. A. A. (2019). *Liquidity Management Instruments for the Islamic Banks in Bangladesh (Special Research Work (SRW-1904))*. Dhaka: Bangladesh Bank.

Suzuki, Y. (2013). A Posttps://www.emerald.com/insight/search?q=Yasushi%20Suzuki" *International Journal of Islamic and Middle Eastern Finance and Management*, 6 (3), 200–210. https://doi.org/10.1108/IMEFM-Sep-2012-0086

US Senate Committee (2021). *Building a Stronger Financial System: Opportunities of a Central Bank Digital Currency: Testimony of Hon. J. Christopher Giancarlo*. Washington DC: US Senate Committee on Banking Housing and Urban Affairs. Retrieved from https://www.banking.senate.gov/imo/media/doc/Giancarlo%20Testimony%206-9-21.pdf

Ward, O. and Rochemont, S. (2019). *An addendum to "A Cashless Society- Benefits, Risks and Issues (Interim paper)": Understanding Central Bank Digital Currencies (CBDC)*. Institute and Faculty of Actuaries. Retrieved from The Cashless Society Working Party: https://www.actuaries.org.uk/practice-areas/finance-andinvestment/finance-and-investment-research-working-parties/cashless-society-working-party.

World Economic Forum (WEF). (2019). *White paper: Central Banks and Distributed Ledger Technology: How Are Central Banks Exploring Blockchain Today?* Cologny/Geneva, Switzerland: World Economic Forum.

11
TAKAFULTECH REFLECTS THE MAQASID AL-SHARIAH ETHOS IN TAKAFUL

Amirul Afif Muhamat and Norfaridah Ali Azizan

1 Introduction

"It's not a faith in technology. It's faith in people."

Steve Jobs

The words of wisdom from Steve Jobs about technology implies that the raison d'être of technology is to lift up the mankind quality of life which is also the ultimate purpose of Shariah. In this chapter, the discussion will be centred on the connection between the takaful operators and the implication of technology to assist the takaful operators to better serve the takaful participants (policyholders) and ultimately to achieve the maqasid al-Shariah.

The chapter is structured into several sections, which is immediately after this section is an overview on the takaful industry, followed by discussion on the maqasid al-Shariah. Subsequently after that are arguments on the dilemma faced by the takaful participants and then deliberation on the examples of takafultech technologies such as drone and blockchain as well as their potentials. Gradually, discussion will be focusing on the challenges of takafultech and linking towards the maqasid of Shariah. Last but not least is the conclusion to bring into focus the essential points of discussion in this chapter.

2 Overview of *takaful*

Takaful is one of the main components in the modern operations of Islamic finance. The importance of *takaful* can be seen when it was developed after the Islamic banking, particularly in the Muslim countries that have dual banking systems. *Takaful* provides the necessary protection scheme that is *Shariah* compliant for individual, group and corporate.

Islamic Financial Services Industry Stability Report 2020 by Islamic Financial Services Board mentions that the global *takaful* industry has recorded approximately at 8.5% in terms of the compound growth rate from 2011 to 2018, and five countries, Iran, Saudi Arabia, Malaysia, the UAE and Indonesia, contributed 91% of the global total contributions. The same report also highlighted that in 2018, the general *takaful* represents higher contribution, 82.6% compared to family *takaful* at 17.4%. This is mainly due to the different market features in which the Gulf Cooperation Council countries focused more on the general *takaful* compared to the Muslim countries in South-East Asia such as Malaysia and Indonesia, which gained more from the family *takaful* business.

The total global *takaful* assets in 2019 as reported by ICD-Refinitiv in the Islamic Finance Development Report 2020 is estimated to be at USD51 billion with 336 *takaful* operators (including windows) actively servicing the *takaful* participants all over the world, and 80% or the Top Three markets' share in 2019 for the global *takaful* assets are Saudi Arabia, Iran and Malaysia.

The industry is now equipped itself with the necessary knowledge, skills and capacity to respond to the takafultech requirements. Takafultech which derives its name from the words *takaful* plus technology (*takaful*+technology) represents the contemporary era of the industry brought by the disruption to the incumbents facilitated by the sophisticated technological tools such as data analytics, internet of things (IoT), clouds and others – most important, it must be Shariah compliant.

The general insurance and *takaful* business are expected to face stiff competition from the standalone insurtech/takafultech (PWC, 2016). In 2016–2017, insurers and *takaful* operators mostly uncertain in terms of consumers readiness for digitalisation. EY (2020) suggests several major areas that will be influenced by the "tech", which are:

i   Underwriting and risk
ii Claims and data management
iii Products and customer experience

This chapter discusses two takafultech technologies which are drone and the blockchain, and their potentials to assist the *takaful* operators to enhance their fulfilment of the *maqasid* al-Shariah.

3 Maqasid al-Shariah in the context of *takaful*

Takaful products and services are financial instruments that are closely related to the fulfilment of the *maqasid Shariah*. This is not peculiar since the early inception of *takaful* which can be traced back to the old Arab tribal practices, the *aqilah* system, to contribute funds that will be used to pay as compensation to the victim from another tribe. In most cases, this has helped to avoid tribal dispute (which normally leads to fighting) from happening. Eventually, when Islam came and spread all over Arabia, the practices which are compatible with the Islamic tenets are remained to be practiced.

Therefore, such form of protection which has managed to avoid the tribal conflict from happening, and in today's modern *takaful* operation, the services and products offered by the *takaful* operators have fulfilled the five components of *maqasid* of *Shariah* which are to protect and preserve the religion, life, progeny, intellect and wealth (Auda, 2008).

3.1 To protect and preserve religion

It is important to note that in *takaful*, the concept of *tawakkal* is pertinent because it emphasises the effort put by the Muslims to ensure the next of kin will be living in a respectable condition if the breadwinner or spouse dead as a result of unfortunate event. In addition, such planning is also accompanied by the intention to gain blessings from Allah while at the same time hoping that such calamity will not happen.

Likewise, if the calamity occurs, the next of kin will be compensated accordingly. This is important so that their current condition can be maintained and not deteriorated. It will be bad if the breadwinner dies, and the family suffers financially due to lack of financial protection in the form of *takaful*. This terrible condition has possibility to cause the victim's family in disarray which perhaps leads the kids to be involved in immoral and criminal activities because they want to "run" from the delicate situation or to find easy yet wrongful way to get money to survive post-death of the breadwinner. In other words, there are possibilities that the next of kin becomes the victim of situation which causing them to do something against the Islamic teachings.

Therefore, *takaful* is essential to ensure the one of the *maqasid* of *Shariah* which is to protect and preserve religion is upheld. This is consistent with the Prophet Muhammad S.A.W. hadith[1]:

> Narrated from Amir bin Sad bin Abi Waqqas that his father said, "In the year of the last Hajj of the Prophet I became seriously ill and the Prophet used to visit me inquiring about my health. I told him, I am reduced to this state because of illness and I am wealthy and have no inheritors except a daughter (in this narration the name of Amir bin Sad was mentioned and in fact it is a mistake; the narrator is Aisha bint Sad bin Abi Waqqas). Should I give two-thirds of my property in charity? He said, no. I asked, half? He said, no. Then he added, one-third, and even one-third is much. You'd better leave your inheritors wealthy rather than leaving them poor, begging others. You will get a reward for whatever you spend for Allah's sake, even for what you put in your wife's mouth..."

3.2 To protect and preserve life

This is another facet of *maqasid* of *Shariah* that is closely related to *takaful*, being a business that manages risk on behalf of the *takaful* participants. This element of *maqasid* is empowered in *takaful* on the basis that in the event of difficulty, *takaful* operators will compensate the unfortunate participant from the pooled funds contributed by other fellow participants. The compensation will be used to assist and to ensure that even though the unfortunate participant experienced deterioration of health or being a victim to any disaster such as fire or flood; it will not cause the unfortunate participant and the next of kin to give up on their lives or stop from getting the necessary treatment for the disease.

Figure 1 shows the global figures of victims who died from suicide. There are various reasons that contributed to this such as depression, notably as a result of the rising costs of living including medical costs, domestic relationships, jobless and others.

3.3 To protect and preserve progeny

In the context of *takaful*, to protect and preserve progeny can be best described by ensuring the next of kin to have proper life even after the demise of the breadwinner. This concern is especially relevant in maintaining the family lifestyle so that other social illnesses do not infiltrate the family, particularly the

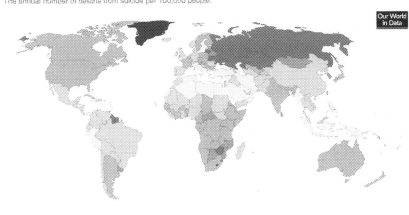

FIGURE 1 Death rate from suicides 2017.
Source: https://ourworldindata.org/suicide

children. There are various reports depicted that those children who lost their family members are prone to psychological issues such as inferiority complex, anger management and others. While *takaful* might not be directly related to the situation; but maintaining or providing assistance in the form of compensation (monetary) will assist the surviving family members to continue with their current lives without having to adjust too much.

3.4 To protect and preserve intellect

This objective emphasises on the needs for Muslims to be able to exercise their freedom to think independently and at the same time to protect their physical and mental from element that can harm them. In the context of *takaful*, when a *takaful* participant faces an accident that can harm his mental capacity and even body, then through the assistance rendered by the *takaful* operators, such an unfortunate situation can be improved and perhaps to be reinstated to the initial condition.

3.5 To protect and preserve wealth

The last element of *maqasid* of *Shariah* which is to protect and preserve wealth can be realised when the compensation received from the *takaful* operators is used to maintain the standard of living prior to the unfortunate event or disaster happened. Moreover, some products such as investment-linked funds are aimed to generate wealth for the *takaful* participants while at the same time offers protection package. Likewise, the hospitalisation benefits shall assist the *takaful* participant to regain the health condition to continue life as before which eventually permits the person to work again – to build individual's wealth.

4 Dilemma of the *takaful* participants

If we regard *takaful* participants to be in the dilemma, it can be controversial subject to some *takaful* practitioners because it focuses on the grievances of the *takaful* participants towards *takaful* operators. Surely, it is not a favourable topic when you are having a cup of tea in the early morning or even a glass of milk before you sleep. Nevertheless, the discussion on this issue should not be dropped rather should be brought to the mainstream discussion.

Therefore, as highlighted earlier, this chapter presents its perspectives from the lens of *takaful* participants. Therefore, the following discussions describe the issues faced by the *takaful* participants.

4.1 'Love–hate' relationship

This relationship becomes critical for *takaful* operators that are setup as stock form *takaful* due to the existence of two principals apart from the *takaful* participants – the shareholders. These two principals play different roles but the onus of bearing most of the risks are on the *takaful* participants (without neglecting the role of shareholders). Yet, the direction and decision of *takaful* operators are being decided by the management of *takaful* operators who being more incline towards the shareholders.

While no one should argue on the role of shareholders who provide the seed capital to setup the business (infrastructure, manpower and paid-up capital) and required by the central bank to fork out funds in the event of financial difficulty faced by the *takaful* operator in form of benevolent financing or *qard hassan*. Yet, one also must realise the heavy burden borne by the *takaful* participants (Mohd Kassim, 2013; Muhamat et al., 2019).

The *takaful* participants who are the intended beneficiaries from the *takaful* operation bear two types of risks; underwriter and investment risks while the shareholders, who are the founders of the *takaful* operator, bear three types of risks which are expense risk, operational and investment risks.

At a glance, the shareholders seemed responsible for more risks compared to the *takaful* participants but if we trace back the source of funding to address these risks, then we will notice that most of the risks are actually being mitigated by the *takaful* participants through the "contribution or premium" that they paid. Perhaps, only investment risk is the only one that being uniquely related to the shareholders – much as the exposure of the invested funds.

Thus, we can delineate the risks that are borne by the *takaful* participants in two circumstances:

i   Directly from the *takaful* participants (from the Participants Account)
ii   Indirectly from the *takaful* participants through the contribution they pay (Participant Special Account)

The pricing mechanism for *takaful* product will take into consideration various costing elements, among the major costs are marketing, reserve requirement, re-*takaful*, service fee (manpower cost) of *takaful* operator and others.

Likewise, if we postulate an event of financial difficulty due to the skyrocketing of *takaful* claims by the *takaful* participants that require *retakaful* operator to intervene, we have to recognise that such service is actually funded (to some extent) by the *takaful* participants. Only if the situation worsening, then the shareholders will be required to provide *qard hassan* financing which is also must be repaid from the *takaful* participants' fund in the future. It can be recommended to be written-off if the financial position of the Participants Account cannot be recovered after a significant period.

Undeniably, the shareholders have important roles in *takaful* operation, but at the same time, *takaful* participants are also at the heart of *takaful* operation being the focus of the business – thus more should be done to get the involvement of *takaful* participants in the *takaful* operator's strategic decision-making process especially matters that concerning them such as investment of the funds, price or charge of the *takaful* policies as well as the benefits or compensation package.

First and foremost, the cost of *tabarru'* or contribution that keep on increasing for both businesses, family and general *takaful*, although the former might be more serious than the latter. While medical card policies are exposed to such issue, but *takaful* operators must work in tandem with the medical providers to reduce the medical costs. For instance, in the long run, may be *takaful* operators can have their own hospital which will be different from the panel hospital because the in-house hospital (funded by the *takaful* operators) will be more transparent when treating the *takaful* participants and able to charge reasonable price for such treatment.

Next is on the *takaful* compensation, which is battling year in and year out, to ensure it is able to meet the current economic condition. This is important although the *takaful* products have been structured diligently by the actuarial and product development staff, but it might not be sufficient to sustain the *takaful* participants' requirements and lifestyle; either as investment return or underwriting surplus.

Customer service must be put as priority because it is the first contact that the *takaful* operators have with others. Furthermore, one of the purposes of information communication and technologies (ICT) that has been adopted and embraced by the *takaful* operators is to increase customers' satisfaction. The fourth concern is to pave way for the *takaful* participants to be involved with the operation of *takaful* business.

Reflecting the core business of *takaful* operators is to service the *takaful* participants, but it seems that the *takaful* participants lack choice apart from expressing their dissatisfaction by leaving the *takaful* operator and becoming client to a new one. Importantly, this should not be the case since the wave of the Industrial Revolution (IR 4.0) has affected all types of businesses involving *takaful* sector, hence the takafultech becomes a theme that should be heeded by all *takaful* operators. The takafultech should empower *takaful* operators to encourage more involvement of *takaful* participants in *takaful* operation particularly to address the issues as highlighted in Diagram 3 above.

5 Takafultech empowers *takaful* participants

This section discusses the possible impacts that takafultech is able to bring to the *takaful* participants if the *takaful* operator decides to implement proper takafultech strategies in the company. The takafultech is subcomponent of financial technology or colloquially termed as fintech, which is a new business landscape that has shaped financial markets all over the world. This new phenomenon requires responsive and agile management of the companies to continuously cope with the changes.

The evolutions of mankind in terms of creativity and innovation marked the transition of activities that are highly dependent on manpower to machine power, to electrical and electronics machines, followed by digital revolution through computers and now through the automation of processes with the IoT, cloud computing, big data, etc. – from IR 1.0 to IR 4.0. *Takaful* industry which is part of the essential component of Islamic financial system needs to adopt and adapt to this new environment as well. Moreover, they must ensure such changes are compliance with *Shariah*.

Two major areas under the takafultech that will be discussed in this chapter are:

- Drone
- Smart contract (utilises the blockchain technology)

These two initiatives bring holistic impacts to the *takaful* participants as well as to the *takaful* operator, hence benefit the shareholders as well.

5.1 Drone

Drone is also called unmanned aerial vehicle (UAV) that has been used for various purposes such as recreational, scientific and commercial issues. An autonomous insurance drone can include additional drone body, with a sensor device allocated on the drone and it saves sensor input that can be disseminated wireless to the insurance processer that will display the data for inspection or analysis (Luciani et al., 2016). It has been widely used in the insurance sector, especially in developed countries, but such adoption can be considered as still negligible for developing countries.

Preliminary research by Muhamat et al. (2021) informs that for instance in Malaysia and Indonesia, drone is yet to be adopted as part of the *takaful* operator's mechanism for either underwriting or damage (loss) assessing procedure. In general, drone has many benefits that can be obtained by the *takaful* operators. However, the discussion in Table 1 solely focuses on the underwriting process, damage inspection and disaster victim identification (DVI).

5.2 Smart contract upon the blockchain technology

The smart contract works well with the blockchain technology by virtually allowing another party of the agreement to access, read and eventually sign the details. Thus, it works well with the blockchain technology by enhancing and protecting the sensitive information of the contracts. The blockchain can be briefly defined as a database that shares nodes of computer network and distributes and stores the information in a digital format. The information is stored confidentially in a group; or known as block. Once the capacity is maximised, it will be closed and another block is created and tagged to the previous block. The process continues until a long chain of blocks, or simply "the blockchain" is created (VanderLinden et al., 2018).

TABLE 1 Benefits of drone in *takaful* operation

	Underwriting	Damage inspection	DVI
Purpose	Drone can be used to assess the risk of the property before determining the appropriate pricing scheme to be charged to the potential participant.	Drone can be navigated to inspect the damages that are remote and difficult to access such as damages either natural disaster or man-made disaster that happened on the rooftop or high rise building or covers huge land area.	In the event of mass disaster, the golden 48 hour is critical to be adhered because beyond that the dead victim's body will be decayed and hard to be identified. Drone (special customised version) can be flown to the disaster area to identify the victims.
Benefits to *takaful* participants	**Fair charge** By flying drone to assess the risks and condition of the property it will be able to provide details which possibly cannot be obtained through manual inspection by staff especially if it involves huge area or difficult to access site.	**Transparent damage inspection** Claim fraud is a common problem in insurance and *takaful* sectors. Drone can assess the damages and provide transparent details of damages for analysis. Likewise, it reduces human involvement in the investigation of damages.	**Fast disbursement of financial claims** Victims who can be identified in a short period of time by using drone during mass disaster will assist the *takaful* operator to process the claim soonest which eventually leads to fast disbursement of compensation.
	Time Drone is able to cover huge area and remotely access site in a short period of time compared to manual process by staff.	**Time** Drone expedites the investigation of the damaged properties hence shorten the time period of investigation. This can increase customer satisfaction which is important for *takaful* business.	**Time** *Takaful* operator needs sufficient time to investigate financial claims that being submitted. Therefore, if the victim identification can be managed quickly, it will facilitate the investigation process; hence significant reduction of time.

(Continued)

Underwriting	Damage inspection	DVI
Price differentiation Pricing structure can be attractive to potential clients because drone as mentioned earlier is able to provide details that can contribute to better decision-making before charging contribution/ premium to the potential client.	**Efficient use of Participant Account funds** If the damages due to accident or disaster can be determined as precise as possible, it can contribute to better compensation received by the *takaful* participant and at the same time, proper used of funds because by using drone, the compensation can be lesser.	**Reduce the psychological burden** When disasters happened, victims will face psychological stress due to high uncertainty concerning their lives. They require the compensation money to re-build their lives or businesses. In the case of death of any family member, the compensation is critical to ensure the family can maintain the current life style like pre-disaster situation.

The security feature of smart contract through the blockchain makes it attractive to companies like takaful operators which is required by the central bank to maintain the privacy of the takaful participants' data. Likewise, the smart contract offers such confidentiality through the cryptography process, and such process also exists in the Bitcoin (which uses blockchain technology as well) that makes it to be independent and unable to be duplicated (this chapter does not intend to discuss the issues of Bitcoin from the Shariah perspective).

While the smart contract has its own appealing features, yet we need to understand how this technology can benefit the takaful participants. Financial claim (due to the medical requirement or damage to a property) is one of the critical functions that exist in the takaful. The claim process varies in terms of time taken to review, investigate and approve the claim, although some takaful operators delineate the minimum time allocate to process the claims.

Smart contract is suggested to be able to reduce such process; and at the same time, it permits such information to be shared with the intended takaful participant so that the person is aware about the claim process; but as per today's standard operating procedure of the financial claim, such information is confidential.

Having said that, if such critical information of the financial claim is being made accessible to the takaful participants, it reduces the anxiety to wait for the approval because the person is able to track and to check the milestones of financial claim. For a person who is really in need of compensation due to unfortunate event, emotionally, the person is in a depressed condition and should be calmed – smart contract through blockchain technology offers this.

Furthermore, it can assist to reduce, at least, if not being able to entirely eliminate fraud from the claim process. While we are not subsiding the pure intention of financial claim by the takaful participant, the industry is prone to claim fraud and the industry losses millions of dollars. The blockchain, due to its inherent features, provides better security and confidentiality of data by making it transparent and unique (hard to be duplicated) (Nienhaus, 2019). If the takaful operators embrace the blockchain in its system (and operation) and make it mandatory for the associates to use it, for instance the loss adjusters, panel workshops and solicitors, this will create a safe and sound ecosystem that will resist the claim fraud.

All these potential benefits should be directed to the takaful participants by lowering the price or tabarru' of the takaful policy, expediting the financial claim, better engagement with the takaful participant and increase of financial returns in the forms of underwriting surplus and investment profit.

Hence, the smart contract promotes fairness that will realise the social justice especially in term of relationship between the takaful operators and the takaful participants which has been highlighted before, tend to bend towards the shareholders of the takaful operators. Therefore, by being able to deliver the benefits of smart contract to the takaful participants, it will reduce the anxiety of the takaful participants and enhance the maqasid of Shariah in the takaful operations.

6 Challenges

Takafultech as being highlighted above offers various benefits to the *takaful* operators, and such positive effects have shaped the way *takaful* operators engage with their stakeholders, especially the *takaful* participants. Nevertheless, from an independent perspective, not all changes that brought by the takafultech are embraced and adopted; even though they are positive changes. The crux of this issue is the inherent cost that is tagged along with the new method, system or device – who will bear the cost?

This is an interesting dilemma that needs to be investigated further whether changes that produce benefits will be adopted at the expense of cost. Previous sections have highlighted the positive impacts brought by drone and in this section, discussion is directed towards the main challenges that affect potential adoption of drone.

6.1 Financial commitment

Takaful operator as one of the Islamic financial institutions is subjected to the perimeter of profit and loss which influence every decision that the firms choose. Therefore, consideration to adopt drone and the blockchain in *takaful* operation will be based on the potential profit or loss that the firms make. Likewise, if the proposed methods (or devices) are better than the current process, but the costs are high, yet the benefits are more, will the *takaful* operators opt towards that, or the *takaful* operators contend to continue with the current process?

Truly, the question cannot be answered directly because they are intertwined between the issues and considerations that must be thought deeply, again, *takaful* operators is a commercial entity that has shareholders who must be prioritised (since they are the co-principal in *takaful* business). Nevertheless, it must be emphasised here as well that the *takaful* participants are also the other co-principal in *takaful* operation and the ultimate beneficiaries of the *takaful* business.

6.2 "Experiencing" the benefits brought by takafultech

There are several benefits that have been highlighted before on the drone and blockchain. The benefits can be broadly segregated into:

- Monetary benefits (such as an increment of sharing for underwriting surplus, cash rebate, higher investment profit and less contribution or *tabarru'* charge)
- Non-monetary benefits (such as faster claim process, better customer relationship management, more engagement from the *takaful* participants and better transparency process)

Both benefits can be experienced concurrently, or any one of them depending on the improvement that is made. It is important to ensure that such benefits can be felt and enjoyed by the *takaful* participants because if they cannot experience such positive outcome as promised or expected when changes happened, then such changes can be regarded as futile.

For instance, *takaful* participants have witnessed the transformation the *takaful* operators have underwent such as implementation of the modern ICT tools and strategies, with the ultimate objectives to facilitate better customer service and reducing costs, as well as time to phase out manual processes that can be automated. Nevertheless, in the case of family *takaful*, specifically on the product of medical card cum investment, benefits from the ICT transformation have not really been "felt" by the *takaful* participant. Yet, over the years, the products have shown several increments of the *tabarru'* or contribution charges. For instance, in 2019, the medical costs in Malaysia have surged to 13.1%, only to be surpassed by Vietnam, 16.3% while the Philippines and Indonesia were 11.5% and 10.8% respectively (Kwang Zhe, 2020).

It is commonly understood that the medical costs have risen tremendously parallel with time (New Straits Times, 2019; Merhar, 2020), but with the adoption of latest ICT, such costs are touted and can be pressed down – as being propagated by the *takaful* operators in their press conferences every time when the companies unveiled their strategic initiatives to the public. Unfortunately, it does not happen.

While it is not fair to direct all the criticisms of medical costs to the *takaful* operators because they are not the medical service providers; yet a critical assessment should be applauded! Every year, *takaful* operators register annual profit, at least in the case of Malaysia (global trend depicts the same pattern though). On the other extreme, such positivity is hardly felt by the *takaful* participants (in the context of family *takaful*).

The *tabarru'* or contribution charge is never reduced, nonetheless, the *takaful* participants noticed spikes of it. Again, while we acknowledge that the risks associated with the product of medical card cum investment are increasing in tandem with age, but, with the positive changes that happened in and around the *takaful* operators, can't the *tabarru'* being reduced even once?

6.3 Takaful participants' rights

Takaful participants must be made to realise their rights as one of the principals in the *takaful* business, in the case of stock form *takaful* operator. While in the context of the governance model of the Anglo-Saxon, their rights are represented by the Independent Board of Directors, but a collective voice of the participants is rarely being made known to the management. Thus, the regulators and the management of *takaful* operators need to think of the best alternative to rally the participation of the *takaful* participants in the operation of *takaful* operators.

For instance, the *takaful* participants can be represented by the institutional *takaful* participants such as companies that are clients with the respective *takaful* operators, hence they can be nominated to be in the board of directors to represent the rest.

7 Takafultech links to the Maqasid Shariah

While this chapter does not evaluate the impacts of takafultech extensively since the components of takafultech are wider, based on the examples given previously on the drone and smart contract, we can understand the potential and magnitude of the impacts that can be brought by the takafultech which can enhance and facilitate the *takaful* operators to perform better to achieve the *maqasid* Shariah. It has been highlighted earlier that at this current state, *takaful* operators have achieved their raison d'être as prescribed by the *maqasid* Shariah; but through takafultech, their ability is enhanced, and they can be better. Figure 2 shows the major *maqasid* of Shariah which is linked to the takafultech of drone and blockchain.

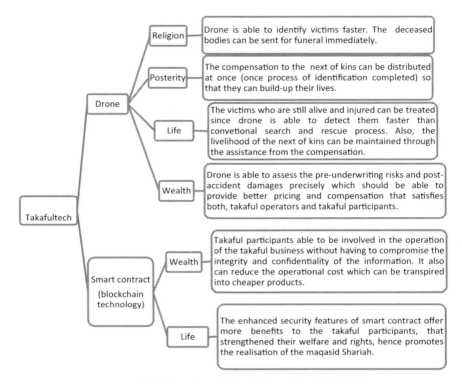

FIGURE 2 Major *maqasid* al-Shariah and their link to the takafultech.

8 Conclusion

This chapter presents discussions from the lens of *takaful* participants and connecting them to the takafultech particularly drone and blockchain. The positive impacts brought by the two takafultech tools indicate insights on the bigger potentials of the takafultech to the *takaful* participants and the *takaful* operators. Hence, it facilitates the *takaful* operators as the Islamic financial institutions to realise their *maqasid* al-Shariah obligations as expected by the stakeholders.

In addition, the challenges are important to be considered because they affect the intended objectives that the *takaful* operators try to achieve. Financial will always be the main hindrance but *takaful* operators must also balance such position with their roles as value-based intermediaries and as the Islamic financial institutions that derived the strength from Islam – they have to behave like one.

Acknowledgement

The authors would like to acknowledge the Ministry of Higher Education (MOHE) Malaysia for the research grant awarded that has contributed to some extent to this chapter. The research grant file number: 600-IRMI/TRGS 5/3 (001/2019)-3.

Note

1 Sahih Bukhari, Book 23: Funerals (Al-Janaa'iz) Translation of Sahih Bukhari, Book 23.

References

Auda, J. 2008. *Maqasid al-Shariah As Philosophy of Islamic Law*. Herndon: The International Institute of Islamic Thought (IIIT).

EY. 2020. *Asia-Pacific insurance outlook: Driving innovation and transformation to seize opportunities and sustain growth*. https://www.ey.com/en_gl/global-insurance-outlooks/how-innovation-can-help-insurers-in-asia-pacific-seize-opportunities (retrieved 14 December 2021).

Kwang Zhe, K.S. 2020. *Insurance: Medical insurance premiums rising at an unsustainable rate, says LIAM*. The Edge Markets. https://www.theedgemarkets.com/article/insurance-medical-insurance-premiums-rising-unsustainable-rate-says-liam (retrieved 14 December 2021).

Luciani, T., Distasio, B., Bungert, J., Summer, M., & Bozzo, T. 2016. *Use of Drones to Assist with Insurance, Financial and Underwriting Related Activities*. Available online: http://www.freepatentsonline.com/y2016/0063642.html (retrieved 30 May 2021).

Merhar, C. 2020. *8 reasons health insurance costs continue to rise*. https://www.peoplekeep.com/blog/8-reasons-health-insurance-costs-continue-to-rise (retrieved 14 December 2021).

Mohd Kassim, Z.A. 2013. The primary insurance models. In Gonulal, S. O. (Ed.). *Takaful and mutual insurance: alternative approaches to managing risks*. Washington DC: World Bank Publications, pp. 1–204.

Muhamat, A.A., Zulkifli, A.F., Sulaiman, S., Subramaniam, G., & Mohamad, S. 2021. Development of social cost and benefit analysis (SCBA) in the maqāsid Shariah framework: Narratives on the use of drones for *takaful* operators. *Journal of Risk and Financial Management* 14(8): 387.

Muhamat, A.A., Jaafar, M.N., & Md Saad, M.S. 2019. *Essential components of takaful operation*. Melaka: UTeM Press.

New Straits Times. 2019. *Why do my medical, health plan premiums/contributions keep increasing?* https://www.nst.com.my/lifestyle/heal/2019/10/532287/why-do-my-medical-health-plan-premiumscontributions-keep-increasing (retrieved 14 December 2021).

Nienhaus, V. 2019. Blockchain technologies and the prospects of smart contracts in the Islamic finance. In Oseni, U.A., & Ali, S.N. (2019). *Fintech in Islamic finance: theory and practice* (1st ed.). Oxon: Routledge

PWC. 2016. *InsurTech: the road ahead*. AICB-PWC Fintech survey: Insurance cut. https://www.pwc.com/my/en/assets/publications/2016-aicb-pwc-insurtech-the-road-ahead.pdf (retrieved 14 December 2021).

VanderLinden, S.L., Millie, S.M., Anderson, N., & Chishti, S. 2018. *The insurtech book: the insurance technology handbook for investors, entrepreneurs and fintech visionaries*. Chicester: John Wiley & Sons.

12
DIGITAL TRANSFORMATION AND IFRS 17 ACCOUNTING ISSUES IN TAKAFUL INDUSTRY

The case of Indonesia

Ersa Tri Wahyuni

1 Introduction

Islamic finance has been a growing industry over the last decade and has been attracting financial practitioners in both of the Muslim and non-Muslim countries. The Islamic Finance Development Report 2021 revealed that the global Islamic finance asset has been growing 70% over the last six years (2014–2020) and is expected to reach almost USD 5 billion in 2025. Nevertheless, most of the Islamic finance assets are distributed to Islamic banks (70%) while takaful industry contributes only 2% to the Islamic finance asset growth (Refinitiv, 2021).

Although takaful industry is relatively small compared to other Islamic financial institutions (IFIs), the industry is also growing globally and its future prospect is optimistic (Abdul Rahman, 2009; CIBAFI, 2018). CIBAFI (General Council for Islamic Banks and Financial Institutions) global takaful survey in 2018 to the 55 takaful operators in 24 countries revealed that most of industry players are optimistic about the takaful industry's prospect. 62% of respondents are fairly optimistic while 36% are very optimistic (see Figure 1). Interestingly, takaful operators from Southeast Asia (seven companies in Malaysia, Indonesia and Brunei) were the least optimistic of all region groups (CIBAFI, 2018).

There has never been a more challenging period for the global insurance industry, takaful included, than the period of 2020s. Firstly, the business landscape of insurance is changing tremendously due to the Covid-19 pandemic and the digital disruption (Capegemini & EFMA, 2021). Secondly, the global insurance industry is facing enormous pressure from the implementation of the new international accounting standard, IFRS 17 Insurance Contract. The standard was issued by the London-based International Accounting Standards Board (IASB) and to be effective globally in 2023. The two major challenges, digital transformation and the accounting issues, faced by the takaful industry are the

DOI: 10.4324/9781003262169-15

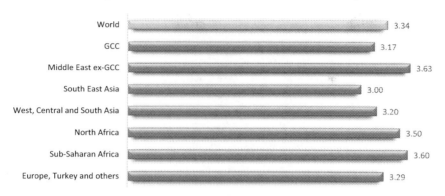

FIGURE 1 Optimism level on overall insurance industry.
Source: CIBAFI (2018).

main discussions for this chapter with a deeper look into Indonesia as the fourth largest democracy with the most populated Muslims.

The motivation of this chapter arises from various new issues and challenges in the takaful industry. The Covid-19 pandemic has been a key driver for various digital transformations in many industries, but the takaful industry seems to be slow in response to these opportunities as technology transformation remains a major challenge (Husin, 2019). Other challenges of the takaful industry are weak regulation (Maf'ula & Mi'raj, 2022), governance issues and the lack of effectiveness of the shariah supervisory board (Nomran et al., 2018; Zain et al., 2021). Lastly, the lack of details of AAOIFI (Accounting and Auditing Organization for Islamic Financial Institutions) standards on takaful contracts also raises concerns of the quality of takaful companies' financial reports (Nahar, 2015; Zain et al., 2021).

The lack of debate and discussions about a proper accounting policy for takaful contract, both nationally in Indonesia and internationally, is quite concerning. The acquiescence of takaful practitioners to the IFRS 17 should raise a fundamental question if takaful contract actually has economic differences with the insurance contract at all. A survey by Nahar (2015), for example, provides empirical evidence that financial report users in Malaysia (proxied by final year accounting students) could not see the difference between takaful companies and insurance companies' financial reports. 96% of respondents could not see the operational difference between takaful and insurance from their financial reports. 100% of respondents perceived the 2012 financial reports of both companies are so similar and the only difference is the terminologies for the same substance. This finding raises a concern whether the financial reports of takaful companies have failed to exhibit the difference of the economic substance of takaful contract.

2 The concept of takaful and takaful models

Takaful comes from the Arabic word *Kafala* which means "guarantee" (Pasha & Hussain, 2013). Takaful is the Islamic alternative to conventional insurance which is based on the idea of social solidarity, cooperation and joint indemnification of losses of the members. Takaful contract is not only involving two parties, but an agreement among a group of people who agree to jointly indemnify the loss that may inflict upon any of them out of the collective fund they donate (Hussain & Pasha, 2011). The main purpose of takaful is not merely making profit, but to provide equity to all participants involved, and the objective of the contract is to support the member of the group when they suffer from disadvantage or calamity.

The takaful model is derived from the concept of *ta'awun* which means to help each other or mutual assistance; the risk being borne among the participants. A takaful contract in accordance with the shariah principle should not contain *gharar* (fraud), *maysir* (gambling), *usury*, *zhulm* (persecution), *risywah* (bribery), *haram* (illicit) goods and *immorality* (Maf'ula & Mi'raj, 2022). Participants of takaful donate money to a *tabarru* fund which will be used to pay the claim should an insurance risk occurs to one of the participants. The company manages the fund and also develops the fund by investing it in the various shariah investment.

There are several contract models of takaful for example *mudharabah* (partnership), *wakalah* (agency) model, *waqf* model, mutual model and hybrid models such as *wakalah-waqf* and *wakalah-mudharabah* (CIBAFI, 2018; Pasha & Hussain, 2013). According to Global Takaful Survey, more than 50% takaful companies use the *wakalah-mudarabah* (Hybrid) model, one-sixth follow a pure *wakalah* (Agency) model, while about 10% each adopt the *wakalah-waqf* (Hybrid) model

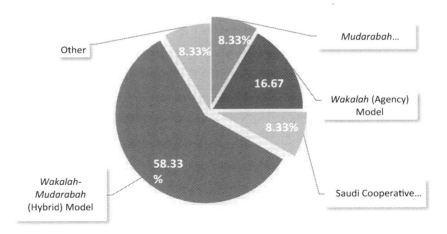

FIGURE 2 Takaful models used globally.
Source: CIBAFI (2018).

or the *mudarabah* (Partnership) model (CIBAFI, 2018). The survey by CIBAFI is conducted on 55 takaful companies in 24 countries (see Figure 2).

Takaful contract under *mudarabah* principle sees the relationship between participants and the companies similar to partnership, where the participants supply the fund and the companies supply the expertise. Both parties shared profits in a pre-determined ratio, similar to any classic partnership contract (Pasha & Hussain, 2013). *Wakalah* model is slightly different from *mudarabah* principle as the company acts as a *wakeel* of the participants and receives a management fee. Risk sharing only occurs among participants where a takaful operator does not participate or share in any underwriting results as these belong to participants as surplus or deficit.

3 The takaful industry and the digital transformation of the insurance industry in Indonesia

Insurance industry in Indonesia in general is an interesting case due to the major insurance scandals over the last decade, which reflects the vulnerability of the industry and the weak supervisory from the regulator (Adinugroho et al., 2022). The bankruptcy of PT Asuransi Jiwasraya (Persero) in 2019 shocked the nation as it was the oldest insurance company in the country (160 years old), the largest customer-based (5.5 million policy holders) and a state-owned enterprise company (Gusti, 2019; Setiawan, 2020). There was also the bankruptcy of PT Bumi Asih Jaya Life Insurance in 2013 (Adinugroho et al., 2022) and the default of PT Asuransi Jiwa Kresna in 2020, PT Asuransi Bumi Putera in 2018 and PT Asuransi Jiwa Bakrie Life in 2008 (Hastuti, 2020). All these scandals have a detrimental impact on the insurance industry as the people's trust to the insurance industry and the effectiveness of regulator supervisory decline.

The Indonesian Islamic finance industry is currently lagging Malaysia and other countries in Asia. For example, in total Islamic finance assets, Indonesia is only number seventh rank out of top ten countries with USD 99 billion of total Islamic finance assets (ICD, 2021). Malaysia is in the third rank with total assets of USD 570 billion. Iran and Saudi Arabia both ranked first and second in the Islamic Corporation for the Development of Private Sector (ICD) ranking (Figure 3).

The takaful industry in Indonesia has been developing since 1994, started with the establishment of PT Syarikat takaful Indonesia. However, a specific regulation on shariah insurance business was only issued 16 years later through Ministry of Finance decree PMK Number 18/PMK.010/2010 concerning the Implementation of Basic Principles for the Implementation of Insurance Business. In 2014, the law about insurance industry was ratified and the law also regulates the takaful industry. The Law Number 40 Year 2014 on Insurance provides a definition of takaful, as follows:

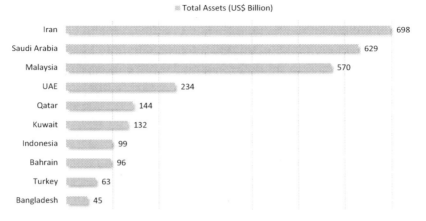

FIGURE 3   Top countries in Islamic Finance Assets 2019.
Source: ICD (2021).

Takaful is a group of agreements, comprising agreements between takaful companies and policyholders and agreements between policyholders, in the framework of managing contributions based on shariah principles to help and protect each other by:

i   Provide replacement to consumers or policyholders for loss, damage, costs incurred, loss of profits, or liability to third parties that may be incurred by consumers or policyholders due to an uncertain event; Or
ii Provide payment based on the death of the user or payment based on the user's life with the benefit of which has been established and/or based on the results of the fund management.

The contribution of takaful industry in the Indonesian economy remains insignificant, less than 2% (Bappenas, 2019). A country with the largest Muslim population in the world does not necessarily warrant a burgeoning Islamic finance industry. The total assets of Islamic banking in Indonesia have been growing by only 13.11% in 2020 but no additional players in the industry. The Islamic stock index was also declining in 2020, mostly due to the Covid-19 pandemic. The takaful industry or the shariah/Islamic insurance industry in Indonesia has been stagnant for the last five years. Since 2017, there is no additional company in the Islamic life insurance industry and even the number is declining for the Islamic general insurance industry (see Table 1).

The decline of the shariah industry creates concern if the Islamic finance industry in Indonesia would be able to tap the opportunities of the new digital era. Digital transformation has been on-going since the last decade with improvement in the telecommunication infrastructures around the world. The Covid-19 pandemic and lockdown encourage digital transformation in many sectors even more, for example, in education sector, entertainment, and even tourism.

TABLE 1 Total Islamic insurance industry players in five years

Industry type	2016 Full	2016 Number of shariah investment package companies	2017 Full	2017 Number of shariah investment package companies	2018 Full	2018 Number of shariah investment package companies	2019 Full	2019 Number of shariah investment package companies	2020 Full	2020 Number of shariah investment package companies
Islamic insurance industry										
Islamic Life Insurance Industry	6	21	7	23	7	23	7	23	7	23
Islamic General Insurance Industry	4	24	5	25	5	24	5	24	5	21
Islamic Reinsurance Industry	1	2	1	2	1	2	1	2	1	3

Source: Annual report OJK (2020).

Everyday transactions were conducted electronically through e-commerce or other digital multi channels as people could not go out from their homes. Business transactions become smoother, faster, more effective and more efficient.

In the new digital era, customers expect 24 hours convenience in doing transaction and demand quick response from the sellers. That would include the policy holders of insurance industry. According to the Insurtech World Report 2021, most of the respondents (80%) who participated in their survey put high value on the convenience factors, namely value for money and insurer's responsiveness as catalyst to switch insurance products. Complicated registrations, high premiums, ineffective claim processing, complicated paper works of the contracts, etc. are greatest problems for Indonesian considering an insurance product. These problems are now being addressed by tech-driven insurance start-ups which provide a faster and smoother customer interaction with the insurance provider.

In Indonesia, the insurtech is also growing but most of the players are not shariah institutions. For example, PasarPolis, one of the largest on-demand insurtech in Indonesia enjoyed a significant increase of new customers since establishment in 2015. In 2020, PasarPolis booked four million new customers and every month they issued about 70 million insurance policies. 90% of the PasarPolis customers are first-time buyers who never bought insurance product before and 40% of its customers work in informal sectors like courier drivers and online SME buyers/sellers (Catriana, 2021). However, PasarPolis insurance partners are mostly conventional insurance companies. Syariah insurtech seems to lag behind the conventional. One of the on-demand syariah insurtech is YukTakaful which was established in 2019. YukTakaful offers full service from new registration to claim through its mobile application. All contracts in YukTakaful are using shariah contract (*akad*).

The growing number of digital market aggregators allows customers to compare premiums and benefits easily before deciding to buy insurance product. Price comparison is something which is very challenging for the customers before the new era. In the past, the way customers can get a premium quote is by contacting an insurance agent and it may take few days to get quotes from various insurance companies. Insurtech allows this process to be completed within minutes. For example, in Indonesia, customers can go to the comparison sites such as cekaja.com, cekpremi.com or asuransiku.com to compare premium prices from several insurance providers.

Although the digital transformation in the insurance industry seems promising, the syariah institution presence is very weak in the Indonesian insurtech. Most of the players in the insurtech industry are non-syariah companies. The slow development of the takaful industry in Indonesia may limit the industry to grab the prospective opportunity from insurtech and the digital transformation which is happening globally. As transforming into a digital company needs investment, not only on the hardware and software but also the brainware, this could be a challenge as well. Lack of regulation can also be a challenge for the insurance company to grow as the regulator is still considering many aspects of insurtech, especially for shariah insurance (Puspaningtyas, 2021).

Nevertheless, the growing development of insurtech should be perceived as an opportunity for shariah insurance as well because the market aggregator also offers takaful products to their prospective customers. As insurance product is becoming more accessible for potential buyers, especially the first timers, the whole market is expanding and so does the market of the takaful products. Potential buyers can easily compare insurance contract and takaful contract in the market aggregator website. This may encourage more potential customers to be exposed with the takaful products and consider buying it.

3 Takaful versus conventional insurance contracts: the accounting challenges

The basic principle of the insurance contract is that the insurance company absorbs the insured risk of the policy holders. The insured risk can be health problems (illness), deaths, accidents or loss of properties because of the fire. As the insurance company absorbs the inherent risk from the policyholders, it creates a challenge to manage the risk effectively for the insurance company to make profits out of their business. As the insurance contract can have a long period of contract, for example, a life insurance contract can have a contract period up to 25 years. Then, the insurance companies are required to assess their risk based on the probability of occurrence of the incident risks from a pool of policyholders.

As the insurance companies absorb the risks and they promise to pay the compensation when the incident risks occur, this creates a liability in their balance sheets. In accordance with the duration of the insurance contract, this liability for remaining claim can be a long-term liability (for example a life insurance contract) or a short one. Measuring these liabilities, especially for the long-term contracts, can be significantly challenging because it involves many actuarial assumptions and calculations in terms of the probability of risk.

The accounting standard for insurance contract has been a challenge because every country has different type of accounting standards which make financial report of insurance companies across jurisdictions incomparable. It is only recently that IASB issued a comprehensive insurance contract standard, the IFRS 17 Insurance Contract in 2017. These IFRS 17 would be effectively adopted by many countries in 2023, with some countries decided to adopt it with one year or two-year gap.

The debate if IFRS should also be adopted by IFIs for the benefit of comparability has been heated over the last few years (Ibrahim & Hameed, 2007; Zain et al., 2021). There also has been a warm discussion among preparers and standard setters if IFRS 17 is also suitable for takaful contract. Takaful or shariah insurance contracts and conventional insurance contracts have slightly different basic concepts. While the globally accepted concept of insurance contract is where one party (the issuer) accepts significant insurance risk from another party (policyholder), takaful concept is more of a mutual guarantee where the insurance risk is shared among all members.

In the takaful contract, the insurance companies act on behalf of the policy holders and they only receive management fee (in the *wakalah* model). Thus, the risk in the shariah insurance contract is not absorbed by the insurance company but is shared among all the policy holders in the group. The insurance company does not necessarily have liabilities to the future claim, but the group of policy holders does. This fundamental difference encourages some scholars to propose that takaful contract should have its own accounting standard and should not adopt IFRS 17.

The fund collected from the policy holders (*tabarrru* fund) should aim to be sufficient in covering the risk calculated future claim. This *tabarru* fund does not belong to the company but belongs to the participants in the group. If one day in the future the fund is not enough to pay the claim, the insurance company then need to step in and give a loan based on a *Qard* agreement (akad) to the group. *Qard Hasan* is an interest-free loan intended to allow the borrower to use the loaned fund with or without a specific period (AAOIFI, 2021). Once the *tabarru* fund has sufficient money, then the loan should be repaid back to the company.

The same challenges apply for the shariah insurance groups. In order for the *tabarru* fund to have sufficient money, the company should sell enough number of policies as more participants joining would mean more funds will be available. The shariah insurance company as the manager of the fund on behalf of the novice policy holders, manage the risk of the *tabarru* fund as well to ensure that the fund is sufficient.

In general, the accounting standard for shariah insurance is less mature than the accounting standard for conventional insurance. Among many Muslim countries, only Indonesia has developed their own accounting standard for takaful contract by an independent syariah accounting standard board. AAOIFI, an international body headquartered in Bahrain also has developed takaful accounting standard which became a major reference in other countries. However, many countries which have a lot of takaful activities, such as Malaysia, or Saudi Arabia or Pakistan, do not develop their own accounting standard for takaful. Some countries stipulate certain additional disclosure or guideline for takaful operators such as issued by Bank Negara Malaysia (BNM) in 2013 or by Malaysian Accounting Standards Board (Nahar, 2015).

In term of developing school of thought of the application of IFRS 17 for takaful contracts, Malaysia seems to be the most progressive country. Where some countries are considering if IFRS 17 should be adopted for takaful contracts, Malaysia has taken a step ahead. In 2021, Malaysia decided to adopt IFRS 17 for the shariah contracts as there is no scope exclusion for takaful contract. During 2021, the MASB (Malaysian Accounting Standards Board) has issued three technical bulletins[1] to accompany the application of IFRS 17 to Takaful Contracts: (1) Applicability of IFRS 17 to takaful, (2) Presentation using Column vis-à-vis IFRS 17 and (3) Qard (loan) accounting under IFRS 17. Other Muslim

TABLE 2 The adoption of IFRS 17 on takaful contract across some jurisdictions

Country	IFRS 17 adoption year	IFRS 17 application to takaful contract
Malaysia	2023	Yes, no exclusion for takaful in the IFRS 17 scope and three guidance have been issued for takaful
Indonesia	2025	No. Takaful contract apply local standard PSAK 108. Takaful contract is excluded in the scope of IFRS 17/PSAK 74
Pakistan	Under consideration to adopt in 2023	Yes, no exclusion for takaful in the IFRS 17 scope is under consideration
Saudi Arabia	2023	Yes, no exclusion for takaful in the IFRS 17 scope. No special guidance for takaful contract
Syria	2023	Yes, no exclusion for takaful in the IFRS 17 scope. No special guidance for takaful contract

Source: Asian-Oceanian Standard-Setters Group/AOSSG 13th annual meeting, November 2021.

countries do not issue any guidance or technical bulletins on how to apply IFRS 17 for the takaful contract (see Table 2).

AAOIFI recently, in 2021, issued exposure draft to amend its existing two accounting standards for takaful. One standard is for recognition and measurement of takaful contract, and another standard is for presentation disclosure for takaful institution. Both standards are proposed to be effective 1st January 2024, one year after IFRS 17. AAOIFI observed the development of global standard for insurance contract and would like to align their standards to IFRS 17 which will effective globally on 1 January 2023.

IFRS 17 implementation can be a challenge for any insurance company for at least three reasons. Firstly, the general model of measurement in IFRS 17 requires the company to make group aggregation of the contracts, based on their three variables: shared risk, annual cohorts and level of profitability profile. Since the beginning of the group recognition, the company should calculate the unearned profit for each group or in IFRS 17 which is called Contractual Service Margin (CSM). CSM is then released slowly during the duration of the contract. However, if there is any group which suffers a loss in the long run, the company should acknowledge the loss right away. This smaller granularity level can be challenging for the company as it was never required before by the previous standard (IFRS 4). Most of the companies already grouped their contract based on the class of business (COB). For example, the group of health insurance would be managed separately from the group of insurance for vehicle accident. However, companies may not break down the COB into annual cohorts and profitability (onerous or profitable group). The smaller level of granularity under IFRS 17 requires more sophisticated IT systems in order to automate the accounting process.

Second challenge of IFRS 17 is the model for revenue recognition for the insurance contract. In the current practice, insurance company book revenue in accordance with the premium they receive or when the insurance coverage started and then they create premium reserve as a reduction of the revenue. The way revenue is recognised would be significantly different under IFRS 17. Revenue is only recognised over time when the liability decreased as the company provide the service. The accrual concept of insurance revenue under IFRS 17 is similar with revenue recognition in other industries. However, the fundamental change may make regulator more anxious as the industry size has been mainly calculated using total premium revenue.

The third challenge is the level of disclosures required by IFRS 17. The standard required more detailed disclosure than the previous standard. More detailed disclosures may require a more detailed database and more sophisticated accounting IT systems to ensure the data is tallied to the smallest unit of information. A better database and IT systems may be expensive and the investors of takaful insurance companies may have less appetite to invest a significant investment due to the small size of the industry.

4 The accounting standard for insurance and shariah insurance contract in Indonesia

Before adopting IFRS in 2012, Indonesia has already had two accounting standards for insurance industry. One standard is for life insurance and one standard is for general insurance. The two accounting standards were developed by Indonesian Financial Accounting Standard Board (DSAK) by considering the domestic industrial practice. These two standards were amended when IFRS 4 was adopted in 2011 into the Indonesian standard PSAK 62.

IFRS 4 as an interim IFRS standard for insurance contract stipulates the company to make liability adequacy test and provides guidance on how to calculate Best Estimate Liability (BEL). However, IFRS 4 does not provide guidance on how a revenue from the insurance contract should be recognised and how the insurance contract should be grouped. The standard also did not provide enough guidance on which discount rate to be used to present value the liability. Thus, all these flaws were remedied by IASB in IFRS 17 with more rigorous principle on how to calculate liability for remaining coverage and also the revenue recognition.

However, for the takaful contract, Indonesia has its own accounting, shariah accounting standard. PSAK 108 Accounting Transaction for Shariah Insurance was issued in 2016. The Shariah Accounting Standard Board (DSAS) decided at that time that the shariah insurance contract cannot satisfy the definition of insurance contract under IFRS 4, thus a different standard is needed. Takaful insurance companies should apply PSAK 108 and deviated from IFRS 4. The basis for conclusion of PSAK 108 provides argument of why DSAS believes that the definition of insurance contract under IFRS 4 cannot be applied to the takaful contracts. Firstly, there is no risk transfer from the participants to the insurance company, only risk sharing among participants. Secondly, the *akad* or agreement under shariah insurance is using *takaful akad*, which implies helping each other and not *tijari akad* which is for commercial purposes like in the insurance contract.

Under PSAK 108, insurance company which issues shariah contract acts as a representative of the participants to manage the participant's funds. Some percentage of participant funds are allocated to investments using shariah principles. The company's role can be perceived as a representative with a contractual agreement. In addition, the company can play a role as a *mudharib* (manager) to generate profit sharing from the management of participant funds (Hendra, 2021). When there is a claim from the participant, the company manage the transfer of the claim amount to the policy holders. If the number of claims is less than expected, the funds are allocated back to *tabarru* funds, which over time can keep improving.

Joining the global IFRS wagon, Indonesian Financial Accounting Standard Board (DSAK) has adopted IFRS 17 to be mandatory applied in Indonesia by 2025; but early adoption is permitted. There will be two-year gap of Indonesia

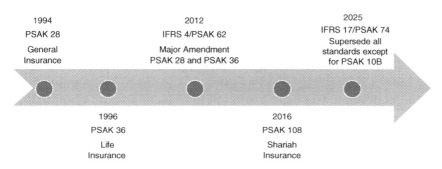

FIGURE 4 Timeline of accounting standards for insurance contracts in Indonesia.

and international field as IASB-stipulated IFRS 17 should be adopted in 2023. Some joint venture insurance companies in Indonesia may decide to adopt IFRS 17 as early as 2023, following their global parent companies which adopt IFRS 17 in that year. The timeline of accounting standards for insurance contracts in Indonesia is detailed in Figure 4.

The adoption of IFRS 17 in Indonesia is identical word by word except in the scope of standard and the effective date. The Board added one exclusion in the scope of the standard and the effective date is 2025. During the transition year until 2025, insurance companies can continue using PSAK 62 (IFRS 4) and also PSAK 28 and PSAK 36 for some elements which are not required in PSAK 62. For shariah insurance contract, PSAK 108 should be applied until the shariah board revises it or makes any further decision.

5 Moving forward: the adoption issues of IFRS 17 for takaful contract

A survey conducted by a global accounting firm KPMG in 2018 to the 160 insurers in 30 countries revealed that the companies believe the implementation of IFRS 17 will give high impact to their IT Finance systems, actuarial systems and their core business systems (KPMG, 2018). This survey was conducted one year after IFRS 17 was issued by IASB in 2017. By that time, IASB's initial planning was to implement IFRS 17 in 2021 globally, but then upon feedback from its constituents, the implementation year was pushed back to 2023. Nevertheless, one year after the standard was issued, many insurance companies have already calculated the impact of the standards to their business operations. The industry expectation at that time was that the implementation is not going to be cheap, nor simple (KPMG, 2018). The similar global survey in 2021 by KPMG revealed only half of the respondents have fully adopted IT systems (KPMG, 2021).

Conventional insurance industry in Indonesia is also marching on the preparation stage of implementing IFRS. As the implementation year of 2025 getting closer, companies are analysing the gap and preparing the budget for IT investment in 2022. Many insurance companies aim to do parallel running between old and new accounting system in the year of 2023, one year before the transition year of 2024. IFRS 17 requires retrospective approach for transition figures; thus, insurance company tries to be ready to implement the standard one year before the mandatory year.

Most insurance companies in Indonesia also have shariah insurance product (or shariah business unit) and they are wondering if the takaful contract will also apply IFRS 17 or remain using the current standard of PSAK 108. The decision is important in the planning and implementation period as the companies are preparing for IT infrastructure for IFRS 17 implementation. Should the takaful contract applies IFRS 17, the IT system of the company would need to maintain two parallel systems of accounting at the same time. This could mean more resources required to run and maintain two systems simultaneously.

On the other hand, there are shariah insurance companies which only sell shariah insurance products. These companies do not sell conventional insurance products. According to the 2020 annual report of Indonesian Financial Service Agency (OJK or Otoritas Jasa Keuangan), there are seven syariah general insurance companies, five life insurance companies and one shariah reinsurance company. For these full-fledged shariah institutions, they may have interest to maintain PSAK 108 model as long as possible to avoid IT investment in adopting IFRS 17. PSAK 108 that mainly in parallel with IFRS 4 has less rigorous measurement model for insurance liability and revenue.

It is interesting to note that DSAS had made decision that when IFRS 4 is adopted, the takaful contract is not the same with insurance contract. IFRS 17 adopts identical definition of insurance contract with IFRS 4. Thus, *ceteris paribus*, DSAS may end up with similar conclusion in which takaful contract should be scoped out from the IFRS 17. It will be a good idea if DSAS and other Muslim countries standard setters discuss about these important issues.

As some countries have already decided to adopt IFRS 17 also for takaful contract, DSAS may also move toward similar directions in the future. At least the board will consider the implementation of IFRS 17 when they revise the current standard of PSAK 108 as they also included IFRS 4 into consideration when they issued PSAK 108. At the time, this chapter is written DSAS has not made any clear decision if the IFRS 17 will also be applied to the takaful contract.

Nevertheless, the lack of debate among preparers of takaful financial report may also indicate the insignificance of the industry. MASB's uncontested decision to adopt IFRS 17 maybe due to the small size of the shariah insurance compared to the conventional. For example, the market share of Malaysian shariah insurance industry is only 16.99%, which is 5.82% in Indonesia as of 2019 (Mutmainah et al., 2022). Most of the shariah contract issuers are also part of a bigger conventional insurance company which are already allocating their resources in the preparation of IFRS 17. Thus, it could be in the interest of the preparers to adopt IFRS 17 also for takaful contract to avoid the unnecessary extra burden of two system parallel running.

However, in a spirit of innovation and independence of the accounting standard setting, the decision to adopt IFRS 17 for shariah contract (or to create a separate standard) should not be based heavily on the conveniency of the preparers. Accounting standard setters need to consider if takaful contract is indeed fall under category of insurance contract in IFRS 17. Malaysian MASB made it clear that takaful contract falls under the definition of insurance contract in IFRS, while Indonesian DSAS stood in the opposite position. On the other hand, a separate standard should not be exercised just for the sake of distancing the syariah with the conventional contract just because the contract name is different. If the economics of the contract is similar then the same accounting policy should be applied to communicate the economics of the transaction, despite the difference in the contract name. *Substance over form*, one of the virtues of accounting, should be upheld in the decision-making of IFRS 17 application for takaful contract. For example, the argument that takaful contract is different from insurance contract should also examine the mutual insurance company which almost has similar economic substance with the takaful contract.

IFRS is a principle-based set of standards and has been used widely and accepted globally as international accounting standard. Indonesia also has adopted IFRS since 2012, including IFRS 17 which will be applied in 2025. Nevertheless, Indonesia retains its right to develop shariah accounting standard for shariah transaction. The fact that IFRS 17 has been adopted by many countries for takaful contract, this could be a sign that IFRS 17 is flexible enough to be adopted also for takaful operators. AAOIFI's recent amendment of their accounting standard for takaful contract also apply IFRS 17 logics with different terminologies. For example, AAOIFI standard uses similar way to aggregate the contracts and the initial recognition takaful residual margin which is a similar concept of CSM in IFRS 17. If Indonesia also adopts IFRS 17 for takaful companies, this will improve comparability across jurisdictions and also encourages the companies to invest in their IT systems.

6 Conclusion

Takaful industry is a growing industry globally and has a prospective future. However, in Indonesia, takaful industry has been stagnant over the last five years. This chapter has addressed two major issues in the takaful industry in Indonesia which are the digital transformation and accounting issues. The digital transformation in the takaful industry is much slower than the conventional insurance. Takaful operators are not present in the insurtech ecosystem in Indonesia. The small size of the industry may contribute to the lack of appetite to invest in the IT system to embrace the insurtech opportunity.

The second issue is the adoption of IFRS 17 for takaful contract. Takaful industry in Indonesia is facing a significant uncertainty from the nondecision to adopt IFRS 17 by the DSAS. The takaful operators in Indonesia mostly operate as a takaful wing of conventional insurance companies, thus they are marching on preparation of IFRS 17 for the insurance contract. As IFRS 17 will be adopted in 2025, Indonesian insurance companies are preparing their IT systems for the implementation. A different set of systems for the takaful wing will complicate the implementation of IFRS 17 in Indonesia. This chapter recommends for the accounting standard in Indonesia to consider the adoption of IFRS 17 also for takaful contract. If a separate standard still deems necessary, harmonisation to IFRS 17-like AAOIFI approach will be beneficial to the preparers to improve the comparability of the financial reports.

Acknowledgement

The author would like to thank the contribution of Prof Dian Masyita for the initial discussion of the chapter and the research assistant for this chapter, Rijal

Firmansyah. The author is also grateful and acknowledges for the input from Prof. Yasushi Suzuki and Dr. Mohammad Dulal Miah for the chapter revision.

Note

1 The bulletins can be downloaded in this link: https://www.masb.org.my/pages.php?id=206

References

AAOIFI. (2021). *Exposure Draft of the Financial Accounting Standard Accounting for Takaful: Recognition and Measurement*. In *2021*. Accounting and Auditing Organization for Islamic Financial Institutions.

Abdul Rahman, Z. (2009). Takaful: Potential demand and growth. *Journal of King Abdulaziz University: Islamic Economics*, 22(1), 171–188.

Adinugroho, I., Rauf, R., & Sucipto, N. (2022). The role of the financial services authority in supervision of fraud prevention in life insurance companies in Indonesia. *Jurnal Economic Resource*, 4(2), 320–324.

Bappenas. (2019). *Indonesia Islamic Economic Master Plan 2019–2024*. https://knks.go.id/storage/upload/1560308022-Indonesia%20Islamic%20Economic%20Masterplan%202019-2024.pdf

Capegemini, & EFMA. (2021). *World Insurance Report 2021*. https://worldinsurancereport.com/

Catriana, E. (2021). Insurtech Ini Catat 4 juta Pelanggan Baru pada 2020 (This Insurtech Record 4 millions new customers in 2020). *Kompas.com*. https://money.kompas.com/read/2021/01/14/174252026/insurtech-ini-catat-4-juta-pelanggan-baru-pada-2020

CIBAFI. (2018). *CIBAFI Global Takaful Survey*.

Gusti, G. P. (2019). Analysis of the cause of loss of PT. Asuransi Jiwasraya (Persero). *Jurnal Manajemen Dan Bisnis Sriwijaya*, 17(4), 199–206.

Hastuti, R. K. (2020). Kacau! Gagal Bayar 5 Asuransi Ini Bikin Nasabah Teriak (Disaster, The Default of Five Insurance Companies makes the policy-holders Sreams). *www.Cnbcindonesia.com*. 7-180132/kacau-gagal-bayar-5-asuransi-ini-bikin-nasabah-teriak

Hendra, G. I. (2021). Determinants of financial stability of Islamic insurance companies listed on Indonesia Financial Services Authority. *Share: Jurnal Ekonomi Dan Keuangan Islam*, 10(2), 253–278.

Husin, M. M. (2019). The dynamics of Malaysian takaful market: Challenges and future prospects. *Journal of Islamic Finance*, 8, 131–137.

Hussain, M. M., & Pasha, A. T. (2011). Conceptual and operational differences between general takaful and conventional insurance. *Australian Journal of Business and Management Research*, 1(8), 23–28.

Ibrahim, S. H. M., & Hameed, S. (2007). IFRS vs AAOIFI: The clash of standards? *Munich Personal PepPEc Archive (MPRA) Paper, 12539*.

ICD Refinitiv, I. R. (2020). *Islamic Finance Development Indicator*.

KPMG. (2018). *In It To Win It : Feedback from Insurers on The Journey to IFRS 17 and IFRS 9 Implementation One Year in*.

KPMG. (2021). *Testing Times: Feedback from Leading Insurers on The Front Line of IFRS 17 Implementation*.

Maf'ula, F., & Mi'raj, D. A. (2022). Islamic insurance in Indonesia: Opportunities and challenges on developing the industry. *Journal of Islamic Economic Laws*, 5(1), 116–138.

Mutmainah, M., Sukmadilaga, C., & Nugroho, L. (2022). Development of Islamic insurance in Southeast Asia (Malaysia, Brunei Darussalam, and Indonesia): The progress perspective. *Sosyoekonomi, 30*(52), 243–255.

Nahar, H. S. (2015). Insurance vs takaful: Identical sides of a coin? *Journal of Financial Reporting and Accounting, 13*(2), 247–266.

Nomran, N. M., Haron, R., & Hassan, R. (2018). Shari'ah supervisory board characteristics effects on Islamic banks' performance: Evidence from Malaysia. *International Journal of Bank Marketing*.

Pasha, A. T., & Hussain, M. M. (2013). Takaful business models: A review, a comparison. *Business Management Dynamics, 3*(4), 24.

Puspaningtyas, L. (2021). Insurtech Jadi Peluang Asuransi Syariah (Insurtech become the opportunities of syariah insurance). *Republika*. https://www.republika.co.id/berita/q4kbug423/insurtech-jadi-peluang-asuransi-syariah

Refinitiv. (2021). *Islamic Financial Develoment Report 2021*. https://www.refinitiv.com/content/dam/marketing/en_us/documents/gated/reports/report-2021-all-color2.pdf

Setiawan, I. (2020). Bedah Kasus Gagal Bayar dan Kerugian PT. Asuransi Jiwasraya (Persero). *Jurnal Akuntansi Dan Bisnis Indonesia (JABISI), 1*(1), 34–41.

Zain, F. A. M., Abdullah, W. A. W., & Percy, M. (2021). Voluntary adoption of AAOIFI disclosure standards for takaful operators: the role of governance. *Journal of Islamic Accounting and Business Research*.

13
DILEMMA AND CHALLENGES FOR FINTECH APPLICATION IN *WAQF* ADMINISTRATION/REGULATION IN CONTEMPORARY MUSLIM MAJORITY COUNTRIES

A case of Bangladesh

A. K. M. Kamrul Hasan

1 Introduction

Waqf is not a new terminology in Islamic traditions, but rather embedded with the Islamic financial system from the early Islamic period. No doubt that the objectives of *waqf* were to contribute to the social welfare through collective efforts of faithful Muslims along with state run programs and supports. However, when we look at the *waqf* estates and administrations in developing Muslim majority countries nowadays, the weak and inefficient management structures of *waqf* properties probably are seen in most of the places which obviously undermines its' glorious past. Bangladesh is a South Asian country with ninety percent of its population is Muslim (BBS, 2011). The country had a rich story of successful *waqf* estates, which once established for humanity and social welfare. However, the *waqf* estates seem not fulfilling its objectives due to several constraints.

We should note that a couple of issues are needed to be addressed regarding *waqfs* and management systems of *waqfs* in Bangladesh. For instance, a good number of *waqfs* properties are still not registered at the 'Office of the Administrator of Waqfs Bangladesh'. The manual process of documentation and supervision of the registered properties seems unproductive; it requires to reexamine the check and balance of the power of administrator in the regulations to ensure good governance in *waqfs* properties. Contemporary scholars have addressed the multiple *waqfs* issues from East Asian and Middle Eastern countries context. However, there is a little academic debate and discussion from modern Bangladesh's perspective in the contemporary literature. Indeed, the issues that we have mentioned earlier have not been well tackled in the global literature due

DOI: 10.4324/9781003262169-16

to lack of availability of data and information. Hence, it is urgent to address the barriers that hinder the maximum utility/welfare of waqf properties, as the ultimate *maqasid* of those properties is to enhance social welfare. Therefore, the main objectives of the chapter are to analyze those issues in depth from an academic point of view and offer a couple of recommendations to the decision makers for adopting fintech as a solving instrument. In short, we attempt to analyses the *waqf* discourse from the developing Muslim majority countries' perspective especially in Bangladesh context in this chapter. We present here a model to resolve the issues related with *waqf* administration in Bangladesh with modern fintech revolution. The structure of the chapter is as follows. Section 2 discusses the definitions of *waqf*, the past and present trends of *waqf* in Bangladesh and the definition of fintech. Section 3 presents a comprehensive discussion on *waqf* administration act and governance structure in Bangladesh. Section 4 presents a critical evaluation on *waqf* act and administration from two perspectives namely monitoring cost and governance. Section 5 provides ways for building a digitalized and efficient *waqf* administration to resolve the issues discussed in prior discussion, whereas Section 6 contains a conclusion.

2 *Waqf*: definition, roles, trends in past and present

The word *waqf* (plural *awqaf*), derived from an Arabic word, literally means 'hold or stop' (Ihsan & Ibrahim, 2011). In general, *waqf* is defined as voluntary and dedicating fixed type assets to Allah SWT and devoting its income for the benefit of human beings (Ali, 1976; Kamaruddin & Hanefah, 2020). *Waqf* can be defined as 'holding certain property and preserving it for the confined benefit of philanthropy and prohibiting any use or disposition of it outside its specific objective' (Kahf, 2003). The tradition of *waqf* is deeply rooted with early Islamic era. Historians cited two *waqf* stories (one is religious *waqf* and other is philanthropic *waqf*) as evidence to describe the importance of *waqf* in Islamic tradition since the prophetic era. First, a well-known *waqf* is the mosque of Quba in Madinah which was built upon the arrival of the prophet (pbuh) in Madinah from Mecca in 622 AD (Kahf, 2003). This was an example of 'religious *waqf*'. Second is *Bir Rumah* well. During the period of Prophet Muhammad (pbuh), many Muslims were continued to migrate to Medina from Mecca to save themselves from the religious prosecutions in Mecca. However, due to high demand and scarcity of supply of drinking water, the price of drinking water in Medina was so high and it is quite difficult for the migrant Muslims to afford the price for drinking water. Seeing this, prophet (pbuh) wishes to buy *Bir Rumah* well so that all people would get the drinking water free of cost and on the request of prophet, one of his companions, Uthman ibn Affan, purchased the well from the owner and made it into a *waqf* property so that all people (both Muslims and non-Muslims) get water from it. Indeed, this philanthropic *waqf* saves many lives and money and created an illustration for next generation Muslims to do *waqf* for the welfare of the society. Although this was done to solve a specific problem faced by the

Muslims, later the concept extended into 'philanthropic *waqf*' such as supporting the public utilities, establishment of hospitals, roads, bridges, and dams.

In fact, next generation Muslims follow the footstep of their ancestors and developed the concept of *waqf* in broader forms. We have observed a variety of *waqf* estates in Umayyad dynasty, Abbasid dynasty, Ayyubid dynasty in Egypt and in the era of the Ottoman dynasty which controlled most of the Arab region and Europe. Cizakca (2002) well documented while analyzing the history of *waqf* that the *waqf* institutions have managed to provide social welfare services that many current states struggle to offer. Specifically, during the Ottoman period, the financing of health, education and welfare services were entirely entrusted to the *waqf* system (Baskan, 2002). In modern days, many Muslim societies and several humanitarian projects are operated through the *waqf* fund. These include the development of springs to provide water for public consumption, building houses for the needy, building bridges, helping the poor and the handicapped, financing the marriage of young people in need and financing orphanages and homes for the elderly (Zuki, 2012).

According to *Waqf* Ordinance 1962 that applicable in Bangladesh,

> '*waqf*' means the permanent dedication by a person professing Islam of any movable or immovable property for any purpose recognised by Muslim Law as pious, religious or charitable, and includes any other endowment or grant for the aforesaid purposes, a *waqf* by user, and a *waqf* created by a non-Muslim.
>
> *(Waqf Ordinance 1962, section 2(10))*

Waqf can be defined from economic sense, 'as investment of funds and other assets in creative properties that provide either usufruct or revenues for future consumption by individuals or groups of individuals' (Pirasteh & Abdolmaleki, 2007). In fact, *waqf* costs nothing to government; rather it supports the government to enhance its public services by engaging wealthy citizen in socio-economic development. Philanthropy-oriented *waqf* has filled gaps in the socio-economic system by appealing to the piety of wealthy individuals (Zuki, 2012). Zuki (2012), while referring to Cizakca (2011), mentioned,

> the key role of the *waqf* sector in providing public services meant significant reductions in government expenditure and borrowing which led to a reduction in the tax burden on the public and increased the potential for savings to be spent on private investment and growth. *Waqf* also offered the opportunity to provide welfare services without involvement of the state. This resulted in the development of an active civil society, assisting in redistributing resources and reducing inequality in society.

In South Asia, *waqf* also played an important role in socio-economic development since the establishment of Muslim rule in 12th century in South Asia.

Particularly during the Mughal period family members of Mughals and elite Muslims made *waqf* to establish schools (madraas), bridges, ponds, etc. During the British colonial regime, South Asian Muslims were almost abandoned from the state's power and support. Besides, the financial conditions of middle-class Muslim population went down and a few new estates had been added within the existing *waqf* properties during the British rule in South Asia. Despite this, during the British colonial rule, few wealthy Muslims continued to donate their properties as *waqf*. Indeed in 1913 'The Mussalman Wakf Validating Act 1913' is a kind of legal acknowledgment by the British ruler to the *waqf* properties. Currently the *waqf* estates in India are administered by Central *Waqf* Council under Ministry of Minority Affairs, Governments of India. In case of Pakistan, *awqāf* properties belong to religious institutions such as mosques, religious schools (madaris), shrines (dargahs), and graveyards (janazagahs) (Abbasi, 2019). After Independence, West Pakistan *Waqf* Properties Ordinance 1959 and the West Pakistan *Waqf* Properties Rules of 1960 considered a breakthrough to regulate and organize the *waqf* in Modern Pakistan (Abbasi, 2019). The history of *waqf* in Bengal (the present day of Bangladesh and some parts of Bengali-speaking regions in Indian provinces) has a long tradition. Since the Bengal Sultanate period (14th to 16th centuries) a lot of *waqf* estates had been established. For instance, during the period of Sultan Nasiruddin Mahmud Shah (1435–1459), there was an endowment to establish mosque at Navagram, Sirajganj, Bangladesh. Besides, several mosques were established in Sylhet District of Bangladesh under *waqf* estate during Sultan Shamsuddin Yousuf Shah period (reigned from 1474 to 1481). Sultan Alauddin Husain Shah, during his reign (1493–1519), allotted many rent-free lands to religious leaders of Bengal in several parts (Alamgir, 2020). Besides, the 'Lalbagh' in Dhaka (presently known as the Lalbagh Fort) and the 'Bara Katra' in Dhaka were *waqf* properties of Mughal subadar Shaista Khan and Sultan Shah Shuja respectively who ruled Dhaka in 16th century (Alamgir, 2020). During the British colonial rule, the *waqf* properties of Haji Mohammad Mohsin (1732–1812) and the *waqf* properties of the Nawabs of Dhaka still exist and serve for the humanity as a symbol of philanthropic *waqf*. In the present day, the buildings of Dhaka University, Dhaka Medical College and Bangladesh University of Engineering and Technology were built on the land donated by the Nawab family of Dhaka. However, after independence in 1947, many *waqf* estates were acquired by the government due to lack of documents which were at that time kept in Calcutta, India and could not be retrieved (Alamgir, 2020). Finally, The *Waqf* Ordinance, 1962, an exhaustive law regulating *waqf*, introduced in Pakistan (including East Pakistan, now Bangladesh) to manage and regulate the *waqf* properties. There is a department established under this Ordinance in which the *waqf* administrator is appointed as the head of the department and his office named as 'Office of the *Waqf* Administrator' under the Ministry of Religious Affairs. After being independent in 1971, the present-day Bangladesh has managed all *waqf* properties under 'Office of the Administrator of *Waqf*s

Bangladesh' which is attached with Ministry of Religious Affairs, Govt. of the People's Republic of Bangladesh.

On the other hand, the now trendy word fintech was coined by CITI group in the early 1990s (Arner et al., 2015; Hochstein, 2015a, 2015b). Arner et al. (2015) rightly noted, '[t]he term's origin can be traced to the early 1990s and referred to the 'Financial Services Technology Consortium', a project initiated by Citigroup to facilitate technological cooperation efforts'. After conducting a semantic analysis on definition of fintech from more than 200 scholarly articles over the last forty years, Schueffel (2016) mentioned, 'Fintech is a new financial industry that applies technology to improve financial activities' (p. 45). According to OECD (2018), 'Fintech involves not only the application of new digital technologies to financial services but also the development of business models and products which rely on these technologies and more generally on digital platforms and processes'. The FSB defines fintech as 'technology-enabled innovation in financial services that could result in new business models, applications, processes or products with an associated material effect on the provision of financial services' (FSB, 2019, p. 1). Scholars argue that fintech companies are filling a gap left by traditional financial institutions and companies, including in Silicon Valley, the United Kingdom and China (IMF, 2020). The reason is

> traditional financial institutions typically provide services through brick-and-mortar establishments and rely on legacy technology that are costly to operate, and even more costly to upgrade and adapt to fast-changing technology; whereas Fintech companies are often better positioned to use the latest technology and data analytics to target niche markets, including lower-income groups, and orient their products to maximize consumer satisfaction.
>
> *(IMF, 2020, p. 13)*

To keep our discussion on track, we leave the detailed discussion on fintech here rather examine how fintech will be helpful in managing *waqf* administration and lowering monitoring cost. The following sections are devoted on these issues.

3 *Waqf* administration act and structure: a case of Bangladesh

In Bangladesh, the *waqf* administration mainly runs under two major regulations such as (a) *Waqf* ordinance 1962 (which is amended in 2013) and (b) *Waqf* special (property transfer and development) act 2013 (Hasan and Siraj, 2016). Below, we summarize the key points of both regulations.

3.1 *Waqf ordinance 1962*

Waqf ordinance 1962 (hereafter Ordinance) is considered as a key regulation in *waqf* administration in Bangladesh. As discussed, the ordinance was first initiated

TABLE 1 Salient features of *Waqf* Ordinance 1962

S. no.	Chapter	No. of sections	Descriptions
1	Preamble	1–6	This chapter discusses the definition of several terminologies used in the ordinance, the scope of the ordinance and the right of records of the *waqf* properties.
2	Appointment of administrators of *waqf*, officers and staffs, and constitution of the committee	7–26	How to appoint an administrator of *waqf*, terms and conditions of appointment, removals and remuneration are briefly discussed in the chapter. Besides, appointment of officers and other staff are discussed. Most importantly, it highlights in detail on how several committees are formed.
3	Powers and functions of the administrators and the committee	27–46	The chapter briefly explains the administrative power and functions of the administrator and the committee. How to appoint an official *mutawalli* is also described here.
4	Enrollment of *waqfs*	47–52	Enrollment, registration of *waqf* estate is discussed in this chapter.
5	*Waqfs* accounts	53–55	Chapter 5 specifies how to maintain the accounts of the *waqf* and conduct audit are highlighted.
6	Transfer of *waqfs* properties	56–58	Regulations on transfer of *waqf* properties are discussed here.
7	Mutawallis	59–70	Chapter 7 solely discussed on remuneration and duties of *mutawallis*.
8	Finance	71–78	How to manage the '*waqf* fund' is discussed in Chapter 8.
9	Judicial proceedings	79–86	How to deal with the legal issues related with *waqf* properties are well explained in this chapter.
10	Amendment and repeal	87–94	Amendment and repeal of the ordinance in Bangladesh is explained here.
11	Miscellaneous	95–103	Several miscellaneous issues such as procedures of conducting meetings, special directions to the administrator's and officers are mentioned in this chapter.
12	Rules and by laws	104–105	The power to government to make rule and power to the administrator to make by laws are explained in detail in the final chapter of the ordinance.

in 1962 to manage the *waqf* estates in the West Pakistan and East Pakistan (now Bangladesh). After its independence in 1971, Bangladeshi *waqf* estates were regulated under this act until 2013 when it was slightly modified in few sections. There are 12 chapters and 105 sections in the ordinance. Table 1 shows the key points of each section.

It is evident from Table 1 that the ordinance briefly discussed on several institutional settings, powers and provisions related with *waqf* and *waqf* properties. We should note that the amendment in the ordinance that conducted in 2013 is not so vast; rather, few sections were included in the text and rest of the text is similar to that was incorporated in 1962.

From the ordinance, it is also clear that there are three parties involved in supervision and monitoring system that established in *waqf* properties as per the ordinance (see Figure 1). First, the 'Office of the Administrator of *Waqfs* Bangladesh' is the supreme authority in *waqfs* in Bangladesh and another is *Mutawalli*-based monitoring and supervision of *waqfs* at bottom level. As there are multiple monitoring structures, it presumes that the system is not cost effective rather crates an expenditure burden on the income on the *waqfs* fund. Besides, there is the manual-based report filling system which creates bureaucracy in the property management system. What is more, it is found that there is no specific qualification or guidelines on appointment of *Mutawalli* and the administrator has empowered with extraordinary power. There is no check and balance, neither for administrator nor for *Mutawalli*. Those monitoring and governance issues are briefly explained in Section 4.

Besides, we observed from the ordinance that the administrative organogram of the office of the *waqf* administrator is quite bureaucratic (see Figure 2) and there is less automation in the office. As a result, it takes much more time to establish a new *waqf* or settle any claim of the *waqf* properties. Finally, it is found that there is a '*waqf* committee' in the ordinance for assisting and advising the administrator in administrating the *waqf* and their funds and in the exercise and performance of the administrator's powers and duties (see *Waqf* ordinance 1962, section 19). We consider this a costly and bureaucratic process in decision-making (see Figure 3).

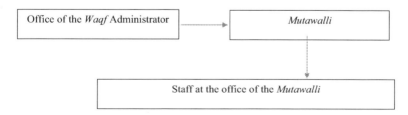

FIGURE 1 Parties involved in *waqf* estates management.

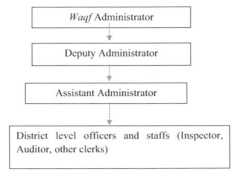

FIGURE 2 Administrative structure of the Office of the *Waqf* Administrator.

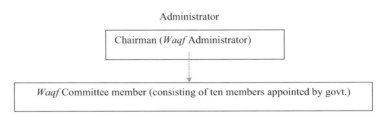

FIGURE 3 Decision-making process at the Office of *Waqf*

3.2 Waqf special (property transfer and development) act 2013

'*Waqf* special act 2013' is enacted in 2013 by the government of Bangladesh to clarify the transfer of *waqf* properties and development. The act has 26 sections of which 13 are related to transfer of *waqf* properties, and the rest are related to *waqf* property development, related lawsuits and miscellaneous issues. It clarifies how *waqf* properties could be transferred and developed/constructed for further use under the existing Bangladeshi laws.

4 A critical evaluation of *Waqf* ordinance 1962: monitoring cost, governance issues and transaction cost perspective

Monitoring cost and transaction cost are widely discussed by the scholars in the field of corporate governance and institutional economics. It is argued to install a good governance system in the organization so that the agency cost will be lowered. Traditional agency theory (see Fama, 1980; Jensen, 1986; Jensen & Meckling, 1976; Jensen & Murphy, 1990) advocates creating a well design compensation contract between agent and principal to minimize the agency problem. Hence, it could be imagined that the office of the *waqf* administrator and *mutawalli* act as an agent appointed by the *waqif* (the founder of the *waqf*) which we may consider as principal. Based on the argument, the monitoring cost can be justified. However, the main issue is that the *waqf* properties have different features than any other business entity. For instance, muslim scholars have viewed the ownership of *waqf* that the property of *waqf* is owned by Allah or by its beneficiaries, however in any case the beneficiaries cannot sell or give away the *waqf*, except few exceptions (Zuki, 2012). Besides, *waqif* should define all the conditions in a written document which must be followed as long as they follow *shariah* principles (Ibrahim, 1996). In addition, *waqf* is used for public utility, it is not a private consumption, but rather we can consider the *waqf* properties as a common asset/property to all. In addition, 'trust' and 'traits' are two key components in *waqf* contract framework. 'Trust' is important because those who pay philanthropy cannot examine products physically, evaluate the use of philanthropic paid and have limited access to information, which shows that the relationship between philanthropic institutions and philanthropic payers are having the nature of uncertainty, dependence and risk (Usman et al., 2022, p. 397). In practice, *waqif* puts his trust on administrator (government/regulating body) and manager of the property (mutawalli) that they will provide their best efforts to maintain the *waqf* estates and maximize its utility to the humanity. And the personal 'traits' (morals) is another key component of *waqf* contract and governance (in section five we have discussed those traits). Although there is a provision to take punitive action against any dishonest/corrupt *mutawallis* by administrator, however if state power supports the former one, it is difficult to bring discipline in the *waqf* governance by the administrator alone. A good number of unregistered *waqf* properties and illegal occupation and encroachment of *waqf* lands are the evidence of our claims (see more in Ahmad & Safiullah, 2012; Hasan & Siraj, 2016). Hence, in such a case, there is no way except morals that could prevent the corruption in management level as *waqif* is no longer to monitor the management. Having these unique features, the existing monitoring system and governance system described in the ordinance are not compatible with the objectives and mission of *waqf* properties. In short, we can conclude that the monitoring costs are important in corporations because there is an existence of incomplete contract (due to agency problems), whereas monitoring costs of *waqfs* properties depend on two T's such as 'trust' and 'traits' of the agents instead of incomplete contract.

We should note that *waqf* administrator office charges five percent of net income from the *waqf* estates and the mutawalli remuneration is fixed at one tenth (10%) of the income from the estate. Besides, there are other administrative expenses to be covered from the income of the estates. As a result, the beneficiaries' proportion is reduced by such kind of structural monitoring cost approved in the ordinance. Readers could raise question about what the role of the government is to ensure the welfare from the *waqf* estates. Unfortunately, there is no single section in the ordinance that indicates to cover any expenditure by the government, rather all governmental staffs are working in the monitoring level with the cost of *waqf* estates. This is the major loopholes within ordinance that state has skipped its financial responsibility to maintain *waqf* properties. What is more, the ordinance has empowered the administrator as a super powerful person in *waqf* estate and controlling the properties. However, scholars argue that *waqf* institutions should have a flexible organizational structure so that the person in charge of administering the *waqf* (a manager/mutawalli) can shape it as he wishes (Ahmed, 2004). It is the mutawalli's moral obligation to protect the *waqf* property and to maximize its profit (Zuki, 2012). As we discussed, the ordinance rather makes it difficult for the mutawalli to take any innovative initiative to enhance because it requires a heavy bureaucratic process to get permission from the Office of the *Waqf* Administration. Indeed, these increase the overall monitoring cost and in turn reduce the welfare from the *waqf* estates.

However, the irony is, although the strict regulations enforce in the country since 1962, the governance of the *waqf* estates is very poor and great number of *waqf* properties are captured by local musclemen and political elites. We can presume that weak governance and monitoring could be a reason for this. A previous study on the tragedy of Bangladeshi *waqf* supports our claim. For instance, Chandan (2018) mentioned after his field visit report at the Office of the *Waqf* Administrator,

> Besides, corruption is also rife in the office of the *waqf* administration and the *waqf* administrator himself confessed this. He says our manpower is so scarce that we could not enforce transparency and accountability in the office. We don't have any officer to cross-check and monitor performance of the inspectors, other staffs and mutawallis.

The legal and religious scholars also stressed on the weakness of the ordinance. One of the legal experts of the country commented in this way

> The law is outdated and does not describe how the rights of the *waqf* property will be protected. It only describes how the *waqf* administration will perform. We need a substantive law which will describe how the cases under the law can be handled and how crimes are to be charged.
> *(Chandan, 2018)*

Religious scholars still have countless objections against the law and the decaying system. For instance, one of the *shariah* researchers explains,

> There is no concrete policy of the *waqf* administration to survey, identify, enlist, and audit the *waqf* properties in Bangladesh. Particularly, it has minimal or no supervision on family *waqf* property. The most significant issue is there is no sharia board for investigating, regulating, or advising the administration for its activities. The *waqf* administration is basically run by the civil servants who don't have knowledge about Islamic law.
> *(see Chandan, 2018)*

Therefore, we could presume that one of Bangladesh's greatest instruments of social service has completely collapsed due to high monitoring cost within the legal framework and weak governance within the administration potentially.

The second issue is the high transaction cost of maintaining a *waqf* property. The *ex-ante* cost is registration fees and stamp fees whereas *ex post* costs are audit fees, *waqf* administrator fee (five percent of net income), mutawalli's remuneration. We presume that high transaction cost eats up the profits generated from the property. There is no specific policy to minimize the transaction cost rather the ordinance fueling to increase the cost. It seems that the *waqf* properties in Bangladesh are facing a 'tragedy of the commons' (Hardin, 2009; Ostrom, 1990). In the next section, we attempt to develop a framework for reducing monitoring and governance cost by applying using fintech in *waqf* estates.

5 Toward a digitalized and efficient *waqf* administration

In fact, academic research provides evidence that *waqf* is a well-accepted instrument for socio-economic development in Organizations of Islamic Cooperation countries (see Medias et al., 2022) and there is no doubt that if *waqfs* are well-managed and properly monitored, the society will reap more benefits. For instance, Islamic Development Bank's (IsDB's) Awqaf Properties Investment Fund (APIF), which has 15 investors, could be an example of well-managed *waqfs* that have high-level impact on enhancing social welfare in South Asia to African countries. APIF uses a unique model to manage the fund and it is reported that, in the APIF portfolio, as of the end of 2018, includes 55 completed or active projects, totaling US$1.04 billion. Of this, IsDB's contribution includes US$161 million from APIF and US$370 million from the IsDB line of financing and the remaining is from the beneficiaries (see details in IsDB, 2019, pp. 33–35). IsDB adopts a modern and transparent administration system using information technology. In academic circle, scholars argue that fintech could be used for multiple purposes in the case of *waqf* to maximize its utility and social benefits. To illustrate, Yusuf et al. (2021) show how fintech is used to cash *waqf* management in Bangladesh, Yoshida (2019) describes a framework of the 'fintech enabled cash *waqf*' as an effective tool for social finance. Usman et al. (2022) in an empirical study found that fintech could convince donors to increase their trust and attitude toward philanthropic institutions, whereas Hapsari et al. (2022) offer a crowdfunding *waqf* model in providing financing resource to develop *waqf* lands. In short, it is evident that fintech or digitalization of waqf administration could enhance the welfare of *waqfs* properties. However, in our previous discussion, we argue that the governmental executive trusteeship on *waqf* properties in Bangladesh contributes to increase monitoring cost and transaction cost. Besides, there is a room to reform the existence ordinance to improve the *waqf* governance structure. We advocate fintech as an effective instrument to resolve those issues. Below we elaborate on how fintech is a viable alternative to settle two issues described from Bangladesh context.

5.1 Fintech: a viable solution to reduce monitoring cost and transaction cost of waqf properties

Bangladesh government has taken several initiatives in recent years to digitalize the governmental services to maximize the public utility and efficiency of the governmental services (see ICTD, 2021). However, the progress seems to be too far from the expectation and many services could be provided under digital system, 'The Office of the Waqfs Administrator' for an example. As discussed in Section 2, fintech has a fast-moving trend in the emerging economies; we suggest adopting fintech in *waqf* administration to increase the welfare from the *waqf* properties. The following discussion elaborates the concept.

In case of cash waqf: In case of cash *waqf*, the *waqif* can open a bank account and instructs the bank to remit the profit/interest at the year end to the *waqf* Fund of the Office of *Waqf* Administrator. Next, the administrator will allocate the fund to the eligible heads (as instructed by *waqif*). We explain this in Figure 4.

In Figure 4, we observe that there is no need/roles for mutawallis for maintenance of fund and thus can reduce the fees paid to mutawalli.

In case of non-cash Waqf: When the *waqf* is conducted for fixed assets or other tangible assets, *waqif* can use fintech to lower monitoring cost and transaction cost. For instance, in the case of new *waqf*, *waqif* can directly conduct the *waqf* registration process in favor of ministry of lands and the property could become a state property instead of Mutawalli-based system which could cut the transaction cost. However, the utilization of the property could base on the instruction/wishes of the *waqif*. In the case of existing *waqf* estates, fintech could be used to reduce the traditional reporting systems and monitoring process. For instance, the mutawalli could remit any financial benefit from the estates to the beneficiaries through mobile financial services and could also remit five percent of income to the *waqf* administrator through mobile financial service. In addition, introducing electronic filing system could help both mutawalli and administrator to cut administrative cost and transaction cost. Figure 5 describes this theoretical framework.

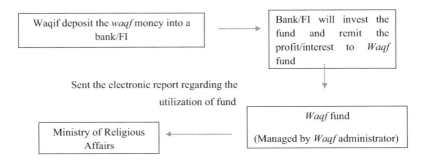

FIGURE 4 Adaptation of fintech in cash *waqf*

5.2 Improving governance system in waqf administration by updating the ordinance

Although conventional and Islamic governance are similar in terms of definition, objectives and good practices, Kamaruddin and Hanefah (2020) documented several principles for Islamic *waqf* governance system which are vital to ensure good *waqf* governance in *waqf* administration. These include *tawhid* (oneness of Allah), *adalah* (justice), *mas'uliyyah* (accountability), *amanah* (trust), *shura* (mutual consultation), *taqwa* (Allah-consciousness), *hisbah* (enjoining virtue and avoiding evil) and *maqasid shariah* (objectives of shariah) (Kamaruddin & Hanefah, 2020, p. 457). We shall note that the *waqf* governance system differs from countries to countries. For instance, in Malaysia, *waqf* governance administered under two ways such as state level and national level, whereas the *waqf* administration follows two guidelines: (i) the guidelines issued by Securities Commission Malaysia in 2014 (see details in SCM, 2014) and (ii) 'Code of Governance and Transparency for *Waqf* Fund' issued by Islamic Banking and Financial Institutions Malaysia (AIBIM) in 2017 (see details in AIBIM, 2017). On the other hand, in Kuwait, a separate ministry named 'Ministry of *Awqaf* and Islamic Affairs' look after the *waqfs*-related issues and formulate different regulations related with *Awqaf*. As we mentioned earlier, the existing ordinance seems to much more bureaucratic type and administrator appears as a supreme authority in the ordinance (in other words, state supervision turns into an executive trusteeship). Hence, we recommend two suggestions: (i) establishing a central *shariah* board at the

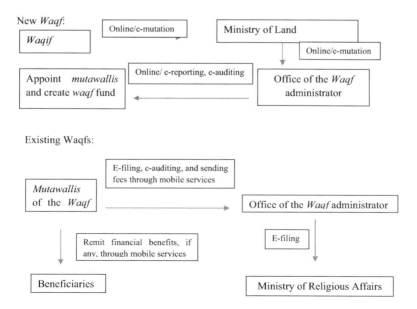

FIGURE 5 Adaptation of fintech in non-cash *waqf*

Office of *Waqf* Administrator replacing the existing committee system in the ordinance. Eminent Islamic scholars could be member of the board to provide shariah opinion regarding *waqf* properties and their revenues. (ii) We suggest following the Accounting and Auditing Organization for Islamic Financial Institutions newly adopted Governance Standard 13 namely '*Waqf* Governance' to ensure good governance in Bangladeshi *waqfs* and adopt full automation in *waqf* administration.

6 Conclusion

In this chapter, we briefly discussed the concept of *waqf* and the historical perspective of the evolution of *waqf* in Muslim majority countries including Bangladesh. Next, we discuss the salient features of the two *Waqf* regulations of Bangladesh. We have proceeded with our discussion to the critical evaluation of the two regulations from monitoring cost and governance issues. Based on our findings we provide a couple of theoretical frameworks to apply fintech in *waqf* administration to minimize monitoring cost and ensuring transparent governance. To recap, we have observed that *waqf* is an important instrument that is used by early Muslim generations to modern Muslim generations mainly to enhance social welfare and philanthropic mind set. The wealthy and kindhearted Bengal Muslims have a long tradition to create *Awaqf* from their properties for creating religious establishments, schools, orphanages, digging ponds, and so on for the betterment of society. As a result, a huge number of *waqf* properties exist in Bangladesh. According to Hasan and Siraj (2016), there are 150,593 *waqf* estates in Bangladesh of which only 97,046 estates are registered. It shows that a good number of non-registered *waqf* properties are in Bangladesh which are not under the monitoring of the government. We have pointed out that there is a huge monitoring cost and transaction cost for registered *waqfs* which are accumulated at the Office of *Waqf* Administrator and at the office of Mutawalli. We presume that high monitoring cost and transaction cost might eat up the incomes of the *waqfs* estates. We suggest that fintech and automation could minimize the costs. It is long overdue to make the *waqfs* properties an efficient income generation asset and bring a transparent governance system in those estates. We also argue that it requires a structural and institutional reform in *waqf* ordinance and governance to adopt fintech in *waqf* properties in Bangladesh. In fact, we should aware that *Awaqf* would not be an example of 'tragedy of the commons' in Bangladesh.

References

Abbasi, M. Z. (February 1, 2019). *Waqf in Pakistan: Rebirth of a Traditional Institution*. Malaysia: Kalalau. SSRN: https://ssrn.com/abstract=3327092 or http://dx.doi.org/10.2139/ssrn.3327092

Association of Islamic Banking and Financial Institutions Malaysia (AIBIM) (2017). *Code of Governance and Transparency for Waqf Fund*. Malaysia: Kuala Lumpur.

Ahmed, H. (2004). *Role of Zakat and Awqaf in Poverty Alleviation*. Jeddah, Saudi Arabia: Islamic Development Bank Group, Islamic Research and Training Institute.

Ahmad, M. M. M., & Safiullah, M. (2012). Management of Waqf estates in Bangladesh: Towards a sustainable policy formation. In *Waqf Laws and Management (with Special Reference to Malaysia)* (pp. 229–262). New Delhi: Institute of Objective Studies.

Alamgir, K. (2020). Awqaf properties in Bengal since the period of Muslim Rule. *Journal of the Asiatic Society of Bangladesh (Humanities)*, 65(2), pp. 103–121.

Ali, S. A. (1976). *The Law Relating to Gifts, Wakfs, Wills, Pre-Emption, and Bailment* (Vol. 1). Lahore, Delhi: Law Publishing Company.

Arner, D. W., Barberis, J. N., & Buckley, R. P. (2015). *The Evolution of Fintech: A New Post-Crisis Paradigm?* (2015/047). Hong Kong: University of Hong Kong, Faculty of Law.

Bangladesh Bureau of Statistics (BBS). (2011). *Population and Housing Census* (p. xiii). Dhaka, Bangladesh: Bangladesh Government.

Baskan, B. (2002). *Waqf System as a Redistribution Mechanism in the Ottoman Empire*. Paper presented at 17th Middle East History and Theory Conference, May 10–11. Center for Middle Eastern Studies, University of Chicago.

Chandan, M. S. K. (2018, February 23). *Waqf*: A forgotten legacy. *The Daily Star*, Star Weekend, p. 3.

Cizakca, M. (2002). Latest developments in the Western non-profit sector and the implications for Islamic Awqaf. In *Islamic Economic Institutions and the Elimination of Poverty* (pp. 263–287). Leicester: The Islamic Foundation.

Cizakca, M. (2011). *Waqf* in history and its implications for modern Islamic economies. In Kahf, M. and Mahmood, S. M. (Eds.), *Essential Readings in Contemporary Waqf Issues* (pp. 43–70). Kuala Lumpur: CERT Publications Sdn. Bhd.

Fama, E. (1980). Agency problems and the theory of the firm. *Journal of Political Economy*, 80(2), pp. 288–307.

Financial Stability Board (FSB). (2019). *FinTech and market structure in financial services: Market developments and potential financial stability implications*. Accessed on 8 March, 2022. https://www.fsb.org/2019/02/fintech-and-market-structure-in-financial-services-market-developments-and-potential-financial-stability-implications/

Hapsari, M. I., Thaker, M. A. B. M. T., Mohammed, M. O., & Duasa, J. (2022). A qualitative investigation into crowdfunding framework as a source of financing for waqf land development. *Journal of Islamic Accounting and Business Research*, 13(3), pp. 425–443.

Hardin, G. (2009). The tragedy of the commons. *Journal of Natural Resources Policy Research*, 1(3), pp. 243–253.

Hasan, R., & Siraj, S. A. (2016). Complexities of *Waqf* development in Bangladesh. *Journal of Emerging Economies and Islamic Research*, 4(3), pp. 17–26.

Hochstein, M. (2015a). *Fintech (the Word, That Is) Evolves*. Accessed 7 March 2022. https://www.americanbanker.com/opinion/fintech-the-word-that-is-evolves

Hochstein, M. (2015b). *Friday Flashback: Did Citi Coin the Term 'Fintech'? Gems from Our Archives*. Accessed 7 March 2022. https://www.americanbanker.com/opinion/friday-flashback-did-citi-coin-the-term-fintech

Ibrahim, M. (1996). *The Concept of Waqf (Endowment), Gifts and Wills in Islam*. Qatar: Islamic Book Development and Translation Council.

Ihsan, H., & Ibrahim, S. H. H. M. (2011). WAQF accounting and management in Indonesian WAQF institutions: The cases of two WAQF foundations. *Humanomics*, 27(4), pp. 252–269.

IMF. (2020). *The Promise of Fintech: Financial Inclusion in the Post COVID-19 Era*. Accessed on 8 March 2022. https://www.imf.org/en/Publications/Departmental-Papers-Policy-Papers/Issues/2020/06/29/The-Promise-of-Fintech-Financial-Inclusion-in-the-Post-COVID-19-Era-48623

Information and Communication Technology Division (ICTD), Government of the People's Republic of Bangladesh. (2021). *Annual Report 2020–21.* https://ictd.gov.bd/site/view/annual_reports/Monthly-Annual-Reports-

Islamic Development Bank (IsDB). (2019). *The Development Impact of the Awqaf Properties Investment Fund A Model for Sustainable Development.* Jeddah, Kingdom of Saudi Arabia: Islamic Development Bank.

Jensen, M. (1986). Agency costs of free cash flow, corporate finance and takeovers. *American Economic Review, 76*(2), pp. 323–329.

Jensen, M., & Meckling, W. (1976). Theory of the firm: Managerial behavior, agency costs and ownership structure. *Journal of Financial Economics, 3*(4), pp. 304–360.

Jensen, M., & Murphy, K. (1990). Performance pay and top-management incentives. *Journal of Political Economy, 98*(2), 261–262.

Kahf, M. (2003). *The Role of waqf in Improving the Ummah Welfare.* In Paper presented at the International Seminar on *Waqf* as a Private Legal Body, Medan, 6–7 January.

Kamaruddin, M. I. H., & Hanefah, M. (2020). An empirical investigation on *waqf* governance practices in *waqf* institutions in Malaysia. *Journal of Financial Reporting and Accounting, 19*(3), pp. 455–473.

Medias, F., Rahman, A. A., Susamto, A. A., & Pambuko, Z. B. (2022). A systematic literature review on the socio-economic roles of waqf: Evidence from organization of the Islamic cooperation (OIC) countries. *Journal of Islamic Accounting and Business Research, 13*(1), pp. 177–193.

OECD. (2018). *Financial Markets, Insurance and Private Pensions: Digitalisation and Finance.* Accessed on 8 March 2022. https://www.oecd.org/competition/financial-markets-insurance-and-pensions-2018.htm

Ostrom, Elinor. (1990). *Governing the Commons: The Evolution of Institutions for Collective Action.* Cambridge: Cambridge University Press.

Pirasteh, H., & Abdolmaleki, H. (2007). *Developing Awqaf Properties and Islamic Financial Engineering: A Conceptual and Empirical Analysis.* Paper presented at first Singapore International *Waqf* Conference: Integration of Awqaf (Islamic Endowment) in the Islamic Financial Sector, 6–7 March. Singapore.

Schueffel, P. (2016). Taming the beast: A scientific definition of fintech. *Journal of Innovation Management, 4*, pp. 32–54.

Securities Commission Malaysia (SCM). (2014). *Waqf Assets: Development, Governance and the Role of Islamic Capital Market.* Malaysia: Kuala Lumpur. https://www.sc.com.my/api/documentms/download.ashx?id=a0b2d65d-07ac-4932-a956-70004a93650c

Usman, H., Mulia, D., Chairy, C., & Widowati, N. (2022). Integrating trust, religiosity and image into technology acceptance model: the case of the Islamic philanthropy in Indonesia. *Journal of Islamic Marketing, 13*(2), pp. 381–409. https://doi.org/10.1108/JIMA-01-2020-0020

Yoshida, E. (2019). FinTech-enabled cash waqf: Effective intermediary of social finance. In: Ali, K., Hassan, M., and Ali, A. (Eds.), *Revitalization of Waqf for Socio-Economic Development* (Vol. I). Cham: Palgrave Macmillan. https://doi.org/10.1007/978-3-030-18445-2_4

Yusuf, H., Amelia, K. R., & Rahmah, S. (2021). A construction of cash waqf management in Bangladesh. *Al-Bayyinah, 5*(1), pp. 86–97.

Zuki, M. S. M. (2012). *Waqf* and its role in socio economic development. *ISRA International Journal of Islamic Finance, 4*(2), pp. 173–178.

14

BREAKING THE BARRIERS OF ZAKAT MANAGEMENT SYSTEM THROUGH ISLAMIC FINTECH

The case of Bangladesh

S. M. Sohrab Uddin and Afroza Sultana

1 Introduction

Zakat (obligatory payment), the third of the five pillars of Islam, is the most influential Islamic tool for reducing poverty and ensuring socio-economic justice (Ibrahim & Shaharuddin, 2015). Though the ultimate goal of paying *zakat* is to achieve the pleasure of Allah, its socio-economic contributions cover a vast area, from ensuring social security to reducing extreme poverty. Poverty alleviation has become a fundamental concern of governments of all economies, especially the emerging and low-income ones. 8.6% of the world's population living at the extreme poverty level (World Bank, 2018) experienced their worst time during the worldwide corona pandemic in 2019. Though 2021 was expected to be the recovery year from the Covid-19 induced new extreme poverty that affects 97 million people, the developing and low-income countries are yet to meet the expected goal of poverty reduction (World Bank, 2021). The macroeconomic policies of emerging economies are mainly concentrated on poverty alleviation and equitable wealth distribution. Complementing the governments' fiscal policies, *zakat* redistributes the income efficiently, reduces poverty, and increases growth (Ahmed, 2015). It is evident that being a part of the comprehensive Islamic economic system, *zakat* positively affects consumption, poverty eradication, saving, and economic growth (Wahab & Rahman, 2011). Acting as a poverty-reducing Islamic tool, *zakat* eventually creates a positive effect on increasing the purchasing power of citizens, inducing aggregate consumption, and ensuring social security.

    The heart of the entire *zakat* management system is the *zakat* institutions, which are charged with collecting 2.5% Islamic tax from Muslim individuals and business owned by Muslims when their wealth reach *nisab* (zakatable wealth) and distributing the same to the eight categories of *al-mustahiqqin* (beneficiaries)

DOI: 10.4324/9781003262169-17

mentioned in *surah at-Towba* (Verse 60). These eight *al-mustahiqqin* of *zakat* are the poor, the needy, the Muslim *zakat* administrator, the new converted Muslim, the enslaved people, the financially indebted, *Fi sabilillah* (those in the way to Allah), and *Innu Sabil* (those in the warfare). The institutionalisation of the entire *zakat* management has the objectives of better community development, empowerment, and financial inclusion (Adachi, 2018). Unlike the other Islamic institutions (Islamic banks, Islamic insurance), which concentrate on wealth creation, *zakat* institutions focus on wealth distribution. *Zakat* Institutions complement the financial institutions by promoting the aggregate demand and supply in the economy (Saad & Farouk, 2019). With increased purchasing power by receiving the *zakat* money, the beneficiaries demand more goods in the economy. On the other hand, increased savings and improved health of the beneficiaries promote the aggregate supply of capital and labour.

The efficiency and governance of *zakat* institutions are the concern of a country's entire *zakat* management system to achieve its novel objectives (Wahab & Rahman, 2011). An efficient *zakat* management system is needed to ensure the proper distribution of its collected money. To reach a systematic and efficient *zakat* management system, adequate technology is required to collect, manage, and distribute the *zakat* money. Though technological integration into the *zakat* management system is not new, it gains a new speed in the ongoing fourth Industrial Revolution. Financial technology (fintech) is now considered the solution to most previous mismanagement problems in organisations, including the *zakat* management system.

World Bank defines fintech as the fourth Industrial-Revolution–driven technologies exponentially enhancing and/or disrupting 20th-century financial services, operations, business models, and customer engagement (World Bank, 2020). The efficiency of financial services and social welfare is the key moto of the fintech industry worldwide. In the case of Islamic fintech's adaptation in the Islamic finance scenario, it is of the solid opinion of Islamic scholars that if a transaction is not related to *riba* (loan with interest), *gharar* (speculation), and Islamic prohibited products (alcohol, pork, gambling, pornography), the finance plan is allowed to be included in the Islamic finance jurisdiction (K. Hasan et al., 2005). It is expected that a *Halal* (legitimate) financial service will be more efficient, less costly, and less painstaking with the adaptation of fintech. So, right after its inception, fintech was appreciated by the Islamic finance jurisdiction. In this regard, the expectations of the Muslim world of reducing poverty through the efficient collection and distribution of *Zakat* through fintech solutions demand an exploration of the existing and probable fintech-adopted *zakat* management system.

In Bangladesh, due to the Covid-19 effect on macroeconomic aspects, the poverty rate increased to 18.1% in 2022 from 14.4% in the previous year (World Bank, 2021). Being one of the fastest-growing economies in the world over the past decades, from among the tenth lowest per capita GDP in the world in its birth year of 1971 to the lower-middle-income country status in 2015, Bangladesh's poverty reduction efforts may catch the interest of the worldwide poverty reduction aspiration of the emerging economies. One critical study showed that relying only on the macroeconomic policy will never achieve Bangladesh's poverty reduction goal; instead, effective *zakat* management will complement the spirit (Ahmed, 2015). Another study showed that *zakat* funds in Bangladesh could replace the government's budgetary expenditure by 43% of the Annual Development Plan (ADP) in 2004/2005 (Hassan & Khan, 2007). From the religious outlook, Bangladesh is the fourth largest Muslim-populated country globally, where 90.40% of the population is Muslim, which is 9.2% of the total world Muslim population (World Population Review, 2022; Wormald, 2013). On the other hand, from technological outlook, mobile phone users increased by 14% (from 157.54 million in January 2019 to 180.78 million in January 2022), and individual internet users increased by 33.92% (from 91 million in January 2019 to 121.87 million in January 2022) within only four years in Bangladesh (Bangladesh Telecommunication Regulatory Commission, 2022). Hence, the full utilisation of the *zakat* system riding over the fintech solutions to reduce the poverty rate in Bangladesh also needs an overview of the current scenario here.

Considering the above aspects, the chapter has attempted to link the barriers of the entire *zakat* management system to *Shari'ah-compliant* Islamic fintech models, which may have the possibility to overcome the barriers. The study has considered the current practices worldwide and fintech models proposed by different scholars in this field of knowledge. Barriers like anti-Islamic sentiment (Obaidullah, 2015) and others that fintech models cannot overcome have been ignored intentionally for the scope of the study. Following the introduction section, this chapter presents an overview of the existing *zakat* management system, followed by a description of the Islamic fintech used or can be used in the *zakat* management system. After exploring fintech models' scope to overcome the barriers and the scenario of fintech to the *zakat* management system in Bangladesh, the chapter ended by highlighting the challenges that fintech might face in full-fledged applications and concluding the whole discussion.

2 Overview of the existing zakat management system

Zakat means growth, cleanliness, blessing, and praise in the Arabic language. In *Shari'ah*, *zakah* refers to the determined share of wealth prescribed in the Holy Quran to be distributed among deserving beneficiaries. This obligatory payment is found in Holy Quran in *sura* (Chapter) : 7:156, 19:31 and 55, 21:72, 23:4, 27:3, 30:39, 31:3, and 41:7. The word *zakat* is individually traced thirty times, among which it came in the same *ayat* (verse) with *salah* (prayers). *Zakat* is applicable to the zakatable amount of cash, assets, livestock, gold, silver, business inventory, agriculture products, animal products, minerals, sea products, exploited assets, and business inventory (Qardawi, 2000).

There are differences in opinion regarding the payment of *zakat* directly to the beneficiaries or to the state government. Most Islamic scholars opined that the best practice is to pay *zakat* to the state or *zakat* agency. Still, there will be no sin in giving *zakat* directly to the beneficiaries (Owoyemi, 2020). An extensive study on Muslim-majority countries showed among the 40 predominantly Muslim countries, 24 did not legally institutionalise *zakat*, 10 countries created laws to establish a voluntary *zakat* system, and the rest 6 countries enforced mandatory *zakat* (Powell, 2010). Though this study did not find positive economic contributions from the application of compulsory *zakat* enforcement, it recommended that the Government should play a promoting role in creating a voluntary *zakat* system. There was proof of the reduced quality of functionality in the entire *zakat* management system with the involvement of the Government also (Saad & Farouk, 2019).

Privatisation of *zakat* institutions is another aspect of zakat management. Privatisation of *zakat* institutions in Malaysia ensures using a specific computer software system to allocate the appropriate beneficiaries into the database and reduce the bureaucracy that might slow the distribution process of *zakat* money (Razimi et al., 2016).

A survey was conducted by the World Zakat Forum from May to July 2020 on its forty member countries' representatives to overview the *zakat* administration at the time of the Corona pandemic. Among the forty countries' representatives, only twelve submitted their responses. When searching the websites of the *zakat* organisations, who were the country representatives, it was found that publishing annual *zakat* performances online was not a regular practice. Still, projects to distribute *zakat* money were posted on the websites. Only five representatives had a yearly report on their websites. But all of them had a digital *zakat* payment gateway. The year-by-year *zakat* collection and disbarment also showed some inconsistent data (Table 1).

It was found that most of the *zakat* money collected by the above representative organisations of its member countries was for providing the education of poor students, scholarships to brilliant students, financial help to the widow, effective development programmes, and other socio-economic causes (Puskas Baznas, 2021). These *zakat* funds were paid in cash, food, and health-related bits of help.

Zakat innovation at the time of the worldwide pandemic of 2020 was more significant in the collection of *zakat* rather than the distribution of the same. The survey of BAZNAS showed among the 14 respondents, 64% of the *zakat* management organisations recorded innovations for collecting *zakat*, while 36% of them created distribution innovations (Puskas Baznas, 2021).

TABLE 1 Zakat collections and disbursements (rounded in a million) of key representatives of the member countries of the World Zakat Forum

The National Board of Zakat the Republic of Indonesia (BAZNAS)

Year	2021 (Projected)	2020 (Projected)	2019	2018	2017
Collection (Rupiah)	12,338,289.93 (9.35%)	11,283,116.87 (10.32%)	10,227,943.80 (25.99%)	8,117,597.68 (30.41%)	6,224,371.27
Distribution (Rupiah)	10,576,303.33 (9.80%)	9,632,262.28 (10.86%)	8,688,221.23 (27.76%)	6,800,139.13 (39.92%)	4,860,155.32

Center for Zakat Management (CZM) in Bangladesh

Year	2021	2020	2019	2018	2017
Collection (Tk.)	–	409.29 (41.36%)	289.54	2018	2017
Distribution (Tk.)	–	352.84 (29.46%)	272.54	–	–

National Zakat Foundation (NZF) in Canada

Year	2021	2020	2019	2018	2017
Zakat collection ($)	–	–	1.83 (38.89%)	1.32 (85.48%)	709,736
Distribution ($)	–	–	1.83 (158.82%)	0.70 (25.88%)	0.56

National Zakat Foundation (NZF) in the United Kingdom

Year	2021	2020	2019	2018	2017
Collection (£)	–	4.47 (61.80%)	2.76 (–18.02%)	3.37 (4.74%)	3.22
Distribution (£)	–	3.80 (27.56%)	2.98 (–5.58%)	3.15 (–10.39%)	3.52

South African National Zakah Fund (SANZAF)

Year	2021	2020	2019	2018	2017
Collection ($)	–	110.15 (12.05%)	98.29 (1.95%)	96.41 (–13.58%)	111.56
Distribution ($)	–	99.99 (3.85%)	96.28 (6.03%)	90.80 (–14.63%)	106,349,880

Source: Constructed by the authors based on the annual reports of the respective representative *zakat* institutions.

3 Fintech and Islamic fintech models for the Zakat management system

Fintech, which is now used as a noun, refers to the application of computers and related digital technologies in financial services (Sangwan et al., 2020). It is the technology used to provide financial markets with a financial product or service characterised by sophisticated technology relative to existing technology in that market (Knewtson & Rosenbaum, 2020). In practice, fintech is an umbrella term that includes innovative methods, technologies, services, and firms that reshape the landscape of future financial benefits. Acting as both partner and competitor of the traditional banks, fintech firms have ensured increasing efficiency, customer centricity, and transparency in the financial service sector (Gomber et al., 2018). It has been proved that fintech firms serve the areas which previously were out of the grip of the traditional banks (Jagtiani & Lemieux, 2018). These findings hint at a potential Islamic fintech market for OIC (Organization of Islamic Cooperation) member countries, where 53.7% of people are unbanked compared to 3% of unbanked people worldwide (OIC, 2018).

The fintech technologies include artificial intelligence (AI), blockchain, robotics, quantum computing, and the Internet of things. In 2019, the top-ranked United States (US) invested $9.4 billion in fintech industries, followed by the United Kingdom (2.29 billion) and Singapore (735 million). The investments mainly were on payments, B2B fintech, security, personal finance and wealth, lending, and blockchain (Findexable, 2019). Another investigation of the worldwide fintech investment showed $210.1 billion in 2021, which was $213.8 billion in 2019. The US accounted for 80% of the total (Statistica, 2022).

The adaptation of *Shari'ah*-compliant fintech technologies into Islamic finance is also growing significantly. It is expected that *Shari'ah*-compliant financial institutions, which are growing to serve the 1.8 billion Muslims worldwide, will increase their Islamic finance assets to $3.5 trillion by 2024 (World Bank, 2020). On the other hand, the estimated Islamic fintech market size for OIC countries in 2020 was $49 billion, which was 0.72% of the current global fintech market size. In 2020, the Islamic fintech market of top ranker Saudi Arabia was $17.9 billion, followed by Iran ($9.2 billion) and United Arab Emirates ($3.7 billion) (Global Islamic Fintech Report, 2021). Besides the other Islamic finance dimensions, Islamic social finance as the forms of *zakat* (obligatory payments), *Sadaqah* (voluntary payment), and *Waqf* (Islamic endowments) possess a significant place in Islamic finance as they justify the Islamic principles to help the less fortunate people of the society by each capable Muslim individual. *Zakat* can raise estimated funds between $200 billion and $1 trillion globally, which will assist in achieving the sustainable development goal of reducing extreme poverty (Rehman & Pickup, 2018).

An extent literature, reviewing the fintech eco-system, proposed the three dimensions of fintech; financial industry (crowdfunding, P2P platform, digital finance cube, shadow banking), entrepreneurial /innovative (AI, big data, blockchain, initial coin offering, initial cryptotoken offering), and legal (RegTech, regulatory sandbox) (Sangwan et al., 2020). Incorporating the current and probable practices of the technologies in the *zakat* management system, some of the fintech services are discussed here.

3.1 Crowdfunding

Crowdfunding is an innovative, disruptive, and democratising method of raising funds for a project from a diverse set of audiences called as the crowd (Langley & Leyshon, 2017). Crowdfunding can take one of the four forms: donation-based (raise funds without offering material incentives), royalty-based (Crowdfunder receives a percentage of revenue from the project they support), equity-based (Crowdfunder gets the shares of a company and are entitled to the dividend), and debt-based (Crowdfunder gets the debt instrument with or without interest) (Nivoix & Ouchrif, 2016). As the platform here is an intermediary one, linking the fundraiser and Crowdfunder, this model entered into the fintech scenario through the use of the internet-enabled channel (website or app) for reaching the Crowdfunder.

The donation-based crowdfunding may be *zakat* (mandatory donation calculated on the salary) or *sadaqah* (voluntary donation). The royalty-based crowdfunding may be *istisna* (manufacture contract). *Musharaka* (profit-loss sharing) and *Mudaraba* (profit-sharing) contracts can be used in equity-based crowdfunding. *Qard hassan* (loans without interest) and *ijara* (leasing contract) can be used in debt-based crowdfunding (Nivoix & Ouchrif, 2016).

In the case of zakat, crowdfunding should be donation-based, whereas *muzakki* (zakat payer) would not get any incentive. Digital social media can be used to reach the area uncovered (Ashiq & Mushtaq, 2020; Bin-Nashwan & Al-Daihani, 2020). According to Milli Gazette, an Indian Muslim newspaper, in 2021, a web-based *zakat* crowdfunding platform IndiaZakat.com raised Rs. 2 Crore within ten months of its inception, mostly distributed as Covid-19 pandemic relief. Between 2013 and 2015, donation-based crowdfunding in Malaysia raised $4.68 million, which was 92.4% of the total crowdfunding platform's funding (Thaker et al., 2019).

3.2 Initial coin offering/initial cryptotoken offering

Cryptocurrency is a digital currency operating on a technology innovation platform that mimics a globally unified financial system without a designated central bank (Abubakar et al., 2019). Though there are many other cryptocurrencies, Bitcoin and Ethereum are two of the most influential cryptocurrencies at the current time. Though used interchangeably, the term crypto coins are used for mineable currencies and cryptocurrencies for non-mineable currencies (Yusof et al., 2021).

There are differences in the opinion of Islamic scholars over the *Shari'ah* complaints issue of cryptocurrency. As Islamic scholars seek the intrinsic value attributes of money, crypto in the form of digital money may gain its intrinsic value backed by two assets, electricity and human resource. Another opinion indicated that as cryptocurrency is a unit of account, medium of exchange, free from *riba*, inflation, and debt, it is acceptable in Islam (Abubakar et al., 2019).

Collecting zakat using cryptocurrency and on the *nisab* amount of cryptocurrency has been a new practice in the Islamic world since 2018 by Blossom Finance in Indonesia (Muneeza, 2020) and by Masjid Ramadan in Turkey (Khatiman et al., 2021).

In the case of Blossom finance, the US-based company acts as an intermediary to channel cryptocurrencies from crypto-rich individuals on his/her nisab crypto to zakat-eligible cooperatives and non-profit organisations in Indonesia that support the poor and needy people, especially widows and orphans. The cryptocurrencies are converted into Indonesian Rupiah through the *zakat* wallets controlled by Blossom finance company on a cryptocurrency exchange in Indonesia. Shakelwell Lane mosque in London started to accept cryptocurrencies as *zakat* and *sadaqah* in 2018 and exchanged them as fiat currency in the crypto exchange platform LocalBitcoin UK through cryptocurrency hard wallets (Yusof et al., 2021). Several authors recommended that Bitcoin, Ethereum, and Tether be used as cryptocurrencies for zakat payment, as they pose less value fluctuations.

3.3 Blockchain, smart contract, and P2P platform

A blockchain is a distributed ledger system where no single entity has absolute control over the database. The transaction occurs in a peer-to-peer transmission system, and the record here is permanent and chronologically ordered (Ozili, 2019). Important requirements in each blockchain step are the smart contract and P2P platform. Smart contracts are a set of rules, including protocols within which the parties were secured on a digital platform without the requirement of a third party (Zulfikri et al., 2021). A P2P platform is an alternative transaction network between two parties without the involvement of any financial and regulatory intermediary (Sangwan et al., 2020). Blockchain has made cryptocurrency channelling a more transparent and easier one. Pseudonymity is maintained, and records are irreversible (Ozili, 2019).

The definition of blockchain could be divided as 'block' and 'chain'. Each block represents digital information (date, time, and transaction information), the block creator's digital signature, and a digital cryptographic hash (previous block data). The chain represents a decentralised database of chronological blocks, validation by participants and transparency, and auditability by all users (Alam et al., 2019).

In *zakat* management, the use of blockchain needs the adoption of a cryptocurrency that will be used as a medium of exchange. A fixed parity system of one local currency to one cryptocurrency unit will be fixed to avoid value fluctuation. The *Amil* (zakat administrator/institution) must have the prospective *mustahiqqin* (beneficiary) database, which will be known as a blockchain account. *Amil* will collect fiat money from *muzakki* and transfer them as cryptocurrency. It will also check the *nisab* amount attainability of *muzakki's* fund. The smart contracts between *muzakki* and *amil* will ensure *amil's* power to cut the funds while it reaches the *nisab*. *Mustahiqqin* will collect the cryptocurrency and convert it into fiat money through an exchange platform (Hamdani, 2020; Rejeb, 2020). The prospective model can be modified based on the socio-economic context of a country.

3.4 Artificial intelligence

Artificial Intelligence (AI) refers to the complex machines which substitute human intelligence with technology (Sangwan et al., 2020). It covers a vast area, from machine translation and chatbots to self-learning algorithms. It improves organisational (finance, marketing, and administration) and process-level performance (Wamba-Taguimdje et al., 2020).

A study by Fajar Nurgaha captured the holistic scenario of AI's application in *zakat* management consisting of current practice and possible AI applications in this field. The current practice indicated the introduction of Rania Chatbot by Rumah Zakat Institution in Indonesia, an AI capable of interacting with *muzzaki* and providing *zakat* education. The study divided the role of *amil* as *katabah* (recorder of zakat), *Hasabah* (estimator and calculator of zakat), *Juba'h* (collector of zakat), *Khazanah* (maintainer of zakat money), and *Qasa'mah* (distributors of zakat). It then highlighted the available AI's that could replace these Amils in future or increase efficiencies of the existing *Amils* (Nugraha et al., 2019).

3.5 Big data

Big data refers to the evolution and application of technologies that enable the right users to receive the correct information at the right time from a mass of data that has been growing exponentially for a long period. Five characteristics of big data are volume, veracity, velocity, variety, and value (Paizin, 2021).

As the fintech applied *zakat* management will mostly concentrate on the genuine profile of the protective *muzzaki*, the big data management mechanism should be a major instrument in the entire *zakat* management system (Paizin, 2021; Taylor et al., 2015).

3.6 Regulatory sandbox

Through the regulatory sandbox, startups maintain a balance between freedom to innovate in fintech and necessary consumer protections (Sangwan et al., 2020). Blockchain, AI, and big data analytics need to develop, test, and deliver a vast array of innovative financial services; these may disrupt the existing financing channel. Regulatory sandbox hedges the systematic risk by reducing the consequence of testing the financial innovation on the clients. It approves time limiting licensing exemption to the fintech firm to test the new fintech solutions and works with public institutions to improve the shape of the sandbox (Alaassar et al., 2021). In 2019, Bank of Indonesia published a regulatory sandbox for *zakat* management that guides a digital *zakat* transaction to be criteria-based, fair, transparent, equal, forward-looking, and proportional (*Bank Indonesia*, 2019).

4 Contribution of fintech for breaking the barriers of *Zakat* management system

A review of the existing literature showed some barriers to the current *zakat* management system worldwide. The authors have made an attempt to link the benefits of Islamic fintech to the challenges faced by the *zakat* management system worldwide and to indicate the probable solutions to the problems.

4.1 Unsystematic and inefficient zakat collection and distribution

Several scholars point out that the current *zakat* management system suffers from the unsystematic and inefficient collection and disbursement. These include:

a   Absence of organisational structure: Zakat's request, screening, and distribution procedures are unsystematic and informal (Ibrahim & Shaharuddin, 2015; Widiastuti et al., 2021).
b   Lack of publicity and bureaucratic delay: Lack of publicity for collecting funds keeps the appropriate recipient out of the system. Also, the bureaucratic problem makes the disbursement delayed, especially for poor students (Ab Rahman et al., 2012; Razimi et al., 2016).
c   Inefficiency in identifying prospective payers: The process of identifying and approaching future *zakat* payers is unclear and not well-stated in the entire system (Ab Rahman et al., 2012; Razimi et al., 2016).
d   Lack of priority list: Unequal allocation of *zakat* money to the prospective beneficiaries considering their preferences of need is detected (Saad & Farouk, 2019). There is a lack of a priority-based list of real, needy people to distribute *zakat* funds (Ashiq & Mushtaq, 2020).

The introduction of a web-based crowdfunding platform recently increased the collection and distribution of *zakat* money in Indonesia. It also ensured a better income distribution (Sonial Manara et al., 2018). The potential of *zakat* receipts is positively affected by the digitalisation of *zakat* payments. It hits at a more formal systematic *zakat* system replacing the old informal one (Abidin & Utami, 2020).

Creating smart contract of the *Muzzaki* (zakat payers) *mustahiqqin* (beneficiaries) at each point of *zakat* collection might ensure a systematic request, screening, and distribution of *zakat*. The distributed ledger system allows tracking the destination of the paid *zakat* money, reducing the fraud and bureaucratic problems of the entire system.

Reaching the previously uncovered area of cryptocurrency holders' *zakat* payment through blockchain platforms will increase *zakat* revenue. Also, the priority-based list of the most desirable *zakat* recipients would only be made in the blockchain model. The United Nation's 'Building Block' could be an instrumental example of using a blockchain-based pilot programme.

4.2 Human resource management problem

An investigation over the zakat management system found *Amil's* (*Zakat* administrator) limited number and inability to use technology are great concerns for optimising the zakat governance. The study also indicated *Amil's* inability to identify *Mustahiq's* actual needs and to detect the potential *Muzakki* (Widiastuti et al., 2021). It is recommended that *zakat* institutions' human resource management practice corresponds to the goal of efficient collection and disbursement of *zakat* (A. Hasan et al., 2019).

AI automates repetitive, monotonous tasks by discovering patterns of massive data and helps in quantitative decision-making by suggesting actionable endeavours. So better work outcomes and enhanced employee–customer interactions are achieved (Ramachandran et al., 2022).

The new fintech platform will concentrate more on searching for eligible recipients than the conventional collection, fund management, and disbursement activities of *zakat*. These will reduce the human resource's efforts. There will be more time for gaining training on new technologies, and comparatively fewer human resources might serve the regular activities. AI technology may take most of the duties of *Amil* (Nugraha et al., 2019).

4.3 Lack of coordination between zakat institutions

There is a lack of coordination among several *zakat* institutions to collect and distribute *zakat*. Lack of uniformity in *zakat* management has a massive loss in *zakat* revenue (Saad & Farouk, 2019; Widiastuti et al., 2021). Through blockchain, integrated data management is ensured that all the institutions, even the international ones, can participate in a better-coordinated manner. Uniform *zakat* management could be built in this process.

4.4 Lack of trust of the zakat payers

The lack of trust of zakat payers derives from the following three reasons:

a   Undistributed funds: A significant amount of undistributed *zakat* funds (RM288 million in 2008 and RM176.1 million in 2007) in Nigeria questioned the accountability of the *zakat* institutions (Saad et al., 2014). A conference in 2019 revealed that though the zakat collection is increasing, 26% of collected *zakat* money by the *zakat* institutions remains undistributed each year in Malaysia (Thaker et al., 2019).

b Lack of transparency of the zakat institutions: A study identified the mindset of *zakat* payers as considering *zakat* as an individual, not collective duty. It creates non-cooperation with *zakat* institutions, but *zakat* payers hint at a transparent *zakat* system publishing the collection and distribution fairly could improve the cooperation and trust (Ibrahim & Shaharuddin, 2015).

c Lack of information on the *zakat* institutions: Lack of information on the available zakat institutions in a particular jurisdiction drives the zakat payers' trust. Institutions' disclosure of their own identity and formation rules is a must (Ahmad, 2019; Widiastuti et al., 2021).

So, an internet-enabled crowdfunding platform would ensure transparency in the *zakat* fund distribution. As in crowdfunding, the information on uses of the *zakat* funds is better documented and has access to everyone; it proves a positive correlation with accountability and channelling funds to crowdfunding projects (Rahmah, 2021). Building trust was one of the other positive and significant motivation variables among the millennial Muslim population of Indonesia who pays *zakat* in a crowdfunding channel through kitabisa.com, a popular and efficient crowdfunding platform there (Dzulfikar et al., 2022; Knewtson & Rosenbaum, 2020). But there was also an exception of the thinking as one study showed the insignificant effect of trust on the overall use of this digital platform (Rahmah, 2021).

On the other hand, the *zakat* blockchain technique records a transaction in near real-time, and the *Muzzaki* may trace the channelising of the funds at each point. So, transparency is fully ensured in the *zakat* blockchain through crypto proof (Khatiman et al., 2021; Santoso et al., 2020).

4.5 Lack of capacity building

Some studies necessitated the role of *zakat* as building the capacity of the recipient rather than giving a sum of money for buying their regular necessity (Ab Rahman et al., 2012; Razimi et al., 2016).

Donation-based crowdfunding platforms can reshape the *zakat* system from the consumption-based *zakat* to the development of *zakat* projects.

4.6 Lack of zakat education

There is a lack of *zakat* education in the rural area regarding *zakat* calculation and *nisab* amount. Paying *zakat* only during Ramadan and not at reaching the point of *nisab* amount is a misconception that well prevailed (Ahmad, 2019).

The barrier could be reversed by creating awareness and serving education about *zakat*. A study showed that a crowdfunding platform is not merely a fundraising tool; instead, it could be used to create awareness (Junge et al., 2022). The use of AI in calculating *zakat* on *nisab* amount may also be the best solution to the ignorance of *zakat* payers (Nugraha et al., 2019).

4.7 Low Shari'ah compliance

The study indicated the leftover *zakat* money to be carried over to the next year in an inefficient conventional *zakat* distribution system, which is against the *shari'ah* compliance (Muneeza, 2020).

As the owner of the blockchain platform has to affiliate with a regulatory authority that will deal with *zakat* money, there will be an instant distribution of the *zakat* money to the recipient and no carry forward of the same to the following year. The regulatory sandbox of the *zakat* management may also ensure that the *zakat* principles are better served.

5 Zakat management in Bangladesh

The Asian Development Bank (ADB) statistics showed that in 2019 the population living below the poverty line in Bangladesh was 20.5%. Besides the government's social safety net programmes, indigenous non-government organisations (NGOs) like BRAC, Grameen Bank's collateral-free micro-credit and other programmes made a magnificent improvement in solving multidimensional and multifaceted problems of poverty in Bangladesh. Dr. Yunus's new 'Social Business' concept after the worldwide acclaimed micro-credit and the Government's ongoing financial inclusion programmes are in the experimental stage of reducing poverty in Bangladesh. But the potentiality of alternative Islamic tools like *zakat* and *Wakf* is overlooked in practice here (Ali & Hatta, 2014).

In Bangladesh, *zakat* is regulated by Government, but the contribution is not mandatory by the state law. On June 5, 1982, the ministry of religious affairs, under the supervision of the Islamic Foundation, formed the *zakat* board through *Zakat* Fund Ordinance 1982. The Ministry of Religion regulates the total system with the help of the *zakat* board. As the socio-political scenario does not approve of the government collecting *zakat* on a compulsory basis, dependency on the private sector becomes a practice here. Social enterprise and voluntary organisations (VO) collect and distribute *zakat* in Bangladesh within the organisational structure. Islamic commercial banks create their own *zakat* funds here. Islamic NGOs also serve the endeavour here but ignore the term *zakat* instead use *donation* for collecting overall funds. The expected benefits of giving zakat through these institutional channels are building capacity rather than distributing daily necessities, less effort from the payers' side and reaching the best-suited beneficiaries.

In 2020–2021, the government's zakat funds operated by Bangladesh Islamic Foundation collected Tk.35.3 million, which was a meagre one compared to its operating jurisdiction. Though the major cause cited was peoples' will to pay zakat to the near and dear ones, other causes were lack of manpower, peoples' trust in privately run entities, and absence of efficient digital mechanism (The Financial Express, 2021).

Commercial banks are the most influential financial institutions in Bangladesh. With strong public demand and continued robust growth, Islamic banks in Bangladesh are becoming the frontliners here. There are ten full-fledged Islamic banks in Bangladesh. Nine of the conventional commercial banks have 41 Islamic banking branches. Also, 13 conventional commercial banks have 368 Islamic banking windows. After the inception in 1983, with strong policy support from central banks like lower statutory liquidity ratio and higher loan–deposit ratio, Islamic banks in Bangladesh now capture 27.89% in terms of deposits and 27.88% in terms of investments at the end of December 2021 of total market share of the banking industry (Bangladesh Bank, 2020) (Table 2).

Besides commercial banks, NGOs are also trying to solve the poverty-driven social problems in Bangladesh. According to the NGOs affairs bureau under the prime minister's office, by February 2022, there are 2,516 NGOs in Bangladesh, among which 260 were foreign, and 2,256 were local NGOs. The actual number of faith-based NGOs is not recorded in the list. Renowned International Islamic NGOs, Islamic Relief Bangladesh and Muslim Aid Bangladesh have been working in the jurisdiction of Bangladesh for a long. Besides, some local Islamic NGOs like Al Markazul Islam Bangladesh, Allama Fazlullah Foundation, Islamic Aid Bangladesh, Social Agency for Welfare and Advancement in Bangladesh (SAWAB), etc., are working to solve several socio-economic problems. These Islamic NGOs serve the ultra-poor in different ways and grant interest-free loans (S. R. Chowdhury et al., 2020). Though they collect *zakat* funds, the amount received is recorded as foreign and local grants or donations in their annual financial statements. So, the actual *zakat* fund could not be detected.

A giant leap in *zakat* management was the foundation of the social enterprise 'Center for Zakat Management' in 2008. The entity is now working with 'Bidyanondo', another giant voluntary enterprise that serves the poor, to institutionalise zakat management for efficient zakat collections and distributions.

The previously detected barriers were also the reality of the *zakat* management system in Bangladesh. Scholars found unsystematic and inefficient zakat collection and distribution (Islam, 2016; Obaidullah, 2015), human resource management problems (The Financial Express, 2021), lack of trust of the *zakat* payers (Uddin, 2016), lack of capacity building instead distributing piecemeal single cloths (Hossain et al., 2020), lack of *zakat* educations like paying zakat only based on conjecture (Obaidullah, 2015; Rony & Karim, 2021) and only at the time of *Ramadan* (Hossain et al., 2020) in the context of Bangladesh also.

It is common to distribute some specific cheap clothes (Sharee, lungi) on a particular declared date by the affluent segment of society for *zakat* purposes.

TABLE 2 Contributions of Islamic banks of Bangladesh to the *zakat* funds for the last ten years (figures are rounded to a million)

Islamic Bank Bangladesh Limited (IBBL)

Year	2011	2012	2013	2014	2015	2016	2017	2018	2019	2020
Zakat expenses (Taka)	262.93	324.77	385.750	425.98	421.31	494.97	519.57	601.56	719.19	817.49
Total operating expenses (Taka)	7,268.44	8,724.64	11,039.14	12,074.13	13,466.17	17,687.22	18,751.44	19,357.24	21,276.17	24,908.15
Percentage of total operating expenses (%)	3.61	3.7	3.49	3.52	3.12	2.79	2.77	3.10	3.38	3.28

Shahjalal Islami Bank Limited (SJIBL)

Year	2011	2012	2013	2014	2015	2016	2017	2018	2019	2020
Zakat expenses (Taka)	59.22	60.65	76.55	92.99	93.31	101.96	113.71	124.66	140.73	160.82
Total operating expenses (Taka)	1,632.45	1,822.08	2,337.59	2,683.05	2,778.20	2,998.95	3,541.88	4,076.43	4,640.85	4,710.67
Percentage of total operating expenses (%)	3.62	3.32	3.27	3.46	3.35	3.40	3.21	3.05	3.03	3.41

Social Islamic Bank Limited (SIBL)

Year	2011	2012	2013	2014	2015	2016	2017	2018	2019	2020
Zakat expenses (Taka)			50.48	63.58	71.84	89.79	111.42	129.66	149.52	165.69
Total operating expenses (Taka)			557.93	515.94	3,400.07	3,931.91	4,686.22	5,408.41	2,065.92	2,029.75
Percentage of total operating expenses (%)			9.04	12.32	2.11	2.28	2.37	2.39	7.23	8.16

First Security Islamic Bank Limited (FSIBL)

Year	2011	2012	2013	2014	2015	2016	2017	2018	2019	2020
Zakat expenses (Taka)	12.50	18.80	28.08	36.49	42.175	50.24	71.58	88.14	98.34	126.54
Total operating expenses (Taka)	1,146.19	1,792.72	2,434.13	2,989.69	3,696.36	4,298.82	5,038.14	5,777.78	6,301.79	6,130.71
Percentage of total operating expenses (%)	1.09	1.04	1.15	1.22	1.14	1.16	1.42	1.52	1.56	2.06

Union Bank Limited

Year	2011	2012	2013	2014	2015	2016	2017	2018	2019	2020
Zakat expenses (Taka)			3.00	4.62	6.00	15.00	20.00	26.50	36.00	44.00
Total operating expenses (Taka)			155.27	526.88	1,016.47	1,403.83	1,738.30	2,110.02	2,499.98	2,740.69
Percentage of total operating expenses (%)			1.93	0.87	0.59	1.06	1.15	1.25	1.44	1.60

Source: Constructed by the authors based on the annual reports of the respective banks.

The practice contradicts the *Shari'ah* compliance, which urges to pay *zakat* without declaration on reaching the *nisab* amount of resource. It also does not follow the capacity building moto of the *zakat* objective. The zakat seekers' crowd also resulted in unwanted death.

Handling zakat through commercial banks, Islamic NGOs, VO, and social enterprises at a time creates a coordination problem between the institutions as these organisations are running under different ministries. One extra contextual barrier of ignoring rural area for *zakat* collection and distribution was found in the context of Bangladesh (Hassan & Khan, 2007; Obaidullah, 2015).

A holistic effort to bring individual donors, government, banks, and non-profit zakat institutions has introduced an internet-enabled crowdfunding fintech product named 'EkDesh'. It is an online crowdfunding platform where an individual may pay and receive zakat money through banking channels or mobile financial services (bKash, Nagad, Rocket, etc.). The voluntary enterprise, Bidyanondo, is currently running several internet-enabled *zakat* crowdfunding campaigns. The website-based Islamic crowdfunding fintech platforms have the capacity to reach the unserved rural areas of Bangladesh as they can link cross-geographical stakeholders into the system (Hendratmi et al., 2020). The mobile wallet, Bkash, has made the channelling of funds much easier in Bangladesh.

Blockchain is in a nascent stage in Bangladesh. The use of blockchain technology has been achieved in the banking sectors of Bangladesh through HSBC bank's cross-border blockchain letter of credit (L/C) for importing 20,000 MT of fuel oil by United Mymensingh Power Limited, Bangladesh from Singapore, for their power plant. Later, HSBC made an inter-bank blockchain contract with Prime bank limited with Contour's technical support, the global trade finance blockchain network. The beneficiary was AnantaGroup to import raw materials for the ready-made garments industry from Tamishna Group, a customer of HSBC Bangladesh. The Information Communication Technology Division of Bangladesh has published the National Blockchain Strategy highlighting the regulatory and strategic aspects of applying blockchain to the organisations of Bangladesh (ICT Division, 2020). The division also published a draft law for using AI in several areas of industries in Bangladesh (Digital Bangladesh, Cabinet Division, A2i, USAID, 2019).

Cryptocurrency is not yet allowed in Bangladesh as it is too decentralised, which is against the financial regulation of Bangladesh. Several big data analytics companies in Bangladesh, like MicrodreamIT, Light Castle, Professional Scrapper, etc., work in Bangladesh's healthcare, retail, insurance, entertainment, and business sectors.

As most of the fintech solutions are still in the initial stage in Bangladesh, it needs campaigns like seminars, advertisements, conferences, and workshops to develop the platform. In the future, the adaptation of the fintech solutions in the zakat management system would be inevitable to keep pace with other sectors of the economy.

6 The challenges ahead

The positive results of adopting fintech into the zakat management system are yet to see as it is still under construction in several countries. A study over the front-runner of fintech adopters National Board of Zakat the Republic of Indonesia (BAZNAS) showed that digitalisation of the zakat payment system has a 55% potential of increasing the *zakat* money. But the realisation of the potential is still low there (Abidin & Utami, 2020).

Crowdfunding application into Islamic finance jurisdiction needs a *shari'ah* board consisting of high-profile Islamic finance erudite (Hendratmi et al., 2020; Nivoix & Ouchrif, 2016). It also requires regular surveys of the users to check whether the projects are *Shari'ah* compliant or not (Nivoix & Ouchrif, 2016). The remuneration of the board members and review process are off-course costly, and they should not eat up the *zakat* proportion of the poor population.

Blockchain applications are also characterised as relying solely on computer codes and the absence of human-controlled institutions. The regulators may ask for full authority to set blockchain rules, the right to veto unfavourable principles and the power to enforce, update and change the rules for its full approval (Ozili, 2019). The pseudonymity of users may promote illegal trading and laundering activities (Alam et al., 2019).

In Bangladesh, though the number of mobile phone users and internet users have been increased significantly, comparative data showed that in 2020 the percentage of the total population using the internet was much lower (25%) than in other Muslim majority countries like Indonesia (54%), India (43%), and Pakistan (25%); the percentage was even lower than in Nigeria (36%), which is just below Bangladesh on the list of Muslim majority countries (World Bank Data, 2022; World Population Review, 2022). The scenario hints a challenge for the development of fintech as the total system relies on the internet.

Also, the fintech adaptation into the zakat management system in Bangladesh needs the collaboration of the Ministry of Religion with the Ministry of Finance (Raquib, 2011) and the ICT division of the Ministry of Information. The recently introduced EkDesh app has some complaints of slow working from the users' reviews.

An application of the technology acceptance model (TAM) for identifying the behavioural aspect of both zakat payers and beneficiaries is needed for the best use of fintech platforms. A TAM model application in Bangladesh's adaptation of fintech shows that it needs more time and effort from the government and fintech providers to educate the low-income and uneducated users of the technology (N.H. Chowdhury & Nida Ussain, 2022). It creates a challenge for blockchain and P2P platforms in *zakat* management as the poor *mustahiqqin* also need to use an internet-enabled device to get the benefit. So, the internet cost should be reduced in this respect.

7 Conclusion

The entire *zakat* management system worldwide has been experiencing a digital transformation. Though some countries like Indonesia and Malaysia have adopted the most sophisticated fintech technologies into their *zakat* management, countries like Bangladesh have yet to progress. It is also evident that the entire system has been suffering from the perennial problem of unsystematic and inefficiency, lack of coordination, lack of trust, dependency on consumption-centred *zakat*, high administrative costs, and low compliance issues. The barriers to ensuring vibrant *zakat* management are expected to be solved by adopting the fintech solutions available in the current business arena with regulatory support from the government. Blockchain, crypto platforms, AI, and crowdfunding may apply to the whole process of *zakat* management to reduce the age-old documentation complexities and ensure efficiency. But the users' awareness and regulators' policy formulation to monitoring the entire process are the challenges that should be better checked before introducing the fintech solutions to the existing one.

References

Abidin, A., & Utami, P. (2020). The regulation of Zakat digital technology in creating community welfare impact on economic development. *Journal of Legal, Ethical and Regulatory Issues, 23*(5), 1–9.

Ab Rahman, A., Alias, M. H., & Omar, S. M. N. S. (2012). Zakat institution in Malaysia: Problems and issues. *Global Journal Al-Thaqafah, 2*(1), 35–41. https://doi.org/10.7187/GJAT122012.02.01

Abubakar, M., Hassan, M. K., & Haruna, M. A. (2019). Cryptocurrency tide and Islamic finance development: Any issue? *International Finance Review, 20*(October), 189–200. https://doi.org/10.1108/S1569-376720190000020019

Adachi, M. (2018). Discourses of institutionalization of Zakat management system in contemporary Indonesia: Effect of the revitalization of Islamic economics. *International Journal of Zakat, 3*(1), 25–35. https://doi.org/10.37706/ijaz.v3i1.71

Ahmad, M. (2019). An empirical study of the challenges facing zakat and waqf institutions in Northern Nigeria. *ISRA International Journal of Islamic Finance, 11*(2), 338–356. https://doi.org/10.1108/IJIF-04-2018-0044

Ahmed, H. (2015). Zakah, macroeconomic policies, and poverty alleviation: Lessons from simulations on Bangladesh. *Journal of Islamic Economics, Banking and Finance, 4*(2), 81–105.

Alaassar, A., Mention, A. L., & Aas, T. H. (2021). Exploring a new incubation model for FinTechs: Regulatory sandboxes. *Technovation, 103*. https://doi.org/10.1016/j.technovation.2021.102237

Alam, N., Gupta, L., & Zameni, A. (2019). *Fintech and Islamic Finance: Digitalization and Disruption in the Financial Sector*. Palgrave Macmillan. https://doi.org/10.1007/978-3-030-24666-2_1

Ali, I., & Hatta, Z. A. (2014). Zakat as a poverty reduction mechanism among the Muslim community: Case study of Bangladesh, Malaysia, and Indonesia. *Asian Social Work and Policy Review, 8*(1), 59–70. https://doi.org/10.1111/aswp.12025

Ashiq, M., & Mushtaq, U. (2020). The convergence of crowd funding and Zakat system in India: An integrated approach for human welfare. *Ihtifaz: Journal of Islamic Economics, Finance, and Banking, 3*(1), 27. https://doi.org/10.12928/ijiefb.v3i1.1879

Bangladesh Bank. (2020). *Developments of Islamic Banking in Bangladesh (October–December 2020)*. December, 14. https://www.bb.org.bd/pub/quaterly/islamic_banking/jul_sep_2019.pdf

Bank Indonesia. (2019). Zakat Development in the Era of Industrial Revolution 4.0.

Bangladesh Telecommunication Regulatory Commission. (2022). Information and Statistics. http://www.btrc.gov.bd

Bin-Nashwan, S. A., & Al-Daihani, M. (2020). Fundraising campaigns via social media platforms for mitigating the impacts of the COVID-19 epidemic. *Journal of Islamic Marketing, 12*(3), 576–597. https://doi.org/10.1108/JIMA-07-2020-0200

Chowdhury, N. H., & Ussain, N. (2022). Using technology acceptance model for acceptance of FinTech in Bangladesh. *International Journal of Internet Technology and Secured Transactions, 12*(3), 250–264. https://doi.org/https://dx.doi.org/10.1504/IJITST.2022.122104

Chowdhury, S. R., Islam, M. R., & Wahab, H. A. (2020). Challenges of faith-based NGO intervention in community development: A case study in Bangladesh. *Global Social Welfare*, 301–313. https://doi.org/10.1007/s40609-020-00176-2

Digital Bangladesh, Cabinet Division, A2i, USAID, U. (2019). *Draft version 3:0 national strategy for artificial intelligence of Bangladesh* (pp. 1–53)

Dzulfikar, M. Z., Santosa, P. B., & Gunanto, E. Y. A. (2022). Analysis of millennial Muslim preferences on the crowdfunding platform. *Indonesian Interdisciplinary Journal of Sharia Economics, 5*(1), 24–47

Findexable. (2019). *The Global Fintech Index 2020. December 2019*, 120.

Global Islamic Fintech Report. (2021). Global Islamic Fintech Report. *Cdn.Salaamgateway.com*, 56. https://cdn.salaamgateway.com/special-coverage/islamic-fintech-2021/Global-Islamic-Fintech-Report-2021-Executive-Summary.pdf

Gomber, P., Kauffman, R. J., Parker, C., & Weber, B. W. (2018). On the fintech revolution: Interpreting the forces of innovation, disruption, and transformation in financial services. *Journal of Management Information Systems, 35*(1), 220–265. https://doi.org/10.1080/07421222.2018.1440766

Hamdani, L. (2020). Zakat blockchain: A descriptive qualitative approach. *EkBis: Journal Ekanomi Dan Bisnis, December 2020*, 492–502

Hasan, A., Hassan, R., Engku Ali, E. R. A., Engku Ali, E. M. T., Abduh, M., & Noordin, N. H. (2019). A proposed human resource management model for zakat institutions in Malaysia. *ISRA International Journal of Islamic Finance, 11*(1), 98–109. https://doi.org/10.1108/IJIF-10-2017-0036

Hasan, K., Kayed, N. R., & Oseni, U. A. (2005). *Introduction to Islamic banking & finance principles and practice*.

Hassan, M. K., & Khan, J. M. (2007). Zakat, external debt and poverty reduction strategy in Bangladesh. *The Muslim World, 4*, 1–37

Hendratmi, A., Ryandono, M. N. H., & Sukmaningrum, P. S. (2020). Developing an Islamic crowdfunding website platform for startup companies in Indonesia. *Journal of Islamic Marketing, 11*(5), 1041–1053. https://doi.org/10.1108/JIMA-02-2019-0022

Hossain, M. S., Hasan, K. M., & Khan, S. M. (2020). Factors influencing proper Zakah payment in Dighalia Upazila of Khulna District, Bangladesh. *European Journal of Business and Management Research, 5*(2), 1–6. https://doi.org/10.24018/ejbmr.2020.5.2.292

Ibrahim, S., & Shaharuddin, A. (2015). In search of an Effective Zakat distribution system in Kano State, Nigeria. *Journal for Studies in Management and Planning, 1*(7), 259–285. http://edupediapublications.org/journals/index.php/JSMaP/article/view/2579

ICT Division. (2020). National blockchain strategy: Bangladesh Information and Communication Technology Division. *ResearchGate, January*. https://www.researchgate.net/publication/343574573_National_Blockchain_Strategy_Bangladesh

Islam, M. S. (2016). Towards an establishment of Zakat Institution in Bangladesh based on Malaysian experience: A juristic and analytical study. *The Muktamar Waqf Iqlimi III 2016 (IQLIMI2016), 2016*(October), 13–14

Jagtiani, J., & Lemieux, C. (2018). Do fintech lenders penetrate areas that are underserved by traditional banks? *Journal of Economics and Business, 100*(April 2018), 43–54. https://doi.org/10.1016/j.jeconbus.2018.03.001

Junge, L. B., Laursen, I. C., & Nielsen, K. R. (2022). Choosing crowdfunding: Why do entrepreneurs choose to engage in crowdfunding? *Technovation, 111*(June), 102385. https://doi.org/10.1016/j.technovation.2021.102385

Khatiman, N. A. B., Ismail, M. S. B., Muhammad, & Yahya, N. (2021). Blockchain-based Zakat collection to overcome the trust issues of Zakat payers. *International Journal on Perceptive and Cognitive Computing (IJPCC), 7*(1), 1

Knewtson, H. S., & Rosenbaum, Z. A. (2020). Toward understanding FinTech and its industry. *Managerial Finance, 46*(8), 1043–1060. https://doi.org/10.1108/MF-01-2020-0024

Langley, P., & Leyshon, A. (2017). Capitalising on the crowd: The monetary and financial ecologies of the crowdfunding. *Environment and Planning A: Economy and Space, 49*(5), 1019–1039.

Muneeza, A. (2020). Pandemic innovation for Zakat: The potential of Crypto Zakat. *INCEIF*, 19–25. https://ikr.inceif.org/handle/INCEIF/3537

Nivoix, S., & Ouchrif, F. Z. (2016). Is crowdfunding sharia compliant? *International Perspectives on Crowdfunding*, 185–198. https://doi.org/10.1108/978-1-78560-315-020151011

Nugraha, F., Permadia, S., Gunawan, A. R., & Saeful, E. (2019). Artificial intelligence usage in Zakat optimization. *International Conference of Zakat*, 14–24. https://doi.org/10.37706/iconz.2019.144

Obaidullah, M. (2015). Zakah management in rural areas of Bangladesh: The Maqasid al-Shari ' ah (Objectives of Islamic Law) perspective. *Middle East Journal of Scientific Research, 23*(1), 45–54. https://doi.org/10.5829/idosi.mejsr.2015.23.01.22032

OIC. (2018). *OIC Economic Outlook 2018 challenges and opportunities towards.*

Owoyemi, M. Y. (2020). Zakat management: The crisis of confidence in zakat agencies and the legality of giving zakat directly to the poor. *Journal of Islamic Accounting and Business Research, 11*(2), 498–510. https://doi.org/10.1108/JIABR-07-2017-0097

Ozili, P. K. (2019). Blockchain finance: Questions regulators ask. *International Finance Review, 20*, 123–129. https://doi.org/10.1108/S1569-376720190000020014

Paizin, M. N. (2021). Big data analytics for Zakat administration: A proposed method. *ZISWAF: Jurnal Zakat Dan Wakaf, 8*(2), 104–121.

Powell, R. (2010). Seattle University School of Law Digital Commons Zakat: Drawing insights for legal theory and economic policy from Islamic jurisprudence economic policy from Islamic jurisprudence. *Pittsburgh Tax Review, 7*(1), 43.

Puskas Baznas. (2021). *Indonesia Zakat Outlook 2021 Center of Strategic Studies the National Board of Zakat.* www.baznas.go.id.

Qardawi, Y. Al. (2000). Fiqh Al Zakah: A comparative study of Zakah, regulations and philosophy in the light of Qur'an and Sunnah. *Fiqh Al Zakah (Vol. I)*, 1–351.

Rahmah, F. (2021). *Factors Affecting the Society's Preference Using Zakat, Infaq and Alms Based Crowdfunding Platform*, 4(1). https://doi.org/10.21093/bijis.v4i1.4162

Ramachandran, K. K., Apsara Saleth Mary, A., Hawladar, S., Asokk, D., Bhaskar, B., & Pitroda, J. R. (2022). Machine learning and the role of artificial intelligence in optimising work performance and employee behaviour. *Materials Today: Proceedings, 51*, 2327–2331. https://doi.org/10.1016/J.MATPR.2021.11.544

Raquib, A. (2011). Islamic Banking & Zakat: An alternative approach to poverty reduction in Bangladesh. *Journal of Islamic Economics, Banking and Finance, 7*(2), 11–26.

Razimi, M. S. A., Romle, A. R., & Erdris, M. (2016). Zakat management in Malaysia: A review. *Journal of Scientific Research, 11*(6), 453–457. https://doi.org/10.5829/idosi.aejsr.2016.453.457

Rehman, A. A., & Pickup, F. (2018). Zakat for SDGs. *United Nations Development Program*.

Rejeb, D. (2020). *4th International Conference of Zakat Proceedings Blockchain and Smart Contract's Contributions to Zakat Management System*.

Rony, J. H., & Karim, N. (2021). E-Zakat: An approach for Zakat management to eradicate poverty. *International Journal of Islamic Banking and Finance Research, 8*(1), 29–40. https://doi.org/10.46281/ijibfr.v8i1.1521

Saad, R. A. J., Aziz, N. M. A., & Sawandi, N. (2014). Islamic accountability framework in the Zakat funds management. *Procedia - Social and Behavioral Sciences, 164*(August), 508–515. https://doi.org/10.1016/j.sbspro.2014.11.139

Saad, R. A. J., & Farouk, A. U. (2019). A comprehensive review of barriers to a functional Zakat system in Nigeria: What needs to be done? *International Journal of Ethics and Systems, 35*(1), 24–42. https://doi.org/10.1108/IJOES-06-2018-0090

Sangwan, V., Harshita, Prakash, P., & Singh, S. (2020). Financial technology: a review of extant literature. *Studies in Economics and Finance, 37*(1), 71–88. https://doi.org/10.1108/SEF-07-2019-0270

Santoso, B., Amilahaq, F., Ahmad, S., & Nasir, N. (2020). *Study on Block-Chain Implementation in Zakat Management (Case Study in Indonesia)*. https://doi.org/10.4108/eai.27-8-2020.2303244

Sonial Manara, A., Rachman Eka Permata, A., & Heru Pranjoto, R. G. (2018). Strategy model for increasing the potential of Zakat through the crowdfunding-Zakat system to overcome poverty in Indonesia. *International Journal of Zakat, 3*(4), 17–31. https://doi.org/10.37706/ijaz.v3i4.104

Statistica. (2022). *Investments into fintech companies globally 2010–2021*.

Taylor, K., Woodcock, R., Cuddy, S., Thew, P., & Lemon, D. (2015). A provenance maturity model. *IFIP Advances in Information and Communication Technology, 448*, 61–66. https://doi.org/10.1007/978-3-319-15994-2_1

Thaker, M. A., Thaker, H., A.Pitchay, A., & Khaliq, A. (2019). A proposed Integrated Zakat-Crowdfunding Model (IZCM) for effective collection and distribution of Zakat fund in Malaysia. *International Journal of Zakat and Islamic Philanthropy, 1*(2), 1–12.

The Financial Express. (2021). *Bangladesh; s Zakat Fund couldn't mobilise even 1.0pc of the potential charity amount*. https://doi.org/https://doi.org/10.1108/FS-06-2020-0058

Uddin, A. E. (2016). Through Islamic Banks' Zakat House (IBZH): Investment of Zakah funds in microfinance to remove poverty in Bangladesh: A new model. *International Journal of Islamic Economics and Finance Studies, 2*(1), 1–25. https://doi.org/10.12816/0036592

Wahab, N. A., & Rahman, A. R. A. (2011). A framework to analyse the efficiency and governance of zakat institutions. *Journal of Islamic Accounting and Business Research, 2*(1), 43–62. https://doi.org/10.1108/17590811111129508

Wamba-Taguimdje, S. L., Fosso Wamba, S., Kala Kamdjoug, J. R., & Tchatchouang Wanko, C. E. (2020). Influence of artificial intelligence (AI) on firm performance: The business value of AI-based transformation projects. *Business Process Management Journal*, *26*(7), 1893–1924. https://doi.org/10.1108/BPMJ-10-2019-0411

Widiastuti, T., Cahyono, E. F., Zulaikha, S., Mawardi, I., & Al Mustofa, M. U. (2021). Optimising zakat governance in East Java using analytical network process (ANP): The role of zakat technology (ZakaTech). *Journal of Islamic Accounting and Business Research*, *12*(3), 301–319. https://doi.org/10.1108/JIABR-09-2020-0307

World Bank. (2018). Poverty and Inequality Platform.

World Bank. (2020). Leveraging Islamic fintech to improve financial inclusion. In *Leveraging Islamic Fintech to Improve Financial Inclusion*. https://doi.org/10.1596/34520

World Bank. (2021). *The World Bank in Bangladesh overview*.

World Population Review. (2022). *Muslim Population by country 2022*. https://worldpopulationreview.com/country-rankings/muslim-population-by-country

World Bank Data. (2022). *Individuals using the Internet*. https://data.worldbank.org/indicator/IT.NET.USER.ZS?

Wormald, B. (2013). *The World's Muslims: Religion, politics and society*. Pew Research Center.

Yusof, M. F., Ab. Rasid, L., & Masri, R. (2021). Implementation of Zakat payment platform for cryptocurrencies. *AZKA International Journal of Zakat & Social Finance*, *2*(1), 17–31. https://doi.org/10.51377/azjaf.vol2no1.41

Zulfikri, Z., Hj Kassim, S., & Hawariyuni, W. (2021). Proposing blockchain technology-based Zakat management model to enhance Muzakki's trust in Zakat agencies: A conceptual study. *Journal of Accounting Research, Organization and Economics*, *4*(2), 153–163. https://doi.org/10.24815/jaroe.v4i2.20467

15
AN INQUIRY INTO THE APPLICATION OF ARTIFICIAL INTELLIGENCE ON *FATWA*

Ali Polat, Shoaib Khan and Usman Bashir

1 Introduction

The unprecedented developments in technology in the last few decades are radically changing corporate life as well as individual life. Innovative technologies such as Artificial Intelligence (AI), Smart Contracts (SC), and Blockchain (BC) will have a huge impact in the financial industry as much as in other industries (Mat Rahim *et al.*, 2018). The mentioned innovative technologies can help the evolution of any field and such blend, i.e., the merge of any applied business field and technology, will create a new way of looking at the matters, solving the problems, require being more creative to reach the necessary knowledge. AI- and SC-related technologies are shaping all over the business and even coining new terms as the existing terms are not enough to convey the intended change of these emerging concepts, ideas, technologies, and activities. That is why some relevant neologisms, such as "FinTech" in finance, "InsurTech" in insurance, "RegTech" in regulation, "LegalTech" in legal affairs, and so on, help us to keep up with digital innovation. For instance, Fintech is considered as the marriage of technological innovation and finance which can be a disruptive technology for conventional operations as much as it may be cooperative (Zavolokina *et al.*, 2016, Hasan *et al.*, 2020). LegalTech refers to the adoption of innovative technology and software which streamlines and enhances legal services (Corrales *et al.*, 2019).

The innovative technology including AI can change the way of the practice with immense changes which sometimes can cause a paradigm shift, perhaps, in Islamic finance and business (IFIs), too. Increasing awareness on the AI approach and asking the question that "AI is getting ready for IFIs but are they ready for AI?" needs to be answered. This chapter aims to trace the existing debate on how the adoption of digital transformation including AI is expected to help facilitate accurate and timely *fatwa* delivery. *Fatwa* is considered one of the sensitive areas of Islamic finance. In Shari'ah-based commercial transactions (*muamalat*), there are certain issues that require scholarly interpretation regarding their compliance with Shari'ah, because Qur'an and Hadith do not always clearly and directly articulate about them. Only qualified Islamic scholars can assess the compliance or non-compliance of a particular financial transaction with Shari'ah. This is known as *fatwa*.

Fatwa process is inherently a human activity, and its nature does not require *mufti* to provide a pinpoint accuracy but to stick with the primary and secondary sources of Islamic law and provide a formal rule or interpretation on a specific case. *Mufti*, as a domain professional, should provide his best effort with his available knowledge and depending on prior sources and cases he should provide an opinion. Without a scholarly opinion, *fatwa*, modern IFI's products, instrument, or applications will be suspicious whether they are Shari'ah compliant or Shari'ah-based. There are methods of providing a *fatwa* for an IFI and depending on the jurisdiction either individual fatwa, a committee decision, or fatwa council, as a higher authority, can provide an opinion. These decisions need to be integrated with the corporate governance structure of IB. Going through the literature and the developments of the key technologies including AI, Machine Learning (ML), and Natural Language Processing (NLP), Fintech or LegalTech does not replace the scholar or the auditor but leads to disruptive change of the profession.

In the book *The 4th Revolution: How the Infosphere is Reshaping Human Reality*, Luciano Floridi (2014) suggests that interpretations of the politics of technology's in-betweenness may swing between two extremes. At one extreme, one may interpret technology's in-betweenness as a deleterious kind of detachment and a loss of pristine contact with the natural and the authentic. On the other extreme, there is the enthusiastic and optimistic support for the liberation provided by technology's in-betweenness. The idea of technological in-betweenness is not seen as a dangerous path toward the exercise of power by some people, systems, or even machines over humans, but as an empowering and enabling form of control. "Clearly, neither extreme position is worth taking seriously. However, various combination of these two single ingredients dominates our current discussion of the politics of technology" (Floridi, 2014, pp. 39–40). In the context of IFIs, we should discuss on how AI is expected to be used for enhancing the Shari'ah Governance upon *fatwa* in accordance with *maqasid al-Shari'ah*. For this purpose, this chapter aims to trace how the current discussion on *fatwa* and AI is going between the extreme positions in the academic literature.

This chapter has four parts. After the introduction, we look at the available research which is related to Islamic corpus and AI. Shari'ah Governance and AI section traces how the current discussion is expecting AI to contribute to not only helping *fatwa* issuance but also enhancing the whole Shari'ah governance. The subsequent section looks at the current discussion on AI- and *fatwa*-related issues from several perspectives. The last part puts concluding comments.

2 Research in *fatwa* and AI

In the mid-1980s, legal expert systems were available as early forms of AI software. They incorporated the knowledge and expertise into software to replicate them. But in the 1990s, they were considered as a failure as they seem to work only if (a) the legal rules are straightforward enough, (b) there is no ambiguity or vagueness regarding the inputs, and (c) there is clarity about which rule applies in each situation (Bues & Matthaei, 2017). The 1990s also saw the developments of formalizations of domain conceptualizations and ontologies. They can be used to create a common gateway for information retrieval. This important spadework contributed a lot to the development of legal reasoning which needs to produce accurate, appropriate, helpful, and useful results which could be considered intelligent.

Muhammad and Muhammad (2003) is one of the early studies to show how Information and Communication Technologies (ICT) are beneficial in disseminating the understanding of Islamic jurisprudence and juridical opinions. Of course, such discussions are on a different level of ICT at an introductory level. A lot of platforms, websites, and software are created to serve the purpose of disseminating Islamic knowledge. In Islamic jurisprudence, *fiqh* has central importance. Imam Abu Hanifah defines *fiqh* as "the ability of oneself to know what he must possess and what is required from him" (Zuhayli, 1997). So, such knowledge should be rapidly and clearly available to all Muslims. That was the help of ICT, and it is still needed perhaps with another vision again. However, using AI and advancing computer learning to a level that does some functions of humans is another level that we want to discuss more.

AI and law will help a new type of computer applications that can make legal arguments. It also can be used to predict the outcomes of legal disputes. A computational model for a legal argument may analyze a situation and answer a legal question, predict the outcome meaning making a legal argument. If that is efficiently possible many complex tasks of human intellect can be done with the help of AI-led technologies (Ashley, 2017). Of course, in the IFIs context, we need to add that muftis, Shari'ah scholars, or audit personnel should have the training and capacity to utilize AI-led tools to decide. Even they need to make these tools available to use. Therefore, it is essential for them to be ready for such technologies.

An important strand of AI- and IFIs-related literature discusses developing case-based reasoning (CBR) system where a system comes up with a *fatwa* which is based on earlier *fatwa*s for similar questions. CBR can have two different approaches: problem-solving and interpretative (Nouaouria et al., 2006). Therefore, CBR learns to find similar *fatwa*s for the same questions. The following research is to be noted in this regard:

Nouaouria et al. (2006) implemented an AI model specific to the domain of drinking (alcohol) and smoking. Such a system requires indexing, extraction, adaptation, validation, and storage modules. When the situation is described, as input, the architecture will provide an answer with its arguments as output.

Mutawa and Al-Terkait (2011) implement a knowledge-based expert system to automate the process under restricted constraints by applying the origins of the Islamic jurisprudence domain (*Usoul al-fiqh*) to verses in the Qur'an alone. Their system was correct in 96% of its judgment when compared to human experts in the field.

Elhalwany et al. (2015) investigate the possibility of a question-answering system based on CBR where an intelligent system responds to a natural language question that was already answered before for the Egyptian Dar al-Ifta Fatwa system. As the model they used for question-answering system does not require the domain knowledge and allows automatic discovery, it provides a scalable ground and language independence. Their modeling shows that AI can be used for Islamic *fatawa (pl of fatwa)*.

For AI to learn easier applying the best AI technique is crucial but not enough as the close to perfect application will be available depending on the abundantly obtainable number of the former cases in the system, *fatwa* in different languages, better root extraction algorithms and removing word's prefix or suffixes depending on the syntax of the language (Elhalwany et al., 2015).

Marir et al. (2019, 2020), inspired by the blockchain-like structure of the Qur'an, presented a recursive co-occurrence text mining algorithm to mine the Holy Qur'an to build a corpus that can be further processed to develop IB business processes complying with Shari'ah. Compliance with Shari'ah law has not been researched or explored from a business process management perspective and the current literature lacks a well-defined methodology for integrating Shari'ah compliance controls into Islamic Shari'ah business processes.

Sa'ad et al. (2020) provide a detailed discussion of the potential of integrating a robo-advisory mechanism for Islamic financial institutions. The legal requirements and the future of AI as a disruptive technology are also discussed.

Fitri (2020) designed an android-based fiqh consultation application. Based on their survey, many Muslims have experienced problems in understanding fiqh knowledge and many of them stated that finding a solution to their problem is important.

Khan et al. (2021) propose an AI-based Fintech model to provide a solution for the affected SMEs and individuals to fight the economic consequences of this pandemic and survive. The findings suggest that Qardh-Al-Hasan must be used in combination with Fintech like AI to save the poor and affected SMEs from this pandemic. Similar topic is also discussed by Syed et al. (2020).

Gazali et al. (2020) examine AI applications for Islamic Investments. In their conceptual discussion, they discussed text mining, algorithmic trading, stock pick and robo in Investment (robo advisor, robo Islamic advisor and robo financial advisor).

Ahmed (2021) discusses whether AI will fulfill the conditions of *Ijtihad* and, in case of so, will it be allowed as a legitimate *mujtahid*, interpreter of Islamic law, simply mufti. As Islam considers that all things are permissible unless otherwise clearly indicated; that rule can be extended for AI too. AI should not be seen as an invention but an extension of the intelligence of man given by Allah to us. The discussion of Ahmed (2021) is more on the applicability of AI for *fatwa* processes and needs to be highlighted. He considers that human-made technologies are a part of human knowledge and intellect. Therefore, as long as there is no clear disagreement with Islamic principles, the default principle is their permissibility.

Munshi (2021) presents a system using AI and deep learning NLP methods to build an automated *fatwa* system. The system performs topic/intent classification and question-answer retrieval. Khazani *et al.* (2021) also show semantic knowledge representation by using *Surah Al-Imran* by setting rules to build a semantic graph, a graph that represents semantic relationships between concepts. Bendjamaa and Talep (2017) analyze the ontologies of Islamic legislative sources which help scholars to provide a *fatwa*. NLP is a specific domain of AI and applying this to Arabic language to extract knowledge is another problem. As Farghaly (2004) indicates, average ambiguity of a token in many languages is 2.3, but in modern standard Arabic, it reaches 19.2 which makes a big challenge for NLP systems. Sheker *et al.* (2016) propose an ontology-based QA for *fatwa* delivery. They reached approximately 90% of the F-measure.

The knowledge of the Qur'an is represented by conforming to an ontology within a system framework. A comprehensive review of concepts in the Qur'an is interrelated with each other and is essential for information extraction, AI, NLP, and knowledge management (Rusli *et al.*, 2018). Therefore, gathering all the existing ontologies to build an ontology representing Islamic knowledge is a prerequisite for creating an argument extraction system. Without a framework and ontological approach to Fintech, generated knowledge and suitability of all products and tools will create an additional burden. Rather than working on a different language, first English and then Arabic should be the default languages on which all these NLP activities work.

Alsabban *et al.* (2021) attempt to tackle the problem of automatic categorization of Islamic jurisprudential legal questions using deep learning techniques. It is a reasonable logic to say that Muslims represent 25% of the earth's population in 51 countries, and while there is a scarcity of muftis, on one hand, there is an explosion of social media channels on the other hand. Such a gap creates a supply-demand problem which calls for automation solutions including AI. Therefore, the potential of AI for automated Q&A systems, Chatbots, and Question topic classification is huge.

While we concentrate on the use of AI for fatwa, Singer (2021) discusses the fatwas on Robotics and AI technologies that were given by scholars. Her research shows that there needs to be more discussion and scholarly gatherings to understand the position of AI from the point of Islamic scholars. The literature review shows that there are many pieces of research that each one is trying to cover a specific problem for the application of AI to IFIs.

3 Shari'ah Governance and AI

Shari'ah Governance is the framework to reach Shari'ah compliance. Lack of it will create reputational problems and Shari'ah Compliance Risk which is unique to IFIs. Yasini and Yasini (2019) mention that most Fintech solutions in IFIs do not sufficiently provide Shari'ah assurance to their clients. They may feel not obligated to provide such assurance and expose themselves to reputational risk in the current environment where absence of a proper regulatory regime and governance standards.

The convergence of AI and BC will be inevitable, and they create both new challenges and opportunities for IFIs. Both technologies deal with data and value. Employing AI will generate insights from data and will generate value (Shroff, 2020). ML models can be improved on blockchains by collaboration and AI models can create new financial instruments over a blockchain. Such developments will make IFIs stakeholder's job harder in terms of Shari'ah compliance.

Corporate governance and prudent compliance are prerequisites of financial stability and customer satisfaction for both the conventional banks and Islamic Banks (IB). The Islamic Financial Services Board (IFSB) and the Accounting and Auditing Organization for Islamic Financial Institutions (AAOIFI) have specific concerns on the issues which focus on compliance with Shari'ah of the corporate governance. A robust Shari'ah governance will build trust and confidence of stakeholders of IB. This will impact the stability, capacity, and performance of IB at the bank level. Increasing the knowledge of the stakeholders is also important for them to make informed decisions. Therefore, Shari'ah compliance should also have a dimension of a disclosure of information that is timely, accurate, and adequate for all parties. Non-availability of proper governance mechanisms will lead to Shari'ah risk which can create additional risks like credit, legal and compliance, reputational risk, and market risk (Ginena & Hamid, 2015).

Lahsasna (2014) classifies the tools which can help identify the incongruences in Shari'ah compliance. These are (i) Accounting and Financial Reporting Techniques, (ii) Legal Technique, and (iii) Shari'ah Technique. There are also techniques like observation, sampling, interview, or testing which are used to capture risky points for non-compliance risk too. All these tools and techniques are necessary; however, we have to suggest that it is becoming difficult to capture the full control of Shari'ah compliance as the number of transactions, the number of documents, and the total amount of digitized transactions are increasing beyond human computational capacity. Setting principles and giving *fatwa* is a necessary condition, however, we must always monitor if it is enough to have a healthy development of IFIs. Under our bounded rationality, AI should help us to facilitate the growth and to improve the quality of IFIs in several dimensions. Ginena (2014) clarifies internal (arising from people, processes and systems) and external causes of possible Shari'ah risks and many of these causes can be minimized with Fintech, specifically AI and other means.

Hilb (2020) discusses the possibility of artificial governance where the role of AI in shaping the future of corporate governance is discussed. There are different lenses to analyze the issue, the business, technology, and society lenses. The article also proposes five scenarios of artificial governance, i.e., assisted, augmented, amplified, autonomous, and autopoietic intelligence. Without improving digital and data capabilities, the benefit of AI will be limited for IFIs. To reach that level, rather than individual Islamic banks, a workgroup can be created under the legitimate international organizations for IFIs (like AAOIFI or *Fatwa*-Related Bodies) and set up both frameworks, prerequisites, and other requirements.

For instance, Islamic Development Bank prepared a report specifically on AI and IFIs, for how to use it for financial inclusion within IFIs context. Accessing finance as a goal of the UN is related to the financial sector (IsDB, 2021). A part of this might be related to *fatwa* but what we see is that in these specific product or technology developments, Shari'ah conformity, audit, etc. are usually disregarded.

Shari'ah-Tech can automate some processes that required once significant human error. This will provide an incremental value to scholars. But it might sometimes innovate the way that the task is done. Although many of the solutions available today are in the category of increasing efficiency with higher quality and fewer costs compared to performing these tasks manually, the technological advancement will provide a shift to more innovative solutions very soon.

We can create a simple framework where Shari'ah conformity is the sum of transaction conformity and technology conformity. Although it is hypothetic, a technology can be non-conform to Shari'ah because of its underlying design principles (Table 1).

A *fatwa* is not only a technical or legal tool but also a social tool that has a relation with society and human behavior. By sticking with Shari'ah principles, the development and deployment of technology-driven *fatwa* solutions are necessary for the future of IFIs. It will be an essential requirement to understand human-machine and human-contract interactions for a mufti as machine code (as a clause of a contract or a condition of a contract) needs to be either approved or analyzed from a Shari'ah conformity basis. The conventional way of contracts is human-made, and AI can be approximate rather than certain. Therefore, a Shari'ah scholar or audit will be in the loop who will check things and provide a second-level review. Such a system will minimize the Shari'ah risks and perhaps

TABLE 1 Shari'ah conformity matrix

Transaction conformity	Technology conformity	Shari'ah conformity
Yes	Yes	Yes
Yes	No	No
No	Yes	No
No	No	No

minimize the time and cost variables during the processes by accelerating *fatwa*/audit lifecycle. All the discussion leads us to somewhere that AI on *fatwa* will not bring any end to mufti but will enrich *fatwa* processes.

Shari'ah compliance assessment should include the procedural processes from the beginning until the end of the product lifecycle. Before launching any product, it should be scrutinized as per fiqh guidelines of Shari'ah Committees. Shari'ah scholars need to be adept with technological developments to adequately assess Shari'ah compliance. A multidisciplinary approach is also required to reach a sound Shari'ah Governance practice (Mohamed, 2020). For Shari'ah assurance the platforms may appoint a Shari'ah Supervisory Board (SSB) (Yasini & Yasini, 2019).

4 Looking forward: AI and *Fatwa*-related processes

The literature and application on AI are going forward increasingly both in conventional Fintech and I-Fintech fields. To understand the capability of AI, strong and weak AI should be clarified. Strong AI is different from weak or narrow AI. The first has the ability "to reason, represent knowledge, plan, learn, communicate in natural language and integrate all these skills toward a common goal". There is no such system yet and AI tools used in LegalTech are far away from such target. Weak AI cannot perform autonomous reduction while strong AI can understand a problem domain. On the other hand, the human brain uses deductive or inductive reasoning while computers have a data-driven approach to describe information processing that cannot be articulated as a mere series of logical steps. These inductive rules are in the form of statistical equations, estimated or trained with samples of historical cases, that model the relationship between the information inputs and the processed output (Bues & Matthaei, 2017).

Shari'ah scholar has a highly complex work that requires processing convoluted sets of circumstances. A scholar must consider all rights and obligations in the domain and render reasoned opinions and provide guidance depending on this information. Understanding the background and context, having a general information, keeping relevant, and filtering the irrelevant noise are also part of the duty. A weak form of AI cannot handle all these duties even some of the scholars cannot have enough background to provide a *fatwa* for complicated cases. Still, we should look at this matter from another perspective. If the IFIs ecosystem gets the bias that (Susskind & Susskind, 2015) refers to as "technological myopia" which is the tendency to underestimate the potential of tomorrow's applications by evaluating them in terms of today's enabling technologies, it will not be easy to update the changes if they come sooner than expected. In this regard, Moore's law states about CPU processing power, the power that is required for AI engines, the technological progress is not going linear but exponential. IFIs should not underestimate the potential of tomorrow's applications.

There might be limitations today but that does not mean these limitations, (a) will exist in a decade, (b) will not have any efficiency or benefit on today's *fatwa* production.

As evidence, we can mention about a new generation AI tool promise to help anyone to prepare, review, and monitor both contracts and legal documents. A San Francisco-based company, Open AI, has a state-of-the-art language model called GPT-3, Generative Pre-trained Transformer 3, released in May 2020, using deep learning to produce human-like text with a capacity of 175 billion ML parameters (Corrales Compagnucci et al., 2021). As Heaven (2020) indicates the quality of GPT-3 generated text is so high that cannot be easily distinguished from a text written by a human being. GPT-3 opened a new era in general in AI-powered solutions. Meanwhile, using AI also brought opportunities and challenges for the legal community and profession in general. For instance, a requirement of a new professional, as Cummins and Clack (2022) call, computable contract designer, will emerge to help this task.

Muhammad and Muhammad (2003) indicate that if many systems available now can mimic doctors, financial analysts, engineers, lawyers, etc. why an expert system cannot imitate the expounder of Islamic law (mufti), mujtahid, jurist, or Muslim judge (*qadhi*)? At the time of discussing this topic, CBR was available. Past experiences of human specialists are represented as cases. When a user encounters a new case with similar parameters of the earlier one which was stored in a database for later retrieval, the user searches for the stored cases with question attributes similar to the new one, finds the neighboring fit, and applies the solutions of the old case to the new case. Users can tag the successful solutions to the new case, and both are stored together with the others in the database. A case conflicting with another one is also important, and they are also appended to the case database with explanations as to why the solutions did not work.

Muslim software developers need to be proactive in developing such AI-based tools. However, a working AI model needs really a big investment in terms of labeling in supervised learning and a huge cost of processing power. AI research is currently either academic or market driven due to its nature of monetary benefits. A system which mutually agreed upon by *ulama*, AI specialists, and perhaps linguists can create additional systems which can go beyond CBR-type applications.

Ashley (2017) asks the question if there will be a software service for "generation of explanations and arguments in law: assists in structuring explanations of answers and supportive legal arguments?" such service has not happened yet though research on how to extract semantic information necessary for AR (argument retrieval) and research on applying this information to cognitive computing to answer the question is still going on.

Alkhamees (2017) refers to inconsistency in SSB rulings which occur in the same bank over time and among different SSBs in one country which leads us to the problem of lack of consistency among *fatwa*s. Therefore, IFIs having a standard framework for *fatwa* is essential to reflect the potential of IFIs activities. We are using "standard framework" not to indicate the juristic differences which are inevitable due to many reasons from variable Quranic recitation to different interpretations of the meanings of the words to lack of knowledge of a *Hadith* or different requirements for adopting *Hadith*. Disregarding *Maslahah* or adopting or not adopting some principles are also effective in these differences. In addition to these, the structure of the *Fatwa* question is also important to have a unified, standard framework. The differences among *fatwa*s can still be available but at least making sure of two things. (1) The stakeholders can differentiate and justify the reasons behind it. (2) The same mufti is not conflicting with its own verdict over time or over the country.[1]

Legal design thinking is a trending term that combines legal expertise, design, and visual thinking to solve a legal problem with a human-centered approach (Neota Logic, 2019). Such innovation in approach can create additional information for *fatwa* processes and benefit for Shari'ah scholars which is currently lacking. Such an approach will not only help identification of the problem but how an overall process works.

From AI perspective, *fatwa* texts are unstructured data, NLP and some additional tools can help find, extract, and present key data in *fatwa* documents. Once the approach changes, additional tools can be used as google Contract Doc AI does (Artificial Lawyer, 2021). By using decision tree algorithm, an expiry date can be extracted depending on other data in the contract although an explicit expiry date is not mentioned in a contract. In IFIs, a contract is not valid after the expiry date, and therefore, it is a part of the Shari'ah audit.

Any development in deep learning and language modeling for general and specific domains, AI will serve better. Still, highly complex, high-risk contracts require humans in the loop. Therefore, AI in current technology still needs humans for the foreseeable future. LegalTech leads to disruptive change in the Shari'ah scholar's profession though it does not replace it. ML and NLP can be used to provide services related to E-Discovery/Forensic Investigation, Legal Search, Automated Document Assembly and Analytics, Online Dispute Resolution/Mass Procedures, Standardized Claim Management, and Legal Predictive Analytics.

Regulatory Technology (RegTech) is a fundamental value addition that can enhance both Fintech and LegalTech developments. Developing and re-conceptualizing of existing regulations by regulators will pave the way for further speed up in both Fintech and LegalTech. Meanwhile, in most of the countries, the regulatory framework is still evolving and conflicts with some of the existing regulations (Rabbani et al., 2020).

As Alam et al. (2019) indicate, RegTech is not a buzzword and its most significant role is to disrupt the regulatory landscape of the financial sector by providing solutions that are technologically advanced. Such fulfillment will help to the ever-increasing demands of compliance within the financial industry, particularly after the 2008 global financial crisis.

5 Conclusion

This chapter shows that there are some introductory studies which are trying to explain a specific part of the AI-related tools or trying to solve some problems in Shari'ah-related domains. By combining both perspectives of Fintech and LegalTech, we looked how Shari'ah compliance in broader terms can benefit from these technologies and how *fatwa* production can be efficiently made. What we suggest here is that the whole *fatwa* process and Shari'ah compliance can be changed in a way that Shari'ah compliance can be a 360-degree solution providing help to each stakeholder – including capital owners, Islamic banks, employees, government, customers, external stakeholders, regulators, rating agencies, international organizations, takaful operators, and lawyers – depending on their needs. One of the advantages of dealing with technology is that it is expected to extract more data from already available data by employing AI, big data analytics, and new tools for virtualizations. Therefore, connecting *fatwa* process and Shari'ah compliance with internal and external Shari'ah audit and analyzing the document for consistency are expected to provide speed, accuracy, and transparency in the Shari'ah compliance process.

We look at the *fatwa* creation process where there is a *fatwa* supply (internal or external, requested or unrequested as *fatwa* can be issued in any way) and *fatwa* demand. AI can be used before and during the *fatwa* supply and AI can be used after the issuance of the *fatwa* on the demand side. Once a *fatwa* is issued, its control, audit, and corporate governance aspects are also related with the demanding party. In its simplest form what we can expect from AI is that

- AI can analyze the past cases from available *fatwa*s and generate a new *fatwa* depending on earlier ones. In this case, AI infers an answer based on the earlier cases.
- AI can also be used to back up a mufti to make the cases available for an easy and fast decision-making or retrieval of *fatwa*.

AI promises many features for corporate governance of Islamic financial institutions although the developing literature covers more on individual *fatwa* demand. For instance, AI can be used for due diligence of the contracts to make sure the appropriateness of the contracts to Islamic rules and principles. Another benefit can be for the specific questions about which there is a consensus of the muftis. A similarity map created by AI can be beneficial to extract specific answers for specific questions. A *fatwa* as a ruling need to be issued by a legitimate scholar but still, this scholar can make a mistake. As long as the mufti intends to provide a solution to a specific problem depending on principal resources, AI can help to find if there is any conflicting *fatwa* for the same problem. Finally, in standard application, a *fatwa* provided by a mufti can be written on different media whether internal or external to the corporation. Still, the originality of the question and the answer needs to be authentic. Such originality can be obtained by blockchain-based AI technologies.

If we see the examples of Bitcoin or altcoins, many scholars are rejecting them on different grounds. Similarly, any AI solution can be accepted or rejected depending on the understanding of the scholar. If there is no framework or R&D on this issue, how the scholar is going to decide? Therefore, certain issues are still inconclusive like the evolution of technology. But in this study, we reviewed the use of technology to overcome certain issues related to the use of AI for fatwa. It can be concluded that the use of AI and ML can be very helpful to save the time and speed up the transactions by retracting *fatwa* from the already issued and stored databases for similar or related cases. The storage and retrieval of case-based *fatwa* using these technologies and keeping the track of rule-based laws can contribute to the development of IFIs. Moreover, the use of technology by religious scholars can help them to address the gray areas in Shari'ah compliance practices. Moreover, we further assume that the use of AI, ML, and Fintech will further revolutionize the relevant fields and can evolve the ways of accomplishing new frontiers in the future, like the revolutions we have seen recently.

Note

1 The flexibility of Shari'ah comes here with the principle, "It is undeniable that the rules change with the change of time." Therefore, a conflicting verdict of a mufti is a matter of discussion but we can simply say that if the premise or reason of a situation is almost same for two different cases, it should create the same conclusion. If there is a difference in conclusion, it means they are not exactly same and the difference is justifiable.

References

Ahmed, B. (2021). The status of the use of artificial intelligence in Ijtihad. *Journal of Socio-Economic and Religious Studies*, *1*(1), 1–15.

Alam, N., Gupta, L., & Zameni, A. (2019). Fintech and Islamic finance: Digitalization, development and disruption. In *Fintech and Islamic Finance: Digitalization, Development and Disruption*. Springer International Publishing. https://doi.org/10.1007/978-3-030-24666-2

Alkhamees, A. (2017). Standardisation of Fatwās to Reduce Creative Sharī'ah Compliance. In *A Critique of Creative Shari'ah Compliance in the Islamic Finance Industry* (pp. 87–116). Brill | Nijhoff. https://doi.org/10.1163/9789004344433_006

Alsabban, W. H., Alotaibi, S. S., Farag, A. T., Rakha, O. E., Sallab, A. A. Al, & Alotaibi, M. (2021). Automatic categorization of Islamic jurisprudential legal questions using hierarchical deep learning text classifier. *International Journal of Computer Science and Network Security*, *21*(9), 281–292.

Artificial Lawyer. (2021). *Google Tells Artificial Lawyer about Its Contract DocAI Strategy*. https://www.artificiallawyer.com/2021/11/18/google-tells-artificial-lawyer-about-its-contract-docai-strategy/

Ashley, K. D. (2017). Artificial intelligence and legal analytics. In *Artificial Intelligence and Legal Analytics*. https://doi.org/10.1017/9781316761380

Bendjamaa, F., & Taleb, N. (2017). Decision making approach using ontologies: Application on sacred texts. *2017 Computing Conference*, *2018-Janua*, pp. 1043–1047. https://doi.org/10.1109/SAI.2017.8252220

Bues, M.-M., & Matthaei, E. (2017). *LegalTech on the Rise: Technology Changes Legal Work Behaviours, But Does Not Replace Its Profession.* https://doi.org/10.1007/978-3-319-45868-7_7

Corrales, M., Jurcys, P., & Kousiouris, G. (2019). Legal tech, smart contracts and blockchain. In *Legal Tech, Smart Contracts and Blockchain, Perspectives in Law, Business and Innovation* (Vol. 4, Issue 2015).

Corrales Compagnucci, M., Fenwick, M., & Haapio, H. (2021). Digital technology, future lawyers and the computable contract designer of tomorrow. *SSRN Electronic Journal.* https://doi.org/10.2139/ssrn.3908370

Cummins, J., & Clack, C. D. (2022). Transforming commercial contracts through computable contracting. *Journal of Strategic Contracting and Negotiation, 6*(1), 3–25.

Elhalwany, I., Mohammed, A., Wassif, K., & Hefny, H. (2015). Using textual case-based reasoning in intelligent Fatawa QA system. *International Arab Journal of Information Technology, 12*(5), 503–509.

Farghaly, A. (2004). Computer processing of Arabic script-based languages: Current state and future directions. *Proceedings of the Workshop on Computational Approaches to Arabic Script-Based Languages,* 1.

Fitri, N. M. G., Andreswari, R., & Hasibuan, M. A. (2020). Android-based fiqh consultation application development. In *Digital Economy for Customer Benefit and Business Fairness.* https://doi.org/10.1201/9781003036173-1

Floridi, L. (2014). *The 4th Revolution—How the Infosphere is Reshaping Human Reality* Oxford: University Press.

Gazali, H. M., Jumadi, J., Ramlan, N. R., Rahmat, N. A., Uzair, S. N. H. M., & Mohid, A. N. (2020). Application of artificial intelligence (AI) in Islamic investments. *Journal of Islamic Finance, 9*(2), 70–78.

Ginena, K. (2014). Sharīʻah risk and corporate governance of Islamic banks. *Corporate Governance (Bingley), 14*(1). https://doi.org/10.1108/CG-03-2013-0038

Ginena, K., & Hamid, A. (2015). Foundations of Sharīʻah Governance of Islamic Banks. In *Foundations of Sharīʻah Governance of Islamic Banks.* https://doi.org/10.1002/9781119053507

Hasan, R., Hassan, M. K., & Aliyu, S. (2020). Fintech and Islamic finance: Literature review and research agenda. *International Journal of Islamic Economics and Finance (IJIEF), 3*(1). https://doi.org/10.18196/ijief.2122

Heaven, W. D. (2020). #OpenAI's new language generator GPT-3 is shockingly good — and completely mindless. *MIT Technology Review.*

Hilb, M. (2020). Toward artificial governance? The role of artificial intelligence in shaping the future of corporate governance. *Journal of Management and Governance, 24*(4). https://doi.org/10.1007/s10997-020-09519-9

IsDB. (2021). *Artificial Intelligence and Islamic Finance: A Catalyst for Financial Inclusion.* https://isdbinstitute.org/product/artificial-intelligence-and-islamic-finance/

Khan, S., Hassan, M. K., & Rabbani, M. R. (2021). An Artificial Intelligence-based Islamic FinTech model on Qardh-Al-Hasan for COVID 19 affected SMEs. *Islamic Perspective for Sustainable Financial System, February.*

Khazani, M. M. M., Mohamed, H., Yusop, N. M. M., Sembok, T. M. T., Wani, S., Halip, M. H. M., Marzukhi, S., & Yunos, Z. (2021). *A Framework for Semantic Knowledge Representation of Al-Quran Based on Word Dependencies.* https://doi.org/10.1109/camp51653.2021.9497925

Lahsasna, A. (2014). Shari'ah non-compliance risk management and legal documentations in Islamic finance. In *Shari'ah Non-compliance Risk Management and Legal Documentations in Islamic Finance.* https://doi.org/10.1002/9781118809181

Marir, F., Tlemsani, I., & Majdalwieh, M. (2019). *A Recursive Co-occurrence Text Mining of the Quran to Build Corpora for Islamic Banking Business Processes* In International Conference on Intelligent Human Systems Integration (pp. 306–312). Springer, Cham. https://doi.org/10.1007/978-3-030-11051-2_47

Marir, F., Tlemsani, I., & Majdalwieh, M. (2020). *Correction to: A Recursive Co-occurrence Text Mining of the Quran to Build Corpora for Islamic Banking Business Processes.* https://doi.org/10.1007/978-3-030-11051-2_141

Mat Rahim, S. R., Mohamad, Z. Z., Abu Bakar, J., Mohsin, F. H., & Md Isa, N. (2018). Artificial intelligence, smart contract and Islamic finance. *Asian Social Science, 14*(2), 145. https://doi.org/10.5539/ass.v14n2p145

Mohamed, H. (2020). Beyond fintech: Technology applications for the islamic economy. In *Beyond Fintech: Technology Applications for the Islamic Economy.* https://doi.org/10.1142/11885

Muhammad, M. R., & Muhammad, M. (2003). Using information and communication technology (ICT) to disseminate the understanding of Islamic jurisprudence (Fiqh) and juridical opinion (Fatwa): A view of a technologist. *Seminar on Understanding Islam through Techno-Da'ei*, 1–28.

Munshi, A. A., AlSabban, W. H., Farag, A. T., Rakha, O. E., Al Sallab, A. A., & Alotaibi, M. (2021). Towards an automated Islamic Fatwa system: Survey, dataset and benchmarks. *International Journal of Computer Science and Mobile Computing, 10*(4). https://doi.org/10.47760/ijcsmc.2021.v10i04.017

Mutawa, A. M., & Al-Terkait, S. M. (2011). Al Usouly: An expert system in the origins of Islamic jurisprudence domain. *Kuwait Journal of Science and Engineering, 38*(1B).

Neota Logic. (2019). *Legal Design Thinking Demystified.* https://www.artificiallawyer.com/2019/11/19/legal-design-thinking-demystified-downloadable-white-paper/

Nouaouria, N., Atil, F., Laskri, M. T., Bouyaya, D., & Amari, A. H. (2006). A case based tool as intelligent assistance to Mufti. *Arabian Journal for Science and Engineering, 31*(1B).

Rabbani, M. R., Khan, S., & Thalassinos, E. I. (2020). FinTech, blockchain and Islamic finance: An extensive literature review. *International Journal of Economics and Business Administration, 8*(2). https://doi.org/10.35808/ijeba/444

Rusli, A. S. M., Ridzuan, F., Zaki, Z. M., Sayuti, M. N. S. M., & Salam, R. A. (2018). A systematic review on semantic-based ontology for Quranic knowledge. *International Journal of Engineering and Technology(UAE), 7*(4). https://doi.org/10.14419/ijet.v7i4.15.21376

Sa'ad, A. A., Alhabshi, S. M., bin Mohd Noor, A., & Hassan, R. (2020). Robo-advisory for Islamic financial institutions: Shari'Ah and regulatory issues. *European Journal of Islamic Finance.* https://doi.org/10.13135/2421-2172/3992

Sheker, M., Saad, S., Abood, R., & Shakir, M. (2016). Domain-specific ontology-based approach for Arabic question answering. *Journal of Theoretical and Applied Information Technology, 83*(1), 43.

Shroff, R. (2020). *When Blockchain Meets Artificial Intelligence.* Medium.com.

Singer, J. (2021). Fatwas from Islamweb.Net on Robotics and Artificial Intelligence. In *Artificial Intelligence in the Gulf* (pp. 279–301). Singapore: Springer. https://doi.org/10.1007/978-981-16-0771-4_12

Susskind, R., & Susskind, D. (2015). *The Future of the Professions How Technology Will Transform the Work of Human Experts.* Oxford University Press.

Syed, M. H., Khan, S., Rabbani, M. R., & Thalassinos, Y. E. (2020). An artificial intelligence and NLP based Islamic FinTech model combining zakat and Qardh-Al-Hasan for countering the adverse impact of COVID 19 on SMEs and individuals. *International Journal of Economics and Business Administration*, 8(2). https://doi.org/10.35808/IJEBA/466

Yasini, S., & Yasini, M. (2019). Current trends and future impacts of fintech in Islamic finance. In *Fintech In Islamic Finance*. https://doi.org/10.4324/9781351025584-20

Zavolokina, L., Mateusz, D., & Schwabe, G. (2016). Fintech What's in a name ? *Thirty Seventh International Conference on Information Systems, December 2016*.

Zuhayli, W. (1997). al-Fiqh al-Islami wa Adillatuhu. In *Damascus: Dar Al-Fikr* (Vol. 57).

CONCLUSION

Yasushi Suzuki and Mohammad Dulal Miah

Digital transformation (DX) is believed to change the course in which financial services are provided historically. The nascent pace of fintech growth around the world bears the testimony that technology has a lot to offer to harness the efficiency and performance of financial institutions. The use of artificial intelligence (AI) and big data for credit screening and monitoring, robo-advising for wealth management, crowdfunding, and peer-to-peer lending to support existing and potential startups, blockchain technologies for recording and archiving information, and digital currency for facilitating quick and easy payments are set to change the future course of finance. This has an important implication for financial service providers. The existing literature makes a laudable attempt to investigate the impacts of technology on financial institutions. However, the focus remains mostly on conventional financial institutions with an emphasis on conventional banking sector, although the DX can have an equal, if not more, disrupting effect on Islamic finance. The Shariah-compliant finance occupies a sizable market share in Muslim majority countries and expanding rapidly in advanced economies. It is, thus, imperative to assess how the disrupting technology affects Islamic finance and Shariah compliance.

From Shariah perspective, technology can be perceived neutral because it simply is an enabler. However, certain fintech innovations for Islamic financial services must comply with Shariah regulations. In general, fintech solutions that need to be adjusted to comply with Shariah are financing and investments, including investment advisory services. From the user's perspective, fintech innovation provides alternatives that are suitable for individual needs. With more choices, users of financial services enjoy competitive service cost. The integration of internet, mobile devices, and social media make financial services more efficient, resulting in greater customer experience. Hence, fintech is likely to

DOI: 10.4324/9781003262169-19

positively contribute to the growth and innovation of Islamic financial products and services. As customers increasingly conduct business online, the sunk cost of Islamic financial institutions (IFIs) may turn burdensome, which can have a devastating impact on traditional financial service providers. Moreover, filtering fintech through the prism of Shariah compliance is a key question that needs to be answered. In the future, competition from small boutique-type tech-based service providers would be heightened, which implies that the financial market is likely to be dynamic and riskier. This book has made a novel attempt to examine how fintech affects IFIs including banks and insurance companies.

Major contribution of the book can be summarized into four broader points. The first line of argument focuses on the theoretical issues as well as conceptualizing fintech. Fintech embodies a vast scope, where different narratives are possible. Hence, the book first focuses on conceptualizing the typology of business models clustering into retail facing – those which focus on consumers, households, and micro, small, and medium enterprises (MSMEs) – and market provisioning, those which enable or support the infrastructure or key functionalities of fintech. In addition, major stakeholders such as commercial and investment banking units are identified as responsible units for each fintech business model. For each of these clusters, opportunities and threats stemming from the adoption of technology are explored. The book relies on traditional theories of financial intermediaries, including asymmetry of information, and transaction costs theories. In light of these theories, it is argued that technology would facilitate financial institutions to reduce transaction cost and mitigate information problem by materializing benefits of AI and big data. However, there is a risk of financial disintermediation as technology would enable tech-based and shadow financial institutions to emerge and share the pie currently belonged to the formal financial sector.

Financial disintermediation would be an issue to ponder from the context of IFIs. Islamic mode of finance (basically Islamic banks) must comply with Shariah, for which an additional Shariah compliance cost is to be incurred *vis-à-vis* their conventional counterparts. Hence, Islamic banks must earn a 'rent', known as bank rent. It is argued that technology-enabled direct finance providers are likely to erode this rent. Hence, it would be difficult for Islamic banks to realize the required rent for strictly complying with Shariah. In addition, expansion of direct finance facilitated by technology would increase wealth distribution but hamper wealth creation, one of the essential roles of financial intermediation. Given the short history of Islamic finance, a focus on wealth creation must be emphasized. From this vantage point, the book argues that instead of blanket adoption of technology, regulatory authorities must consider the effect of fintech on wealth creation. If appropriate regulatory institutions are carefully crafted, fintech would turn into an effective tool for customers' value creation.

The second major contribution of the book underlies its general assessment on the adoption of technologies by financial institutions in the Islamic jurisdictions. Based on survey data, it is illustrated that the adoption of technologies is not uniform across the jurisdictions; rather, IFIs are in different stages of development and implementation of digital Islamic banking. Digital wallets and the use of biometric authentication are the most adopted technologies observed so far. Social distancing rule during the COVID-19 pandemic accelerated the use of mobile-based technologies including digital payment and related transactions, process automation, etc. Some Islamic banks have deployed, limitedly though, more sophisticated technologies including robotics, process automation, machine learning, AI, big data, and cloud computing. Implementation of these technologies helped financial inclusion among the different jurisdictions. However, the penetration of technology is slower in insurance companies compared to their banking counterparts. It is, thus, recommended that Islamic insurance companies can materialize benefit by adopting technologies in premium determination, smart contracting, damage assessment, and fraud detection.

This part of the analysis also points out some obstacles in adopting technologies by financial service providers. Skilled manpower is identified as a primary obstacle that hinders the smooth and quick adoption of technologies. In addition, it is uncertain under the current environmental setting as to how adoption of technology may affect Shariah compliance. For instance, if application of some technologies is not explicitly cleared by Shariah norms, a conventional bank which has Shariah windows struggles to implement such technologies. Similarly, conventional insurance companies which have takaful operation face difficulty in integrating reporting standards between these two clusters of services. This has prompted IFIs (and conventional banks with Islamic banking windows) toward 'wait and see' strategy in adopting fintech. In addition, customers of Islamic banks are worried about security and privacy of their information. This has been attributed to customers' inadequate understanding about the functioning of underlying technology. Mitigation of such obstacles requires the regulatory authority to designing appropriate institutional environment that is complementary to other sectors of an economy and conducive for adoption of technologies by financial institutions.

The third strand of argument brings applications of fintech that are practiced on the ground. One of the cases reveals that data inadequacy of MSMEs acts as hindrance for lending institutes in many developing countries. To overcome such obstacle, P2P lenders can integrate value chain in which all players in the business ecosystem have mutual relationship and contribute to economic value creation. Technology eases the process of connection between parties and ensures the smooth flow of information for the lenders to keep track of borrowers' activities. This, in turn, helps slashing lending risk. Another case shows the potential of blockchain technologies for cost-effective and timely transfer of remittance. Pakistan and Malaysia have already adopted blockchain-based transfer payment to avail the embedded benefits. Other countries can follow the suit for the greater interest of financial service users. In a similar fashion, another empirical study examines the experience and feasibly of crowdfunding in a Muslim country, Bangladesh. Although the initial experience does not draw a rosy picture for Islamic crowdfunding in Bangladesh, participants' enthusiasm is gradually gaining a momentum. However, in the absence of a practicing and appropriate rule of laws, such as property right, investors may shun away from such endeavor, resulting in the failure of materializing the benefits offered by a thriving crowdfunding sector. Another case critically assesses how the central bank digital currency (CBDC) can affect the balance sheet of Islamic banks. It is argued that the fluctuation of digital currency may fall into the category of *gharar* (uncertainty), which Islamic banks are prohibited to be part with. In such a circumstance, a central bank of an Islamic jurisdiction must take uncertainty issue of IFIs stemming from CBDC into account before it aims to develop and circulate CBDC.

The final part of the contribution concentrates on management issues such as Waqf and Zakat management and fatwa-related matters. Waqf offers a great potential to contribute to social welfare through collective efforts along with state-run programs and supports. In explaining the status of Waqf management, it is argued that currently practiced Waqf management in most Muslim countries is inefficient. Assets, under the disposal of Waqf, are not properly managed. Technology can revolutionize modernizing the existing system such as registering, record keeping, monitoring, and managing Waqf assets. Moreover, fintech-enabled cash Waqf management can turn into an effective tool to enhance social welfare. Similarly, Zakat embodies a greater potential to eradicate poverty through its proper collection and distribution. However, this specific tool has failed, so far, to meet the expectations. Analysis shows that Zakat management across Islamic jurisdictions is obsolete and ineffective. Centralized Zakat collection is an absolute meager compared to its potential, which indicates the inability of mobilizing Zakat fund. One of the critical elements of Zakat, highlighted in this book, is trust. Efficient Zakat management enhances the trust of Zakat payers. Technology can function marvelously in this context. Using technology for automation of Zakat collection and distribution would increase trust toward Zakat system by boosting transparency. Like Waqf and Zakat, technology can also remarkably impact *fatwa*. It is mentioned that the use of AI can overcome the shortage of skilled Fiqh scholar to issue *fatwa*. AI can be used to ascertain the compliance of a particular Islamic financial product with Shariah. Hence, the book recommends that the accuracy and speed of *fatwa* issue can be enhanced by using sophisticated algorithm, deep learning, and natural language processing.

Future issues

Ethical considerations

In our four major arguments summarized above, the need for a strong legal and regulatory environment has been emphasized. However, regulation is not the panacea against all odds resulting from adopting technologies by IFIs. Technology has its own limitations. The world is so much dynamic and complex that it is impassable to incorporate all aspects of human behavior into legal codes. History shows that laws more often than not lag behind technical advances. It is more so when we talk about deep and machine learning, algorithm, AI, cloud computing, etc. Predicting *ex-ante* any odd those technologies may bring is infeasible. Hence, remedies to cure those adversaries by enacting appropriate laws are hard to come by. In addition, the letters of any law do not mean a lot if we ignore the spirit, which underlies ethics. This suggests that we must recourse to ethics where law reaches its boundaries.

No doubt, ethics is going to be the major concern in the post-industrial society brought about the fourth industrial revolution. In this book, we have pointed out some existential threats such as persistent wars, food shortage, and famine in third world countries, increasing carbon emission in the atmosphere that constantly poses increasing threat to our living, etc. Data suggests that the benefits of fintech will be lopsided and tilted toward wealthy individuals as well as institutions. Therefore, the divide between the rich and poor is likely to increase as fintech increasingly penetrates businesses. Oxfam recently published a report showing that the world's top eight billionaires are as rich as the world's poorest half. Accumulated assets of these eight billionaires are equivalent to the accumulated wealth of 3.6 billion people who make up the bottom half. Of the top eight billionaires, majority are the owners of tech-based firms.

This inequality will spread in the society through continuous financialization enabled by technology. In the 1950s, profit earned by the US financial corporations as proportion to national income averaged 9.5% which rose to 45% in 2002. In 2013, profits earned by finance and insurance industries accounted for 37% of the profit all other sectors combined. It means that more than one-third of a dollar earned in the US economy goes to the financial sector. Including financial activities of non-financial firms would make the estimation unbelievably high.

The unprecedented financial crisis of 2007–2009 reveals a scary picture about the increased financialization. Following the internet bubble-bust in the early 2000s until the crisis erupted in 2007, top executives and rentier class had pocketed exorbitant pay checks as bonuses, salaries, and dividends. Most of them resulted from the trades of toxic financial assets including derivatives, which were not only risky but also fictitious. As the crisis engulfed financial sectors, veteran financial firms started collapsing. Government rescued them by injecting taxpayers' money. This entails, under the current financial world order, that profit is privatized, whereas loss is socialized. It is absolutely feasible that the finance world comes up with some exotic financial products in the future with the help of AI, big data, and algorithm to create another financial bubble. Laws and regulations alone cannot eliminate this trend unless ethics is put ahead of everything.

Second, the mining and use of cryptocurrency involve with environmental and security concerns. According to the Cambridge Centre for Alternative

Finance, Bitcoin alone consumes about 110 terawatt hours of electricity each year, which is about 0.55% of the world's total electricity generation. Simply put, this use of electricity is equivalent to the annual use of small countries like Malaysia or Sweden. Much of Bitcoin has already been mined, but mining of other cryptocurrencies continues and is likely to grow further in the future. Moreover, the amount of power required to validate a transaction in blockchain technology is largely unknown because large-scale transactions using cryptocurrency remain unaccomplished until now. It is, of course, a moral and ethical concern if the world can environmentally support such an expensive power-consuming technology at a time when climate change has turned into an existential threat to humanity. Another concern raised by cryptocurrency is related to monitoring. Traditional banking system is highly regulated. Anti-money-laundering and anti-terrorist-financing acts prevent banks from entertaining suspicious customers. In contrast, the origin of crypto-based transactions remains anonymous. This may pave the way for illegal and terrorist financing worldwide. Formal regulations may not be so effective in such cases. Only ethics can have a discernible impact.

Third, financial institutions collect enormous data about their customers. There is a growing tendency that those confidential data to be sold without the knowledge and consent of the owners to third parties who analyze them and figure out consumers' preference and choices using a sophisticated algorithm. In 2018, The New York Times and the Guardian reported a huge quantity of Facebook users' data leak by Cambridge Analytics which used the data to make users' psychological profile helpful for the US presidential campaign. As mentioned earlier, the benefit of crypto mining goes to the miners, but the burden of resulting emission is shared by all. Even if financial institutions intend to care about people and society, their interest might not coalesce into social interest. Google failed to sustain its ethics council which aimed to monitor the development of AI. Such a failure is not only shocking but also rings an alarm bell that tech firms are not ready to embrace the spirit of ethics. Even if we assume that when human beings code AI maintaining an ethical standard, the same cannot be expected when algorithm itself codes another algorithm. We should at the same time note that artificial stupidity may rise along with the rise of AI. Only ethical practice can limit such trend.

There is no denying that fintech ushers a new dawn for financial institutions to revolutionize their services. Benefits that can be derived from the ongoing digital disruption are progressive which are well-articulated in this book. At the same time, the urge for a conducive regulatory environment has been emphasized for fostering financial inclusion and development. However, the book has made a point that formal regulation is not the last thing society needs to harvest the maximum benefits from the DX. Regulations should be backed by morality and ethics for a better fintech world.

Toward the political economy of DX Islamic finance

Since the 1970s, Islamic monetary economics and its initiatives to establish Islamic financial institutions, particularly in the Muslim majority nations, have been developed. The idea of Islamization of economics initially manifested in the form of various publishing activities, conference centers, and the establishment of Islamic economics at different universities in the Islamic community. These strategic efforts did not end at the stage of conceptual ideas; the movement of the Islamization of economics also implemented real projects in the form of experiments to establish IFIs based on the principles of Islam. One of the salient features of Islamic finance that distinguishes it from the conventional mode of finance is that the former complies, in objectives and operations, with Shariah. There is little doubt that the role of the board members and advisors in the Shariah Supervisory Board (SSB) or the Shariah Committee, called in general 'Shariah Board' is inevitable in Islamic finance. IFIs are usually governed by two boards: Board of Directors and SSB. The SSB has a unique role of ensuring that all the IFIs are Shariah-compliant; therefore, the SSB members should be Shariah scholars with experience in Islamic banking and financial transactions.

How is the trend of DX going to affect the Islamic mechanism of ensuring the Shariah compliance? This book does not have room enough to answer the question. More or less, as Floridi (2014) points out, the 'democratization' brought about by information and communication technologies (ICTs) is generating a new tension between power and force, where power is informational, and exercised through the elaboration and dissemination of norms, whereas force is physical, and exercised when power fails to orient the behavior of the relevant agents and norms need to be enforced. The trend of DX may undermine the Shariah-compliant mechanism of SSBs and their members because of ICTs' 'data superconductivity' which may further facilitate the frictionless flow of information related to Islamic legal cases to be smoothly shared among the Islamic financial players. To some extent, the SSBs may end by undermining its own future as the only Shariah information agent. On the other hand, we should note that data superconductivity may bring a steady increase in agents' responsibilities.

> The more any bit of information is just and easy click away, the less we shall be forgiven for not checking it. ICTs are making humanity increasingly responsible, morally speaking, for the way the world is, will be, and should be. This is a bit paradoxical since ICTs are also part of a wider phenomenon that is making the clear attribution of responsibility to specific individual agents more difficult and ambiguous.
>
> *(Floridi, 2014, pp. 42–43)*

Perhaps, the democratization of the Shariah-compliant mechanism upon SSBs and their members into a new mechanism upon the frictionless flows of information will be unavoidable. ICTs and DX are supposed to facilitate a more fragmented mechanism while enhancing a just and coherent legal judgment and reasoning for disputing cases in the Islamic commerce and finance, consequently lowering the transaction cost of Shariah compliance in individual IFI levels. The democratization may contribute to intensifying and standardizing the way of complying Shariah within the Muslim community. Simultaneously, ICTs and DX are going to bring the exponential increase in common knowledge of comparing the Islamic mode with the conventional mode of financial intermediation, in which more people are helped to make rational analyses, enquiries, and evaluations to consider a harmonious and complementary or supplementary co-existence of both modes. In parallel, more people are supposed to review upon rational analysis, enquiry, and evaluation on how the Muslim community could expect the economically effective benefit from the Islamic mode. This trend is going to expose more IFIs to a severer competition in global financial markets.

ICTs and DX may contribute to transforming the Muslim community *per se* as an information society, which makes it possible to intensify and standardize the way of Shariah compliance within the community. Simultaneously ICTs and DX may help shift the balance against a centralized mechanism upon SSBs and their members, to respond to the economic demand from the customers and users of IFIs under the global competition. To some extent, ICTs and DX are making the outer economic border of each community *porous*. The Muslim community may face complicated tensions both from the internal force as well as from the external one under the trend of DX. Analyzing these forces – the political economy of DX in Islamic finance – should be a direction of future research in this field.

Reference

Floridi, L. (2014). *The fourth revolution: How the infosphere is reshaping human reality*. Oxford University Press, Oxford.

INDEX

Note: **Bold** page numbers refer to tables; *italic* page numbers refer to figures and page numbers followed by "n" denote endnotes.

Aba, F. 69
ABCBDC *see* asset-backed CBDC (ABCBDC)
Abdullah, A. 176, 195
Abubakar, M. 195
acceptable *gharar* 194
accessibility 154, 155, 174
agent banking 51, 58
Ahmad, S.M. 177
Ahmed, B. 276, 277
Ahmed, D. 21
Ahmed, M.U. 151
Ahmed, N. 145, 149
Ajouz, M. 197
Alam, N. 282
Aliyu, A. 197
Alkhamees, A. 281
Al-Saati, A.R. 193, 194
Alsabban, W.H. 277
Al-Terkait, S.M. 276
altruism 36
Alvia, D.D. 194
Alzubaidi, I.B. 176
Amil 259
Annual Development Plan (ADP) 253
Anwar, M. 176
API 125, 126
Appiah-Otoo, I. 69
Arner, D.W. 239
artificial intelligence (AI) 119, 151, 259, 273; application 280–282; research 275–277; Shari'ah Governance 278–280, **279**
Ashley, K.D. 281
Asian Development Bank (ADB) 263
asset-backed CBDC (ABCBDC) **198,** 198–199
asset-backed *sukuk* 198
asset-based *sukuk* 198
Association for Digital Financial Innovations players in Indonesia (AFTECH) 85, **86**
Auditing Organization for Islamic Financial Institutions (AAOIFI) 227, 278
Auer, R. 193
Ayoungman, F.Z. 145, 150

Bakar, M.A. 176
Bakar, M.D. 5, 17
Bakr, A.M. 176
Bangladesh 101; awareness about fintech 148–149; during COVID-19 pandemic 146; digital services 146; economic growth 145–146; economic infrastructures comparison 107–108; Islamic banks in 146, 149; Islamic crowdfunding opportunities 108–110, **109, 110**; Islamic finance 177–179; literature review 143–145; mobile banking 146; research design and respondents 147, **147**; thematic content analysis 148; *see also* crowdfunding

Index

Bangladesh Government Islamic Investment Bond (BGIIB) 196
Bangladeshi banks 33
Bank for International Settlement (BIS) 191
Bank Indonesia (BI) 181
banking 17, 88–89
Banking as a Service (BaaS) 51, 61n2
Bank Negara Malaysia 181–182
Barclays Bank 1
Bell, D. 64
Bendjamaa, F. 277
big data 259
BigTechs 134
biometric authentication 126–127
'*Bir Rumah*' 236
Bitcoin 2, 197
bKash 148
blockchain 145, 151, 172, 174, 258–259, 273
blockchain-based remittance transfer: challenges 186–187; contribution 185, *186*; defined 174–175; loopholes 184–185
blockchain-powered remittance technology 183
Böhme, R. 193
Bottiglia, R. 102
Bowles 36
Bukhari, S. 217n1
business ethics 31
business risk mitigation 84, 92–94, *94*; demand risk data 95; supply-chain variable 95; supply risk data 95–97, **96,** *96*
Bussche, A. 158

capitalist economy 32
case-based reasoning (CBR) system 275
cashless transactions 2
Central Bank Digital Currency (CBDC) 9, 190–191; ABCBDC **198,** 198–199; architecture 193; definition 191; features and trends 191, **192;** *gharar* 193–197, *196*; precious-metal–backed cryptocurrency 197; Shariah-compliant 197
Central Bank of Nigeria (CBN) 193
Central Bank of the Republic of Turkey (CBRT) 190
CFP *see* crowdfunding
Chandan, M.S.K. 244
Chinn, D. 158
Chowdhury, N.H. 148
Citibank 154
Cizakca, M. 237

climate crisis 74–75
cloud computing 127, 128
commercial banks 22; opportunity for 57–60
commercial capital buys 32
competitive advantage 66, 89
conflicts 72–74
consistency 155
Contractual Service Margin (CSM) 227–228
conventional banks 35
conventional financial model 25
conventional insurance industry 230
copy trading *see* social trading
COVID-19 pandemic 2, 123, 167, 168, 219
credit creation 19, 41n2
Crosby, M. 176
cross-border payments 174–175
crowdfunding 4, 50, 101–102, 257; in Bangladesh 112, **113,** 114; concept of 103; convenient framework of 110–114, *111, 112,* **113;** defined 102; donation-based 102–103; economic infrastructures 107–108; global volume of 102; history and current situation of 105–107, **106;** implementation 114–115; opportunities 108–110, **109, 110;** research methodology 104–105
crowd-led microfinance 49
cryptocurrency 4, 8, 9, 73, 176, 257–258, 266
custody 53, 54, **55**
customer confidence 159
customer satisfaction operational efficiency 122
cybersecurity 155, 164; risk 129

Darussalam, A.Z. 143, 147, 149
data governance 155
Data processing and Notification Requirement Act (WGCM) 164
data protection principles 158–159
data quality 154–155
data security 155; risk 130
decentralized exchange (DEX) 61n4
demand risk data 95
De Nederlandsche Bank (DNB) 156
digital assets exchange 53, **54**
digital banking 51, **51,** 154, 155; age 161, *162;* banking system 156, *157, 158;* COVID-19 pandemic 167; development challenges 163–165; digital banking patronage 156, 159–163, *160–163;* gender 160–161, *161;* technical knowledge 162–163, *163*

digital capital raising 50, **50**
digital currency 176
digital disruption 88–89
digitalization 1, 4, 22
digital lending 19, 47–49, **49**
digital micro saving solutions 52
digital money market/fund *see* digital savings
digital payments 52–53, **53**
digital revolution 1
digital savings 51, 52, **52**
digital transformation 118; challenges 132–134, *133*; COVID-19 123; current status 123–125, *124*; defined 1, 44; implication 135–137; important issues in 125–128, *126*; insurance industry in Indonesia 221–222, *222*, **223**, 224–225; perception 120; prudential risks 129–132, *130*; rationale 120–123, *121, 122*; regulation 134–135, *135*; technology 128–129, *129*
'direct' CBDC 193
disruptive technology 2, 8, 273
Distributed Ledger Technology (DLT) 190
division of work 35
dominant principles 59
doomsday prediction 68
drone 210, **211–212**
Dutch banking sector 156, *157,* 158
Dutch Data Protection Authority 155

economics 5
economies of scale 25
EkDesh 106, 266
El Amri, M.C. 37, 176
Elhalwany, I. 276
Emara, N. 69
emerging market and developing economies (EMDEs) 198
eMoney 51
empirical assessment: digitalisation (*see* digitalisation); research method 119–120
epidemics/pandemics 71–72
equity-based crowdfunding (ECF) 103, 111–112
equity-based finance 4, 18, 34
ethics 5
'e-Tunairakyat' 182
European Union 158–159
eWallet 51

Farghaly, A. 277
Farooq, U. 34
fatwa 38, 274; application 280–282; research 275–277
fiat money 2

financial contracts 4, 6, 46
financial crisis 173
financial disintermediation 5, 17–22, **19,** *20*
financial inclusion 20, 65
financial institutions 1, 15
financial intermediaries 37
financial technology (Fintech) 5, 15, 16, 142–143, 173–174; affect the performance of Islamic banks 22–25; costs 25; development in Indonesia 84–88, *86,* **87**; diversify risks 22; in merchant financing 30–35; for poverty alleviation 69; trend 36–39; value proposition 65–67; *waqf* 246, *246*; working taxonomy and classification **45–46**; *Zakat* management system 256–257
Fintech business model 6, 44, 46, 47, 53
Fiqh scholar 10, 291
Firmansyah, E.A. 176
Fitri, N.M.G. 276
Floridi, L. 4, 274
Fu, J. 2

Gao, Y. 175, 176
Gassner, M. 31
Gazali, H.M. 276
General Data Protection Regulation (GDPR) 158–159
gharar (uncertainty) 193–197, *196*
Ginena, K. 278
The Global Covid-19 FinTech Market Rapid Assessment Study 15
global financial crisis 2
globalization 3

Hadith 10
Halal 252
Hanefah, M. 247
Hanifah, I.A. 275
Hanif, M. 197
Hannigan, R. 158
Hapsari, M.I. 245
hardware wallet 54
Hassan, M.K. 24
Hawking, S. 68
Hilb, M. 279
hilm 37, 38
Holdstock, D. 67
Hussain, N. 148
hybrid CBDC 193

'idle' money 33
ijma 38
Ijtihad 37

Inaba, K. 69
Indonesia: business risk mitigation 92–94, *94*; digital disruption and banking industry 88–89; fintech development 84–88, *86, 87*; insurance and shari'ah insurance contract 228–230, *229*; insurance industry in 221–222, *222*, **223,** 224–225; Islamic finance 180–181; Islamic P2P Lending and MSMEs 89–92, **90,** *90*
Indonesian Islamic finance industry 221
industrial capital 33
inequality 70–71
Information and Communication Technologies (ICT) 275
information & communication technology (ICT) 3–4
infrastructure-as-a-Service (IaaS) 128
insurance contract 225
insurance industry 9; in Indonesia 221–222, *222,* **223,** 224–225
insurtech 1, 10, 44, **55,** 55–56, 224
integrating technology 6
interest-bearing capital 32, 33
interest-bearing CBDC 191
intermediated CBDC 193
International Banker 20
International Financial Reporting Standard (IFRS) 10, 232
International Islamic Liquidity Management 196
internet-based services 154
Internet of Things (IoT) 56
invoice trading 48
Irfan, H. 21
Islamic banking assets 20–21
Islamic banks: bringing and promoting 149; challenges 150–151; innovating and launching 149–150; innovations 144; opportunities 150
Islamic crowdfunding website (ICFW) 111, 112
Islamic Development Bank's (IsDB's) 245
Islamic financial institutions (IFIs) 3, 195, *196*
Islamic Financial Services Board (IFSB) 185, 278
Islamic FinTech 16, 173–174; classification 175
Islamic P2P Lending 89–92, **90,** *90*
Islam, K.M. 145, 148
Islam, M.T. 115
Islam, N. 145, 148
Izutsu, T. 37, 38

Jobs, S. 67, 203

Kafala 220
Kamali, M.H. 37
Kamaruddin, M.I.H. 247
Kaur, B. 154
khair 37
Khan, M.T.A. 115
Khan, S. 175, 276
Khazani, M.M.M. 277
Kissinger, H. 145

Lahsasna, A. 278
Lalbagh Fort 238
Lawrence, J. 31
legal design thinking 282
LegalTech 273
Lendingclub 31
Levy, S. 67
liability 191
Li, C. 44
Linardy, D. 69
London, S. 158
loopholes 184–185
low Shari'ah compliance 263

mal 37
Malaysia, Islamic finance 181–182
Malaysian Accounting Standards Board (MASB) 226
Malaysian Islamic banks 21
Mamun, A.A. 177
mandatory gharar 194
maqasid 16
maqasid al-Shari'ah 16, 204–205; to protect and preserve intellect 207; to protect and preserve life 206, *206*; to protect and preserve progeny 206–207; to protect and preserve religion 205; to protect and preserve wealth 207
maqasid shari'ah 5
Marir, F. 276
market provisioning 15, 46
Marxian tradition 33
Marx's treatment of capital 32
maslahah 38
Mawdudi, S.A.A. 38
M-cash 148
McEvoy, M.J. 93
merchants' capital 31, 33
Miah, M.D. 26, 33
micro, small, and medium enterprises (MSMEs) 84, 89–92, **90,** *90*
Milosavljevic, N. 155

Mishra, M. 2
mobile banking 146
mode of financial intermediation 4
modern technology 69, 172
Mohammed, M.O. 176
Mohieldin, M. 69
Mohsin, H.M. 238
money as capital 32
money as money 32
money supply 9, 19
moral values 5
mu'amalat 4
mudarabah 17
Mudharabah 104
Muhamat, A.A. 210
Muhammad, M 275, 281
Muhammad, M.R. 275, 281
mukallaf 16
Muneeza, A. 176
Munshi, A.A. 277
Murabahah 104
murabaha syndrome 27, 30
Murinde, V. 144
musharakah 17
'The Mussalman Wakf Validating Act 1913' 238
Mustafa, O.M. 37
Mustapha, Z. 176
Mutawa, A.M. 276
Muzzaki 260–261
mWallet 51
MyCash Online 182

Nagel, T. 36
Nahar, H.S. 219
Najaf, K. 143
Naqvi, S.N.H. 38
Nations Bank 154
Natural Language Processing (NLP) 277
Nazim Ali, S. 16
near-field communication (NFC) technology 125
Netherlands *see* digital banking
Network and Information Systems Act (WBNI) 164
'New-Keynesian' 30
new normal 2
Nisar, S. 34
Njagojević, S. 155
North Korea 73
Nouaouria, N. 275

Omar, M.A. 69
online platform 19

Oporajoy.org 105
Optimism Level on Overall Insurance Industry *219*
'Order-book' 61n3
Ord, T. 67
Oseni, U.A. 16
over-the-counter (OTC) 61n5

Pakistan 179–180
PasarPolis 224
peer-to-peer (P2P) lending 19, *20*, 39, 47–48
performance, Islamic banks 22–25
permissible *gharar* 194
Pichler, F. 102
Piketty, T. 70
PLS contract 34
PMBC *see* precious-metal-backed cryptocurrency (PMBC)
Point of access (PoS) 53
policyholders 226
'Post-Keynesian' 30
poverty 68–70
poverty alleviation 251
precious-metal-backed cryptocurrency (PMBC) 197
'Private Banking' 22
profit and loss sharing (PLS) contract 34
profit on sales 26
prohibited *gharar* 194
Project Greenback 2.0 181

Qardh-Al-Hasan 276
Qazwa 84, 92–93, 97
Qiu, T. 175, 176
Quran 10, 277

Rabbani, M.R. 175
Rahman, B. 144
real estate crowdfunding 50
Regulatory and Supervisory Authorities (RSAs) 118–119, 135
regulatory sandbox 259–260
Regulatory Technology (RegTech) 282
Rella, L. 176
remittance 34, 174–175
rent 22–23
respondents, from Bangladesh Bank 147
Retail Facing 15
retail facing 46
revenue/profit share crowdfunding 50
reward-based crowdfunding platform 111, *111*
riba 25

Ripple system 175
'risk fund' 34
risk premium 23
Rizkiah, S.K. 195
robo-advisors 56, 61n8
Robo services 151
Rochemont, S. 195
Rocket 148
Ryan, D. 67

Sa'ad, A.A. 276
Sankaran, A. 64
Satoshi Nakamoto 2
Savings-as-a-service (SaaS) 52
Schueffel, P. 239
Secure Socket Layer (SSL) encryption 165
security threat 8
sells commodities 32
shadow banking 31, 136
Shariah Accounting Standard Board (DSAS) 229, 231
Shari'ah-compliant 25–30; CBDC 197, **198**; financial disintermediation 17–22, **19, 20**; Fintech 16
Shari'ah Governance 278–280, **279**
shariah insurance 226
Shari'ah Supervisory Board (SSB) 185, 280, 294
Shari'ah-Tech 279
Sheker, M. 277
Siddiqi, M.N. 26
Simon, A. 65
Singer, J. 277
small and medium enterprises 24
smart contracts (SC) 210, 212–213, 258–259, 273
social insurance 56
social justice 5, 28, 38
social trading 56, 61n7
Society for Worldwide Interbank Financial Telecommunications (SWIFT) 175, 182
socio-civilizational 68
software wallet 54
Solis, B. 1, 44
Song, N. 69
South Asia 177, **178**
Southeast Asia 180–182
specialization 35
stagnant money 18
stakeholders 6, 47
Strengths, Weaknesses, Opportunities and Threats (SWOT) 176
supply-chain variable 95
supply risk data 95–97, *96*

Suzuki, Y. 23, 26, 28, 33, 193
Szymanski, J. 1, 44

ta'awun 220
Taher, S.A. 150
takaful industry 218, 219; accounting challenges 225–228, **227**; challenges 213; compound growth rate 204; concept of 220–221; contract model 220–221; financial commitment 214; IFRS 17 230–232; importance 203; in Indonesia 221–222, *222*, **223**, 224–225; 'Love–hate' relationship 207–209; Maqasid al-Shariah 204–207, *206*; participants 207, 215; takafultech empowers 209–213, **211–212**; total global assets 204; *vs.* conventional insurance contracts 225–228, **227**
takaful models 220–221
takafultech 209–210; benefits 214–215; drone 210, **211–212**; to Maqasid Shariah 215, *216*; smart contract 210, 212–213
Taleb, N. 277
Tarique, K.M. 151
technical knowledge 162–163, *163*
"technological myopia" 280
technology 67, 68
technology acceptance model (TAM) 159, 267
technology-enabled financial transactions 1, 41n1, 44
technology-savvy customers 66
technomania 67–68
Telenor Microfinance Bank 180
temporary solution approach 5, 17, 18, 21
Thalassinos, E.I. 175
Theory of Innovation Diffusion 159
traditional remittance transfer 182–184, *183, 184*
traits 243
transaction cost 20, 23, 40, 48, 176–177
transfer payments 174–175
Trotter, R.T.II. 147
trust 243
Tsuji, M. 150

Uddin, M. 155
Uddin, S.M.S. 23, 33
unmanned aerial vehicle (UAV) *see* drone
Upay 148
Usman, H. 245
usury 26

"value-chain integrated' financing 93, 94
vendor lock-in risk 131
Voigt, P. 158

wakalah model 221
waqf 10, 35, 235; administration 239; definition 236; digitalized and efficient 245; fintech 246, *246*; governance system 247, 247–248; roles 236; trends 237–239
waqf ordinance 1962 239, **240**, 241, *241, 242*; monitoring cost and transaction cost 242–245
waqf special act 2013 242
war 72–74
Ward, O. 195
wealth creation 37
wealthtech 56–57, **57**
web wallet 54
Wilson, R. 24, 25, 28–29
working taxonomy **45–46**; analyses 46–47; custody 53, 54, **55**; digital assets exchange 53, **54**; digital banking 51, **51**; digital capital raising 50, **50**; digital lending 47–49, **49**; digital payments 52–53, **53**; digital savings 51, 52, **52**; insurtech **55,** 55–56; wealthtech 56–57, **57**
World Bank 252
World Bank study 69–70

Yasini, M. 278
Yasini, S. 278
Yoshida, E. 245
Younus, M. 105
YukTakaful 224
Yusuf, H. 245

Zaher, T.S. 24
zakat management system 10, 35, 251; artificial intelligence 259; in Bangladesh 263–264, **265,** 266; big data 259; blockchain 258–259; challenges 267; collections and disbursements **255**; crowdfunding 257; definition 253–254; efficiency and governance 252; fintech and islamic fintech models 256–257; human resource management problem 261; initial coin offering/initial cryptotoken offering 257–258; innovation 254; lack of capacity building 262; lack of coordination between 261; lack of trust 261–262; lack of zakat education 262–263; privatisation 254; regulatory sandbox 259–260; unsystematic and inefficient collection and disbursement 260–261
Zhang, R. 175, 176
Zuki, M.S.M. 237

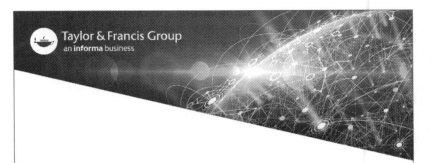

Printed in the United States
by Baker & Taylor Publisher Services